HELLO, HELLO BRAZIL

BRYAN McCANN

Hello, Hello Brazil

POPULAR MUSIC IN THE MAKING

OF MODERN BRAZIL

Duke University Press Durham & London 2004

© 2004 Duke University Press

All rights reserved

Printed in the United States of America

on acid-free paper ∞

Designed by C. H. Westmoreland

Typeset in Minion with Gill Sans display

by Keystone Typesetting, Inc.

Library of Congress Cataloging-in-Publication Data

McCann, Bryan.

Hello, hello Brazil : popular music in the making

of modern Brazil / Bryan McCann.

p. cm.

Includes bibliographical references and index.

ISBN 0-8223-3284-1 (cloth : alk. paper)

ISBN 0-8223-3273-6 (pbk : alk. paper)

1. Popular music—Brazil—History and criticism.

2. Music—Brazil—Social aspects.

I. Title.

ML3487.B7M39 2004

781.64′0981—dc22   2003024989

CONTENTS

ACKNOWLEDGMENTS

This book would not have been possible without access to the rich holdings of the Museum of Image and Sound (MIS) Archive in Lapa, Rio de Janeiro, where I spent several satisfying months listening to broadcasts recorded between the late 1930s and the 1960s. Of the many debts I have incurred in the long process of writing this book, the first is surely that owed to the MIS-Arquivo, whose personnel have been continually generous, insightful, and supportive. Ádua Nesi, Claudia Mesquita, Marilza, Claudio, Lúcia, Laura, and Rita in particular offered me more assistance than any visiting researcher could rightfully expect.

The Yale Council of International and Area Studies, the Mellon Foundation, and the National Endowment for the Humanities Summer Stipend all contributed essential research funds.

I have drawn on the expertise and enthusiasm of a host of Latin Americanist advisers; although this book falls far afield from some of their concerns, it benefits from their example and support. Leslie Damasceno encouraged me to study Brazil, Michael Jiménez held me to a high scholarly standard for the first time, and Sandra Lauderdale Graham taught me to write and to find the mystery in my subjects. Geoffrey Parker and Emília Viotti da Costa reminded me not to lose track of the big questions. Gil Joseph, my doctoral adviser, has been a source of inspiration, a model of generosity, and a good friend throughout.

My fellow students at Yale, particularly Nara Milanich, Amy Chazkel, Tori Langland, Jolie Olcott, Greg Grandin, and Di Paton provided intellectual engagement, commiseration when it was necessary, and celebration at the key moments.

I have been fortunate to study modern Brazil, a field that allows me the camaraderie of a cohort that knows how to find the joy in scholarly inquiry. In Brazil, I enjoyed the good company of Noah Elkin, Tom Jordan, Peter Beattie, Erica Windler, Tamera Marko, and Joel Wolfe. Elsewhere, I have benefited from the friendship and collegiality of Jim

Green, Christopher Dunn, Charles Perrone, Martha Ulhoa, Stuart Schwartz, John French, Jerry Davila, John W. F. Dulles, Oliver Dinius, Brodie Fischer, Seth Garfield, Dain Borges, Marc Hertzmann, James Woodard, Micol Seigel, and Brian Owensby. Many of these scholars have improved this book through their valuable feedback on earlier versions. Barbara Weinstein's support and insight have been vital. Daryle Williams continues to teach me something new about Brazil every time we meet. His warm friendship, along with that of James Rostron, have been among the greatest benefits of moving to Washington, D.C. Jeff Lesser has read the entire manuscript twice, and his comments and enthusiasm have been of inestimable assistance.

Corinne Pernett, Jim Cane, and Michael Conniff joined me on a Conference on Latin American History (CLAH) panel that helped refine my understanding of the relationship between popular culture and populism. Eric Zolov reminded me that popular music is a serious scholarly subject, and also much more. Mark Healey has followed the project from its earliest stages, offering acute comments, enlightening comparisons, and good friendship.

At the University of Arkansas, David Chappell read the manuscript with a sharp eye and helped guide me through revisions. Steve Striffler was a model of good-natured, committed scholarship. Marlie McGovern's able proofreading helped me complete the first draft. The student directors of KXUA FM were foolish enough to give me my own weekly show, where I tested out many of my ideas on an unsuspecting audience, and I salute their adventurous spirit. My students, particularly Susana O'Daniel and Rosario Nolasco, have inspired me with their curiosity, humbled me with their wit, and taught me how to get the point across. At Georgetown, Erick Langer and John Tutino have offered wise counsel on the manuscript, and everything else associated with starting a new job.

Valerie Millholland has been a gracious and encouraging editor, guiding this project through shoals I failed to see until we had passed them.

In Brazil, Luiz Carlos Saroldi, Jairo Severiano, Carlos Didier, and José Ramos Tinhorão went out of their way to help a foreign researcher. Claudia Matos shared her anecdotes and her record collection. D. Norma Tapajós granted entrance to her extensive personal archive.

Acely Fernandes and Alberto at Rádio Nacional generously extended their hours to allow me to complete research at key moments. The archivists at the Centro de Pesquisa e Documentação (CPDOC) of the Fundação Getúlio Vargas, particularly Inés, saved me days of frustrating searches with their advice.

Members of the Marlene Fan Club welcomed me to their celebrations, granted numerous interviews and even bestowed gifts, and I thank them, particularly João Batista and Ciro Gaulo. Lia Calabre de Azevedo gave helpful archival indications. Haquira Osakabe provided key assistance in Campinas. Margareth Rago and her family have been both gracious and informative in São Paulo. Tatiana Librelato has generously provided music and expertise.

Francisco Costa rephotographed the images from the Museu da Imagem e do Som. Peter Reznikoff generously allowed me to reproduce the cover photograph. The saudadesdobrasil listserve has put me in touch with dozens of fans, scholars, and performers of Brazilian popular music. Daniella Thompson, in particular, has saved me from several blunders, and set a high standard of expertise and passion.

Luciana Lopes Delphim, Graça Arruda Fialho, Wilma Custers, and Lígia Mefano have helped to make my visits to Rio as enjoyable as they are enlightening. Angela Magalhães and her family have given me a home away from home on more than one extended trip.

Chris Jennings and Doug Graham have reminded me why live music is better. Jay McCann's historical curiosity has inspired me to refine my arguments. Moira McCann Moderelli has enabled me to laugh through the difficult moments. My mother, Helena Moraski, has been unfailingly generous and utterly invaluable in countless ways. Ray Moraski's support has been a blessing. Sean McCann has had the grace and wisdom to pull me through scholarly and other quandaries, and I thank him. Mary Hunter, my wife, deserves more gratitude than I can hope to offer. Her humor, sage advice, and love keep me going. Booker, the next one is for you. . . .

INTRODUCTION

"Quem foi que inventou o Brasil?" Who invented Brazil? This musical question begins Lamartine Babo's 1933 *marcha* "História do Brasil."[1] The next line offers an answer that toys with history and those who believe in it: "Foi seu Cabral! Foi seu Cabral!" It was Mr. Cabral, or Pedro Alvares Cabral, the errant navigator who in 1500 initiated Portuguese exploration and settlement of the territory that soon became known as Brazil. When Babo wrote these lines, Cabral was certainly understood to be the discoverer of Brazil, but discovery is not the same as invention. The next line raises further historical doubts: "On the 21st of April, two months after Carnival." This suggests that Brazil's tradition of pre-Lenten revelry somehow antedated the arrival of Cabral and the Portuguese. What is the meaning of the deliberate anachronism? Was Babo making fun of textbook history by dismantling its catechism and reassembling it in nonsensical fashion? Was he suggesting that between discovery and invention lies a complex process of mythmaking and occasional misinformation? Or was he merely suggesting, in fine Brazilian fashion, that a naively forthright question deserves a dubious answer?

"História do Brasil" is, at first blush, a trifle, a carnival ditty with a simple melody and exuberantly inane lyrics, the kind of tune that Babo cranked out by the dozens throughout the 1930s. This was among his more successful efforts, and the original recording by the vocalist Almirante became a hit of the 1934 carnival season. By its nature, however, Carnival was a season of festivity, not critical inquiry, and it is likely that the revelers who followed Almirante's open car through the streets, throwing confetti and joining him in song, happily accepted the good-humored incongruities of "História do Brasil" without prolonged reflection as to their meaning. But the tune's initial question echoes across the decades with a deeper resonance. Who, after all, *did* invent Brazil? As interesting, why did Babo want to know? He was by no means alone in this concern. Inquiry into the nature and meaning of Brazilianness was the foremost theme of the 1930s at all levels of intellectual debate. Brazilianness, or *brasilidade*, was commonly understood to mean that collection of qualities which defined the nation, which distinguished Brazilians from citizens of Argentina, Portugal, and the United States—to name three populations whom Brazilians felt it was important to define themselves *against*. Determining the cultural content of Brazilianness, and discovering the best ways to cultivate, express, and preserve it, became an overriding concern. Artists, authors, bureaucrats, popular composers, and, to a surprising degree, everyday Brazilians, shared in an investigation of Brazil's cultural roots and identity—an investigation that in itself became a process of reinvention and reconstruction.

"História do Brasil" is one of many manifestations of this tendency. It was neither the most graceful nor the most influential, but it was one of the earliest explicit inquiries into national identity in the field of popular music. It was also remarkably acute in describing a transition from one set of national myths and symbols, based on a high cultural vision of the marriage of European and indigenous elements to another, based on Afro-Brazilian roots and modern, popular cultural forms. The tune's second verse alludes to José de Alencar's 1857 novel *O guarani*, Brazil's most influential nineteenth-century nationalist work.[2] The novel was later adapted into an opera by composer Carlos Gomes, and both novel and opera were considered obligatory markers of Brazilian high culture in the late nineteenth and early twentieth centuries.[3] In *O guarani*, the Portuguese maiden Cecília, or Ceci, for short, falls for Peri, the Guarani chief of the title, and from their union, allegorically, the nation of Brazil is born. In "História do Brasil," the primordial couple surfaces in the line "Later, Peri kissed Ceci, to the sound of *O guarani*." Again, Babo indulges in playful anachronism by suggesting that Gomes's opera was the soundtrack for the mythic couple's embrace.

O guarani is prototypical of nineteenth-century nationalist literature in its depiction of Peri as a noble, solitary Indian who must give way before the advancing European settlers but whose spirit is symbolically incorporated into their new civilization. It was also typical of nineteenth-century Brazilian thought in the way it pushed Brazil's enormous population of African descent to the margins: African influence cuts no ice in Alencar's national allegory. By the 1930s, such a perspective was clearly antiquated. Reconsideration of the importance of African cultural influence was the single most important element in

Brazil's collective inquiry into national character.[4] Nowhere was that influence more apparent than in popular music, and, partly as a result, popular music became particularly freighted with nationalist meanings. Subsequent lyrics in "História do Brasil" allude to this transition: "Later, Ceci became Iaiá, Peri became Ioiô." Iaiá and Ioiô were Afro-Brazilian terms of endearment, historically used by slaves for the slave-owner's children, but by the 1930s used, or stereotyped, as terms of courtship between older Afro-Brazilian men and women. Babo's marcha thus domesticates the interracial union of *O guarani* and gives it an Afro-Brazilian tinge, implying a new national ancestry.

Babo describes another transition, from *"O guarani* to *guaraná"*—that is, from the high cultural works of Alencar and Gomes to the modern commercial product of guaraná, a carbonated soft drink made from an Amazonian berry. Guaraná, as bottled by the powerful firms Antárctica and Brahma, was fast becoming a staple of the Brazilian popular diet. Babo ushers out the old, refined, elitist Brazil, and welcomes the new, mass-produced, democratically consumable Brazil. In doing so, he astutely links two apparently unrelated aspects of the enormous cultural transformation currently underway—the new emphasis on Afro-Brazilian roots and the rise of a mass market. This link is indeed fundamental: the symbolic capital of Afro-Brazilian authenticity was an important factor shaping the growth of a mass market for popular musical recordings and radio programs. Emphasis on the Afro-Brazilian origins of samba, for example, became increasingly important as samba became a packaged commercial product.

From the vantage point of Carnival, 1934, a Brazil culturally defined by *O guarani* already seemed a distant past. "From there to here," Babo concluded, "everything changed. Grandma's time has gone and now Severa and the horse Mossoró are in charge." This line refers to a melodramatic singer of Portuguese laments and a prizewinning thoroughbred, both of whom were in the headlines in 1933. Babo was wrong about these last two—few Brazilians today would recognize their names. Many, in contrast, would recognize Babo's, although they would likely refer to him only by his first name, and almost all would be able to sing at least a few lines of his most famous tunes, without necessarily attaching a name or a date to them. They are part of a common store of cultural knowledge. As markers of Brazilianness, they are as pervasive as *feijoada*, the black bean stew of African origin, or guaraná itself. Babo was right about a transition in the relative importance of high and popular culture in defining the nation, but he could not be expected to foresee his own importance, or that of his fellow composers and performers of popular music, in formulating the new definition.

Babo and Almirante were members of a foundational generation in the history of modern Brazilian popular music, a generation that turned a small collection of popular musical forms into both a thriving industry and a consistently vital meditation on the nature and contradictions of Brazilianness. Lamartine's nimble marchas—a genre related both to the Brazilian samba and the European march, ideal for carnival parades through the streets of Rio—helped define a generation and served as models for countless subsequent composers. Almirante—the stage name of Henrique Foréis Domingues—was a mediocre singer, but he went on to become Brazil's most inventive radio producer and host from the 1930s through the 1950s. His programs, not coincidentally, were frequently dedicated to investigations of Brazil's cultural identity. Other creative figures, such as the exuberant performer Carmen Miranda, the brilliant melodist Pixinguinha, and the incisive composer Geraldo Pereira, to name just a few, were equally important in creating this generation's body of work. While these figures occasionally collaborated, their approaches to the driving questions of the day were by no means unified. It is the multiplicity of voices and perspectives that makes their collective body of work so rich and continually relevant. Its overlapping branches set the parameters of Brazilian popular music—and to a great degree Brazilian culture more broadly—for the remainder of the century.

Brazilians of all classes were playing music well before the 1920s, of course, and even popular music produced commercially for a national audience already existed, largely through the circulation of sheet music by a few large publishers and the efforts of a fledgling recording industry.[5] But between the late 1920s and the mid-1950s, previously existing themes and practices of popular music, and popular culture more generally, were left behind or radically reinterpreted. By the close of this period a new set of themes and practices had been consolidated, and it is that set which continues to define popular cultural life in Brazil. These themes and practices still inform the ways Brazilians understand their nation, their racial politics, their conflicts of gender—in short, themselves, and they do so at the deepest level—that of a pop song half heard from the window of a passing car and never forgotten.

This book analyzes the creation of that new popular music and explores its deeper implications. Brazilian film, magazines, sports, and other popular cultural forms were also transformed dramatically during this period, and innovations in these fields surface in the chapters that follow. The title, indeed, alludes both to the standard greeting proffered by early Brazilian broadcasters and to *Alô, alô Brasil* (Hello, hello Brazil), a 1935 film demonstrating the intertwining nature of these simultaneous transformations. In the film, a young man travels from the interior to Rio de Janeiro in hopes of meeting his favorite singer. He finds his way into a radio station where, starstruck, he witnesses performances by the top stars of the day, including Carmen Miranda and Almirante. The plot symbolically shows the processes of urbanization and industrialization under way, and dramatizes the unification of heartland and metropolis through the glamorous cultural production of the latter. As a commercial product targeted at an audience demanding the latest in popular music, the film demonstrates the overlapping nature of the broadcasting, recording, and cinema industries in the 1930s.

Popular music was both the common ingredient and the binding glue of these transformations. To a greater degree than cinema, popular literature, or sport, it emerged as a decisive forum for debate over national identity, and Brazilians began to view the exercise of musical preference in the cultural marketplace as an act with enormous consequences. Popular music also became a signature export product, one whose fortunes abroad were anxiously debated back home. These debates played out in radio stations and recording studios, carnival parades, musical revues, and the cafés in downtown Rio de Janeiro where composers shared and sold their inventions. Together, these venues formed a popular musical arena where the evolving body of Brazilian popular music was created and shaped, bought, and sold. Composers, performers, samba schools, fan clubs, advertisers, producers, and critics all participated in this popular musical arena. As *Alô, alô Brasil* suggested, radio stations, above all, proved to be crucial laboratories for popular cultural formation, for it was through radio that most Brazilians made their first and most enduring contact with new sounds, and it was radio that linked the production of the metropolis with the audience of the far-flung hinterlands.

This connection was fundamental, for the emerging popular culture was national in both scope and intent. To begin with, it was marketed primarily to a domestic audience—international success came only unexpectedly. All sectors of this audience were not equal. Because the recording and broadcasting industries were so heavily concentrated in Rio de Janeiro, the preferences of Cariocas dictated larger trends. Nonetheless, national broadcasts and tours of radio stars through the interior brought metropolitan popular culture to audiences from Belém to Porto Alegre with a previously unimaginable immediacy. And as performers from the interior migrated to the capital and broke into broadcasting, Rio de Janeiro's top stations became a clearinghouse for regional styles, broadcasting the nation back to itself—with crucial transformations along the way. Finally, as even a cursory analysis of "História do Brasil" demonstrates, much of the new cultural production was explicitly dedicated to investigating and expressing the nation.

Composers and performers were particularly influential in shaping this culture and, as the following chapters demonstrate, they produced works of subtlety and complexity that repay close analysis. But it would be misleading and superficial to present this popular music as the creation of a series of individual geniuses. Instead, it was the inevitable outcome of broad economic, political, and cultural transformations. Rapid urbanization and industrialization laid the groundwork for a popular cultural market by creating an audience and the means to meet the needs of that audience. Bureaucratic centralization and a political drive to refashion the nation facilitated communication and channeled broader nationalist themes. High-cultural investigations of national identity and reappraisals of Afro-Brazilian influence inspired popular responses. Composers, performers, producers, and fans responded to these deeper trends. In some cases these responses were conscious and explicit, in others unconscious and implicit, but in all cases the influence of these deeper trends was ineluctable. Composers and performers shaped the resulting popular culture, without creating it out of nothing. The audience, too, shaped the culture—again, sometimes through active and even aggressive engagement with cultural producers, sometimes through relatively passive consumption, but constantly and with decisive effects. Understanding Brazil's new popular music, then, requires attention to the connections between cultural expression, the audience's desires, the government's demands, and the inescapable imperatives of the economy.

THE CULTURAL AND POLITICAL
PARAMETERS OF THE NEW POPULAR MUSIC

It is no accident that this period of musical invention largely coincides with the years in which Getúlio Vargas dominated political life in

Brazil. Vargas rose to power in the Revolution of 1930, consolidated dictatorial authority under the Estado Novo, or New State, of 1937 to 1945, fell from power in a 1945 coup, returned as elected president in 1951, and shot himself in office in August of 1954. The dramatic nature of this trajectory coupled with the enormous ambition of his policies made Vargas a metonym for an era. Between the late 1920s and the mid-1950s, Brazil passed from the Old Republic, a period of oligarchic political rule masked by republican window-dressing, through the centralizing gauntlet of the Estado Novo and into the populist fracas that ensued. This was the nation's difficult passage to modernity, and it entailed dramatic change in political, economic, and cultural spheres.

These transformations were intimately related without sharing a perfect correspondence. The cultural reinvention of the nation, for example, was well under way by the time Vargas rose to power. The Modernist movement, which burst on the high-cultural scene with the Modern Art Week in São Paulo in 1922, had already created enormous disturbance and realignment in the belles lettres, visual arts, and concert music. By the close of the 1920s the modernist project of deliberate cultural overhaul had spread from a small and volatile initial cohort to several fractious branches, which varied widely in political affinities and modes of expression, but shared a strong commitment to defining and cultivating Brazilianness.

On the popular cultural level, as well—as subsequent chapters on the development of samba and *choro* will attest—the 1920s witnessed both rapid innovation and conscious pursuit of national expression. Over the course of the decade, moreover, high-cultural modernists and popular musical innovators frequently crossed paths. The erudite modernist composer Heitor Villa-Lobos incorporated the guitar techniques of amateur choro musicians into his compositions. Poet and musicologist Mário de Andrade developed a rich typology of Brazilian folkloric music and kept close tabs on the rapid evolutions of urban popular music. Poet and vanguardist Oswald de Andrade cited samba lyrics in his *Anthropophagist Manifesto* of 1928, implying that popular musicians were leading the way in incorporating foreign influence into a robust national culture. By the late 1920s, intellectuals without close association to the modernist movement, like the anthropologist Gilberto Freyre and the historian Sérgio Buarque de Holanda, had also begun to cultivate ties with popular musicians.[6] To a degree unimaginable in earlier decades, intellectuals and popular musicians began to move in the same circles. They did not necessarily see themselves as equals, but parties from each camp knew that they had something to say to each other, across dividing lines of class and education.

Several of the key elements of the new popular music, then, were in place by the end of the 1920s. Three processes of the early 1930s helped build these elements into a sweeping process of innovation and consolidation. The first and most important was the rapid growth of the broadcasting industry, enabling diffusion of metropolitan popular culture throughout the country. The second was the steady intensification of exchanges between high and popular cultural innovators over the course of the decade. I will explore both of these processes in detail. The third was the rise of the Vargas regime itself, which consciously sought to mold and direct these cultural transformations. While the regime's cultural propaganda often failed, in some cases abjectly, its centralizing energy did serve to encourage and subsidize sanctioned expressions while marginalizing others. Even failed government initiatives brought composers, performers, and producers into direct contact with the state. One might evade that state's directives without escaping its influence.

Vargas recognized the importance of the link between policy and popular culture from his earliest days as a politician. As a junior federal congressman in 1926, he proposed a law requiring movie theaters and radio stations to pay royalties for the use of recorded music. This "Getúlio Vargas Law," eventually passed in 1928, endeared him to musicians.[7] By imposing an expense on the use of recorded music, it encouraged radio producers and theater owners to opt for live entertainment, helping to establish a trend toward live radio programming in radio's infancy in Brazil. Surely this would have happened in any case, as audiences made their preference for live radio clear. But the law prefigured Vargas's later approach to radio: his most effective policies were those that accepted the commercial, popular nature of broadcasting in Brazil and sought to turn those qualities to the advantage of the regime.

In 1930, a coalition of disgruntled regional elites backed Vargas as a presidential candidate. When Vargas lost an election marred by brazen irregularities, his supporters waged a brief, effective military campaign against the existing government and placed him in office. Popular musicians and composers were among the first to perceive his rise to power as an opportunity to strengthen their own hand. Shortly after his arrival in office, a representative group of performers and composers paid a call on the new president to endorse his stated intention to renew Brazil, and to urge him to protect their livelihood by requiring theaters and radio stations to dedicate at least two-thirds of their programming to Brazilian music.[8] As he was to do with so many factions, Vargas magnanimously accepted these recommendations but made no firm commitments. Like the Vargas Law, the episode prefigured later events. The display of homage to the chief set a pattern for submission to Vargas and his bureaucracy that musicians and radio professionals rarely broke over the next fifteen years, at least in public. And the notion that composers, popular musicians, and government officials were all engaged in the renewal of Brazil, and that radio would be a crucial medium for that project, grew increasingly important throughout the first Vargas regime.

During the next half-decade, Vargas gradually assembled the administrative structure that, with occasional alterations, would carry his regime through 1945, constructing a strong federal bureaucracy dominated by the Ministries of Justice, Education and Health, and Labor. He distributed competing cultural projects among these key ministries, creating an intricate and occasionally contradictory network of federal cultural initiatives. Under the Estado Novo, in particular, the regime's intrusions into the field of popular culture through propaganda, subsidization, and censorship brought musicians and composers into an ongoing process of negotiation with federal policy makers.

The 1939 initiation of the Good Neighbor Policy by the U.S. government, with the full support of the Estado Novo, added a new component to this dialogue. Already, North American popular culture had become increasingly present in Brazil over the course of the 1930s, borne on the tide of hemispheric trade and promoted by U.S. advertisers and advertising agents. The Good Neighbor Policy gave new energy to this dissemination, and brought Brazilian popular musicians and composers into increasing contact with U.S. producers. It also enabled some of these performers, Carmen Miranda above all, to embark on successful careers in the United States.

The collapse of the Estado Novo in 1945 and the inauguration of the Eurico Dutra presidency the following year drastically diminished the federal government's attempts to manage popular culture. In the field of popular music, the withdrawal of the government altered but did not diminish the music's deep concerns with Brazilianness. Untrammeled by the propaganda initiatives of a dictatorial regime, popular musical formulations of national identity took on new volatility, reflecting a broader political and cultural turbulence. Vargas's return to office as democratically elected president in 1951 did not mark the resumption of previous state cultural endeavors. Large-scale attempts at federal cultural management had met with myriad obstacles even under the dictatorship and, in the contentious atmosphere of Vargas's second presidency, they were completely impracticable.[9] Instead, popular culture articulated through the market reigned supreme, with little involvement by the government.

Perhaps in concession to this reality, Vargas attempted to increase his personal contact with radio stars, cultivating close ties to glamorous singers like Linda Batista and Angela Maria.[10] Friendship with popular performers, however, could not win him back a public opinion disillusioned by the corruption scandals of 1953 and 1954. During the last, bitter month of Vargas's presidency, visits by musical stars to the presidential residence at Catete Palace ceased—for the first time, associating with the president had become a liability to one's public image. Vargas's suicide, on 24 August 1954, triggered an enormous reversal of popular sentiment, prompting a public outpouring of grief and remembrance. As many of these mourners undoubtedly sensed, his death would come to symbolize the end of a period of political, economic, and cultural construction and consolidation. In the popular musical arena, Vargas's death coincided with a shift toward niche broadcasting and the splintering of the national audience. To a great degree, a window of opportunity for the establishment of deep and lasting patterns of popular musical production and consumption had closed.

This period has long been recognized as central to the establishment of modern Brazil. Over the last two decades, in particular, scholars have developed a rich historiography of the Vargas period, either narrowly defined as 1930–45 or more broadly as 1930–54, and its attendant processes of modernization.[11] Studies of nation building in this period have grown from an early consideration of the formal political sphere and high cultural production to analyses of more subtle and complex manifestations of national reinvention in the midst of rapid modernization.[12] Recent work has brought new sophistication to our understanding of the complex cultural strategies of Estado Novo bureaucrats, as well as the Estado Novo's adoption and transformation of modernist projects.[13]

The emergence of a new popular culture, in contrast, has received relatively little attention. Where it has been treated, it has been understood as relatively separate from political and economic spheres, an autonomous field dominated and directed by individual creators.[14]

Over the last decade, a few scholars have begun to push beyond this foundation, drawing the necessary connections between the popular and the political, without interpreting popular culture as merely a reflection or a consequence of political trends.[15] This book lifts off from these important contributions, offering a more complete picture of the popular musical arena. Participants in this arena lent their contrasting voices to a swelling chorus of musical invention. By exploring the layered meanings that resulted, I hope to reveal the workings of a coherent popular culture—one that offered Brazilians counterbalanced messages of tradition and modernity, community and individuality, nationalist fervor and cosmopolitan flair.

POPULAR MUSIC, BETWEEN NATIONAL COMMUNION AND COMMERCIAL DEBASEMENT

In contrast to the formal political arena during these years, and the Estado Novo in particular, the popular cultural arena was remarkably democratic. This has rarely been understood. Because the popular culture of the 1930s and 1940s shares certain nationalist themes with the political rhetoric of the Vargas regime, it has often been characterized as co-opted or controlled.[16] In this view, audience tastes were dictated by bureaucrats, advertisers, or both. Afro-Brazilian participants in the popular cultural industry, especially, have often been understood as exploited, seduced into selling their authentic creations cheaply to fast-talking producers or strong-armed politicians. But theories of co-optation grant too much control to government propagandists and advertisers, and fail to account for savvy and highly self-conscious popular participation in the cultural arena. Afro-Brazilian *sambistas*, for example, did not merely provide grist for the mill of commercial popular culture. They engaged the cultural market and played crucial roles in shaping new cultural expressions, gaining a cultural influence over the nation that stood in marked contrast to their continued marginalization in the economic and formal political spheres. The critical consumption of popular music, moreover, made connoisseurs of everyday Brazilians, frequently prompting them to join explicitly in the debate over national identity. More broadly, collective manifestations of popular taste offered previously marginalized Brazilians a central role in the creation of a market for cultural goods. In seizing this role and playing it with gusto, they achieved a form of popular citizenship, while full political citizenship—the right to vote, to be free from arbitrary arrest, to speak openly against the government—remained narrowly limited, when not entirely suspended.

The popular musical arena was not as clearly defined as the formal political arena, and did not offer the same tangible access to power, but it was far more accommodating. Everyday Brazilians participated in the creation of the new popular culture by writing samba verses and selling them to professional composers, by joining fan clubs and samba schools, by attending radio shows and writing to trade magazines. They did not necessarily enjoy the benefits of full political citizenship, but nor were they marginalized from modernity as unchanging, essential folk. And the popular culture they helped fashion proved deeply relevant in the formal political and economic spheres, both during and after the Vargas period.

There were limits to this popular citizenship, and they are a crucial element of this history. Afro-Brazilians were not compensated fairly for their decisive contribution. Through much of the Vargas period, radio stations and record labels shied away from featuring black performers, allowing white professionals to become rich and famous while Afro-Brazilian composers often remained relatively poor. Rhetorical praise of African influence served to mask this ongoing racism. Thus, charges that Afro-Brazilians were often exploited by the popular music industry hold weight. Given Brazil's economic stratification, with Afro-Brazilians concentrated heavily in the lower range, this could hardly fail to be the case. Charges that they were co-opted or seduced into acting against their own interests, however, do not stand up to investigation. Instead, Afro-Brazilians seized limited opportunities within the popular musical arena, turning them to their economic advantage. Similarly, key Afro-Brazilian composers availed themselves of their popular cultural citizenship to comment critically on their political and economic marginalization. In these important cases, Afro-Brazilian popular music played a crucial role in revealing the existence of racism in Brazil.

To assert that the new popular music was democratic is not to deny that to a certain extent it reproduced inequalities and prejudices from other areas of Brazilian life. Rather, it is to affirm that this music was collectively created, ultimately bearing the stamp of participants from every economic level. It is also to argue for the relevance of this popular participation in the broad struggle to redefine the nation that characterized the period. In his excellent book on the competing projects of national cultural construction within the Estado Novo, Daryle Williams has suggested that the active participants in such "culture wars" were limited to a small sector of government insiders and modernist intellectuals.[17] The popular musical arena, however, witnessed a crucial extension of this battle for the national soul, marked by broad and vigorous participation. Composers like Luiz Gonzaga and Geraldo Pereira, for example, rose from the humblest ranks of the nonwhite rural poor to positions of enormous cultural influence. Both not only became famous composers but created works that probed the heart of Brazil's knotty racial and ethnic contradictions, adding powerful new voices to ongoing national debates. They achieved an influence that would have been unimaginable for similar figures in formal politics or high culture. Popular participation on the consumption side of the market's equation was also crucial, if more difficult to pin down. This influence is most obvious in cases of mass audience participation, for example, in the choro revival of the 1950s, or the contemporary growth of fan clubs. In both cases, fans made known their expectations regarding both popular music's relationship to national identity and its importance in building community.

Brazilians of all economic levels and political backgrounds were highly conscious of the creation of a new popular music, as well as the role of radio and the recording industry in articulating that music, and greeted both with a combination of hope and fear. Virtually all observers agreed that music possessing authentically Brazilian characteristics was worthy of national dissemination via the mass media, and that music unacceptably tainted by foreign influence or merely commercial in character was to be condemned. But the qualities of authenticity and Brazilianness were not nearly as self-evident as most critics asserted, and the difficulty of pinning down these qualities turned the popular musical arena into a battleground. One's position in that battle tended to reflect one's faith in the market. A small but influential group of actors, most of them industry insiders, considered the market to be not only benevolent but the only suitable laboratory for the distillation of Brazilianness through popular music. A larger group, including many intellectual observers, viewed the market as a realm of perdition: as authentic folkloric creations became commodities, their Brazilianness was inevitably diluted or corrupted.

The successful Carnival films of the Rio de Janeiro studio Cinédia, including *Alô, alô Brasil*, presented the most effusive case for the market's benevolence. Brazilian director Adhemar Gonzaga founded Cinédia in 1930. Later in the decade, working in conjunction with

Wallace Downey, an American who had come to Brazil to run the Columbia recording company's local operations, Gonzaga produced several films set in the milieu of Rio's burgeoning popular music scene. The films, released just before Carnival each year, wedded Rio's nascent film industry to a more advanced popular music industry. For Downey and his recording stars, the films offered an opportunity to cross over into a new medium, borrowing mannerisms from Hollywood along the way. The films were among the first Brazilian talkies, or, as they were suggestively called in Brazil, *cinema cantada*, sung cinema. They mixed the lavish production numbers typical of Hollywood musicals with Brazil's own rich tradition of theatrical musical revues in a hugely popular blend, outgrossing Hollywood imports.[18]

Like *Alô, alô Brasil*, the remaining Cinédia Carnival films depicted a glamorous world of popular musical stardom. In the 1935 production *Estudantes* (Students), Carmen Miranda played an aspiring radio singer who crosses paths with three students fascinated by the music industry. As in *Alô, alô Brasil*, talent and good humor prevail through confusion, and performers and fans unite in the common creation of Brazilian popular culture.[19] *Alô, alô Carnaval* (Hello, hello Carnival) of 1936, produced by Downey and directed by Gonzaga, brought a new tension to the series, dramatizing the protection of domestic cultural resources from the threatened depredations of foreign interlopers. Its plot concerns a pair of poor Brazilian performers whose plans to produce a musical spectacle featuring the best local talent are stymied by the preference of wealthy potential investors for a foreign troupe. The plot pits an emerging Brazilian popular culture against an established, foreign, erudite culture, and suggests that the deck is stacked in favor of the foreigners. By dint of talent, hard work, and luck, the locals pull off their revue, to clamorous success. The implication is that Brazil can only achieve its deserved popular culture through competition on the uneven playing field of the market. In the Cinédia films, the commercial nature of popular culture allows national communion to take place.

Marques Rebelo's acclaimed 1939 novel *A estrela sobe* (The star rises) presents the opposite interpretation of the popular musical arena.[20] The novel traces the life of Leniza Maier from her youth as a poor but strong-willed girl in downtown Rio to her breakthrough as a radio star. Along the way, Leniza betrays and disappoints all those who trust her, traffics in a sordid world of vice and homosexuality, and brings shame on herself and her mother through unwanted pregnancy and abortion.

Rebelo chronicles these passages with a prurient fatalism, suggesting that by embarking on a career in radio, Leniza has inevitably, if not quite knowingly, plunged into a seamy underworld.[21] By taking her golden voice out of the closed world of her poor neighborhood and selling it to commercial exploiters, she corrupts her own talent. In the process, she loses her individuality, becoming just one in a long line of indistinguishable, ruined starlets. In Rebelo's vision, commerce destroys everything of value in popular music, including its capacity to represent the nation.

Most Brazilians adopted a position somewhere between these poles. Whatever their opinion, they needed to be aware of these extreme interpretations, which remained crucial in structuring debate on popular music throughout the period. This high degree of self-consciousness regarding cultural choice is part of what makes the popular musical arena fascinating. Brazilians—including composers, performers, producers, bureaucrats, and fans—consistently justified their musical preferences on the basis of what was good for the nation. In doing so, they struggled to elevate popular music above the level of mere entertainment into the realm of public culture. They sought to turn popular music into the foundation of a unified national culture, one that would bridge long-standing chasms of class and regional distinctions in order to bring Brazilians together on an equal footing with a shared experience. Once engaged in that struggle, they oscillated between poles of optimism and pessimism regarding whether such a culture might be achieved. The more optimistic among them held up the ideal of an inclusive national culture as tangible and attainable, or even as a rightful natural inheritance needing only to be protected. The more pessimistic among them held up this ideal only to show how it had been continually debased and undermined. Their varying perspectives on this crucial subject reflected their differing conceptions of *o popular*, the popular, a vague concept standing at various moments for the popular spirit, the popular citizen body, and the authentic element that gave commercial popular music its legitimacy. The multiplicity of voices in this debate, and the crisscrossing connections between high and low cultural spheres, gave popular music its richness and depth.

This book's title, in referring to a Cinédia film, indicates my optimistic interpretation of the commercial nature of Brazilian popular music. As Eric Hobsbawm—a scholar not overly credulous of the market's tendency to serve the popular interest—has written regarding jazz, "Readers who believe that records make themselves and that horn players are fed by ravens sent down from heaven, like the angel Elijah, are advised to pick themselves a less earthbound music to admire. Jazz musicians are professionals. The prejudice against 'commercialism' among a large section of the jazz public makes it necessary to repeat this obvious truth."[22] Likewise, the musicians who helped fashion a new Brazilian popular culture between the 1920s and the 1950s were professionals, or aspired to be professionals. When they found themselves in a disadvantaged position in the musical market as a result of racial prejudice or a prior condition of economic marginalization, they took steps to improve their position, rather than to isolate themselves from that market. By the mid-1930s, isolation was impossible, in any case. The forms and styles that emerged in this period to enrich and shape the lives of Brazilians did so within the context of the expanding radio and recording industries, and their existence is inseparable from that context. Again, this is not to deny that these industries often underpaid musicians and, in the case of radio, sought to induce consumers to buy products they did not necessarily need. It is to assert that deeper understanding of Brazil's new popular music requires recognizing that the initial expansion of these industries created an enormously fertile climate of invention. By the end of this period, these inventions were consolidated and established as the foundation for subsequent experimentation.

In the late 1920s, Mário de Andrade, a scholar more skeptical than Hobsbawm about the effects of industrialization on popular music, lamented that samba was an urban genre. Its roots in the city, among a fluid population subject to the blandishments of radio stations, condemned it to inconstancy. Because it lacked a "necessary tradition," it could never be fixed, like rural, folkloric music. In the best of worlds, Andrade suggested, Brazilian "national character" would serve as that necessary tradition, providing a stake for the flowering tendrils of urban popular music. But he despaired that this could happen, for the national character remained "undefined, shot through with internationalism and fatal foreign influence."[23]

Andrade's characterization of the popular musical arena was correct. It was indeed shot through with international influence, and the genres and styles defined within it were subject to rapid evolution. He was wrong, however, about the effects of these characteristics: they did not result in watered-down or meaningless music, reduced to mere commodity ("flesh to feed radios," as he described it). Instead, they contributed to the richness of the emerging popular culture, which itself became precisely the necessary tradition whose absence Andrade mourned. It drew its vitality and relevance not from static or folkloric qualities, but from its complexity, its ability to contain a multiplicity of forms and styles, and to yield varying, even opposed interpretations that nevertheless took the same initial premise as their starting point.

Over the course of the period in question, several prominent themes and patterns emerged to give the new popular music shape and continuity. Each chapter in this book analyzes one of these themes or patterns, explaining its meanings to contemporary participants and its continued relevance in subsequent decades. Chapter 1 analyzes the growth of broadcasting and the Vargas regime's attempt to direct popular culture through radio during the Estado Novo. Chapter 2 analyzes the rise of samba as a symbol of national identity in the 1930s and early 1940s, and the transformation of that symbolism in the 1950s. Chapter 3 tracks the emergence of two parallel strains of northeastern regionalism—one of the arid hinterlands, one of the lush coast—in the popular music of the 1940s and 1950s. Chapter 4 examines evolutions in the Brazilian popular musical response to the economic and cultural influence of the United States. Chapter 5 investigates the strong reaction to perceived foreign influence in a wave of defensive popular cultural nationalism during the early 1950s. Chapter 6 analyzes the growth of fan clubs and radio auditorium programs in the 1940s and 1950s. Chapter 7 studies the influence of advertising agencies on radio programming.

The reader will note that my analysis concentrates overwhelmingly on the music produced in Rio de Janeiro, and that where I discuss audience interpretation, I privilege the metropolitan audience. This is unavoidable: throughout the period, Rio was the bureaucratic and cultural capital of the nation, home to the principal recording studios and the most powerful radio stations. Many popular musicians from other areas of Brazil achieved national prominence in this period, but without exception they did so by establishing careers in the capital. The music minted in Rio became the standard currency of national cultural exchange.

▌ RADIO AND ESTADO NOVO

When Getúlio Vargas assumed the presidency following the Revolution of 1930, his authority was tenuous. He had the backing of the regional power brokers who had placed him in office and the goodwill of the majority of Brazilians who had been left disenfranchised by the clubbish political machinations of the Old Republic. But his opponents remained strong, and the economic insecurity brought on by a deepening global depression made for volatile popular sentiments. Vargas recognized the need to embark immediately on strong political and economic reforms in order to stabilize his government. In addition he and his new administrative cohort understood the imperative to reach and inspire a broad population with a message of inclusion and common struggle. Radio seemed the perfect tool for their enterprise: it combined technology and industry, and it harnessed invisible forces in pursuit of triumphant modernity. It was capable of reaching into the private homes of citizens and transforming their lives, placing them in direct contact with their leader. Most important, it offered the hope of linking far-flung territories into a single network of instantaneous communication, and of bridging the gaps of culture and class that divided Brazilians.

Vargas and his underlings frequently gave voice to such sentiments in both public pronouncements and private letters. In a 1936 interview, Lourival Fontes, director of the Department of Propaganda and Cultural Diffusion (DPDC), insisted on the need for greater government attention to the medium. Fontes argued that in other nations—he was thinking of Italy and Germany in particular—government radio stations already served to create a spirit of national unity, and he urged Vargas to establish a similar system in Brazil: "We cannot underestimate the work of propaganda and culture undertaken on the radio . . . it is enough to say that radio reaches where the school and the press do not, to the farthest points of the country, to the understanding of illiterates."[1] As one bureaucrat put it in a 1942 letter to Vargas, "More than in any other part of the world, radio is destined to exercise here a decisive influence in the formation of the culture and the popular character itself."[2] Regime bureaucrats envisioned a propaganda that would go beyond narrow political concerns in order to mold a national popular culture. In his public statements, Vargas suggested that he shared this belief.[3] In his policy, however, he allowed government radio projects to wilt while commercial radio bloomed.

In keeping with the administrative architecture of his regime, which balanced the power of various factions in competing agencies, Vargas distributed radio projects among his three key ministries. The Ministry of Justice, through the DPDC, later to become the Department of Press and Propaganda (DIP), controlled the *Hora do Brasil*, a nightly government program aired on every station. The Ministry of Education and Health (MES) broadcast programming from its own transmitter in Rio de Janeiro. And, late in the Estado Novo, the Ministry of Labor also acquired its own station, Rádio Mauá. The Ministry of Labor station served primarily as a platform for the speeches of Minister Alexandre Marcondes Filho, directed at industrial workers. Its popular musical offerings made up a significant portion of the station's broadcasting schedule, but they were poorly funded and did not differ significantly from those of commercial stations. The programmers within the DIP and the MES, in contrast, deliberately sought to contain and counter what they perceived as the noxious trends of commercial broadcasting. For the DIP this meant censoring radio programs and records for their social and political content, and using the *Hora do Brasil* to mold the popular spirit. For the MES, this meant uplifting the popular audience through the didactic presentation of erudite material. Both enterprises failed miserably. Vargas denied each the resources necessary to achieve preeminence within the regime, much less to challenge the dominance of commercial radio. By the close of the Estado Novo, bureaucrats from both the DIP and the MES were forced to admit that their hopes to influence popular culture through broadcasting had failed.[4]

At the same time, another station owned by the federal government grew into the powerhouse of Brazilian broadcasting. Rádio Nacional was already among the most popular stations in the nation when it was taken over by the state in 1940. New government ownership had little effect on the programming: Rádio Nacional continued to be run as a commercial station featuring popular music and soap operas throughout the Estado Novo and beyond. The great bulk of its programming differed from that of its commercial competitors primarily in its high production values and its star quality—as Brazil's most popular station, Rádio Nacional was able to attract the best producers and the most famous performers. This popular programming, nonetheless—particularly the prime-time musical broadcasts—was often explicitly nationalist, and presented a vision of glorious modernization nourished by Brazilian cultural roots.

As a result, Estado Novo broadcasting presents a contradiction. When the regime sought to direct popular culture through propaganda and censorship, it failed. When it limited itself to providing a structure for commercial broadcasting, it was able to wield a decisive influence. This contradiction is easily explained: it arose primarily from the relative talents and preferences of the respective broadcasters. The *Hora do Brasil* and the programming of Rádio MES were created by bureaucrats interested primarily in satisfying the regime itself, and by high-cultural sophisticates disdainful of popular tastes. Rádio Nacional, in contrast, was staffed by broadcasting professionals with an intuitive grasp of their audience and a deep commitment to Brazilian popular music.[5]

Daryle Williams has demonstrated the importance of "cultural managers" within the Estado Novo, using that term to describe both career bureaucrats and intellectuals recruited temporarily to carry out the regime's cultural projects.[6] As Williams has shown, these cultural managers proved crucial in mediating between the government and the broader population. In spaces where the regime could exercise considerable control, such as museums and international expositions, they were able to carry out effective projects of cultural and civic persuasion. Popular culture, in contrast, and popular music in particular, proved relatively impervious to direct bureaucratic manipulation. Popular music required a different breed of cultural manager—one who might enjoy government protection but paid more attention to market tendencies than to state directives, and one who demonstrated a greater ability to respond to popular taste. The core of producers and performers responsible for creating Rádio Nacional's programming fit this description precisely. They were able to nurture local trends, in turn magnifying them through their broadcast power, turning the local into the national. Their position at the nexus of state and market gave them unmatched influence in shaping Brazil's new popular music.

Rádio Nacional, as a result, came far closer than either the DIP or the MES to molding national popular culture, and it did so primarily through its presentation of commercial popular music. Understanding these contrasting fortunes requires a deeper background in the growth of Brazilian broadcasting.

RADIO B.C.

Radio came to Rio de Janeiro before Christ. It arrived in 1922, when it played a prominent role in an exposition celebrating the centennial of Brazilian independence. Technicians from Westinghouse mounted a radio tower on Corcovado—the sheer peak that became the perch for Rio's famous statue of Christ nine years later—and installed receivers at the exposition plaza downtown. Those attending the centennial festivities on 7 September were jolted by a voice emanating from metal boxes around the main plaza. The voice counted to ten in English and was quickly replaced by that of Epitácio Pessoa, president of Brazil, delivering an independence-day address. Those who remained through Pessoa's speech were treated to a recorded rendition of arias from the Carlos Gomes opera *O guarani*. Brazil's first broadcast thus combined U.S. influence, state propaganda, and Brazilian music, three elements that would mark Brazilian radio profoundly in the decades to come—though neither English lessons, presidential speeches, nor operatic recordings were ever to prove popular fare.[7]

The following year, Edgar Roquette-Pinto, a linguist, botanist, and educator, founded Rádio Sociedade de Rio de Janeiro, the country's first radio station. Roquette-Pinto's apparatus was precarious and there were only a handful of receivers in the city, limiting his audience to a small circle of friends and colleagues. His programming consisted primarily of recordings of erudite music, readings from the daily newspaper, and the occasional high-toned, semiacademic lecture.[8] While this program may have seemed designed to bore a popular audience, Roquette-Pinto envisioned far greater things. As a scholar, he was at the forefront of a vast transformation in the intellectual understanding of Brazil and its prospects. Whereas nineteenth-century elites had suggested that the Afro-Brazilian population would remain a drag on the nation until it was whitened through European immigration and miscegenation, Roquette-Pinto argued that only a lack of education blocked Brazil's inevitable progress. He did not celebrate Afro-Brazilian culture in the manner of intellectuals of the 1930s like Gilberto Freyre, but he believed firmly that all Brazilians, if given the proper intellectual tools, had a valuable role to play in the construction of the modern nation.[9] He viewed radio as the ideal mechanism for the cultural uplift of the population and considered his own didactic presentations on Rádio Sociedade a halting step in the right direction. Roquette-Pinto would later bring this philosophy to his post as director of Rádio MES.

At the end of the 1920s, a convergence of several trends enabled the sudden transformation of radio from society hobby into growing industry—one that would not, however, live up to Roquette-Pinto's ideals. Urbanization and industrialization created new city dwellers and wage earners, increasing the size of the potential audience. Technological innovations dramatically improved the fidelity of recorded music and the transmission of live studio programs. And radios themselves grew far less expensive: by the late 1930s, installment plans and used radios sold through newspaper classifieds put them within reach even of working-class families. By 1945, IBOPE (Instituto Brasileiro de Opinião Pública e Estatística), the Brazilian polling organization, estimated that 85 percent of the households in Rio and São Paulo owned radios. By 1950, that figure had gone up to 95 percent.[10] This prevalence ensured that radio would become the privileged medium for the transmission of Brazil's emerging popular music.

The growth of a broadcasting industry, however, depended on early government initiative. Like all nations seeking to control their airwaves in the early 1930s, Brazil ostensibly had two options: to follow the American model of commercial broadcasting, minimizing government regulation and propaganda, or to follow the British and German model of state control and no commercial sponsorship. In reality, Vargas had little choice. The expansion of Argentine radio presented an immediate challenge: Brazil risked losing control of its airwaves to its neighbor if it did not move to fill them quickly. As Vargas did not nearly have the resources at his disposal needed to create a state broadcasting structure in the short run, choosing some variant of the U.S. broadcasting model was inevitable. It came as no surprise when he legalized radio advertising in 1932 and instructed his civil servants to bestow broadcasting licenses on entrepreneurs dedicated to commercial popular programming.

The legalization of broadcasting advertising gave an immediate boost to the burgeoning entertainment industries of Rio de Janeiro. By the mid-1930s, Rio's broadcasting scene had become a Brazilian Hollywood, characterized by glittering stars and lavish productions. In 1935, there were fourteen stations in Rio, with twelve of them broadcasting primarily popular entertainment, most of it live musical programming. As the decade progressed, the Rio stations extended their reach. Technological innovations enabled the largest stations to broadcast all the way up the Atlantic coast, even before the rise of shortwave radio late in the decade. But the transformation was also a matter of attitude, as producers and performers became conscious that they were addressing a national audience. Magazines and newspapers, as well as records, gave the radio stars of Rio a national presence even before their broadcasts could reach the most distant cities. Their nationwide tours, featuring broadcasts from local stations in a dozen cities, became occasions of mass celebration and public apotheosis.

The importance of broadcasting in transmitting popular culture continued to grow in the following decades. In 1931, there were twenty stations in Brazil. In 1941, nearly a hundred, and in 1950, three hundred.[11] The great majority followed the lead of Rio de Janeiro's most successful broadcasters. São Paulo, while geographically close to Rio, was the only metropolitan area to maintain a relatively independent broadcasting market, a path inspired by local resentment of the capital's overweening predominance and made possible by the city's wealth. At the same time, São Paulo station owners avoided challenging Rio's control of the national entertainment industry. They established a pact setting limits on performers' compensation and refused to hire those performers who broke contracts in search of higher pay, pushing top local talent to the more lucrative market of Rio.[12] São Paulo broadcasters compensated through deliberate localism: whereas the top Rio stations emphasized national visions, São Paulo's most popular stations stressed local color. One of the city's most popular variety shows of the early 1950s, for example, was set among the city's poorer Italian immigrants and featured dialogue in an Italo-Portuguese argot that most non-Paulistanos would have found unintelligible.[13]

Even São Paulo, however, was hardly impervious to the influence of Rio's broadcasters. The stars of Rio performed frequently as guests on the São Paulo stations, instilling a local demand for their glamorous musical productions. São Paulo's orchestras learned to imitate the arrangements of Rio's best radio conductors. Demand for the top names from Rio grew so high that during one period in the 1940s, singer and producer Almirante hosted shows on both Rádio Nacional of Rio de Janeiro and Rádio Record of São Paulo. São Paulo's localism protected a relatively small popular musical market but did not nurture significant variations from the popular musical innovations emanating from Rio.

The growing importance of the polling organization IBOPE in evaluating broadcasting success further undergirded Rio's predominance. IBOPE was founded in 1942 in São Paulo but soon moved the base of its operations to Rio in deference to that city's larger radio industry.[14] IBOPE's audience polls, based on extensive door-to-door interviews, became increasingly important to advertisers looking to appeal to a popular audience. By 1945, the organization produced a highly reliable radio survey for metropolitan Rio, showing audience figures for each half hour, divided by class. Advertisers hoping to appeal to a national audience had little choice but to rely on these figures to inform their campaigns, determining the programs they would sponsor both in Rio and nationally.

The fortunes of the recording industry were closely intertwined with those of broadcasting. Most radio stations depended on records to fill in at least parts of their schedule, and radio stations and recording companies worked together to promote their mutual stars. As radio achieved a national audience in the early 1930s, record sales rose exponentially. In the 1910s and early 1920s, there were several studios in Rio de Janeiro and São Paulo, including locally owned enterprises and multinational affiliates. These studios had already begun to favor popular over erudite music by the late 1910s, recognizing its greater market potential. The low fidelity of their mechanical recording technology and the lack of a national distribution network, however, limited them to small pressings primarily for a local audience. In 1927, the local affiliate of the multinational recording corporation Odeon brought electromagnetic recording technology to Rio de Janeiro for the first time. The new method enabled recordings of significantly higher fidelity, reproducing the sounds of complex instrumentation and allowing vocalists to sing in softer, more nuanced tones.

Even more so than broadcasting, the recording industry was heavily concentrated in Rio de Janeiro. In the late 1920s, Odeon was joined in Rio by three other multinational corporations, RCA Victor, Columbia, and Brunswick.[15] Brunswick quickly retreated, leaving the Brazilian market to Odeon, RCA Victor, and Columbia for the next ten years. The new, more expensive recording technology, as well as the importance of investing in national distribution and promotion, effectively precluded local, independent studios. As a result, throughout much of the highly nationalistic Vargas period, Brazilian recording was controlled by multinational enterprises. But the record labels of Rio de Janeiro were far from the thin stereotype of the foreign investor interested only in exploiting cheap labor, foisting off a cheap product on a desperate market, and extracting the maximum profit. The local affiliates of Odeon, RCA Victor, and Columbia were dedicated to building a market for Brazilian popular music, not for disseminating music from the United States. In this regard, the Brazilian recording industry was one of the must successful Latin American cases of import-substituting industrialization in the 1930s. A percentage of the profits from record sales was funneled back to the U.S. headquarters of Columbia and RCA Victor. But the other economic activities associated with the rise of Brazilian recording stars—the production of public performances and radio shows, the publication of fan magazines, the production of films designed as vehicles for musical stars—were locally controlled and locally profitable. The popular music nurtured by this industry became one of Brazil's most important and profitable export products, bringing receipts from abroad. The most important effects, however, were not economic, but cultural. Instead of becoming dependent on imported popular music, as was the case with most smaller Latin American nations, Brazil nurtured its own production into a thriving collection of multiple genres, marked by vigorous popular participation.

THE RADIO IDEAL AND THE DIP

In contrast to the roaring twin engine of commercial broadcasting and the recording industry, government broadcasting started slowly. Vargas bureaucrats made their first foray into regular radio production in May 1934 with the creation of the *Hora nacional*, which was soon rechristened the *Hora do Brasil*, produced by the new DPDC. Almost immediately, the program became the target of public scorn. In October 1934, one listener sent a letter of protest to the DPDC complaining that the program was so bad that even congressmen turned it off. He referred to the program as the "fala sozinho," or "talks to itself," a nickname that haunted the show for decades. The *Hora do Brasil* was born under the sign of ridicule and never escaped.[16]

All Brazilian stations were technically required to retransmit the program's signal from Rio, but many distant stations did not even receive the signal, and owners of others objected to the program on the grounds that it ate into lucrative commercial hours. Broadcasters in São Paulo, resentful of federal encroachment, simply refused to retransmit the program, broadcasting an "hora do silêncio" instead.[17] MES director Gustavo Capanema, meanwhile, perceived the program as an encroachment on the MES's turf, and sought to undermine the rival agency, advising Vargas that government radio was best left to the MES. Over the next several years, the mutual enmity between Capanema and Fontes grew along with their competing desires to define the cultural project of the Vargas government.[18]

Fontes constantly beseeched Vargas to grant him greater control over the airwaves, and for several years Vargas largely ignored such advice. Even after the inauguration of the Estado Novo, the DPDC remained a relatively minor sector of the government. In 1939, however, Vargas transformed the DPDC into the DIP and named Fontes its general director, greatly extending Fontes's powers—at least on paper. The decree founding the DIP gave the department control over the *Hora do Brasil* and granted extensive powers of censorship over broadcasting and popular music, as well as greater influence over cinema and publishing. The DIP embarked on its mission with tremendous energy, sponsoring contests for patriotic popular music and sending out warnings to stations that had neglected to retransmit the *Hora do Brasil*. Within months, the DIP established a public profile as high as that of any sector of the government.

It did not take much longer, however, for Fontes to start complaining about funding shortages. His protestations were entirely justified. The DIP could only find room in its 1940 budget for nineteen censors for Rio de Janeiro, and twelve of those were only temporary. This small corps was expected to control radio, the recording industry, film, and the press. At the time, Rio was home to ten radio stations, four recording studios, a dozen daily newspapers, and a host of magazines and book publishers. Their total production was well beyond the capacity of nineteen censors. In total, according to Fontes's budget, the DIP only employed 140 functionaries in 1940. These figures left out numerous journalists and writers paid for individual assignments. Still, the numbers were paltry given the DIP's stated mission. The popular commercial station Rádio Mayrink Veiga, in comparison, employed well over 150 people, most of them full-time, and made no pretense of directing the nation's cultural development.[19]

THE *HORA DA FALA SOZINHO*

Although the *Hora do Brasil* was intended to reach a national audience, it operated on a minimal budget and rarely attracted talented speakers and musicians as guests. Despite Fontes's grand cultural aspirations, it remained primarily a source of information on government activities. The program aired from eight to nine in the evening, Monday through Saturday, occupying what would otherwise have been a lucrative prime-time hour, thereby infuriating commercial broadcasters. Vargas speeches often preempted all or part of the regular programming.[20] On those evenings when Vargas had no speech, the program began with news on the president, followed by news from Rio, and then by dispatches from the other states. Most nightly programs included a patriotic trivia segment. Finally, the last few minutes of the program were devoted to musical selections.[21] These segments concentrated primarily on erudite Brazilian composers. Fontes was an ardent admirer of Villa-Lobos, for example, and that composer's pieces were often heard on the *Hora do Brasil*. Military bands were also prominent, as were vast choirs singing "orpheonic song"—simple pieces arranged for hundreds of voices, often children.[22]

Popular music was a less frequent inclusion. Occasionally, stars from Rio's commercial stations made guest appearances on the *Hora do Brasil*. Francisco Alves, for example, sang several times on the program in 1940, shortly after recording Ari Barroso's "Aquarela do Brasil" (Watercolor of Brazil).[23] The DIP was clearly interested in incorporating that nationalist hit into its own propaganda. The samba school Mangueira also performed once on the *Hora do Brasil*, as part of a special 1936 broadcast transmitted directly to Nazi Germany through a temporary telephone hookup. The musicians in the Mangueira school were overwhelmingly poor and Afro-Brazilian, from the *favela* of the same name. Their performance on the *Hora do Brasil* demonstrates that, admiration for Joseph Goebbels notwithstanding, Vargas's bureaucrats had already begun to conceive of their own culture in a manner which contrasted dramatically with Nazi racial purism. It also gives an early indication of the regime's attempt to associate itself with the popular enthusiasm for samba, a strategy that would grow more evident later in the decade. But Mangueira's performance on the *Hora do Brasil* was singularly unusual: samba schools, and Afro-Brazilian popular musicians more generally, were far from regular guests.[24] Infrequent performances by popular singers, moreover, did not alter the fundamentally unpopular, or even *anti*popular nature of the program. By the time the musical segment rolled around, listeners had been subjected to forty-five minutes of sterile bureaucratic reports. They were then likely to be rewarded with parade marches, with only a rare samba to leaven the load. This was not enough to give the DIP currency with a popular audience. The star performers who accepted the invitation to sing on the *Hora do Brasil* did so to curry favor with the regime, and not to reach their adoring public—commercial radio was far more effective for that purpose.

IBOPE, the Brazilian polling organization, ignored the *Hora do Brasil*, refusing to take radio polls during the obligatory broadcast. As a result, it is impossible to gauge with any precision the percentage of listeners who kept their radios on during the *Hora do Brasil*. One later poll, from 1950, suggests that roughly half the listening audience turned off their radios as soon as the obligatory government program came on. Deputy Minister of Labor José de Segadas Viana later recounted his reply when he first met Vargas and the president asked him for his opinion of the program. In contrast to his colleagues, who were eager to please the dictator with sycophantic insincerities, Segadas responded, "Mr. President, they call it the *Hora da fala sozinho* (The hour of it talks to itself) because everyone turns off their radios as soon as it comes on." Impressed by his honesty, Vargas gave him a promotion. As the anecdote suggests, the *Hora do Brasil*'s failure was an open secret.[25]

CENSORS

The DIP's censors were more successful than its producers in shaping the popular cultural landscape. The decree founding the DIP required the department to oversee the "censura prévia," or prior censorship, of all radio programs and musical recordings. In the broadcast realm, stations were theoretically required to submit scripts of every program for review by DIP censors. Because of the department's shortage of personnel, however, this system was often overlooked. Censors were known to review the scripts of a few ribald humor programs closely, and to keep tabs on programs written by authors with known communist sympathies.[26] But they rarely glanced at the vast majority of scripts, if they even received them. Instead, they relied primarily on censorship by *papeleta*—daily edicts prohibiting specific subject matter, circulated to all radio stations.[27] The vast bulk of entertainment programs aired with only nominal prior censorship of scripts.

Popular musical recordings were subject to greater scrutiny. These recordings presented the censors with a choke point. There were thousands of popular songs recorded each year during the Estado Novo, but even this number could be reviewed fairly quickly. And unlike radio programs, which frequently were written only a day in advance, recordings could be delayed for a few weeks with no immediate prejudice to any of the parties involved. The DIP took advantage of this opportunity to review popular music lyrics carefully, and it frequently demanded alterations. In 1940, for example, the bureau insisted on changes to some 373 compositions, and to hundreds more in 1941. The great bulk of these cases involved lyrics which pushed moral and social, rather than political, boundaries. Compositions deemed overtly sexual or celebrating a life of crime were likely targets of the censors.[28]

In marked contrast to the military regime of 1964–85, which generated notable conflict between censors and composers, similar practices under the Estado Novo provoked no open conflict. In public, composers and performers professed to accept the DIP's supervision readily. In 1941, singer Francisco Alves alleged, "The DIP has improved the environment greatly. Censoring, or to put it better, straightening out the lyrics to popular compositions, that department has undertaken a magnificent work toward the better presentation of our national music." Even Wilson Batista, a composer known for his sambas depicting life on the urban margins, agreed: "Sometimes the DIP censors my lyrics. I get upset, but then I realize they are correct. There has to be some control."[29] The dubious sincerity of these statements calls attention to more subtle strategies of evasion. Apparent compliance with the DIP's requirements occasionally masked implicit mockery of the regime's insistence on order and progress. The limitations imposed by censors forced popular music to grow in a different direction than it otherwise might have, but it was not the direction the DIP had planned. The bureau's censorship was more effective than its programming, but still did not amount to control.

Behind the scenes, meanwhile, rival bureaucrats did everything possible to undermine the DIP. The Civil Police had controlled censorship before the creation of the DIP, and resented Fontes's takeover of their turf. Police investigators sought to tarnish the image of the DIP through the circulation of confidential memoranda within the Ministry of Justice. They concentrated their invective on Fontes himself, calling him immoral because of his second marriage, undertaken without Church sanction, and deploring his habit of spending too much money on his wife. More seriously, they charged that he had "no sincerity whatsoever for the Estado Novo and its chief," and alleged that he called Vargas a dictator behind his back. Finally, they lamented that the head of such an influential department "walks down the street with his fly unbuttoned."[30] While the veracity of such accusations is impossible to ascertain, their very existence points to the DIP's precarious authority within the regime and suggests how far short it fell of becoming the omnipotent director of public opinion it once aspired to be.[31]

The police slurs may have contributed to Fontes's ouster: in July 1942, he was removed in a larger ministerial shuffle. The DIP carried on but never again aspired to exert greater influence within the Estado Novo. In May 1945, the department was disbanded and replaced by the National Department of Information (DNI). The *Hora do Brasil* was scaled back to a half hour and renamed the *Voz do Brasil*, airing at 7:30 p.m. The *Voz* was strictly a broadcast bulletin of government information, forsaking any grander pretense of molding culture. In a final assessment at the changing of the guard, Júlio Barata, director of the DIP after Fontes, admitted that the *Hora do Brasil* "lacked . . . essential qualities of content, organization, execution—in sum, radiophonic spirit."[32]

RÁDIO MES

In contrast to Lourival Fontes, Gustavo Capanema was a humanist who believed in the need for a strong state not in order to discipline and control, but in order to educate and uplift. As a counterweight to more authoritarian elements, he accumulated far-reaching powers within the Vargas government, turning the MES, early in 1937, into one of the most influential ministries in the Estado Novo.[33] Capanema observed the growth of commercial radio and the popular music it disseminated with despair, and pinned great hopes on the airwaves' ability to refine national culture. In a 1936 letter to Vargas, he insisted, "In a country like ours, in which the distances between population centers are so great . . . radio has a role of inestimable value to play. Radio should not content itself with giving its listeners information and music, it should help to elevate their level of general culture, and contribute to their intellectual, moral, physical, civic, and professional formation."[34]

Not surprisingly, Capanema turned to the like-minded Roquette-Pinto to define and create the MES's radio project. Roquette-Pinto's own station, meanwhile, was in desperate straits. In 1936, the government had passed a law requiring all stations to make capital improvements in their broadcasting facilities and transmitters. The law was specifically designed to encourage commercial broadcasting: small stations that could not afford to invest in the latest technology would be forced to sell their signal rights to more powerful investors. Because Roquette-Pinto had never permitted commercial advertising on his station, he was unable to make the necessary improvements. Rather than sell his transmitter and broadcast channel, he donated them to the MES.[35]

The donation offered Capanema the opportunity to achieve the broadcast potential he coveted in order to offset the baseness of commercial radio. Partially in an attempt to repay Roquette-Pinto for this gift, Capanema named him director of the new station.[36] From its inception, Rádio MES faced enormous difficulties. As a force for the elevation of the national culture it was absurdly inadequate. In 1937, its reliable broadcast reach was limited to the state of Rio and part of the Atlantic coast. In 1941, the regime granted the station a twenty-five-kilowatt transmitter, ostensibly one of the most powerful in the country. But the mechanism was damaged, and Rádio MES, unable to acquire permission to import the parts necessary for its repair, reduced its power to fourteen kilowatts. Worse, the poor placement of the transmitter restricted its range. MES bureaucrats repeatedly petitioned Vargas for the authorization and the funds to repair and relocate the transmitter, to no avail.[37]

Capanema was also forced to devote much of its energy to fending off his rivals within the Estado Novo. On several occasions, Fontes lobbied Vargas to turn Rádio MES over to the DIP. Capanema successfully fought off these advances, but never succeeded in convincing Vargas of the urgent need for greater funding.[38]

Under Roquette-Pinto's direction, Rádio MES became known for its concentration on erudite culture, primarily through its broadcasts of recorded classical music. Given the station's budget, more ambitious live programming was unfeasible. In 1945, Rádio MES employed one full-time musician, assisted by a handful of part-timers. Rádio Nacional, in contrast, employed over a hundred musicians in the same year, most of them full-time. The Brazilian Symphonic Orchestra was willing to perform for Rádio MES broadcasts, but the station's cramped studios could not accommodate the entire orchestra.[39]

As a result, Rádio MES looked for inexpensive ways to create effective programming. Its live productions were limited largely to programs which required no more than one or two on-air performers. These limitations already put Rádio MES at a disadvantage in comparison with its commercial rivals, which could draw on large bands and lavish production budgets. The tone of MES's programming, willfully out of step with popular tastes, further assured that its audience would remain minimal. The 1944 program *Como falar e escrever certo* (How to speak and write correctly), for example, sought to blend grammar with moral and civic instruction. Lessons occasionally served as a springboard for more ambitious assaults on popular culture. In a period when attending professional soccer games was fast becoming the principle leisure activity of Rio's working classes, the host of *Como falar e escrever certo* condemned the practice: "Bringing together sixty or eighty thousand people to a stadium to boo their countrymen is sad; it is painful; it is antipatriotic; it is everything but sport."[40] Not surprisingly, *Como falar e escrever certo* never attracted an audience large enough to register in the radio polls. Its programming ensured that the station would never reach the popular audience it ostensibly intended to uplift.

Rádio MES was by no means a complete failure. Its recorded classical music programs had a small but devoted audience, one with limited options in the commercial radio market. As one grateful listener put it, "In a country where music of African origin—like samba, marcha, and *frevo*—predominates, a little chamber music, classical, opera, is like a drop of water in the Sahara."[41] Rádio MES's listeners—a small but devoted and generally wealthy group—explicitly demanded an alternative to the popular music heard on stations like Rádio Nacional. Pleasing this small but influential audience necessarily meant sacrificing the station's original goals.

By the end of the Estado Novo, Fernando Tude de Souza, who took over the station's directorship in 1943, was prepared to lower expectations for the station, stressing the minor victories of erudite programming: "Our service does not exist . . . in order to compete with other stations. Its principal goal is to present methods that make possible the elevation of the level of national broadcasting." At the same time, he could not avoid a painful assessment of the station's shortcomings, acknowledging that Rádio MES had accomplished very little in terms of elevating the cultural level of a popular audience.[42]

Meanwhile, commercial broadcasting boomed. By the early 1940s, a hundred private stations competed with the few government broadcasters for radio's growing audience. Although the bureaucrats at the DIP and the MES looked on with a combination of envy and disdain, the growth of commercial broadcasting was a sign not of the state's failure but of successful state policy. From the inception of his first presidency, Vargas sought to balance commercial and state radio, and to foster a broadcasting sphere in which commercial interests would predominate without completely drowning out government voices. One station in particular—the only one with both state affiliation and commercial programming—drew enormous benefits from this policy, and from the benevolent gaze of the regime more generally.[43]

THE LEADER

Throughout the 1940s and for much of the 1950s, Rádio Nacional was by far the most powerful station in the country, creating a model that nearly every other commercial station pursued in vain. Only in the early 1950s did other stations begin to develop approaches to the medium that were at once distinct from that model and successful in attracting an appreciable audience. The station was founded in 1936 by a consortium that also ran the widely read Rio daily newspaper *A Noite* and several magazines. It broadcast from its studios on the top two floors of *A Noite*'s twenty-two story skyscraper in downtown Rio, the tallest building in Latin America at the time. Its twenty-kilowatt transmitter made it one of the most powerful stations in the country, capable of reaching most of the Atlantic coast and much of the interior. Within two years, the station's directors had hired several figures who would play instrumental roles in creating the Rádio Nacional model and, by extension, in determining the shape of Brazilian popular music. Radamés Gnattali, the orchestral director, brought to his post years of classical training, a willingness to experiment, and a fierce dedication to the cultivation of Brazilian music. Almirante, a director, producer, and singer, sought to create a new form of radio that would distance the medium from its theatrical predecessors. He developed ambitious, highly didactic musical programs, extolling the glories of Brazilian culture. Paulo Tapajós and José Mauro became Almirante's disciples, carrying on his work at Rádio Nacional when he departed for other stations. And Victor Costa brought colloquial language and quotidian concerns to radio theater and trained a cadre of radio actors that eventually made Rádio Nacional the country's leading producer of soap operas. All of these producers insisted on exacting standards uncommon in the early years of the medium's growth. Almirante explained their professionalism with a phrase that became the slogan for the station's employees: "Radio is only entertainment for the listener. For those who create it, it is a job like any other."[44]

Gnattali, Almirante, and their assistants left a lasting influence not only on the programming of Rádio Nacional and its imitators, but on Brazilian popular music. They led the way among contemporary broadcasters in treating Afro-Brazilian popular music not as mere entertainment but as both a sophisticated artistic form deserving the highest orchestral standards and as a repository of a national cultural essence. In doing so, they took the ideas and expressions of both an intellectual and popular cultural vanguard, gave them the polish of lavish orchestral production, and disseminated them throughout the nation. In the process, they turned Rádio Nacional into the most important force in the creation and consolidation of national musical trends.

By early 1940, Rádio Nacional was one of the two most popular stations in the country, competing with crosstown rival Rádio Mayrink Veiga for dominance. In March of that year, the station was taken over by the government, along with *A Noite* and its affiliated magazines. The takeover and its consequences have been widely misinterpreted. Rádio Nacional has often been dismissed as state radio, a mouthpiece of the Vargas government.[45] In fact, direct government intrusion in programming decisions was minimal until 1964, when the new military regime scuttled the Rádio Nacional model and fired most employees. But the government takeover did have significant ramifications, giving Rádio Nacional the financial freedom to crush its competitors by hiring away the best performers and raising its high production standards.

Before the takeover, Rádio Nacional and *A Noite* belonged to a consortium consisting primarily of international capitalists. The consortium also owned the Companhia Estrada de Ferro São Paulo–Rio Grande, a railway in southern Brazil that had long been plagued by debt and labor trouble. As the Estado Novo progressed, Vargas grew increasingly uncomfortable with strong foreign interest in Brazilian transport and communications. On 8 March 1940, he used the railway's debts as a pretext to seize all of the consortium's holdings, including Rádio Nacional. He justified his actions on the grounds that such enterprises were better in the hands of the government than in those of foreign capitalists.[46]

Vargas had contemplated such a move against the Estrada de Ferro São Paulo–Rio Grande as early as 1933, three years before the existence of Rádio Nacional. The station was not, therefore, the primary object of the takeover.[47] Instead, it was almost an incidental benefit of Vargas's measures to seize the railway. Vargas designated the newly acquired corporations the Empresas Incorporadas ao Patrimônio da União (Enterprises incorporated into the patrimony of the union) and appointed a superintendent to manage them. This enabled the Estado Novo to swallow private, profit-oriented corporations without substantially altering their structure or purpose. It also enabled Vargas to separate these corporations from the rest of the Estado Novo hierarchy. Beyond that of the superintendent, who reported directly to Vargas, there were no new bureaucratic posts created to administer the incorporated enterprises. They remained relatively free of the habits of political patronage that characterized Estado Novo ministries.[48]

Rádio Nacional drew enormous benefits from this system and became the only truly successful incorporated enterprise. A Noite and its associated magazines all lost money, draining the coffers of the Estado Novo. Rádio Nacional, in contrast, generated immense profits. Between 1940 and 1946, it increased its gross revenue by 700 percent.[49] Because there were no private investors to satisfy, on the one hand, and because the station was kept separate from the rest of the government bureaucracy, on the other, the vast majority of that income was reinvested in the station's infrastructure and productions.

In 1942, while Rádio MES and the DIP were feuding over meager resources, Rádio Nacional purchased a fifty-kilowatt transmitter, by far the most powerful in the country. And at the end of that year, the station inaugurated a shortwave transmitter, increasing its broadcast reach and giving it the capability to air separate, concurrent broadcasts. In contrast to stations in other countries that used shortwave primarily for international purposes, however, Rádio Nacional overwhelmingly broadcast the same programming on both its transmitters. With the exception of a few programs in English and Spanish for international audiences, its shortwave programming was pitched at the Brazilian interior.[50] In the early 1950s, when radio audience polls were conducted in most provincial cities for the first time, Rádio Nacional led the nighttime ratings in cities hundreds of miles away, from Curitiba in the far south to Salvador and João Pessoa on the northern Atlantic coast, and Itabaiana in the northeastern interior. Audience surveys in distant cities indicated that even when listeners gave their preference to local stations, they tended to choose Rádio Nacional's stars as their favorite performers.[51] The station achieved a national profile that surpassed even the high audience ratings of its own programs.

The anecdotal evidence of residents of far-flung provincial cities tuning in Rádio Nacional in the 1940s and 1950s in order to establish some kind of connection to life in the capital could fill a book in itself. Luís da Câmara Cascudo, for example, the foremost scholar of Brazilian folklore in the period, was an assiduous listener. Living in Natal, Rio Grande do Norte, some twelve hundred miles north of Rio, Câmara Cascudo regularly tuned in Almirante's programs on Rádio Nacional, and the pair exchanged correspondence in which Câmara Cascudo gratefully acknowledged Almirante's contributions to his own studies.[52] The example begins to suggest not only Rádio Nacional's importance in creating a national network of information, but its influence in the quest to define and elaborate a Brazilian popular culture.

Rádio Nacional achieved dominance primarily by hiring the best radio talent in the country, drawing its personnel from several different worlds. Gnattali and several of his orchestral colleagues, for example, had trained for the conservatory. Victor Costa, along with most of the radio-theater cast, had worked extensively in the light-hearted musical revues that were the staple of theatrical entertainment in Rio and São Paulo. Many of Rádio Nacional's musicians had cut their teeth in the *dancings*—the low-budget dancehalls of downtown Rio. Others had already established themselves as successful recording artists before moving to Rádio Nacional. The combination of these diverse elements yielded a broadcast palette of tremendous variety and vibrancy, including children's programs, soap operas, comedy, and, above all, popular music in multiple forms. The great majority of these programs dominated their time slots in the Rio de Janeiro radio polls. In 1947, for example, out of a total of 248 weekly time slots, Rádio Nacional led in 171 and came in second in 58. Its control of prime time was virtually complete. Audience response was overwhelming: in 1954, the station received over seven hundred thousand fan letters, the majority from out-of-state listeners. Most of these were not spontaneous letters of appreciation—almost two-thirds were contest entries. Nonetheless, they begin to suggest the size and range of the station's audience.[53]

Not all of Rádio Nacional's programs were equally successful financially. The station aired several large orchestral programs that were enormously expensive to produce, and could not cover their costs through advertising alone. Some of its most popular comedy programs, on the other hand, featured only two performers and required very little investment. But before the 1950s Rádio Nacional never cut individual programs because of losses alone, and it intentionally maintained expensive, high-gloss programs to lend glamour to its overall schedule. According to Tapajós, "The directors never worried about whether any one program was losing money. The totality was what mattered."[54]

The station's explicit project was to bring cultural sophistication and patriotic idealism to popular radio entertainment. As station director Gilberto de Andrade put it in a 1943 interview, "Rádio Nacional is a station that does not merely broadcast programs of a purely popular nature. Although we do not neglect the recreational side of radio, we seek to attract the sympathy of the public with a presentation of a highly patriotic, educational, and cultural foundation. . . . It is a work of national construction."[55]

Andrade's words might well have been spoken by Gustavo Capanema regarding Rádio MES. Like Capanema, he was an Estado Novo insider—before his appointment at Rádio Nacional, he had been a high-ranking official in the regime's National Security Tribunal. In contrast to Capanema, however, Andrade had also worked as a radio announcer, and he understood the medium well enough to refrain from turning Rádio Nacional into an organ of government propaganda.[56] Beyond the obligatory *Hora do Brasil*, the station's only concession to the DIP's frequent requests for airtime was a regular but brief late-night segment written by regime ideologue Cassiano Ricardo. The station gave Ricardo fifteen minutes, from 11:00 to 11:15 p.m., several nights a week, for political and cultural lectures. As radio polls did not cover late-night hours until the late 1940s, it is difficult to gauge the reception of these lectures. They generated no anecdotal popular response, were not reviewed or even noted by critics, and do not appear in any histories of Brazilian radio. They played no part in Rádio Nacional's overwhelming dominance of the airwaves.[57]

Instead, Andrade turned artistic control over to figures like Almirante, Gnattali, and Mauro. These producers had already dedicated their talents to a patriotic treatment of Brazilian popular culture before the takeover, and the tone of their programming did not change after 1940. Rádio Nacional's very success is an indirect indication of its relative independence from government control: as the failure of the *Hora do Brasil* and Rádio MES demonstrate, a heavy bureaucratic hand was enough to sink any broadcasting venture.

Other stations did their best to approach Rádio Nacional's high standards. As early as 1939, before the takeover, Rádio Nacional recorded some of its showcase musical programs on acetate discs and shipped them to Rádio Clube of Fortaleza. That station not only aired the recordings as its featured broadcasts, but used them as models to emulate. As a producer from that station put it in a later interview, "Whatever Rádio Nacional did, we imitated. We followed as closely as we could."[58] Within Rio, Rádio Mayrink Veiga and Rádio Tupi, Rádio Nacional's closest competitors, often produced blatant imitations of Rádio Nacional's musical programs and designed their schedules to echo Nacional's. In 1946, Francisco de Assis Chateaubriand, the owner of Rádio Tupi, successfully lured away Almirante and several other prominent Rádio Nacional personnel, and tried to duplicate Nacional's approach. The attempt largely failed for lack of resources, and most of the performers eventually returned to Rádio Nacional. But Chateaubriand did successfully establish a chain of stations throughout Brazil, most of which attempted in some way to pursue the Rádio Nacional ideal. The advertising trade journal *Publicidade* summed up the situation in a 1951 article: "Because of the predominance that Rádio Nacional has achieved in the broadcasting of the country, dominating not only in Rio but becoming the most popular station throughout the country, its line of action is a standard pursued by a large number of stations."[59]

When Gnattali, Mauro, Almirante, Tapajós, and their cohort began in 1939 to elaborate a programming schedule based on a patriotic celebration of Afro-Brazilian popular music, they could not have known that they were establishing the paradigm for a generation. They also could not have known that their approach would soon be inextricably linked to the Estado Novo, through the regime's acquisition of the station. And yet that acquisition was unquestionably fundamental to the station's enormous influence. Vargas never would have allowed Rádio Nacional to attain the level of influence it reached in the early 1940s if it had *not* been connected to the government. The president could have taken steps to undermine the station by withdrawing its transmitter—as both the DIP and the MES had requested—by siphoning off its budget, or by interfering in its programming. His restraint indirectly indicates his support for the station, and his understanding that its investment in the patriotic presentation of popular culture redounded to the benefit of his administration. Although not state radio, Rádio Nacional undoubtedly flourished in the sheltering embrace of the regime.

Rádio Nacional succeeded where the DIP and Rádio MES failed, using broadcasting to nurture and mold the emerging popular culture.

State protection and commercial savvy were both crucial to that success. The Estado Novo allowed Rádio Nacional to blossom, permitting it to acquire resources that other stations, both state and private, could only covet. Commercial sponsors responded to that protected status, choosing to invest in a station that flourished under the watchful eye of the dictatorship. The programmers at Rádio Nacional, finally, brought both a sense of nationalist mission and a keen understanding of evolving popular tastes to their work. Most presciently, before any affiliation with the Estado Novo, they endorsed Afro-Brazilian popular music as the cultural essence of the nation. The combination of these factors gave the station enormous influence. Nowhere was that influence more apparent than in the elevation of a particular understanding of samba to national prominence. That elevation and its consequences are the subject of the following chapter.

2 SAMBA AND NATIONAL IDENTITY

Between the late 1920s and the early 1940s, samba evolved from a marginal musical genre performed almost exclusively in a few, predominantly poor and Afro-Brazilian neighborhoods of Rio de Janeiro into the mainstay of a burgeoning industry and a widely recognized symbol of Brazilian national identity. This transformation brought with it a vigorous debate over the meaning of the genre and its links to Brazilianness. The completion of the evolution, however, temporarily put an end to that debate: the general acceptance of samba as national symbol discouraged extensive discussion over the meaning of that symbolism and historical investigation of its emergence. The authority of the icon depended on at least the illusion of unanimity and inevitability. Assertions that samba was the principal expression of Brazilianness fostered an ahistorical understanding that samba had always meant Brazil, and vice versa.

By the early 1950s, popular composers began to draw precisely on this generally accepted symbolism to reveal the failures of the nation, returning critical vitality to the genre. These critical sambas, however, only deepened the association of the genre with national identity. For several decades, the historical emergence of that association went largely unexamined. In the 1970s and 1980s, a few works appeared tracking the rise of Rio's samba schools from impromptu clubs in the 1920s to the center of a multimillion dollar industry in the 1970s, but to the degree that these works implied a reconsideration of the question of samba and national identity, they were largely ignored.[1] More recently, scholars have written on changing perspectives toward samba among intellectuals of the 1930s, and on the divergent approaches to nationalism among key samba composers of the 1930s and 1940s.[2] Together, these works constitute an important evolution in the historiography of samba, bringing to light some of the contingencies in the rising importance of the genre. They tend, however, to underestimate the importance of radio as an arena in which samba's trajectory was determined, leaving much of samba's rise to be explained. The most compelling recent account of the evolution of samba, Carlos Sandroni's brilliant *Feitiço decente* (Decent enchantment), stops in 1933, just when samba's rise to national consecration was gaining momentum.[3] To understand the continuing vitality of samba as a symbol of national identity, it is necessary to pick up where Sandroni leaves off, following the genre's evolution from the early 1930s through the mid-1950s.

In the mid-1930s, when samba was still an emerging popular music of Rio de Janeiro, the most prominent samba composers offered several competing understandings of the genre itself and of its links to national identity. These ranged from reductive and romantic fantasies of samba springing from the bosom of an undifferentiated *povo*, or people, to caustic visions of samba as a satire of the pseudo-civilization of Brazilian elites and authorities. Much of the debate in the samba world concerned questions of the origins and nurturing grounds of the genre, with some sambistas claiming that samba was music of the *cidade*, or city, and others contending that it was originally and primarily music of the *morro*, or hill. Both were collective terms, with *cidade* standing for the various working and middle-class, white, and mixed-race neighborhoods of downtown Rio, as well as for the city's radio stations and recording studios, and *morro* for the predominantly black favelas. The polemic regarding these two vaguely defined locations explicitly treated questions of style, and implicitly involved more sensitive questions of class and race.

By the early 1940s, the most reductive understanding appeared to have triumphed. In samba lyrics, in critical reviews, and in popular cultural references, samba was depicted as flowing forth unbeckoned from the favelas, a pure, authentic popular form ennobled by its expression of Brazilianness. The two elements of this vision were corollaries: the more samba was seen as a carrier of national identity, the more it was depicted as arising in its purest form from the morro. Rádio Nacional played a crucial role in transmitting this understanding. In the 1930s, when broadcasting in Rio was characterized by a number of nascent, competing stations searching for a successful professional format, a variety of samba voices coexisted on the air. As Rádio Nacional became the dominant station in Rio and the trendsetter for the entire country, it broadcast several styles of samba, but in its rhetoric it adopted a single, consistent position on the nature and meaning of the genre. Partly because of the station's power, that position became a national standard.

This reductive understanding of samba profoundly influenced perceptions of the music both within Brazil and internationally, and lent credence to a rhetoric of racial democracy which pointed to esteem for Afro-Brazilian culture as evidence that racism did not exist in Brazil. That rhetoric, in turn, was pivotal in the national self-conception in the 1940s and beyond, undergirding a vision of Brazilian exceptionalism and virtue. Its successful propagation has generally been referred to as "the myth of racial democracy," a phrase that became standard currency among scholars who set out to debunk that myth beginning in the late 1950s.[4] But despite forty years of voluminous and utterly persuasive refutation, the idea of racial democracy retains power, and is frequently invoked by Brazilians of all classes and phenotypes. Given this survival, the concept of "myth" has outlived its usefulness, for it implies a fictional story in which people willfully or gullibly invest real belief. It is more illuminating to speak of a rhetoric of racial democracy employed in the service of varying strategies. In certain situations, this rhetoric continues to serve the self-congratulatory purpose of distinguishing Brazil from racist nations—the United States foremost among them. In this usage, the rhetoric indeed serves to gloss over, if not entirely conceal, the real existence of racial discrimination. The consecration of samba as a symbol of national identity remains important to this usage. But as several scholars have shown, the rhetoric of racial democracy can also serve to describe an ideal, deliberately contrasted to a corrupt reality. This ideal is invoked to emphasize the anti-Brazilian nature of a specific racist practice.[5] In this sense, the rhetoric has proved an important, if double-edged, tool for Afro-Brazilians demanding equal treatment. Assertions of samba's link to national identity have *also* served this usage: if samba is the essence of Brazil, disparagement of its practitioners is anti-Brazilian, and therefore to be condemned.

Just as the rhetoric of racial democracy has proved to be more complex than a hollow myth, then, so has its relationship to samba. Patriotic *samba-exaltação*, or samba-exaltation, became the dominant paradigm within the genre in the early 1940s, but it did not remain dominant for long. By the fall of the Estado Novo, a few composers— Geraldo Pereira, in particular—began to use the notion of authenticity ascribed to favela samba to comment acerbically on the marginalization of *favelados*, or residents of the favelas, from other aspects of

Brazilian life. In doing so, they revealed the striking contrast between the civic celebration of Afro-Brazilian culture and the economic and political exclusion of poor Afro-Brazilians. Samba, then, has served both to support and to belie the rhetoric of racial democracy. It is the contrapuntal relationship between these two tendencies that has made samba's link to national identity continually compelling over the last half century. But there is another wrinkle: by composing sambas that probed the knotty dilemma of race in Brazil, sambistas like Geraldo Pereira gave new life to the genre's promise of racial democracy. Through samba, they claimed a powerful role as popular cultural citizens, achieving an influence denied them in the formal political and economic realms.

FROM CIDADE NOVA TO THE PROGRAMA CASÉ

Samba, as a coherent rhythm, dance, and musical genre, emerged from popular dance parties in the downtown Rio de Janeiro neighborhood of Cidade Nova during the 1910s. These parties were held primarily in the homes of several well-known *baianas*, Afro-Brazilian women who had migrated to Rio from the northeastern state of Bahia, around a small square known as Praça Onze de Junho (Eleventh of June Plaza) or simply Praça Onze. In its earliest incarnations, samba drew heavily on both West African antecedents and existing local popular forms like the *lundu* and the *maxixe*, themselves blends of European and African instrumentation and rhythm. Early samba's debt to the maxixe was particularly clear: Like that genre, samba was performed primarily by stringed instruments with percussive accompaniment, and was danced primarily by embracing couples, often with an intimacy which tested the boundary of social propriety. And like maxixe, early samba was often considered the lowest of the many popular genres in Rio, the easiest to play and the most amenable to vulgar displays on the dance floor, and therefore the least worthy of sophisticated musical embellishment. And both genres, in different periods, were subject to repressive measures by authorities cracking down on the disorder of the downtown dance scene. In the case of samba, in particular, however, the extent of this repression was often greatly exaggerated by subsequent observers arguing for recognition of samba as a form of popular resistance.[6]

This political construction calls attention to a notable contrast: it was precisely their unruly characteristics, and in particular their association with marginal Afro-Brazilian communities, that lent first maxixe and then samba to theoretical attributions of national essence. A journalist protesting police repression of the maxixe in 1907, for example, asserted, "Maxixe banished! Maxixe, which is to music what *vatapá* is to our national cuisine!" Vatapá, a paste of ground cashews, dried shrimp, palm oil, and spices, is considered the signature dish of Afro-Brazilian cuisine. The journalist thus based his assertion of maxixe's national importance precisely on its Afro-Brazilian heritage. Similarly, a 1909 advertisement for a downtown dance hall proclaimed maxixe the "marvelous invention of the mulata! . . . The genuine product of the always remembered Pedro Alvares Cabral."[7] In this case, the advertisement attributed maxixe's power to a blend of African and European characteristics represented by the mulata, an iconic figure accorded enormous powers of sexual attraction, and one who would become crucial to formulations of samba's seductive charms as well. The advertisement then further linked this sensual blend to a process of national discovery initiated by Cabral (foreshadowing Lamartine Babo's "História do Brasil"). These are precisely the assertions that would be made for samba in subsequent decades, with the distinction that in 1909, this treatment of maxixe was relatively rare, and by 1942, the analogous treatment of samba was nearly universal. The spread of this conviction from a few local voices to a national choir depended on a massive transformation in the understanding of Afro-Brazilian cultural heritage, as well as the growth of a music industry capable of disseminating its products throughout Brazil. The early attributions of national essence to maxixe indicate that this transformation did not emerge suddenly out of a vacuum in the early 1930s: the seeds of samba's consecration were planted early in the century, before the genre itself had cohered in any meaningful way.

That process of coherence was as much social as musical. In the late nineteenth and early twentieth centuries, in Brazil as in all other countries with developing popular musical markets, genres were fluid and defined more by social attitudes and market considerations than by inherent musical qualities. Maxixe could not be clearly and consistently distinguished from the *tango brasileiro*: composers often labeled their works with the more socially acceptable designation of tango, while their popular audiences continued to call them maxixes. (It bears noting here that the Brazilian tango had very little in common with the Argentine tango, whose international success would soon guarantee it sole claim to that name.) Nor was maxixe clearly distinct from its own predecessor, the lundu, or from Brazilian versions of the polka. And while popular musicians played maxixe or polka on the dance floors in Cidade Nova, when those same musicians took a break in the courtyard, they played *batuque*, a rhythm with clearer West African precedents, characterized by call and response singing and individual dancing within a circle of singers and spectator/participants clapping the rhythm.

Samba emerged from this thick soup and drew characteristics from several preceding genres. As Sandroni has shown, by the early 1920s the designation *samba* had effectively subsumed or succeeded maxixe, tango brasileiro, and batuque. From its inception, samba incorporated two different musical practices: it could be a ballroom dance for embracing couples, accompanied by stringed instruments, woodwinds, and percussion, or it could be a ring dance accompanied predominantly by percussion. Sandroni labels these two practices as the popular and the folkloric, implying with the former an urban origin and a link to the market, and with the latter a rural origin and a separation from the market. He further suggests that this duality gave samba much of its power: as a popular music it grew and prospered along with the musical market, while its folkloric credentials made it dear to the heart of nationalist theorists. This duality also made the genre the subject of endless debate between those who argued for the authenticity of a folkloric samba and those who countered that the genre had always been urban and volatile.[8] These labels are not entirely satisfactory: the static, anonymous category of folklore seems misapplied to the courtyards of Cidade Nova in the 1910s, abuzz with change and invention. And the idea of a pure, folkloric samba invoked by theorists of later decades was, as Sandroni recognizes, artificial. But Sandroni's analysis of the duality within samba and its importance in theoretical constructions of the 1930s is compelling and convincing.

The growing popular music industry gradually enforced greater coherence in rhythm and instrumentation. From the outset, Brazilian music publishers had demanded that popular composers label their works by genre. As recordings gradually replaced sheet music as the primary form of musical dissemination, those labels became more consistent: consumers came to expect a samba recording to feature a 2/4 rhythm and eight-bar melodic phrases, performed either by solo piano or guitar, *cavaquinho* (a kind of ukulele), mandolin, and percussion. The boundaries between samba and other genres became clearer. Among these various genres, samba was well positioned for adaptation on a national scale. Rio was the center of the nascent music industry. As the simplest genre of that city, the one most given to catchy melodic phrases and popular dancing, samba was inevitably favored by the growing record companies and, later, by popularly oriented radio stations. That process was well under way by the mid-1920s, when the pianist Sinhô became known as the King of Samba for his jaunty melodies and his lyrics chronicling the popular transformation of the city. But it was still clearly recognized as a local rhythm of Rio de Janeiro, its national consecration yet to come. In the words of Radamés Gnattali, a classically trained pianist who arrived in Rio from the southern state of Rio Grande do Sul in the late 1920s, "In that time samba was a form of Rio de Janeiro. In São Paulo, no one played it. After the arrival of radio, everyone started to hear it, and now everyone plays it."[9] As the orchestral director of Rádio Nacional in its glory years, Gnattali himself was to play a crucial role in that process of national popularization.

In the late 1920s, a nucleus of composers from the neighborhood of Estácio, adjacent to Cidade Nova, and containing the favela of São Carlos, developed a new approach to the genre. Sinhô's sambas placed a heavy emphasis on the downbeat, in both melodies and his piano accompaniment. The Estácio sambistas, in contrast—led by Ismael Silva, Nilton Bastos, and Alcebíades Barcellos, or Bide—played and sang a more syncopated style of samba, throwing in off-beat accents liberally. To a degree, the new style was merely catching up to the dancers, who had always been "requebrando" to samba—that is, moving their bodies suddenly at odd angles and in unexpected directions, often on the weak beats. The Estácio sound provided more impetus to *requebrar*. In a famous interview late in his life, Silva described this transformation: "Samba was like this: *tan tantan tan tantan*. It wasn't any good. . . . So, we started to play samba like this: *bum bum paticumbumprugurundum*."[10] The quotation concisely expresses the transition from Sinhô's stress on the strong beats of a 2/4 beat to the Estácio group's rhythmic elaboration and dislocation. *Bum bum paticumbumprugurundum* is, in fact, a highly accurate rendition of a percussive phrase typical of the Estácio sound, and all subsequent samba.

The new samba was better for couples on the dance floor or individuals in the *roda*, or ring, but it was particularly well suited to parading through the streets at Carnival in a *bloco*, or informal parade band. To that end, Silva, Bastos, Bide, and others founded a permanent bloco in 1928 in order to rehearse their compositions and present them at Carnival in more polished form. They called their new institution a samba school, partly in jest, and named it Deixa Falar (Let him talk). Sambistas from other neighborhoods quickly transformed their blocos into samba schools as well. Informal competition between these schools soon established the foundation for the more formal Carnival parades of the 1930s and beyond.

The Estácio sambistas, along with other musicians throughout Rio in the late 1920s, also altered the typical samba instrumentation. They gave new prominence to three percussive instruments in particular, the *surdo*, the *cuíca*, and the *tamborim*. The surdo is a large bass drum: the term literally means deaf, suggesting that the drum's tone is so low it is felt in the bones rather than heard through the ears. The surdo anchored the samba rhythm, particularly in the Carnival parades. The cuíca is a hand-held drum with a stick attached to the underside of the drumhead, which produces resonant squeaks when rubbed with a wet cloth. The tamborim is a small handheld drum with a high-pitched tone, usually played with a stick. (Unlike our tambourine, known in Brazil as the *pandeiro*, it has no cymbals.) The cuíca and the tamborim were ideal for providing the syncopated accents of the new sound. This transformation met with enormous popular approval, quickly making the Estácio sound the definitive samba, just at the moment that the music industry of Rio de Janeiro was attaining the capacity to create national trends.[11]

The composers of Estácio were young Afro-Brazilian men of poor and working-class origin. They sold their compositions to the white singers favored by the record companies and radio stations, and thus reached a broader audience only indirectly. Composers from other neighborhoods, meanwhile, adopted their sound, creating their own variations. Vila Isabel—a predominantly white, middle- and working-class neighborhood—nurtured a particularly vibrant samba scene. The composers of Vila Isabel gained easier access to the recording and radio industry than did their Estácio neighbors. A group from that neighborhood known as the Bando de Tangarás (*Bando* meaning group or gang and *tangará* a small colorful singing bird native to Brazil) produced several composers and performers who went on to prosper in the music industry. In 1930, the Tangarás had their first hit with "Na Pavuna" (meaning "In Pavuna," a working-class suburb of Rio), a samba that brought the fluid syncopation of the Estácio sound to the recording studio for the first time. The Tangarás also added their own percussive innovations, principally a repeated bass thump after the refrain that gave the samba an instant rhythmic allure. The record became one of the most popular of the year, inspiring a host of imitations.[12]

Almirante, the group's leader, became a popular singer and the most prominent radio producer of the next two decades. Two other Tangarás attained particular renown: Carlos Braga, better known by his pseudonym João de Barro, who became one of the most successful composers of Carnival samba and marcha of the era, and Noel Rosa, one of the foremost sambistas of the decade and the most influential lyricist in the history of the genre. Rosa's compositions provided the most important expression of the link between samba and national identity in the early and mid-1930s.[13]

Rosa's extraordinary influence depended primarily on his poetic gifts, his ability to chronicle the age with a few deft phrases, but it also depended on his access to the expanding broadcasting industry. He broke into radio precisely at the moment when the *Programa Casé*, named for its founder and producer, Adhemar Casé, was becoming Brazil's first radio showcase for live performances by popular musical stars. From its inception in 1932 through the rest of the decade, the program served as a samba laboratory. Several of the great sambistas played on the program every week, and many more participated occasionally: Carmen Miranda, Francisco Alves, Marília Batista, Silvio Caldas, and Lamartine Babo—all among the most influential singers and composers of the 1930s—were fixtures on the show.[14] The program was strikingly innovative in several respects. It emphasized live performances at a time when many other programs consisted primarily of broadcasts of a phonograph playing in the studio. It was at the forefront of the rise of advertising, weaving jingles and commercial announcements into the program. More important, the income from these advertisements supported the program's other innovation—the payment of substantial regular salaries to a steady cast of performers. Most other producers expected ambitious young performers to work solely for exposure. At most, on other programs star singers made informal arrangements for payment by the song. On the *Programa Casé*, in contrast, each member of the cast signed contracts for payment per show.[15]

This turn to regular contracts had two important effects. The first was simple—it enabled Casé to demand radio exclusivity from his performers, preventing them from performing on other shows and other stations. Stars used various ruses to circumvent this exclusivity clause, and Casé relented in Rosa's case, but to a surprising extent Casé was able to sign the city's best samba talent and control its radio exposure. The second was more subtle: regular contracts fostered both the professionalism and the cohesion of the cast. The contracts required most cast members to perform several times during a show, which began with a four-hour slot on Sunday evenings, expanding to twelve hours in the late 1930s. This kept them in or around the studios throughout the program. Off the air, they rehearsed and worked on new projects, often generating impromptu numbers that later became hits.

Radio exclusivity and a collaborative atmosphere placed the program at the center of the small world of samba. The genre continued its rapid evolution in the early 1930s, and the *Programa Casé* became a crucial site for experimentation and innovation; its ability to broadcast those innovations to a wider audience immediately gave it even greater importance in molding the genre throughout the 1930s. The program's bandleader in the early 1930s, for example, was the composer, flautist, and arranger Pixinguinha (Alfredo da Rocha Vianna), who was also the principal arranger and conductor at RCA Victor. In his work on the *Programa Casé* and at Victor, Pixinguinha pushed the harmonic possibilities of samba, using the full palette of a large brass section to develop counterpoint and complex chordal backgrounds. He did not entirely succeed in transferring the easy swing of the Estácio sound to a big band, a development that would await Gnattali's talents later in the decade. But he did show that samba could be dressed up without losing its soul, helping to bridge the gap between samba's downtown bohemian origins and its expanding, cross-class audience.[16]

Big-band samba was not the greatest of the program's innovations. *Samba de roda*, or informal, impromptu samba, performed on guitar, cavaquinho, and percussion, was an even more fertile area of innovation. On each program, Rosa and his fellow composer, guitarist, and singer Marília Batista led a short segment titled *Samba e outras coisas* (Samba and other things). This mini-program generally featured the latest works of the composers, along with other popular sambas, performed by the stars and their guests.[17] Much of the segment's energy derived from the contrasting personalities of Rosa and Batista. Both were young, middle-class, and white, and both wrote sambas characterized by rapid-fire lyrics of cutting humor and verbal invention. But Batista was only sixteen when she first performed on the program, and was just emerging from the relatively closed world of an upper middle-class teenage girl, sheltered as much as possible from contact with men outside her family, particularly those of a lower class. Rosa, eight years older and accustomed to taking advantage of the far greater social liberties afforded middle-class men, was already intimately familiar with life in the city's rougher neighborhoods. They exaggerated their differences on the program, with Batista playing the daring ingénue plunging into the exotic world of samba, and Rosa the wise-cracking, worldly scoundrel familiar with all of that world's tricks.

They developed their on-air personalities primarily through improvised samba, a skill at which both excelled. This improvisation soon led to further innovation: while trading verses between themselves and their guests, they began to break open the form. After a rhymed ABAB quatrain, for example, Rosa often added another B line. The fifth line was generally spoken, not sung, and provided humorous counterpoint to the quatrain itself.[18] This approach was a close precursor of a style that soon became known as *samba de breque* (from the English "break") so named because the band stopped the music to create space for these spoken asides. Rosa and Batista were among the first to make this acerbic "extra" line a standard feature of samba and to push its humorous possibilities. They did not invent the style—in the same period, composers of the morro were pursuing similar innovations, and one could likely find precedents in the batuque of earlier decades. These processes of invention were intimately linked. Rosa regularly participated in sambas de roda in the favelas of Mangueira and Salgueiro, trading ideas with the composers of those neighborhoods, and bringing ideas to and from the broadcasting studio.

This kind of popularization has frequently been construed as exploitation: middle-class, white radio stars profit by bringing the funky practices of the favela to a mass audience, while the favela sambistas themselves remain relatively anonymous and poor. But this interpretation ignores the importance of the *Programa Casé* as a site of invention, and the innovations of Rosa and Batista themselves. Nor did the program's innovation stop with this duo: in the mid-1930s, Rosa was often joined at the microphone by Antonio Moreira da Silva, another sambista who moved fluidly between the morro and the cidade. Later in the decade, Moreira da Silva became the most famous practitioner of samba de breque. His performances often contained more spoken asides—all rich in streetwise Carioca slang—than they did uninterrupted measures. He attributed the development of his style primarily to the *Programa Casé*'s experimental, collaborative environment.[19] As a nucleus for innovation within the genre, the program was as important as the sambas de roda of Mangueira and Estácio; as a nucleus for popularization, its importance was unsurpassed.[20]

These musical innovations were impossible to separate from the program's commercial nature. One famous Batista/Rosa number, performed every week, matched the composers and whoever was joining them in successive rounds of improvised verses. Both Rosa and Batista often worked references to the segment's sponsor—a local textiles dealer—into their improvisations, particularly in the spoken "extra" line.[21] Upholstery advertisements, then, figured strongly in the early progression toward samba de breque. Again, purists might construe this as a case of the market exploiting communal culture, destroying its integrity—but this misses the point that innovation and advertisement happened together. Advertisers, of course, were always quick to use popular culture to sell commodities, often distorting it and separating it from both its creators and its original audience in the process. But the case of the *Programa Casé* shows that the market did not merely distort and exploit popular culture: it also allowed that popular culture to be born. Samba's development and its rise to national consecration were unimaginable outside the context of the expanding market.

MORRO AND *MALANDRO*

Batista's family viewed her entrance into the world of samba and radio with consternation. As she described it in a 1977 interview, "for a society girl to be a radio artist in that period was, to a certain degree, disreputable."[22] Batista herself, meanwhile, played in her sambas on the expectations created by her pampered childhood. The lyrics of her first hit described a fantasy of being whisked away to a *roda de bamba*, or informal performance by expert sambistas, on the morro: "Malandro, me pega, me leva pro morro pra me diplomar / eu tenho certeza, posso jurar, que na roda de bamba bem dentro do samba aquele é o lugar."[23] ("Scoundrel, take me, carry me to the hill to give me my diploma / I am sure, I swear, that in the roda de bamba, in the midst of the samba, that's the place to be.") The composition's suggestion of cross-class— and by implication interracial—sentimental and cultural education alarmed and intrigued listeners. According to Batista, this explained the samba's success: "It came from that contrast, from a society girl singing that . . . because samba was considered music for black people, and was not accepted by society."[24]

On the surface, lyrics like these presented a fairly simplistic vision of samba as an exotic music of the morro that residents of the cidade could only approach as adventurous outsiders. Performance on the *Programa Casé*, however, gave the samba a second meaning, revealing Batista herself as a legitimate *bamba*, or samba expert in a thriving *roda*, or samba jam, without need of anyone's diploma or stamp of approval. Such complexities were more apparent in Rosa's work. His sambas were overtly nationalistic, and they explicitly linked national identity to samba. But the concept of nationalism they expressed and the understanding of samba which served it were both dense and ambiguous. In his short career—he died young of tuberculosis, drink, and despair—Rosa crafted a body of work that made him the most compelling of the composers exploring the link between samba and national identity.

Early in the 1930s, Rosa concentrated on the figure of the *malandro*—scoundrel, or rogue. The malandro—a flashy petty criminal, disdainful of work and domesticity—was an idealized social type rapidly becoming an iconic figure in Brazilian popular culture, and a stock figure in the samba lyrics of the period. The malandro was usually represented as an Afro-Brazilian man in stylish attire, most frequently a white linen suit and panama hat, living by his wits in the brothels and gambling dens of the city. The stereotype became a symbol of outlaw glamour in the Rio underworld. The malandro also became an ideal to which many sambistas aspired: Moreira da Silva, for example, carefully cultivated an image of himself as a streetwise tough with a touch of nightclub polish, always dressing the part of the malandro in a pressed linen suit and well-shined shoes. The icon of the malandro, as a result, became inseparable from the world of samba, both enriching and constraining the development of the genre.

Rosa's portrayal of malandros differed from that of his contemporaries largely in its ambitions: Rosa's malandros are not merely colorful characters, they are the performers and guardians of the essence of popular culture in its purest form. His 1932 samba, "São coisas nossas" (They are our things), for example, presents a list of essential national characteristics, all of them vital elements of Carioca popular culture.[25] The samba's second verse begins, "Malandro que não bebe, que não come / que não abandona o samba, que o samba mata o fome." (Malandro who does not drink, who does not eat, who does not leave the samba, because samba kills hunger.) The malandro feeds off popular culture and separates himself from other kinds of worldly concerns. In doing so, he embodies a fundamental aspect of national character and becomes one of "our things."[26]

The following year, Rosa extended this association of samba, the malandro and national identity in "Não tem tradução" (Without translation).[27] The lyrics open by blaming "cinema falado," or talking cinema, for the rise of a pernicious fashion for English and French phrases, and then suggest that the favelas and streets of Rio are the source of a culture that is irreducibly Brazilian, and therefore resistant to foreign influence. "Samba has no translation in French," the song insists, "and everything that the malandro pronounces / in a soft voice, is Brazilian / it has gone beyond Portuguese." The malandro is the true voice of Brazil, but even he is potentially seduced by the foreign. The last verse suggests that if he does not remain close to his roots—Carioca popular culture—he will succumb to the absurdity of dancing fox-trot instead of samba, thereby turning his back on his true nature. In Rosa's sambas of the early 1930s, the malandro, and particularly the malandro sambista, is the preeminent mouthpiece of Brazilian culture because he mediates between cidade and morro. Like the Marília Batista composition discussed above, Rosa's sambas romanticize the favelas of Rio as a particularly rich source of popular culture. But in Rosa's work, the inventions of the morro only acquire meaning through contact with the messy, treacherous world of the city streets, and it is the malandro who serves as the go-between for these two poles.

POLEMIC WITH WILSON BATISTA

The malandros in Rosa's early sambas play the same kind of mediating role that Rosa himself played in the development of the genre. Unlike many composers from the cidade, Rosa spent much of his time on the morro and collaborated extensively with composers from the favelas, primarily Ismael Silva, the principal creator of the Estácio sound.[28] More than any other composer of the period, Rosa wrote samba that bridged morro and cidade. In other respects, Rosa had nothing in common with the malandro as popularly represented. He was a scrawny, white, middle-class, medical school dropout, given to difficult loves and more likely to run from confrontation than to display the rough valor of the malandro. In contrast to the dapper malandro, he was physically scarred: at birth, the attending surgeon had crushed the right side of Rosa's jaw with a forceps, leaving him disfigured for life. The painful disability contributed to his poor health, as well as to his preference for the darkness and soft shadows of Rio's nightworld. He was not a streetwise tough but a bohemian poet.

Perhaps as a result, his pronouncements on *malandragem*, the way of the malandro, irritated the young composer Wilson Batista (no relation to Marília). Batista was of working-class, Afro-Brazilian origin, and had grown up in the provincial town of Campos, several hours from the city of Rio. When he migrated to Rio in 1930, he was consequently an outsider to the samba circles of both morro and cidade. Once in the capital, he survived on any number of odd jobs, including lamplighter and messenger, while training for the only two occupations for which he showed any true inclination, malandro and sambista. He started hanging around the bars and brothels of the city, learning the tricks of malandragem and peddling the sambas he seemed to write with ease. His "Lenço no pescoço" (Scarf around the neck), recorded by singer Silvio Caldas in 1933, was a veritable malandro anthem, praising the scoundrel's dapper, carefree vagrancy.[29] When the samba became a surprise hit, Batista's first, Rosa wrote a response in samba form, with the title of "Rapaz folgado" (Idle youth).[30] Uncharacteristically for Rosa, this samba apparently disdained the malandro, or at least Batista's version of that character. Batista perceived "Rapaz folgado" as an attack, and responded with "Mocinho da Vila," (Little boy from Vila Isabel), a samba whose lyrics impugned Rosa's authority in subjects of malandragem. The polemic continued to unfold in samba form over the next two years, prompting Rosa to refine his vision of the link between samba and national identity.

In "Mocinho da Vila," Batista warned Rosa, "You who are a mocinho da Vila . . . If you don't want to lose your name / Take care of your microphone / and leave he who is a malandro in peace."[31] In addition to its meaning of "little boy," *mocinho* is also the term for the hero of a melodrama or adventure film, and invokes images of a white-hatted, chivalrous gentleman—images uniquely ill-suited to the dissolute Rosa. Together with the reference to the white, middle-class neighborhood of Vila Isabel, the description implied that Rosa had no business speaking on topics that were not of his social milieu. Instead, he would do well to look after his reputation—both to the pedigree of his class and the fame he had acquired as a recording star—and concentrate on his microphone, or by extension his radio career (a pursuit largely closed to real malandros). The samba called into question not only

Rosa's authority on malandragem, but his entire project—the composition of sambas that blended the music of cidade and morro in order to express deep national truths.

Rosa let the matter rest for several months, continuing with his radio and recording career and apparently giving Batista no further attention. Then in late 1934 he composed "Feitiço da Vila" (Enchantment of the Vila), a samba that trumped Batista both through its masterful technique and its elevation of the debate.[32] The lyrics of "Feitiço," a samba written in conjunction with the pianist Vadico, suggest that the sambistas of Vila Isabel brought poetry to the form, thereby raising it to the level of high art. "Those who are born in the Vila / do not hesitate to embrace samba" begins the first verse, continuing, "São Paulo produces coffee, Minas produces milk, and Vila Isabel produces samba." The coffee of São Paulo and dairy products of Minas Gerais were, in the 1930s, the backbone of Brazil's economy. By placing samba in their presence, Rosa suggested both that samba was the nation's foremost cultural product and that Vila Isabel was its vital source.

Other verses suggest that Vila Isabel has "transformed samba into a decent enchantment," raising it from its humble origins. That elevation becomes possible because in Vila Isabel, "the *bacharel* (one with an advanced degree) does not fear the bamba." In the Vila, samba is the creation of both the intellectual and the malandro. The combination of erudite and popular culture yields national art. Rosa expanded on this notion in a 1936 interview. He praised the work of several poets who had recently devoted their talents to samba lyrics, and argued, "It is necessary, at the same time, to emphasize that these poets had to adapt also, abandoning a host of literary prejudices. They influenced the public, but they were influenced by the public as well. From the reciprocal action of these two tendencies resulted the elevation of samba as an expression of art."[33]

"Feitiço da Vila" was Rosa's most eloquent statement on the link between samba and national identity, and also became one of the biggest radio hits of 1935. Wilson Batista responded with churlish personal attacks on Rosa's appearance, prompting one more composition from Rosa, "Palpite infeliz" (Unfortunate suggestion).[34] "Palpite," a melodically inventive, upbeat, and enormously catchy samba, surpassed "Feitiço" in its popular success: radio performances and a recording by Araci de Almeida, one of Rosa's preferred interpreters, made the composition one of the defining hits of the Carnival of 1936. Its lyrics largely reiterated the message of "Feitiço," suggesting that in

Vila Isabel samba became poetry, while displaying a somewhat more generous appreciation of other samba hotbeds in the city—Estácio, Salgueiro, Mangueira, Osvaldo Cruz, and Matriz.[35] These compositions marked the culmination of Rosa's nationalist progression. His earlier formulations of a popular cultural essence arising from the urban margins of Rio de Janeiro reached their logical conclusion in these sambas about samba, transformed into art and reaching its full potential as the expression of national identity. They clearly transcended the polemic with Wilson Batista: indeed, the larger public was largely unaware of the disagreement between the two sambistas, as neither "Rapaz folgado" nor Batista's final contributions to the polemic were recorded until years later. "Feitiço da Vila" and "Palpite infeliz," in contrast, were both enormous popular successes, and constituted the state of the art in the evolving debate over the meaning of samba. They also marked the apogee of Rosa's own career. He continued to compose and perform on radio until weeks before his death, but he was erratic and clearly suffering from poor health. He died in May 1937, at the age of 26.

In the short span of Rosa's public career, samba had progressed from the first, tentative manifestations of the Estácio sound to the mainstay of Brazil's burgeoning music industry. The *Programa Casé* remained on the air, having hopped from one station to another in its five years of existence, and was more influential than ever in bringing new samba sounds to a wider public. Every radio station in Rio had several shows dedicated to the genre, featuring a wide range of styles. Carmen Miranda's flirtatious, loquacious samba and marcha catapulted her to superstardom. Francisco Alves's smooth delivery gave a tinge of sophistication to his material. Patrício Teixeira, the only Afro-Brazilian sambista to gain extensive broadcast exposure as a headline performer in the 1930s, played improvisatory samba de roda on Rádio Mayrink Veiga. Together, this profusion of approaches made samba the lingua franca of popular radio in the city of Rio de Janeiro. Folklorist and intellectual Luís da Câmara Cascudo found this broadcasting panorama disappointing. He complained in 1937 that radio brought only musical banality, "broadcasting, with lamentable insistence, sambas and sambas, sambas and sambas."[36] Câmara Cascudo preferred the rural, amateur popular traditions of Brazil's Northeast, and failed to note the invention and diversity of radio's samba offerings, but his testimony does speak to the genre's predominance on the Rio airwaves. By 1937, most metropolitan centers in Brazil were already following

Rio's lead in programming samba above all other popular genres. It would take the rise of Rádio Nacional to make that trend fully national, temporarily winnowing out much of the diversity in the process.

LARGER DEBATE

As the discussion of the *Programa Casé* has made clear, *samba do morro* was never entirely separate from *samba da cidade*. There were always intermediaries absorbing the styles of both camps, carrying messages between them and fostering mutual influence. But there were distinct camps. By 1933, composers of several favelas had followed the example of Estácio and Deixa Falar, founding samba schools to lead Carnival parades and host sambas de roda throughout the year. The schools of Mangueira, Salgueiro, and Portela, in particular, nurtured a samba tradition that developed along lines parallel to the samba on the radio stations and recording studios of downtown Rio.[37]

The differences between these parallel traditions were primarily in performance and instrumentation, rather than in rhythm, structure, or the subject matter of the lyrics. Even before the 1930s, composers of the morro seeking wider fame or greater compensation sold their sambas to recording stars. Not surprisingly, this practice was often exploitative: the true composers were occasionally robbed outright of their songs, and more frequently were induced to share rights with after-the-fact collaborators. The singers who took advantage of such conditions became known as *comprositores* for their habit of buying—*comprando*—other people's work and calling it their own. As Sandroni has shown, however, composers of the morro were often eager to engage in such transactions, understanding perfectly the relative risks and rewards. They sold unproven works for a fixed sum, while the purchasers gambled that their investment would pay off in record sales and radio contracts down the line. Chicanery was not limited to the purchasers: the favela sambistas occasionally sold the same samba to several different buyers. Continued dirty-dealing on either end was enough to destroy one's reputation in this small, face-to-face market. To shield themselves from accusations, many composers and performers established relatively stable partnerships, with composers selling the right to record their sambas, along with nominal coauthor's credits, to the same performers year after year.[38]

As professionalization grew in both the morro and the cidade during the 1930s, these stable partnerships became the rule, and outright theft of the composer's rights became the exception. Such partnerships, and even the exploitative abuses of them, created constant traffic and exchange between morro and cidade. As a result, it would be impossible to distinguish real and consistent compositional differences between these two idealized sectors. The urbane sophisticate Alves, for example, purchased many of his hits from morro pioneer Ismael Silva. This was not, moreover, a one-way street: Silva, for example, attested to the influence of radio singers like Alves and Mário Reis on his evolving compositional style.[39]

Even in terms of performance styles, there was a great deal of crossover. The sambas de roda of Vila Isabel did not differ greatly from the informal samba gatherings of the neighboring favelas. The fundamental link between the samba schools and Carnival, however, did lead to certain innovations which distinguished morro from cidade. Principal among these was the development of large percussion sections, including not only surdos, tamborins, and cuícas, but a wide assortment of other percussive instruments.[40] This array overwhelmed the recording capabilities and the single-microphone radio studios of the era, and therefore remained limited primarily to Carnival and to the samba schools. As a result, the *samba batucada*, or heavily percussive samba, of the Carnival parade bands became perceived as the sound of the morro, when in fact the samba de roda, featuring several guitars and lighter percussion, was far more common throughout most of the year.

In the mid-1930s, this trend was reinforced by the rise of Rio's official Carnival parade. The *Mundo Sportivo*, a Rio sports newspaper searching for a way to sell papers outside soccer season, sponsored the first competitive parade among the city's samba schools in 1932. The parade was held in the Praça Onze, the birthplace of the genre. Nevertheless, the *Mundo Sportivo* depicted samba as music deriving from the favelas, announcing its inaugural competition with the headline, "The sonorous soul of the morro will descend to the city."[41] The idea of two separate spheres of samba, with the morro considered more soulful, was already in place by 1932. The subsequent development of the parade enforced that idea. In 1934, the Rio de Janeiro City Council brought government sponsorship to the parade for the first time, and imposed a new set of rules. First, wind instruments were prohibited. This limited the schools to percussion and stringed instruments, and primarily to the former, as unamplified string instruments were inaudible in the din of the parade. This separated the music of the *escolas* from the orchestral samba featured on records and broadcasts. Second, each school was required to include an *ala das baianas*—a wing of Bahian women. This regulation linked the parade directly to the Baianas who had hosted the first samba parties in the Praça Onze, and indirectly to West African cultural heritage in Brazil, strongly associated with the state of Bahia. In the Carnival parade, the Baianas were expected to wear the white, flowing dresses worn by the street vendors of Bahian cuisine. This attire, directly associated with the Afro-Brazilian religion of *candomblé*, had already become the signature Bahian style. As the Carnival tradition developed, the costume itself stood in for Bahian influence and presence, even when the women wearing it were completely Carioca. A third regulation required schools to perform sambas with "national themes."

As early as 1934, then, parade officials imposed limitations on musical innovation, required folkloric representation of samba's roots, and encouraged patriotic expression. Such efforts were later redoubled when Vargas's federal bureaucracy took over sponsorship of the parade. The schools themselves, for their part, embraced these guidelines. Paulo da Portela, the most influential samba school leader of the 1930s, established models for his colleagues in the creation of patriotic themes and the deployment of the ala das baianas. Tradition, as defined by adherence to these rules, became the schools' principal calling card. At the same time, da Portela advocated stricter hierarchical organization and rigorous training within his own school, and the other schools quickly followed suit.[42] Although musicians within the schools remained "amateur," performing for no direct compensation, their organizational structure was increasingly professional. In truth, by the late 1930s, amateur status was already a fiction—although individual members performed for free, the schools depended heavily on the funds acquired through government sponsorship. The renewed vigor of commercial sponsorship following the fall of the Estado Novo intensified professionalization, funding more lavish and complex spectacles.[43]

In the same years that the parade of samba schools was becoming the highlight of Rio's pre-Lenten season, a loose group of intellectuals began to speak of samba as a uniquely Brazilian popular expression. The Pernambucan anthropologist Gilberto Freyre played a critical role in this transformation. As Hermano Vianna has shown, Freyre witnessed a 1926 performance in a downtown nightclub by Pixinguinha, Patrício Teixeira, and other local notables of Rio's popular music scene. At the time, Freyre was primarily known for his strong defense of the regional cultural autonomy of his native Northeast, a position built on his esteem for the patriarchal role played by white plantation owners. This intellectual background would have seemed incompatible with an embrace of Afro-Brazilian Carioca samba. And yet, Freyre reported enthusiastically on his encounter with Rio's popular music, suggesting that these musicians embodied an authentic, vigorous Brazil unjustly obscured by a corrupt, official Brazil.[44] The vibrant music of the down-at-the-heels cabarets corresponded perfectly to his evolving notions of Afro-Brazilian culture, and he shared this new enthusiasm with his colleagues.

Freyre's response to Pixinguinha and Teixeira prefigured an understanding of Brazil's culture inheritance that he did not fully express until 1933, with the publication of *Casa grande e senzala* (which appeared in English as *The Masters and the Slaves*). That enormously influential tome set forth Freyre's theory of Brazilian exceptionalism, arguing that the blend of Portuguese, indigenous, and African cultural elements, and their endless recombination in a climate of tropical fertility, gave Brazil its great cultural vitality. In Freyre's view, this fertile blend would both power the nation's progress and guarantee its singularity, ensuring a vigorous, unique modernity. In his presentation of this argument, Freyre adduced provocative descriptions of specific aspects of Afro-Brazilian cuisine, language, music, dance, and sexual behavior. Freyre's description of the development of Brazilian culture in *Casa grande e senzala* echoed the one in Lamartine Babo's "História do Brasil," released in the same year. Whereas Lamartine transformed Ceci and Peri into Iaiá and Ioiô, implicitly replacing the difficult marriage of European and indigenous with a suggestion of harmonious Afro-Brazilian domesticity, Freyre described indigenous cultural elements largely giving way before vigorous African strains more suited to tropical hybridity.

Freyre's intellectual turn helped set the tone for the popular cultural investigations of a host of intellectuals. While Freyre himself detailed extensively the cruelty inflicted by white owners on their African slaves, he placed that cruelty within the context of a familial, affective relationship, in which mutual attraction supposedly offset exploitation. His readers often settled on the simplest possible interpretation of this lurid depiction, seeing only a harmonious and productive blend of African and European characteristics. In this interpretation, the real danger posed by elite white society toward popular Afro-Brazilian society lay not in material exploitation, which was accepted as an unavoidable fact of life, but in cultural hostility, which was increasingly perceived as anti-Brazilian.

As this interpretation spread, investigations of Afro-Brazilian folklore became more common, and the will to understand samba as an urban manifestation of that folklore became more compelling. Intellectuals on the left proved particularly receptive to this vision. In 1936, for example, the young intellectual Carlos Lacerda applied rudimentary Marxist theory to samba's evolution. Lacerda would swing precipitously from left to right over the course of his turbulent political career, becoming Vargas's principal nemesis in 1953 and 1954. In 1936, however, he was a member of the Aliança Nacional Libertadora, the legal affiliate of the outlawed Communist Party. Lacerda had also served briefly as a substitute announcer on the *Programa Casé* and should have been intimately familiar with that program's importance as samba laboratory. Nonetheless, in an article for the newspaper *Diário Carioca*, he condemned the commercialization of samba at the hands of radio stations and record companies. Implicitly invoking notions of communal use value in contrast to trade value, he argued that samba was being "deformed in its passage from music of the poor to entertainment of the rich."[45] This position became common among intellectuals with a theoretical interest in the soul of the people but little understanding of the popular musical arena.

During the 1930s, then, several understandings of samba coexisted uneasily. Noel Rosa elaborated a vision of samba as the vital popular culture of the urban margins, elevated into national art. Meanwhile, the sambas de roda of the *Programa Casé* and Patrício Teixeira's show on Rádio Mayrink Veiga embodied an understanding of samba as the creation of composers of both morro and cidade, competing within the market and open to unexpected cross-fertilization and innovation. This understanding was harmonious with Rosa's vision, but not synonymous. At the same time, the city council, in its sponsorship of the official Carnival parade, promoted an understanding of samba as the urban folklore of the favelas, harnessed to a patriotic ideal. The samba schools themselves, linked through sponsorship and bureaucratic regulation to the evolving project of the official Carnival, began to express their own conception of samba as a genre existing in its purest and most important form on the morro. Leftist intellectuals adopted this position eagerly—so long as samba do morro could be separated, at least on a superficial level, from the taint of commerce. And in these same years, many composers of both cidade and morro avoided these larger questions, concentrating only on marketing their sambas and cultivating a popular audience.

Within the milieu of samba, proponents of these various schools competed for preeminence and struggled to define and direct the evolving genre. The Café Nice, a downtown Rio café popular with musicians and industry insiders, became known in the mid- and late-1930s as a locus for debate on the meaning of samba. At the Nice, composers of every stripe met with each other and with radio stars to collaborate, sell their sambas, and learn the latest gossip. By the early 1940s, discussion shifted so frequently to the nature and origins of the genre that one magazine columnist, author of a regular feature on radio, complained about "those sociologists of the Café Nice who try to separate samba da cidade from samba do morro." For the columnist, at least, the distinction was impossible.[46]

Outside the milieu of samba, the understanding of the music as an urban folklore of the favelas became increasingly predominant. After Rosa's death in early 1937, his compositions fell from popularity, leaving no prominent spokesperson for his position.[47] And for observers unfamiliar with the complexity within the world of samba, the reductive vision of the official Carnival was the most readily convincing. Even among those intellectuals purportedly debating the meaning of samba, its characteristic as a musical genre emanating in its purest and original form from the morro went unchallenged, as it did in Lacerda's article. In mid-1939, for example, the historian Pedro Calmon and the novelist José Lins do Rego carried on a fierce polemic regarding samba in the pages of two Rio dailies. Calmon began the dispute with an article arguing that Carmen Miranda's sudden Broadway success was bad for Brazil, as it would create a misleading impression of the country as a land of vulgar music. "This gibberish of carnivalesque tenor will not give a real expression of Brazil, much less define it. It represents, principally, an untruthful and dangerous generalization," charged Calmon. He went on describe Miranda's music as "vulgar and degrading fashion, inevitably banal."[48]

Lins do Rego replied with a stirring defense of popular tradition: "Mr. Calmon is against samba . . . and wishes to extinguish from our life that black and vile thing that is Brazilian music. . . . But the academic who turns against the rhythms of our land and the richness of our psychological substratum would not have the strength to pierce a cuíca, nor to snap the guitar strings of Patrício Teixeira, nor to shut down a samba school."

Calmon responded indignantly: "I warned of the error not of a native dance, but of the unfortunate propaganda being made of Africanism in stylizations and exploitations. Abroad, they will take us for Guinea blacks or Hottentots in striped shirts. . . . Rather than appearing as what we have become—a cultivated and ambitious civilization—we will appear as what we long ago stopped being, even before Abolition, a people rocked to sleep by the monotonous sound of *atabaques* [large, cylindrical Afro-Brazilian drums]. . . . The people, for Mr. Lins do Rego, is not a great thing. Samba school, guitar, and cuíca. The people for me is the Brazilian Homeland, it is not the Morro do Salgueiro. And the Brazilian Homeland is not a pale and feeble reflection of slavery." Lins do Rego closed the debate by dismissing Calmon as a jealous academic, and insisting, "Let us leave samba, which is a far more serious thing than our literature and our vanities."

The pair ostensibly debated whether or not samba was an apt representation of Brazil. Calmon expressed what was, even at the time, an outmoded racist embarrassment regarding African influence on Brazilian culture, and struggled to envision a more classical, erudite Brazil, at the obvious cost of erasing the nonwhite majority. Lins do Rego adopted the perspective that became dominant among a younger generation of Brazilian intellectuals, praising Brazil's mixed heritage as the foundation of a new and vigorous national culture. He began his argument with the assertion that samba represented the entirety of Brazilian music, and went on to suggest that the genre—and in particular the music of the samba schools—was a vital part of the national psyche. Such assertions made him a figure of much greater currency and influence than Calmon in the intellectual circles of the late 1930s, marked as they were by search for the roots of national popular culture. They did not, however, make him an acute observer of samba. As poet, musicologist, and folklorist Mário de Andrade noted with despair, neither contender discussed music itself.[49] And Lins do Rego did not bother to distinguish the samba performed by Carmen Miranda—a white performer in a stylized Baiana costume, backed by an all-white band—from the samba of Salgueiro. Nor did he confront the fact that both Miranda and the samba school of Salgueiro had commercial projects—albeit of vastly different scope—and that both those projects depended on a simplified representation of samba as folklore. This last observation, perhaps, was historically unavailable to Lins do Rego, requiring a greater distance from the Carnivals of the Estado Novo. As the regime matured, real debate on the meaning of samba diminished, partly because of the Vargas regime's successful effort to reform samba lyrics.

THE DIP VERSUS THE MALANDRO

As the polemic between Rosa and Wilson Batista demonstrates, malandragem was a perennial samba theme. Ignoring the exhortations of "Rapaz folgado," Batista continued to write sambas chronicling the malandro's milieu throughout the 1930s. Moreira da Silva continued to interpret these and other malandro sambas, and to act the part to perfection. The success of Batista and Moreira da Silva inspired numerous imitators, making malandro samba one of the most popular subgenres of the late 1930s.[50]

These sambas, portraying outlaw glamour, defiance of authority, and disdain for work, stood in direct opposition to the ideals of the Estado Novo, making them an obvious target for the censors. Beginning in the late 1930s, the Department of Propaganda and Cultural Diffusion (DPDC), active until November 1939, and the DIP, which took its place, concentrated their censorship efforts on defeating the malandro.[51] Given the popularity of malandro samba, one might expect that the censors faced nearly insurmountable challenges eradicating it. But this was not so: the DPDC stepped up its campaign against positive portrayals of malandros in early 1939, passing the torch to the DIP later that year. By 1940, not a single explicit malandro samba was recorded. It is possible that sambistas continued to play and improvise explicit celebrations of malandragem in informal performances, but they made few attempts to bring these into recording studios. Disputes between composers and censors did occur. But there is no evidence, anecdotal or otherwise, that such disputes became prolonged and embittered, as they did under the military dictatorship thirty years later.[52]

The relative facility of the campaign's success seems to have four causes. First, many sambistas supported Vargas and adhered to the broad tenets of the Estado Novo despite occasional friction with its bureaucracy.[53] Second, self-censorship became commonplace: once composers realized that the state was cracking down, they altered their approach before facing the censors in order to avoid conflict. This by no means eliminated official censorship, but it did militate against repeated and prolonged confrontation between composers and censors. Third, apparent compliance often masked subtle defiance. Praise of malandros gave way quickly to sambas about the *malandro regenerado*, or regenerate malandro. Batista was, again, the principal exponent of this style, describing characters who had forsaken vice for virtue. One critic, praising this trend, reported, "There is no longer any place for praise of malandragem. . . . The new lyrics emphasize the advantages of work." But as scholar Claudia Matos has shown in an analysis of malandro samba and its offshoots, these compositions often contained verbal and musical clues providing implicit counterpoint to their explicit praise of work and domestic regularity.[54]

"O bonde São Januário" (São Januário tram), by Batista and Ataúlfo Alves, provides one well-known example. The narrator is ostensibly a happy worker who has renounced his former bohemian ways. Popular anecdotes suggest that the original chorus mocked the worker as a fool, and that, in order to satisfy the DIP Batista merely changed a few words to bring the samba into line with Estado Novo ideology—for example, changing the word *otário*, or sucker, to *operário*, or worker.[55] Whether or not the anecdotes are true, the composition's lyrics can certainly be interpreted as an implicit criticism of the deadening routine of working-class labor, described by a suspiciously happy ex-malandro, suddenly thrilled to be commuting to a low-paying job on a crowded tram.

The fourth and related cause is that enthusiastic portrayals of malandragem had run their aesthetic course by 1939, and innovation of some sort was inevitable. The irony of the DIP's censorship was that open praise of malandragem had *never* been common. Batista's "Lenço no pescoço" was an exception in this regard—perhaps explaining why Rosa disdained it. Instead, since the rise of malandro samba in the late 1920s, most chronicles of malandragem had ostensibly criticized these practices. As in the case of "O bonde São Januário," apparent condemnation of life on the margins was often a thin veil for a celebration of outlaw chic. Many early malandro sambas would have met the DIP's requirements of at least superficially condemning malandragem. The DIP's censorship merely helped make the tale of the regenerate malandro the definitive trend within malandro samba.

While this trend did not radically transform the genre, it did push Rosa's nationalist formulation into the past: praise of the malandro's popular cultural performance, even in conjunction with the poet's erudition, was no longer possible. As a result, compositions exploring the link between samba and national identity required a new approach.

The regenerate malandro partly filled this need, but a new style, which became known as samba-exaltação, went much further in giving voice to the swelling patriotic fervor of the Estado Novo's middle years. Characterized by sweeping orchestral arrangements, samba-exaltação became the most prominent face of samba under the Estado Novo and initiated a decisive stage in its evolution from marginal genre to national symbol.

ARI BARROSO

As a corollary to their censorship of unwholesome samba, the DPDC and the DIP sought to encourage patriotic popular music. Their efforts in this regard dovetailed with the Rio City Council's official Carnival parade. Under the Estado Novo, the federal bureaucracy played a larger role in the yearly celebration. Supervisors of the parade grew more demanding, requiring from each samba school not merely a "national theme," but a historic one that taught some patriotic lesson.[56] Carnival became expressly a festival of civic instruction. The DIP also sponsored popular music contests in the pre-Carnival months, and a yearly "popular music day" celebrating Brazil's musical traditions. Not surprisingly, these contests and festivals soon became occasions to promote patriotic music. Ari Barroso, a composer whose patriotic fervor was equaled only by his immense musical talent, pioneered and defined the style that came to characterize these events.

Barroso was by no means a creation of the DIP. He was a successful, ambitious composer with a diverse body of work well before and after the Estado Novo, and he never perceived his own patriotic sambas as propaganda. He did not write them to please bureaucrats, and they did not meet immediately with the favor of the censors. But their unsullied patriotic enthusiasm coincided neatly with the campaign to clean up samba and with the larger state-building rhetoric of the Estado Novo, making Barroso a figure of tremendous currency in the early 1940s.

Barroso was born and raised in Ubá, Minas Gerais, a provincial town he left in the early 1920s to attend law school in Rio de Janeiro.[57] Like Rosa, Barroso was white and middle-class. Unlike Rosa, he had little interest in the seductions of the brothels, gambling dens, and cabarets of the city—in contrast, he believed deeply in the virtues of work, dedication, and professionalism. His progress as a student was somewhat slowed by his constant work as a pianist, but he succeeded in finishing his degree. He then promptly abandoned law for a career as a popular composer. He was not nearly as gifted a lyricist as Rosa, but he was a peerless melodist, and throughout the 1930s, he wrote a series of hit sambas. In retrospect, it is easy to trace in these efforts the rising arc of his career, moving from simple Carnival refrains to more subtle and complete compositions, and finally to complex works of intricate but instantly memorable melody and harmony. This final musical evolution coincided with a turn to new subject matter in his lyrics, from unexceptional reflections on romance and quotidian life to rapturous effusions on the glories of Brazil.

Barroso's success made him a regular presence on the airwaves, and he embraced radio as fervently as he did composition. More than any other composer, he worked constantly to maintain a broadcast presence, using radio not only to market his own compositions but to militate for the protection and enrichment of Brazilian popular music in general. For years, he hosted Rio's most popular *calouro*, or amateur, show, moving from station to station in the city. Most calouro shows were an opportunity to make fun of the least talented contestants. Barroso, in contrast, used his program to inculcate his understanding of the rules and values of Brazilian popular music in the minds of its newest practitioners. He could be merciless in his sarcastic treatment of contestants who violated those rules, but the focus was always on the music and not on the sarcasm. As a result, Barroso's program was the only calouro show that consistently revealed talents who went on to successful radio careers of their own. This power to anoint the next generation of Brazil's musical stars, along with the success of his own sambas, had already made Barroso the dean of Brazilian popular music by the late 1930s. It was Barroso, for example, who was chosen to deliver the eulogy at Rosa's funeral, a moment that captured the passing of the torch from one composer to the other. His public role in the 1930s set the stage for his rise to even greater prominence in the 1940s.[58]

His patriotic turn was not completely unheralded—from the start of his career he had shown an inclination toward nationalist sentiment. As early as 1930, he synthesized the notion of samba as the urban folklore of the favelas that was later to underpin both his own patriotic music and more general understandings of the genre. In a newspaper interview of that year, he asserted, "I speak of our *caboclo* of the morro, who is born with samba in his heart, with the Brazilian rhythm in his conscience. They are the kings of syncopation, one of the most difficult manifestations of music and yet one which, in the sambista of the morro, is spontaneous. Our people know samba of the salon, embellished with all the harmonic recourses of the orchestra, but are completely unfamiliar with the genuine samba, which, in the tranquil hours of the night, our anonymous composer drums and cries." Barroso was already positing an anonymous, spontaneous, racially linked samba do morro, and categorizing that as the genuine samba, in contrast to the adulterated music of the city.[59]

Barroso's usage of *caboclo* to describe residents of the morro is curious: the term was generally applied to Brazilian Indians living among whites, or descendants of whites and Indians. The favelas were primarily Afro-Brazilian, and there were virtually no Indians living in Rio in 1930. Barroso was apparently transferring the indigenous associations of the term *caboclo* to the Afro-Brazilian residents of the favela, implying that Afro-Brazilian culture was Brazil's true native culture, rightfully displacing any indigenous precedent. His statement prefigured Lamartine Babo's depiction of the transition from Ceci and Peri to Iaiá and Ioiô, as well as Freyre's suggestions regarding the African sources of Brazil's native cultural vitality. Barroso's terminology did not become commonplace—*caboclo* was rarely used in the sense he gave it—but his sentiment did: he was on the cutting edge of Brazilian social thought.

Barroso's condemnation of "samba of the salon" appears highly ironic in retrospect, given that Barroso himself ultimately did more to popularize orchestral samba than any other composer. But in fact this duality was quite common: invocations of an idealized, pure *samba do morro* became more prevalent as the samba commonly heard on the radio and in recordings grew more orchestral. One of the secrets of Barroso's success was his ability to bring both these elements to bear in his greatest compositions: the lyrics evoke a folkloric samba of simpler times, while the backing orchestra supplies soaring strings and jazzy horns.[60]

In the mid-1930s, he cohosted a program called *Horas do outro mundo* (Hours of the other world) on Rádio Phillips. In addition to his own music, Barroso's segments featured his wide-ranging cultural commentary. After the 1934 release in Brazil of the Hollywood musical *Flying Down to Rio*, for example, Barroso took to the airwaves to denounce the film and its representation of Brazil. He was particularly outraged by the film's use of Brazilian popular melodies performed by an American orchestra in a rhythm he disparagingly described as "foxtrot" (at the time, this was the general term in Brazil for American bigband pop music). Henrique Pongetti, a part-time cinema critic on his way to becoming an influential bureaucrat in the Vargas regime, had given the film a glowing review in *O Globo*, and Barroso included Pongetti among the objects of his wrath. The critic responded, labeling Barroso a "sambista do morro resident in the flatlands," and expressing bewilderment over what he considered to be the composer's misplaced protectionism. "If our national anthem had appeared danced to a blues beat, protest would be deserved," Pongetti conceded, but he could not understand Barroso's "agitating the flag over a musical fantasy." The response only increased Barroso's ire, and he continued to lambaste the film and Pongetti until the publishers of *O Globo* asked him for a truce.[61]

AQUARELA DO BRASIL

Pongetti failed to understand that, for Barroso, samba *was* a national anthem. Five years later, Barroso made that clear to all with "Aquarela do Brasil" (Watercolor of Brazil), an orchestral samba that subsequently became Brazil's unofficial national anthem, far more widely known and celebrated than the official anthem.[62] In an interview years later, he described composing the samba, on a rainy evening in 1939:

> I began feeling all the greatness, the value, and the opulence of our land, a giant in its very nature . . . and I essayed the first chord, vibrant, to be sure. It was an emotional clangor. The new rhythm, different, played in my imagination, standing out above the noise of the rain, in syncopated cadences of fantastic hand drums. The rest came naturally, music and lyrics all at once. . . . I felt myself another. From within my soul came forth a samba that I had long desired, a samba that, in brilliant and strong sonority, traced the greatness, the exuberance of the promised land, the good people, hardworking and peaceful, a people that loves the land in which it was born. That samba extolled, in a sonorous apotheosis, that glorious Brazil.[63]

The unrestrained ardor of the description echoes the tone of the composition, which escapes bombast only through its musical perfection. The lyrics are an extended, delirious celebration of lush, tropical grandeur as the source of national vigor. The unabashed redundancy of the samba's famous first words—"Brasil, meu Brasil brasileiro" (Brazil, my Brazilian Brazil)—immediately establish a tone of breathless patriotism. What adjective could begin to describe the greatness of Brazil? Only, of course, *Brazilian*.[64]

The second line—"meu mulato inzoneiro"—begins to describe the source of that greatness, and that Brazilianness, by personifying Brazil as a "tricky mulatto." By 1939, this Freyrean sentiment, implying that racial and cultural mixture was the wellspring of national identity—which, in turn was linked to a certain willingness to evade the rules—was common among intellectuals. It was still too close to malandragem, however, for the bureaucrats of the DPDC, particularly in conjunction with another line from the composition, "terra do samba e pandeiro" (land of samba and the tambourine). The censors, no doubt, would have been more comfortable with lyrics describing Brazil as the land of progress and industry, and initially vetoed the line. Barroso reportedly visited the bureau in person, successfully arguing his case that the samba, in its original form, redounded to the glory and benefit of the nation.[65]

In June 1939, "Aquarela" was included in a musical revue for charity hosted by First Lady Darci Vargas. For all intents and purposes, in its public debut the composition was already incorporated into Estado Novo image-making. The revue, at Rio's posh Teatro Municipal, united radio and recording stars onstage with high-society amateurs. Pongetti, ironically, wrote the script, a trifling sketch linking widely diverse musical numbers. "Aquarela do Brasil" was sung by Candido Botelho, an operatic tenor making a moderately successful bid for crossover success as a popular singer. The performance was reviewed positively, but not to thunderous acclaim.[66] It was not until the composition debuted on Rádio Nacional that it reached a wider audience and attained the form that would make it both famous and a model for a burgeoning subgenre.

Barroso composed "Aquarela" in the same period that Radamés Gnattali, the orchestral director at Rádio Nacional, was searching for a more effective way to bring the swing of samba to a large orchestra. Luciano Perrone, the leading drummer at the station, recommended shifting some of the rhythmic responsibilities from the percussion section to the horn section. Gnattali and Perrone later described this as an entirely autonomous, and Brazilian, invention. In reality, American swing bands had been using a similar technique with jazz rhythms for several years. Gnattali was an admirer of Benny Goodman, Duke Ellington, and Tommy Dorsey, and had already used some of their arranging techniques in his work at Rádio Nacional.[67] The arrangements he developed in mid-1939, using the horn section primarily for rhythmic expression, followed directly from this swing experience.

Their effect on Brazilian music, however, was dramatic, changing the sound of samba on the radio, and consequently the sound of samba in general. "Aquarela do Brasil" gave Gnattali a showcase for the new sound. Barroso's composition overlapped the basic samba beat with a new, two-measure cadence that fit perfectly with Gnattali's swinging, percussive horn arrangement. This backing horn line is the element that immediately identifies the composition for most listeners: *bump bump BUMP, bump budump budump*. Gnattali counterposed this swinging horn line with a vigorous tambourine, melding hip, international sound to down-home roots. As sung by Francisco Alves, the samba quickly became a radio hit and the featured presentation on Rádio Nacional's evening musical broadcasts. Alves, backed by Gnattali's orchestra, recorded the samba in August 1939, bringing both Gnattali's swinging orchestral arrangement and Barroso's patriotic effulgence to the recording studio for the first time.

"Aquarela" did not immediately rise to the status of unofficial national anthem. In January 1940, Barroso entered the composition in a DIP-sponsored popular music contest, and it lost. Heitor Villa-Lobos, Brazil's most prominent erudite composer and a member of the contest's jury, convinced his colleagues that the civic pride of "Aquarela" was incompatible with the spirit of Carnival. Instead, the jury bestowed the prize on "Oh, Seu Oscar," a samba by Wilson Batista and Ataúlfo Alves. Barroso indignantly protested that the event had been billed as a popular music contest, not a Carnival competition, and never forgave Villa-Lobos.[68]

There were several ironies to the contest results. First, Carnival under the Vargas regime was expressly a festival of civic pride, as the jury was well aware. Second, "Oh, Seu Oscar" was the last recorded samba of the Estado Novo to suggest fairly explicitly that malandragem trumped work. (In that samba, Oscar, the hardworking title figure, arrives home to find that his wife can no longer put up with their domestic ritual and has abandoned him in favor of a life of revelry.) Third, Villa-Lobos himself was a rabid nationalist and a part-time Estado Novo bureaucrat. Describing himself in a 1941 interview, he asserted, "I am nationalist all the way to the last strand of my hair. My work is 100 percent Brazil. I have been lauded by President Getúlio Vargas, and I will continue my nationalist action."[69]

It seems likely that Villa-Lobos rejected "Aquarela" because he realized that he and Barroso were competitors. Both sought to give Brazil its true and noble musical expression, and both perceived popular music as the folkloric raw material of their own more sophisticated efforts. Villa-Lobos, in fact, was famous—notorious in some circles—for using popular musical melodies as the themes for his erudite extrapolations.[70] And as much as Barroso admired samba do morro, he perceived his own mission as transforming that samba into a more polished and durable form. As he put it in a 1958 interview, "I want to do what Gershwin did in America with *Porgy and Bess*."[71] Barroso recognized that he and Villa-Lobos had similar projects, and argued on that basis that he deserved the same acclaim heaped on Villa-Lobos by erudite critics: "He does with erudite music what I do with popular music. Our music is the same, Brazilian. . . . If Villa-Lobos is a genius, then so am I."[72]

The ambitions of Villa-Lobos and Barroso, then, were not only alike, they were also like Noel Rosa's. All three aspired to elevate popular music, transforming it into national art.[73] Barroso expressed as much in his graveside eulogy for Rosa: "We were colleagues and rivals. Colleagues, because we were on the same road. And rivals, because we were miners of the same lode, searching for the same jewel."[74] The principal difference in their attitudes was that for Rosa national identity was decidedly ambiguous. Brazil, like a malandro, was attractive and deceptive at the same time. Consequently, he celebrated a scruffy popular culture of the urban fringes. Villa-Lobos and Barroso, in contrast, endorsed an unambiguous, table-thumping patriotism. Their Brazil was the country of the future, destined for a greatness fueled by the bottomless reserves of its cultural vitality. Consequently, the popular culture that emerged in their music was distilled and contained. This made them uniquely timely composers in the early 1940s. Villa-Lobos was continually celebrated by the Estado Novo bureaucracy, and was appointed the director of musical education for Brazilian youth. Barroso never worked within the regime, and in fact eventually served as a congressman for the UDN, the party most fiercely opposed to Vargas, but his patriotic sambas became widely identified with the Estado Novo's civic cult.

THE INFLUENCE OF "AQUARELA"

Rádio Nacional lent the full power of its arsenal to the promotion of "Aquarela do Brasil," playing the composition frequently in both live and recorded versions. The station's embrace of "Aquarela do Brasil" and the trend of samba-exaltação it inspired cannot be ascribed merely to narrow commercial interests or to state intervention. The station's promotion of Barroso and Alves was unusually intense given that neither was under contract with Rádio Nacional at the time. Gnattali was the orchestral director at Rádio Nacional, and was clearly interested in promoting his own work, but he arranged and recorded hundreds of compositions in 1939, giving him no commercial interest that would lead him to stress "Aquarela do Brasil" in particular. More important, given the frequent allegations that Rádio Nacional was a state mouthpiece, the station began heavily promoting "Aquarela do Brasil" a full six months *before* the Estado Novo takeover of the station in March 1940. Clearly, its enthusiasm for samba-exaltação did not follow a state directive. At the same time, both commercial interests and nationalist aspirations informed the station's endorsement of the new samba. The programmers at Rádio Nacional were the first to realize that "Aquarela do Brasil" was potentially a hit of monstrous proportions, and that it would keep listeners tuned in. And their promotion of subsequent compositions in the same vein revealed their conviction that it was their mission to present popular culture that both expressed and celebrated the nation. As producer Paulo Tapajós put it in a 1977 interview, "the name *Rádio Nacional* implied a certain commitment to musical nationalism."[75] The privileged role they gave to samba as the vehicle for that nationalism both preceded and outlasted Rádio Nacional's affiliation with the Estado Novo.

Their efforts paid off, as "Aquarela do Brasil" became a runaway success. In January 1940, *Cruzeiro*, Brazil's most popular magazine, ran a feature article chronicling a day in the life of Ari Barroso, calling him the most popular composer in the country.[76] Imitations were inevitable, and they followed quickly. Barroso himself composed several sambas in the same vein over the next few years, and a host of composers tried their hand at his mix of orchestral flourishes and patriotic lyrics. In a later interview, Barroso professed, "I created the style they call samba-exaltação. Why, I don't know. It's the phase in which I speak of the grandness of Brazil, of its beauties and its riches. There is nothing exalted about it."[77] The assertion reveals both Barroso's influence and the forthright, extreme nationalism of the style. By mid-1941, the fashion had become both widespread and predictable. In July of that year, a critic reviewing "Canta, Brasil" (Sing, Brazil), a samba by Alcir Pires Vermelho and David Nasser, wrote, "The melody of 'Canta Brasil' is worth very little, because it is too much like the other compositions of this patriotic genre that have appeared lately."

Government bureaucrats, naturally, perceived the trend differently. The DIP began using patriotic sambas in its film soundtracks, and in 1942, one DIP functionary wrote an impassioned article welcoming the "evolution" of samba. The titles of some of these works alone betray their bland patriotism: "Where the Blue Sky Is Bluer," "Brazil, Factory for the World," "Where the Coffee Groves Flourish."[78]

Rádio Nacional invested heavily in promoting this trend. In 1942, the station inaugurated an orchestral hit parade titled *Um milhão de melodias* (A million melodies). Gnattali and the Rádio Nacional orchestra led the program and frequently concluded it with a samba-exaltação. During the same period, the station broadcast Almirante's *Aquarelas do Brasil*. That show featured folkloric music, rather than samba-exaltação, but took its title from Barroso's work. Several years later, the station unveiled *Quando canta o Brasil* (When Brazil sings), a program similar to *Um milhão de melodias*, albeit even more dedicated to the samba-exaltação. Each week, the announcer promised "melodies that speak from the heart of our people," and opened the show with the command, "Open the vast yellow and green curtain!"[79] Significantly, *Quando canta o Brasil* did not begin until after the fall of the Estado Novo, showing once again that the station's embrace of samba-exaltação did not merely obey the regime's command. In contrast, Rádio MES, the *Hora do Brasil*, and Rádio Mauá, the official government radio mouthpieces, did not promote samba-exaltação. The *Hora do Brasil* offered patriotic music but—a few performances by Alves notwithstanding—it did not frequently include samba. Again, this suggests that Rádio Nacional's programming philosophy was its own, and not a product of the Estado Novo bureaucracy.

No other samba-exaltação had anything like the influence of "Aquarela do Brasil." As with all musical trends, some examples won the audience's favor, and others failed miserably. Popular success depended at least in part on intrinsically musical factors such as a catchy melody and a compelling arrangement. To a large degree, however, it also corresponded to lyrical content, and specifically to invocations of a primordial link between folkloric samba and national identity. Compositions that hewed closely to the Estado Novo's rhetoric of progress and industry, such as "Brazil, Factory for the World" and "Where the Coffee Groves Flourish," invariably flopped. Compositions that followed "Aquarela do Brasil" in placing a simplistic and romantic vision of Afro-Brazilian culture at the center of nationalist celebration often succeeded. Assis Valente's "Brasil pandeiro" (Brazil tambourine) of

1941, for example, invoked stereotypical markers of Afro-Brazilian culture, including the percussive instrument of the title, batuque, Carnival parade dancers, and—once again—Iaiá and Ioiô, and described that culture conquering the world, and, specifically, the United States.[80] Similarly, "Brasil moreno" (Brown Brazil), composed by Barroso and Luiz Peixoto that same year, featured the lyrics, "Samba, my brown Brazil. . . . Go to the batuque in the evening air. . . . Samba, beat your tambourine. . . . Samba, all the world will listen."[81] "Brasil pandeiro" and "Brasil moreno" both employed the rhetoric of racial democracy, describing a folkloric Afro-Brazilian culture that invigorated the nation, giving Brazil its rightful prominence on the world stage. "Brasil pandeiro" was more specific, suggesting that the United States, far from representing a threat to Brazilian culture, would be helpless before the power of samba.

Barroso made this understanding of a pure, folkloric samba and its connection to the nation more explicit in a 1948 attack on an elitist local radio director: "She has always been a rancorous enemy of samba," he declared, "which is to say . . . an enemy of the very popular soul. Or even, an enemy of the people in what they have that is most sublime, which is their spontaneous musical expression."[82] The "popular soul," however, was not distributed equally among all Brazilians. Barroso and his imitators consistently suggested that the favelas of Rio de Janeiro were the source of samba in its purest and most authentic form. Rádio Nacional played a crucial role in disseminating these ideas. To begin with, the station explicitly ratified Barroso's project. In a 1948 special on the composer and his works, the announcer described him as "the greatest composer of all of South America. . . . A man who lived with samba and for samba."[83] Again, the strength of this support was unusual given the fact that Barroso worked for Rádio Mayrink Veiga, a rival station. In addition, Rádio Nacional gave constant, didactic emphasis to the notion that samba was Brazil's national rhythm. One 1950 program explained the rhythmic foundations of several Latin American genres. When introducing Brazil and its music, the narrator stated succinctly, "Brazil is samba."[84] The station brought this same didactic approach to its portrayal of the morro. In 1947, for example, one of Rádio Nacional's children's programs featured a special show on Mangueira. The program's narrator described the favela as "the morro that is most Carioca, the morro that is truly the soul of samba." Later in the same show, the narrator described a sambista leaving Mangueira for the bright lights of the city: "The sambista when he becomes famous leaves the morro and comes to the city, an ingratitude that the morro cannot pardon. But in the city the sambista is lost. . . ."[85] Pure samba, the show suggested, is samba of the morro, out of place in the city below.

In material terms, Rádio Nacional's commercial and critical success gave it every incentive to continue its promotion of samba-exaltação. During the 1940s, Rádio Nacional became far and away the most powerful and influential station in the country. Programs like *Um milhão de melodias* and *Quando canta o Brasil* played an important role in that success. They were never the station's most lucrative programs, partly because they demanded significant contract expenses for a large orchestra and Brazil's most popular singers, but they garnered tremendous critical attention, reinforcing the station's reputation for both lavish productions and patriotic grandeur. Regardless of what underlay its approach, Rádio Nacional's ability to broadcast to almost the entire nation and its immense popularity were fundamental to spreading the messages of samba-exaltação. The subgenre became a fundamental element in the widely imitated Rádio Nacional broadcasting model.

Samba-exaltação also flourished internationally. Walt Disney became a fan of Barroso's on a 1941 trip to Brazil and subsequently included "Aquarela" in the film *The Three Caballeros*. (Disney continued to work with Barroso in subsequent years, even convincing him to move briefly to Hollywood.) Carmen Miranda also frequently performed the composition in the nightclubs of New York and Los Angeles. In the United States the samba was given English lyrics, largely unrelated to the original set, and titled simply "Brazil." In this guise, it became an international hit, one of the most internationally successful Brazilian compositions of all time.[86] Along with samba-exaltação, the vision of Rio's favelas as the source of the purest samba also gained international adherents. Orson Welles, sent to Brazil in 1942 on a Good Neighbor Policy initiative, planned a long segment on samba for his unfinished epic *It's All True*. In the surviving fragments of the film, Welles describes samba as "the rich, deep, Brazilian music rolling down to Rio from the hills."[87]

The international success of samba-exaltação was crucial to Brazil's evolving rhetoric of racial democracy, and consequently to a larger sense of self-definition. The notion that racial prejudice did not exist in Brazil flourished in the wake of Freyre's *Casa grande e senzala*. As numerous scholars have pointed out, that notion depended heavily on an implied contrast with segregation in North America: those who pointed to a putative Brazilian racial harmony as the key to a uniquely vital approach to modernity did so through invidious comparison with the United States.[88] Samba-exaltação was itself a part of this flourishing rhetoric, celebrating as it did Afro-Brazilian culture as the source of national identity, albeit in a way that consigned Afro-Brazilians themselves to a folkloric, idealized, and static past. The international success of this music put racial democracy on a world stage, proving to all observers that Brazil cherished its Afro-Brazilian roots, and demonstrating the irresistible popular culture that prospered in its sunny, harmonious clime. By 1942, the success of samba-exaltação at home and abroad had brought samba to its apotheosis.

THE REBIRTH OF CRITICAL SAMBA

Despite the fact that he was the world's preeminent composer of samba, Ari Barroso did not consider himself a sambista. "I am not a sambista," he insisted on several occasions in the late 1940s, "Geraldo Pereira is a sambista."[89] Pereira was born in rural Minas Gerais but had spent most of his youth in the favela of Mangueira, and was known for his sambas chronicling life on the morro. With this assertion, Barroso suggested that he was both less and more than sambistas like Pereira. Less, because his work was not spontaneous or natural—even sudden inspirations like "Aquarela" were, in their elaborate finished versions, the hard-won triumphs of the artist. And more, because he took samba in the raw—the jewel of the national lode—and polished it. Barroso's refusal of the label "sambista" reveals much about his understanding of the genre. It also calls our attention to Pereira, who in Barroso's view fulfilled the requirements of the true sambista—Afro-Brazilian, of poor background, a composer of sambas that appear on first audition to be artless, extemporaneous accounts of his social milieu. In fact, Pereira was a composer of great depth and subtlety, a brilliant melodist and lyricist, bringing together Barroso's and Rosa's strengths. Along with Wilson Batista, he was largely responsible for the rebirth of critical samba in the late 1940s and early 1950s, for its transformation from the fervent patriotism of samba-exaltação to a penetrating inquiry into the failures of the Brazilian nation. In particular, the new critical samba explored the gap between samba-exaltação's depiction of happy and productive Afro-Brazilians, rejoicing in their role as the nation's cultural stewards, and the messy reality of the economically marginalized favelas.

The trajectory of Laurindo, another iconic figure from samba's gallery of stock characters, illustrates the origin of this transition. In 1935, Noel Rosa and Hervê Cordovil composed a samba entitled "Triste cuíca" (Sad cuíca), which told the story of Laurindo, a two-timing cuíca player done in by his vengeful girlfriend.[90] The character of Laurindo, disreputable in his romantic affairs but capable of awakening profound passion with his music, attracted the sympathy of other sambistas. He soon surfaced in other compositions, thrust into new surroundings. This process of communal invention of a stock character was relatively common during the genre's formative period.

His next recorded appearance came in Herivelton Martins's 1943 samba, "Laurindo."[91] In that composition, the title character is the director of harmony for a samba school from an unspecified morro.[92] Laurindo refuses to believe that the Praça Onze has been destroyed—although in reality it had been truncated and paved over to make way for Avenida Getúlio Vargas in 1942, and the Carnival parade moved to an adjacent street. Laurindo climbs the morro, rallying his school for a last performance in the imagined plaza. In the last verse, the musicians lay down their instruments and head off to join the war effort—Brazil had joined the Allies in 1942. Martins's "Laurindo" is a samba-exaltação, depicting a harmonious Afro-Brazilian folkloric past that both undergirds and gives way before a noble future in which Brazil takes its place among the world's leading nations.

The samba was relatively successful, and local film studio Cinédia resolved to include it in an upcoming film, and to use its poignant narrative as the basis for an extended segment. Geraldo Pereira was chosen for the role of Laurindo. At that time, Pereira was recognized for his talent within Mangueira but little known in the city below. He won the part of Laurindo on the basis of his credible samba background and his good looks—he was tall, muscular, and Afro-Brazilian, perfect for the part. The film appeared in 1944 with the inapposite title *Berlim na batucada* (Berlin in the batucada), again in order to link it to Brazil's war effort.[93] The film was not tremendously successful, and there is no complete surviving copy, making it impossible to evaluate critically. It did serve to link Geraldo Pereira with the character of Laurindo in the mind of the public, and perhaps his own. And it also gave him easier entrance into the world of the cidade, with its film studios, record companies, and radio stations.

As Pereira began to peddle his sambas in those circles, the character of Laurindo continued to evolve. In 1944, 1945, and 1946, Wilson

Batista composed three sambas taking Laurindo from director of harmony to corporal in the Brazilian Army, to budding politician on the morro. These compositions—"Lá vem Mangueira" (Here comes Mangueira), "Cabo Laurindo" (Corporal Laurindo), and "Comício em Mangueira" (Rally in Mangueira) firmly locate Laurindo in the Mangueira samba school, perhaps in deference to Pereira's ties to that neighborhood.[94] In the first, Mangueira parades without Laurindo, because he has gone off to war. (Batista makes a clever play on Laurindo's departure from the front of the parade for the front of the Italian campaign.) In the next, Corporal Laurindo returns covered with glory. All the favelas of Rio celebrate, and "they say there will be a transformation on the morro": implicitly, the return of Laurindo, the "defender of equality," will bring better conditions for his own neighborhood. In the last, Laurindo speaks at a rally in Mangueira, remembering those from the neighborhood who died at the front, and promising that their deaths will not be in vain.

The trajectory of Laurindo in Batista's compositions suggests the rising expectations of favelados, who were led to believe, based both on the importance accorded them in the rhetoric of samba-exaltação and their contribution to the war effort, that they would at last be integrated into the political and economic nation. These expectations were not to be met. The government of Eurico Dutra, elected president following the fall of the Estado Novo, promised a democratization that would not leave poor Brazilians behind, but it failed to deliver. The favelados were largely excluded from the brief period of exuberance and openness in the first postwar and postdictatorship years. The return of Getúlio Vargas as elected president in 1951 changed little in that respect. Again, promises of inclusion were unfulfilled. The population of the favelas continued to grow, and it remained cut off from basic social services. The favelados' very existence, in unplanned, precarious neighborhoods outside the grid of the formal city, demonstrated the failure of successive government modernization projects. While the cidade engaged the future, the Laurindos of the morro encountered only exacerbated marginalization and a growing gulf between the rhetoric of racial democracy and reality. Geraldo Pereira, the favelado who had played Laurindo on screen, experienced those frustrated aspirations *na pele*, in the Brazilian expression, meaning literally "in the skin," or intimately. He continually found that talent and perseverance were not enough to bring him prosperity, and that Laurindo's footsteps, from samba school drummer to broadly respected public figure, were extremely difficult to follow. He and Wilson Batista became the most incisive chroniclers of those betrayed expectations.

RETURN OF THE MALANDRO

Several years before Pereira's appearance as Laurindo, Batista and Pereira had collaborated on "Acertei no milhar" (I hit the jackpot), a successful samba of 1940.[95] The narrator of that composition dreams that he has won the lottery and that he will be able to quit his dreary workaday job to enjoy a life of luxurious ease. In the final verse, he wakes, horribly disillusioned. Typical of Batista's work of the early 1940s, the samba conceals a criticism of working-class drudgery in a satirical package that DIP censors found unobjectionable. Although it calls attention to class differences, it is not bitter. Its narration of a frustrated dream, however, already hints at the more acerbic commentaries Batista and Pereira would pursue later in the decade.

Pereira was decidedly the secondary composer of "Acertei no milhar," and its success gave little boost to his career. Over the next several years, he wrote a series of conventional sambas, all of them unsuccessful. His first real hit was "Falsa baiana" (False Baiana) recorded by vocalist Ciro Monteiro in 1944.[96] "Falsa baiana" signaled his innovative approach to melody, and presaged the critical turn he would develop further toward the end of the decade. The melody skips along the rhythm like a stone over rolling waves, diving suddenly and rising just as unexpectedly. Its quality of buoyant swing and its use of phrases of unequal length became Pereira's trademarks as a composer. In "Falsa baiana" and in his subsequent work, the vocal line first establishes a regular relationship to the underlying rhythm, then disrupts that relationship with a rapid roll of stressed consonants falling in between the rhythm's strong beats. In his recording of the samba, Monteiro brought an effortless, unhurried ease to this melodic syncopation. Along with Moreira da Silva, the inveterate malandro, he became Pereira's preferred interpreter.

The lyrics of "Falsa baiana" compare the title character, who merely puts on the costume of a Baiana for Carnival, to the real Baiana, who has samba in her every movement. When the false Baiana enters the samba circle she just stands there, not knowing what to do. No one claps, no one sings, and the samba dies. When the real Baiana enters, in contrast, she swivels her hips and leaves her onlookers with their mouths watering, saying "Hail, Bahia!" "Falsa baiana" takes samba-exaltação as its starting point, accepting that trend's celebration of a folkloric Afro-Brazilian culture. But whereas samba-exaltação suggests that all Brazilians take nourishment from that culture, feeding off its authenticity, in "Falsa baiana" there is a clear division between those who share it and those who do not. The samba mocks the notion that Brazilians can suddenly overcome all separations at Carnival, joining in common revelry, and claims samba as something separate, which belongs to some Brazilians but not to all. It accepts the premise of samba-exaltação only in order to deny its conclusions: samba is the soul of the nation, but that soul is misused and corrupted by those who only try to put it on once a year. Here, the adoption of Afro-Brazilian rhythms and symbols is not evidence of racial democracy, but a phony, unconvincing gesture.

Pereira was allegedly inspired to write "Falsa baiana" by the wife of one of his friends, a taciturn, reserved white woman who chose the common, but in this case unsuitable, costume of a Baiana for Carnival. Nonetheless, it is striking that "Falsa baiana" was released when Carmen Miranda's importance as unofficial Brazilian cultural ambassador to Hollywood and the world was at its height. Miranda had gained her international fame precisely as a false Baiana, wearing a stylized costume and acting out an exaggerated version of tropical exuberance. In Miranda's case, at least, the false Baiana had rhythm to spare, and could samba with the best of them. But although she may have been perceived abroad as the perfectly authentic representative of Brazilian sensuality, there was considerable grumbling at home about her misrepresentations and distortions of Brazilian music. Whatever the circumstances of its composition, "Falsa baiana" clearly echoes these grumblings, using the very ideal of folkloric Afro-Brazilian samba to reveal the artifice of nationalist representations like that of Miranda.

Over the course of the next decade, Pereira's reflections on the divisions of class and race in Rio became progressively bitter. His "Golpe errado" (Unfair blow), also recorded by Monteiro and released in 1946, for example, marks the return of the shameless malandro to recorded samba in the wake of the fall of the Estado Novo.[97] But Pereira does not celebrate this return: instead, he presents a stinging portrait of the malandro as a cog in the machine of social exploitation. The lyrics begin with a brief, quasi-cinematic description of the malandro strolling with his new girlfriend: "Here he comes in his starched white suit / bringing another brown woman by his side." They go on to note that while he cheats, his wife is off working as a maid in a white man's house, and will even bring him supper later. This complex chain of social relationships is expressed in four remarkably concise lines. The first three are sprinkled with references to color, referring to the malandro's white suit, to his brown girlfriend, to his black wife, and finally to her white employer. This quick survey of the spectrum starts by showing us the malandro's flashy style, and ends by reminding us who holds the real economic power in Brazilian society.

The refrain then observes that the malandro's callous exploitation of his wife amounts to an "unfair blow," or swindle. This moral judgment is unusual in Pereira's work—he usually limited himself to apparently dispassionate reportage on the lives of his characters. The explicit condemnation of "Golpe errado" seems to stem not so much from the malandro's mistreatment of his woman but from the fact that this mistreatment forces her to work as a maid to sustain his lifestyle and his adulterous affairs. His independence is an illusion: in reality, his dependence on his wife perpetuates her exploitation at the hands of white employers. The lyrics suggest that she is "se acabando," finishing herself, wasting away to support his illusory freedom.

In Wilson Batista's "Comício em Mangueira," Laurindo speaks at a rally, entering the formal political arena to praise the nation and claim his place at its center. In this regard, Pereira parted ways with the character he played on screen. He generally avoided the realm of formal politics, unless one counts the free shows he gave to public functionaries in order to guarantee his sinecure as a truck driver for the Department of Sanitation.[98] This *osso*, or bone, in the Brazilian phrase for nominal public employment, provided him with at least a minimal salary in lean years, but it also reminded him of the limitations placed on the social ascension of ex-favelados like himself. The expanding government bureaucracy could absorb him at a menial level, but even if he had chosen to work hard at this job—something he strictly avoided, as a matter of principle—he was not likely to rise through the ranks. Perhaps as a result, on the rare occasion when he did offer explicit political commentary, it was with the stinging sarcasm of an outsider. His "Ministério da Economia" (Ministry of the Economy) of 1951, for example, satirized the proposed creation by the recently elected Vargas of a Ministry of the Economy to guard against inflation.[99]

The lyrics take the form of an open letter to the president, praising him for taking the measures that will doubtless lift favelados out of poverty. In contrast to samba-exaltação, however, here the praise of development policy is clearly tongue-in-cheek: "Mr. President . . . now everything will be cheap / the poor will be able to eat / I won't have to eat cat anymore." It was a standard joke on the morro that eating cats was the ultimate act of economic desperation: here Pereira adds bite to his satire by sarcastically suggesting that the practice was common. The real power of the lyrics, however, comes from the speaker's exultation that now he will be able to call home his "nega bacana," his excellent black woman, who has gone to work as a maid in a rich woman's apartment in Copacabana. As in "Golpe errado," the economic marginalization of the favela has forced this black woman into menial labor in a wealthy, and by implication white, home. In its sarcasm, the samba suggests that Vargas's new economic overtures toward the working class would do nothing to change this basic, demeaning truth. Pereira was correct: the minimum-wage increase pushed through several months later did not apply to domestic labor.

In "Escurinha," a samba of the following year, Pereira returned to the theme of the Afro-Brazilian woman who has left the favela to work as a maid.[100] "Escurinha" means something like darky girl, or little black girl, although it is clearly applied here to a grown woman. This diminution of the black subject was common in both the United States and Brazil—witness "boy" and "neguinho," or blackie, as applied to black men—with the distinction that, by the late 1940s, the practice was already recognized as racist in the United States, whereas it carried no apparent deprecatory charge in Brazil. Candor about phenotypic difference itself was often invoked as twisted evidence of racial democracy: the ability to frankly mock one's fellow Brazilians about color showed that there was ostensibly no real prejudice and therefore no hard feelings. In truth, the regular application of the diminutive form to Afro-Brazilians served to reduce their public stature, and apparently good-natured jokes often carried stinging disparagement. That said, Pereira clearly uses "escurinha" in a tone of affectionate intimacy—the speaker is one favelado wooing another—but in a way that immediately calls attention to her color. Similarly, the speaker refers to himself as a *nego*, or black man, again making race explicit.

The speaker is director of harmony of a favela samba school—although unnamed, he shares Laurindo's position. He pleads with the title figure, urging her to leave her work as a maid and to return to the favela. Instead of promising her a palace, he promises to share his *barraco*, or shack, honestly listing its bare appointments—four earth walls, zinc roof, a floor of wooden slats. The rigorous literalism here seems designed to contrast the real physical confines of the favelas with the idealized image of samba-exaltação. More important, he promises to make her the queen of the samba school. By returning her from the favela to the city, he will invert her status from maid to queen—but her reign will only last through Carnival and will offer no material wealth. Like "Falsa baiana," "Escurinha" takes as its initial premise the notion of pure, essential samba do morro as a vital resource. But it makes explicit that investing in that cultural glory will only bring the favelado a life of economic deprivation. At the same time, it shows that the only alternative is menial employment in the city. As in "Falsa baiana," samba is no longer a national treasure nurtured by Afro-Brazilians and then shared by all Brazilians, it is a separate cultural sphere owned by favelados, and *not* shared.

Also as in "Falsa baiana," these subtle lyrics, offering an acute criticism of Brazilian social realities, are carried by a deceptively buoyant, irresistible melody. In "Escurinha," the sound of those lyrics adds another dimension to their meaning. The opening lines, sung in a rough Portuguese typical of the favelas, offer a dense string of sibilant consonants, recalling a samba percussion section at full strength: "Escurinha tu tens que ser minha de qualquer maneira / te dou meu boteco / te dou meu barraco" (Escurinha, you must be mine, any way, I'll give you my bar, I'll give you my shack.) The director of the samba school, fittingly, speaks in pure samba. His rhythm is inevitable and spontaneous, like the music of the morro described in the lyrics of samba-exaltação. In this case, however, its implications of a racially divided Brazil are quite different.

Pereira continued his indictment of the marginalization of Afro-Brazilian favelados in several other sambas of the early 1950s. In "Cabritada malsucedida" (Unfortunate goat stew) of 1953, for example, the narrator is a favelado who is unjustly arrested for attending a party where the guests are served a meal of stolen goat.[101] He is saved from jail not through his innocence but through the intervention of his girlfriend's employer. This is far from racial democracy, at least as the official rhetoric described it: in "Cabritada malsucedida," the state has no reverence for the spontaneous favela festivities celebrated in samba-exaltação. Instead, the state disrupts and crushes samba at its root. To free himself from the clutches of this oppressive mechanism, the favelado, by implication Afro-Brazilian, is forced to call on the patronage of the powerful elite, by implication white. The ostensibly colorblind institutions of the modern state are shown to be distorted by archaic networks of patronage where power is concentrated among white elites.

At the same time, the favelado does not lack entirely for resources. The final line, "O patrão da Sebastiana é quem foi ao Distrito e mandou me soltar" (it was Sebastiana's boss who went to the station and ordered them to let me out) is emotionally ambiguous. It can be read as a humiliated admission of dependence or an outraged denunciation of the abuse of power. But it can also be read as a boastful demonstration of the narrator's elite connections, albeit a boast tempered by acknowledgement of vulnerability. Pereira's own 1953 recording of the samba gives most weight to the latter interpretation: in one of his finest vocal performances, Pereira breathes a jovial ease into the narrator's shaggy tale—he is the untouchable malandro more amused than insulted by the machinations of the cidade. In "Cabritada malsucedida," racial democracy does not exist, but even the poorest favelado can pull strings to evade conviction. The narrator's *jeito*—his way, his rhythm, his samba—flourishes in spite of the depredations of the official Brazil, arising from his clever movement through the interstices of power.

THE MALANDRO'S DILEMMA

This description of Brazilian society was more perceptive and realistic than that offered in samba-exaltação. Its recognition of the relationship between power and race was also highly unusual. Pereira's sambas prefigured a criticism of the rhetoric of racial democracy that would not take shape in academic circles until late in the 1950s, and would not play a significant role in formal political debate until much later. In the early 1950s, popular music may have been the only way to bring such criticism into the public sphere, however covertly. When Pereira denounced racial discrimination openly, among his colleagues in popular music, his complaints fell on deaf ears. His acquaintances found them tiresome and unseemly. As one fellow composer put it, "He had a persecution anxiety, and he thought color was the problem."[102] His critical sambas, with their subtle, potent investigations of race and power, were hits with the public, however, selling tens of thousands of copies and receiving extensive radio broadcast.

Pereira himself was unsatisfied with this success, and grew disillusioned with the music industry he had struggled desperately to penetrate. His frustration stemmed largely from his inability to translate his growing fame into greater material prosperity. "Falsa baiana" made him a household name in Brazil, but recording royalties arrived slowly, and Pereira was convinced he was being cheated. He tried to double his royalties by recording more of his own compositions, and those of other sambistas, after 1951. His own recordings, however, tended not to sell, a failure he attributed to racial discrimination within the industry.

There were other reasons: Pereira's voice was thin, and he lacked the easy swing of Ciro Monteiro (with the notable exception of his recording of "Cabritada malsucedida," which reveals Pereira as a vocalist deeply influenced by Monteiro). It seems doubtful that he would have succeeded as a singer even had his skin been lighter. Nonetheless, he was certainly correct about racial discrimination in the radio stations and recording studios. The early 1950s were relatively open in comparison with previous decades—in the 1930s, Afro-Brazilian musicians had been almost entirely limited to backup roles—but Afro-Brazilian representation in featured roles remained minimal considering the Afro-Brazilian foundation of the music being performed.[103] Mixed-race performers of relatively light skin, such as Moreira da Silva and Ciro Monteiro, had been headliners for years. Dark-skinned performers, in contrast, rarely received the kinds of promotional benefits—like magazine covers, newspaper features, and radio specials—that turned talented singers into national stars.

At a time when a host of adored vocalists reigned supreme in the Brazilian popular musical pantheon, only two of those stars had dark skin.[104] The first was Ataúlfo Alves, who might be characterized as the antimalandro. As a samba composer and vocalist, Alves cultivated a relentlessly professional, even managerial air. In his composition, he generally avoided the kind of probing social commentary favored by Pereira, limiting himself primarily to conventional domestic dramas.[105] As a singer, he had the same limitations as Pereira but effectively set his own voice against an excellent backing vocal trio, the Pastoras (Shepherdesses). The Pastoras shared equal billing with Alves, and together they became one of the most reliable acts of the 1940s and early 1950s.

The other was Blecaute, who became famous in the late 1940s as a singer of good-natured Carnival hits. His nickname, a Brazilian phonetic spelling of the English word *blackout*, itself demonstrates the unusual nature of Afro-Brazilian stardom—it was uncommon enough to call attention to itself. Blecaute recorded two compositions by Pereira, one of which became the best-selling single of the composer's career. "Que samba bom" (What a good samba), released early in 1949, was uncharacteristically simple and upbeat by Pereira's standards, describing a hot samba jam with plenty of booze flowing and women to spare.[106] Pereira was ambivalent about the record's success, resenting Blecaute's triumph despite sharing in it. Soon after, he prevented Blecaute from recording another of his compositions, giving it to another singer at the last minute.

Blecaute, meanwhile, ran up against the same obstacles. Despite reigning over Carnival for several years running, he never appeared on the cover of the *Revista do Rádio*, the most popular music and radio fan magazine. Late in 1954, he accused the magazine's editors of keeping him off the cover merely because of his dark skin. They responded with a taunt that revealed both their racism and the difficulty of confronting it: "What's that, *neguinho*? You know there is no prejudice!"[107] They employed the racial diminutive to belittle him and his claim of discrimination, while invoking the rhetoric of racial democracy to put him back in his place: there is no racism in Brazil, so let the samba continue. This knee-jerk condemnation of any explicit denunciation of racism reveals the value of the dense, subtle criticism implicit in Pereira's works. He used samba, the most cherished symbol of racial democracy and national identity, to show that both were rife with contradictions.

Wilson Batista was also unsatisfied with a composer's royalties and tried to make it as a singer. He formed the Dupla Verde-Amarelo—the Green-Yellow Duo—with Erasmo Silva, and recorded several of his own and other composers' works, with middling success. The pair's invocation of the colors of the Brazilian flag, a gesture typical of samba-exaltação, already begins to suggest the difference between Batista and Pereira. Batista was less likely to criticize racial discrimination, and more likely to invoke the rhetoric of racial democracy and nationalism when it was to his strategic advantage—as in the Laurindo sambas. He also had a much longer career in the public eye, from "Lenço no pescoço" of 1933 through the mid-1950s, and his work was more diverse. By the late 1940s, when Pereira was fashioning a new critical samba, many of Batista's best works were almost a decade old. In 1950, however, he wrote one of his best sambas, a composition that by itself justifies his inclusion in any discussion of samba as criticism of the failures of the nation.

"Chico Brito," like Pereira's "Golpe errado," is a portrait of a favela malandro. Recorded by Dircinha Batista, one of the leading female vocalists of the day, and released late in 1950, it became one of the hits of the pre-Carnival season.[108] Its popular success was unexpected, given its ambiguous message. Like "Golpe errado," it begins with a quasi-cinematic description of the malandro in motion, although in this case, the title character is coming down the morro in the hands of the police. His crime is unspecified: we learn only that he is a card-sharp, a strongman on the hill, and a smoker of "an herb from the north." Batista, the former composer of regeneration, thus added marijuana to the list of the malandro's vices. Then the lyrics tell a different story: when Chico Brito was a child, he went to school and studied hard. When the boys played soccer, he was always chosen as captain. This account of his promising childhood sets his marginal adulthood in greater relief. What happened to steer him from the path of leadership and achievement? Chico himself answers: "But life has its reverses, / says Chico, defending a thesis / If man was born good / and did not stay good / the fault is in society, / which transformed him."

The last quatrain sets a puzzle for the listener that cannot be resolved. Is Chico the victim of prejudice and exclusion, forced into a life of crime by the foreclosure of other opportunities? Or is he just a hoodlum looking to blame his crimes on society? Batista concisely predicts decades of sociological debate, and implicitly mocks the sterility of that debate at the same time. The malandro who invokes Rousseau on his way to jail has already outwitted his analysts. (If Chico's words seem farfetched, it should be noted that they were written by Batista, who had even less formal schooling than the character he invented.) The one thing that is clear about Chico Brito is that he is *not* the beneficiary of a racially democratic society. Instead, his story of failed promise and/or smug deviance challenges the listener to reevaluate that rhetoric and its implications. This was the epitome of malandro samba, employing a language as shifting and inscrutable as its characters.

Batista himself had much in common with Chico Brito—he was quick with a clever story and good at getting himself into and out of difficult situations without ever seeming to suffer deeply from their consequences. Pereira, in contrast, grew increasingly angry, frustrated, and volatile over the course of the early 1950s. In a state of wretched health, suffering from various ailments brought on by his hard-drinking life, he died after a barroom brawl in 1955. In his last years, his life closely resembled that of one of his own inventions, the title character of "Escurinho."[109] Pereira's last great samba, released in the year of his death by Ciro Monteiro, was a companion piece to "Escurinha." Again, Pereira named a character with the racial diminutive, although this time in more ambiguous fashion—it is unclear whether the tale of the Escurinho's self-destruction related in the lyrics is told by a friend or a patronizing outsider. The former may be more likely, as the lyrics are, like most of Pereira's sambas, rich in streetwise slang. Nonetheless, in this case the diminutive clearly carries a charge of disparagement, or at least disappointment.

Like Chico Brito, the Escurinho once had a promising future: we learn in the first line that in the past he was "um escuro direitinho," a straight-up dark man. Again, something went awry, this time with more disastrous consequences. The Escurinho gets out of jail—as with Chico Brito, the offense is unspecified—and immediately goes from one favela to another provoking trouble, like a man possessed. He hits on another man's woman, topples the Baiana vendor's food tray because she won't give him credit, and beats up a bamba. Worst of all, he climbs the Morro do Pinto, one of Rio's oldest favelas, and brings the samba to an end with his violent disruptions.

The malandro who destroys samba destroys himself. Instead of mediating between morro and cidade and thereby fostering a national culture, as in Noel Rosa's early sambas, he obliterates that culture. As in "Chico Brito," the listener is left to wonder whether jail has twisted the Escurinho, or whether he is responsible for his own decline. It is surely significant, however, that in both cases, the direct cause of the character's imprisonment is never mentioned: it is taken for granted that the favelado will have trouble with the law. And the Escurinho's violence against the Baiana and sambistas indicates a frustration with the folkloric roles thrust on favelados by samba-exaltação. Once he was "um escuro direitinho," implying a docility and an acceptance of prevailing social codes—but not anymore. In the decade between Laurindo of 1945 and the Escurinho of 1955, the malandro had returned, more elusive and ambiguous than ever.

NEOREALIST SAMBA

The new critical samba did not have the obvious, immediate effects of samba-exaltação. It was not a trend, temporarily captivating composers, critics, and fans, but a tendency, slowly filtering into the genre and accruing a density of meaning. Certainly, the compositions of Pereira and Batista received significant airplay and sold tens of thousands of copies. This exposure had the immediate effect of spreading favela slang throughout the country—not a trivial achievement, given the marginalization of favelados in most other respects. But there were no radio specials celebrating the new tendency, no eager acclamations of a novel manifestation of the essential national culture, and certainly no official endorsement. Yet the tendency did spread, surfacing in surprising and compelling formulations.

In 1955, just a few months before Geraldo Pereira's death, the young Paulistano filmmaker Nelson Pereira dos Santos completed his first film, *Rio, 40 graus*.[110] Following in the footsteps of the postwar Italian neorealists, Pereira dos Santos created a serious, overtly political, quasi-documentary portrait of exploitation and class conflict in Rio de Janeiro. The film follows the experiences of five boys selling peanuts on the streets of the city on the hottest day of the year, as the thermometer climbs above 40 degrees Celsius. The camera follows these interlacing stories to offer a cross section of life in the city, from the idle white elite of Copacabana to the exploited Afro-Brazilian poor of the favela. The opening credits play over aerial footage of the city, concentrating on its postcard views, its sparkling beaches, its enormous soccer stadium. On the soundtrack, Radamés Gnattali's orchestra plays a lavish instrumental arrangement of the samba "A voz do morro" (The voice of the hill). Later in the film, we hear the lyrics, as well: "Eu sou o samba / A voz do morro sou eu mesmo, sim senhor . . . Sou eu quem leva a alegria / Para milhões de corações brasileiros." (I am samba, the voice of the morro, that's me, truly, yes sir. . . . I am the one who brings happiness to millions of Brazilian hearts.)[111]

Zé Keti, a young Afro-Brazilian composer of modest means, himself a member of the vaunted samba school Portela, had written "A voz do morro" earlier in 1955.[112] The lyrics, and the arrangement on the film's soundtrack, are standard samba-exaltação. But when heard as the accompaniment to the film's blistering criticism of racial polarization in Rio, the samba takes on an entirely different meaning. Pereira dos Santos, as filmmaker, turns samba-exaltação into critical samba. This becomes more apparent in the film's final scene, depicting an exuberant samba gathering in a favela. Here the film is at its most documentary: the storyline begins to slip away, and the camera simply follows the action, taking in the impassioned singers, the sly percussionists, and the effortlessly graceful dancers. The implication is that despite the economic marginalization revealed over the course of the film, despite machinations within the samba school itself, the morro continues to nourish an authentic Brazilian culture that stands in noble contrast to the oppression and inequality of official Brazil. Like Geraldo Pereira's sambas, the film takes the understanding of samba do morro as an authentic, folkloric expression of Brazilianness as its initial premise, and uses that notion to underpin a stinging indictment of the exploitation of the favelados.

Pereira dos Santos continued this theme in his next film, *Rio, Zona Norte* (Rio North Zone) of 1957.[113] The main character, Espírito da Luz Soares, is a sambista from a favela in Rio's northern suburbs. Through a series of flashbacks, the film narrates his exploitation at the hands of a cruelly efficient music industry that appropriates his music and offers him nothing in return. He dies tragically, leaving only the refrain of an unfinished composition: "It's my samba, and Brazil's too." The refrain is at once an affirmation of samba's link to national identity and a rebuke of the nation's failures, for Espírito's story is one of suffering at the hands of white exploiters. Again, through manipulation of context Pereira dos Santos turns an apparent gesture toward samba-exaltação into critical samba.

Rio, 40 graus and *Rio, Zona Norte* extend the tendency of new critical samba to film. At the same time, their depiction of favelados, and of samba itself, is less complex than that offered by Geraldo Pereira and Wilson Batista. In the sambas of Pereira and Batista, the favelados have jeito—the ability to maneuver through tricky situations—but in Pereira dos Santos's films the favelados have no jeito. They exist only to be exploited. In *Rio, Zona Norte*, for example, Espírito's son Norival is a malandro much like Chico Brito, but the film shows clearly that society, and not Norival himself, is to blame both for his petty crimes and his death. The compelling ambiguity of Chico Brito's departing lines is absent. Similarly, the depiction of a strictly exploitative music industry with no redeeming characteristics in *Rio, Zona Norte* merely equates commerce with debasement, and lacks the subtlety of, for example, "Escurinha." In his sympathy for the plight of favelado sambistas, Pereira dos Santos failed to perceive the way real-life Espíritos operated successfully within the popular musical market. Zé Keti, for example—one of the inspirations for the character of Espírito—was, in the mid-1950s, fast becoming one of the most sought-after composers in Rio. As in the case of Geraldo Pereira and Wilson Batista, success did not bring him fabulous wealth, but it left him far from the anonymous, miserable fate faced by Espírito.

Nonetheless, Pereira dos Santos's extension of the new critical tendency set a crucial precedent for the continued evolution of the genre. Samba was again available as a critical form, accommodating innovative uses. Those in power quickly recognized the corrosive power of this tendency. In a period when political censorship was relatively rare, in comparison with the Estado Novo or the later military dictatorship, the Federal Police banned *Rio, 40 graus*. Only after several months of protests and back-channel negotiations was the film cleared for public showing. Its experience of the blacklist helps explain why manifestations of the new critical tendency in samba remained predominantly implicit.

Between 1930 and 1955, samba's link to national identity evolved in three stages. In the first, roughly from 1930 through 1937, composers, critics, intellectuals, and fans increasingly came to accept, and even to cherish, the notion that samba expressed or represented national identity. Several interpretations of the meaning of that expression or symbolism coexisted. Among these, the most important was Noel Rosa's vision of a popular samba, created through the common efforts of morro and cidade as brought together by the mediating actions of malandros, and ennobled into national art by poets. Rosa's nationalist vision was ambiguous, and skeptical of the institutions of work and authority, describing samba flourishing in opposition to these institutions. Another interpretation, one that became increasingly influential among intellectuals, was that pure samba, a kind of unsullied national essence, arose in a folkloric form in Rio de Janeiro's favelas. The Carnival parade of samba schools served to reinforce and institutionalize that perception. The radio stations and recording studios of Rio de Janeiro, meanwhile, were open to various competing interpretations of samba and its link to Brazilianness.

In the second stage, roughly from 1937 to 1945, the samba field narrowed. Fewer interpretations of its meaning became acceptable. The dominant interpretation derived from the folkloric vision of samba do morro as national essence, hooking that understanding to a patriotic celebration of Brazil's march to a bright, exceptional, racially democratic future. Samba-exaltação, a trend that united folkloric descriptions of samba do morro with lavish orchestral arrangements, expressed this dominant interpretation and was beloved by critics, fans, and the Estado Novo. Rádio Nacional played a key role in disseminating and popularizing this interpretation.

The few scholars who have studied the rise of samba as a symbol of national identity have stopped here. Consequently, their analysis runs toward allegations of co-optation by the state, or collective amnesia regarding samba's initial connections to the market and its dependence on mediation between morro and cidade.[114] These interpretations carry some weight: certainly, the Estado Novo attempted to encourage samba-exaltação and to use it as propaganda. Nevertheless, it was never terribly successful at controlling samba. Popular composers continued to do their own thing, often altering the state's message to suit their own purposes. And samba-exaltação achieved its real success in the market, through record sales and commercial radio broadcasts. Fans notably stayed away from those compositions that smacked of regime propaganda. The second strain of interpretation is more convincing: the consecration of samba-exaltação and its folkloric myth did obscure samba's previous growth within the market, and the complex forces contributing to its rise. And these factors remained obscure to most observers in subsequent decades. But the evolution of samba's relationship with the nation did not end there: if the simplicity of "Brasil moreno" had marked the endpoint of samba's growth, it seems likely that the understanding of samba as the foremost expression of Brazilianness would have lost its currency and power.

Instead, a third stage of evolution, roughly from 1945 to 1955, witnessed the rebirth of critical samba. The new tendency offered compelling analysis of the failures of the Brazilian nation, and in particular the failures of its ostensible racial democracy. That critical tendency revitalized samba, explaining its enduring power. The new approach did not negate the implications of samba-exaltação. By 1944, these were too deeply embedded to be uprooted. On the contrary, the new critical samba took the premise of samba-exaltação as its starting point, accepting uncritically that trend's celebration of a folkloric samba do morro as national essence. This implicit acceptance, however, then served as the basis for an indictment of Brazil's social inequalities, its failures to live up to its own rhetoric. The new critical tendency rose in counterpoint to the triumphalist strain of samba-exaltação, in a minor mode. This contrapuntal tendency would then swell and ebb over successive decades, as younger generations of composers embraced the critical visions of Pereira and Batista and put them to new uses.

The implications of samba-exaltação and the new critical samba are contradictory. The first celebrates racial democracy and a national culture built on Afro-Brazilian foundations but shared by all harmoniously. The second shows the contradictions and ambiguities behind the rhetoric of racial democracy, and reveals the networks of power that structure Brazilian society. Nonetheless, over the past fifty years these two contradictory approaches to the genre have coexisted. Samba serves both as uncritical celebration of the nation and profound inquiry into its failures. The romantic myth and the gimlet-eyed self-reflection have proven equally attractive. The same composers, performers, and fans are likely to invoke both. It is the coexistence of both strains, their contrapuntal relationship, that gives the link between samba and Brazilianness its continued vitality and power.

3 THE RISE OF NORTHEASTERN REGIONALISM

My dream is to write a folk rhyme, a little folk rhyme,
something that gets lost among the people.

—Dorival Caymmi

And then I couldn't tell if it was folklore or not, because
I didn't know what folklore was. It was something I had
sung as a boy, and there in the *sertão* we didn't have
that business of knowing who the author was. I think
it was mine. I think it was my father's. I think it was
everybody's. I don't know.

—Luiz Gonzaga

In 1945, seven years after leaving his native Bahia for Rio de Janeiro, Dorival Caymmi wrote "Peguei um Ita no Norte" (I caught a ship in the North), a song chronicling a similar emigration.[1] Like Caymmi, the narrator sells most of his possessions to secure passage on an "Ita," a ship in the commercial fleet that shuttled along the Brazilian coast. The names of the ships—the Itapé, Itaparica, Itaquera, and others—explain their popular nickname. Like Caymmi, the narrator bids good-bye to his mother and father, sets out for Rio, and finds success in the capital. He gives up the idea of returning to the North, and his native city remains only a fond memory. The song was neither one of Caymmi's best nor his most successful commercially, but it immediately became a sentimental favorite among the legions who had left the impoverished lands of northeastern Brazil for the expanding cities of the Southeast.

Seven years later, Luiz Gonzaga and Guio de Morais offered another version of this migrant pattern. Their "Pau de arara" (literally, parrot's perch) takes its title from the popular name for the rickety, open trucks that transported both cargo and passengers in the Brazilian interior.[2] In this case, the narrator—considerably more down-at-the-heels— catches a ride on a flatbed out of his dusty, provincial town, carrying only a small sack containing all his worldly goods. As in Caymmi's case, the song stands out in Gonzaga's vast repertoire primarily for senti- mental reasons, and for its obvious historical resonance.

Migration from the Northeast to Rio and São Paulo was one of the fundamental trends in the social, political, and economic upheavals that reshaped Brazil in the decades approaching mid-century. Drought, economic stagnation, and a landholding structure that virtually pre- cluded the existence of viable small farms pushed hundreds of thou- sands of rural laborers out of the Northeast. Expanding industrial opportunity, political centralization, and cultural allure pulled them toward the big cities. Between 1920 and 1950, Rio de Janeiro doubled in population, much of that the result of migration from the Northeast. São Paulo's growth was even faster (although European, Middle East- ern, and Japanese immigration were at least as responsible as domestic migration). By mid-century, the journey from Northeast to Southeast itself was iconic, a passage representative of more complex movements, appearing in numerous forms in both high and low culture. Graciliano Ramos's brilliant social-realist novel *Vidas secas* (Barren lives), for ex- ample, chronicles the travails of one family leaving drought-stricken hinterlands for a nebulous future.[3] *Literatura de cordel*, a form of popu- lar chapbook poetry, frequently treated similar migrations.

It is no surprise that the journey out of the Northeast surfaces in the work of both Caymmi and Gonzaga, the two most prominent north- eastern popular musicians of the era. These composers were seen as the cultural emissaries of the Northeast in the capital, and it was to be expected that they would put the migrant experience into song. In the words of the announcer who introduced a sweeping, orchestral version of the Caymmi tune on a 1949 broadcast of *Um milhão de melodias*—A Million Melodies, flagship program of Rio's Rádio Nacional—"This is the story that synthesizes the history of thousands of those who caught the Ita." As both composers recognized, moreover, northeastern migra- tion was transforming the popular culture of Rio and São Paulo, and, by extension, that of Brazil itself. The narrator of "Pau de arara," for example, carries nothing with him but three percussive instruments—a triangle, a bell, and a drum—and sings, "I brought . . . the *maracatu* and the *baião*." These northeastern rhythms were, at the time of the song's release, becoming nationally popular, largely through Gonzaga's own success. The narrator comes bearing nothing but culture.[4]

Despite overarching similarities, however, these two versions of migration were markedly different, most obviously in their contrast in class. The Itas were not cruise ships, and conditions of travel were often uncomfortable and precarious, but passage was limited to those who could afford the substantial fare. Hitching a ride on a pau de arara, or more likely on any number of trucks on a journey of many stages, was for most migrants the only way out of the interior. The Caymmi song is also by far the more jaunty and optimistic. As the composer himself described it, "It tells an ideal story, it doesn't talk about misery. The guy even gets over his *saudade*." Saudade, the lyrical, bittersweet nostalgia so frequently mentioned in Brazilian song, was a crucial theme for both Caymmi and Gonzaga in their evocations of the Northeast, but particularly for the latter. "Pau de arara," on the other hand, is written in a foreboding minor key, and the narrator insists, "I suffered, but I arrived."

These contrasts begin to reveal more profound differences between the artists. While both proposed to speak for the Northeast, they did not speak for the same Northeast. They packaged themselves as representatives of starkly different cultural identities, to great effect. Each drew on a wide array of popular images, folk traditions, and elite literary formulations of regional character and, to some degree, their constructions corresponded to existing regional stereotypes. But in many respects they created the regional identities they claimed to represent. The coherence and imaginative detail of their parallel cultural projects, coupled with tremendous commercial and critical success for both, insured them privileged roles in the redrawing of the Brazilian popular cultural map that accompanied the period's political and economic transitions. To put it succinctly, Dorival Caymmi was not just *baiano*, he was, and is, the ur-Baiano, and Luiz Gonzaga was not just *nordestino*, he was the ur-nordestino.

Baiano designates someone from the northeastern state of Bahia, and usually suggests a more specific cultural grounding in the state's capital, Salvador da Bahia. Stereotypes of the region emphasize West African cultural heritage, erotic delights, and seaside tropical languor. *Nordestino* literally designates anyone from the Northeast, but in practice designates one from the sertão, the arid hinterlands of the northeastern interior. Stereotypes of the sertão, its inhabitants, and refugees emphasize hardship, rugged self-sufficiency, and tendencies to banditry and religious fanaticism. (*Sertanejo*, one from the sertão, is frequently used as a synonym for nordestino, and in the 1940s Gonzaga and his peers were more likely to use that term to describe themselves. More recently, however, sertanejo has come to mean countrified in general, and has become particularly associated with *música sertaneja*, a blend of Mexican *ranchera*, southeastern Brazilian country, and international pop that has almost no relation to the music of Luiz Gonzaga.) Caymmi and Gonzaga used, redefined, and reformulated these stereotypes in their music and performances, and in the process, came to be seen as embodiments of these respective regional identities. This understanding can be found in countless critical appraisals of their music, of varying eloquence and insight. In the words of novelist Jorge Amado, Caymmi's compatriot and sometime collaborator, "I know of no artist more important. . . . In Caymmi's music is the master spring of the life of the Bahian people, of our blacks and our fishermen." Folklorist Luís da Câmara Cascudo assessed Gonzaga in remarkably similar terms: "He himself is the source, headwater, and fountain of his creations. The sertão is him. The Pernambucan landscape . . . forgotten times in sentimental villages, return to live, to sing, and to suffer when he puts his fingers on the accordion."[5]

Both artists are seen simultaneously as influential creators and as inevitable spokesmen of a larger culture. Their canonization among a select few founding fathers of Brazilian popular music has not resolved the ambiguity over the degree to which they compiled original bodies of work and that to which they merely channeled a regional identity which spoke through them—or, in less charitable formulations, the degree to which they stole their compositions from anonymous folk sources. Indeed, their critical stature depends on that very ambiguity.[6] Their parallel formulations of Baiano and nordestino identity acquired their extraordinary power because they appeared to be at once chthonic and inventive. Their representations of a rural Northeast, created within the context of the metropolitan popular musical market, resonated with both fellow migrants and residents of the Southeast assimilating their arrival. Disseminated throughout the nation in broadcasts and records, these representations proved to those who had remained in the Northeast that the metropolis had felt their influence. These songs appeared to bridge the gap between the folkloric—rural, collective, anonymous—and the popular—urban, individualist, commercial—and in the process to introduce Brazil to itself.

THE ORIGINS OF NORTHEASTERN REGIONALISM

As Getúlio Vargas consolidated his regime in the early 1930s, one of his primary goals was to break down the regional strongholds that dominated Brazilian politics. First, he disrupted and dismantled the political machines of Minas Gerais and São Paulo which had controlled the presidency for the previous two decades. After crushing rebellion in São Paulo in 1932, he turned to the Northeast, seeking to dissolve tightly knit landholding clans by incorporating key members into his government and pushing others to the political margins. The inertia of the rapidly expanding federal bureaucracy itself also worked to undermine regional power structures, creating a greater federal presence in the provinces. By 1937, Vargas's goal had been largely accomplished—political and economic power and momentum lay with the federal government and its allies in Rio, and not in the far-flung regions. Still, when Vargas arrogated dictatorial powers to himself in 1937, inaugurating the Estado Novo, he justified the move largely with reference to the continued fight against persistent regional dissent. The ceremonial incineration of the state flags, shortly after the declaration of the Estado Novo, symbolized Vargas's antipathy toward regionalist sentiment. He railed against *"caudilhismo regional"*—the parapolitical, semifeudal control of land and labor by regional strongmen, and scorned "the regionalisms that in every area sought to place themselves before the interests of the nation in general."[7]

Given this strong centralist political strain, the rise of cultural regionalism may seem unlikely. Yet the regime's own cultural projects seemed to carry it inevitably back toward northeastern regionalism. The Vargas government sought to encourage patriotism through national civic ritual and instruction and to elaborate a unified Brazilian culture. Like many of their contemporaries in populist dictatorships around the globe, Vargas bureaucrats sought the wellsprings of a national culture in folklore, and looked for opportunities to disseminate throughout the nation any local folk customs deemed appropriate to the ethos of the regime. Following the inauguration of the Estado Novo, officials at the Department of Press and Propaganda (DIP) delineated a plan to broadcast folkloric programs on the government's radio stations. And in a 1940 letter to Câmara Cascudo, Brazil's leading folklorist, DIP director Lourival Fontes wrote, "No other culture expresses, like folklore, the master lines of nationality, fixing the physiognomic shape of a population in its various dimensions."[8] Interest in folklore logically led back to questions of regional characteristics. But for Fontes and his companions in the DIP's quasi-fascist pursuit of the master lines of national identity, regional variations were easily sheltered under an overarching nationalist umbrella. In the words of Agamemnon Magalhães, a participant in the Revolution of 1930 and a former minister of labor, "Brazilian folklore consists of regional motives, all informed by sharp nativist sentiment." But for Magalhães, the step from regionalist nativism to nationalism was short and inevitable: with the establishment of a national community, regionalist sentiment would naturally transfer to the nation. Not all regions were created equal, however, and in the process of national consolidation some regions would inevitably appear more "Brazilian" than others. Not surprisingly, Magalhães made the case for his native Pernambuco: "Its music is profoundly Brazilian. It has the accents of bravery of our people in its exaltation and its defense of the land." When Vargas named Magalhães *interventor*, or presidentially appointed governor, of Pernambuco shortly after the inauguration of the Estado Novo, one of his first official acts was to initiate a folklore program on the state's principal radio station. Inevitably, the program emphasized local folkloric music.[9]

Fontes and Magalhães, particularly the former, were deeply influenced by the Mussolini regime, and in retrospect their initiatives appear ham-handed and distasteful. Other sectors of the Vargas bureaucracy, however, put forth more coherent and perceptive programs for folkloric study and preservation. Poet, novelist, and musicologist Mário de Andrade, for example, worked for several years in an uneasy alliance with the Estado Novo as the head of its National Service of Historic and Artistic Patrimony (SPHAN). Before he split with the increasingly repressive Vargas dictatorship in 1939, Andrade delineated a host of initiatives for folkloric research, most of which were undermined or drastically transformed by his successors.[10] Although Andrade differed radically from Magalhães in his intellectual concerns and political leanings, he shared his understanding of the Northeast as a critical site for folkloric research, and energetically sought to commission northeastern research for SPHAN journals. In a 1937 letter to Câmara Cascudo, Andrade encouraged the independent scholar to abandon his historical research of Brazilian nobility and to concentrate more completely on the folklore of his native Rio Grande do Norte: "You have folkloric richness passing in the street every moment. You have all your acquaintances in your state and throughout the Northeast. . . . write about the habits you find in homes, and hovels, in gambling dens, at festivals, in the fields, on the pier, in the popular bars."[11]

The origins of this notion of the Northeast as a particularly rich folkloric repository are more difficult to trace. Undoubtedly, they spring in part from the geographical movement of Brazilian history. The northeastern provinces, particularly Bahia and Pernambuco, were the center of colonial Brazil. Salvador was the colonial capital until 1752. In the late eighteenth and nineteenth centuries, the great sugar and tobacco economies of the Northeast declined, and economic and political energy shifted to the Southeast. The inertia of the decadent structure of monocrop export agriculture slowed economic and social transformation in the Northeast. Rapid industrialization of the Southeast in the early twentieth century made regional contrast ever starker, undergirding the understanding of the Northeast as a place to study the tradition behind Brazil's southeastern modernity.

Euclides da Cunha's 1902 work *Os sertões* (translated into English as *Rebellion in the Backlands*) furnished a tremendously influential expression of this vision. An epic in every sense, da Cunha's book describes the 1898 military campaign to destroy Antônio Conselheiro's millenarian community at the dusty Bahian outpost of Canudos. Da Cunha's description of the campaign serves primarily as a springboard to his larger investigations of the contradictions between the archaic, fanatical, but oddly noble involutions of the northeastern hinterlands and the cosmopolitan, self-important modernity of the coastal southeast. Over the first decades of the century, the work became recognized as a classic, a touchstone of intellectual formulations of national identity.[12]

Trends of the 1930s gave this vision ever greater currency. Gilberto Freyre's 1933 work, *Casa grande e senzala* (translated into English as *The Masters and the Slaves*) described a Northeast strikingly different from da Cunha's, but equally archaic. Whereas da Cunha's exemplary cell of northeastern essence was the nordestino, Freyre's was the sugar plantation. He then boldly extrapolated from the world of the Pernambucan sugar plantations with which he was familiar to offer sweeping appraisals not only of the Northeast, but of all Brazil. Freyre's theory of hybrid cultural inheritance placed particular importance on the sensual attractions of the Afro-Brazilian Northeast. The erotic allure of the *mulata*, the call of the *batuque*, the savory spice of fish stew in palm oil—these were both the fruits of Brazilian fertility and the engines of further cultural recombination, tempting and drawing together Brazilians of all backgrounds. Within a few years of its publication, his work was already as influential as da Cunha's.[13]

This thumbnail description already begins to suggest that Luiz Gonzaga in some sense followed da Cunha, and Caymmi followed Freyre, and this would be broadly accurate. But while da Cunha and Freyre may have been the most influential theorists of the Northeast, they were by no means isolated. The great northeastern migration brought a host of talented elite and popular artists to Rio. Once established in Rio, these artists attained national influence. Northeastern regionalism, written largely by emigrants to Rio, was the dominant Brazilian literary trend of the 1930s. Between 1930 and 1938, Graciliano Ramos, José América de Almeida, José Lins do Rego, and Rachel de Queiroz all published critically acclaimed novels set in the sertão. In the late 1930s, Jorge Amado began to publish the first works in his long series of literary investigations of Afro-Bahian culture. The northeasterners so completely dominated the literary scene that in 1941 the cultural weekly *Diretrizes* (Directives) invited Ramos, Lins do Rego, Queiroz, and Amado to write alternating chapters of a serial novel. Only one non-northeasterner, Aníbal Machado, was invited to participate.[14]

The literary regionalism of the 1930s helped to establish the context for the emergence of Gonzaga and Caymmi. Ramos and Amado proved particularly relevant to their regionalist formulations, and were closer forebears of their work than da Cunha and Freyre. The songs by Gonzaga and his various collaborators echo Ramos in both subject matter and in the spare tones of their social realism. And Caymmi and Amado offer strikingly similar celebrations of Afro-Bahian popular culture, not surprising considering their long friendship and occasional collaboration.

Gonzaga and Caymmi were not the first artists to exploit a popular vein of northeastern regionalism. In the late 1920s, traveling bands like the Turunas de Pernambuco created a brief vogue for northeastern popular music in the capital. Poet and lyricist Catulo da Paixão Cearense, another northeastern emigrant to Rio, frequently explored northeastern themes. With the rise of popular radio in the 1930s, readings of Catulo's romantic, sentimental poetry and performances of his lilting ballads became standard fare on Renato Murce's *Alma do sertão*, a weekly, hour-long, sertanejo-themed broadcast. Murce explained his long-standing commitment to the program, which remained on the air for two decades on various stations, with a sentiment that might have come directly from a reading of da Cunha: "I saw in the man of the backlands the true pith of our nationality." Despite his attraction to the subject matter, however, Murce found Catulo's long-winded sagas unwieldy and inappropriate for broadcast without extensive cutting. Catulo was neither a popular artist nor a folklorist—his intent in adopting sertanejo themes was to raise them to an erudite level through his own high-flown, romantic reflections.[15]

The 1930s also witnessed the rise of a contrasting trend in regionalist broadcasting, the *dupla sertaneja*, more commonly known as the *dupla caipira*, or hillbilly duo. Jararaca and Ratinho (Milksnake and Ratso, roughly), two former members of the Turunas de Pernambuco, established one of the first hillbilly duos. They dressed in a slightly exaggerated version of northeastern attire, largely symbolized by a leather hat with the upraised brim of the nordestino cowboy, performed folk tunes and their own humorous narrative songs, and told tongue-in-cheek anecdotes contrasting the ways of country and city folk. Their radio programs and theater performances were widely popular in the mid-1930s, but their dominance of the genre was soon eclipsed by the duo of Alvarenga and Ranchinho. The latter pair professed an identity not of the Northeast but of the interior of São Paulo. As the decade wore on, both of these duos, as well as their many imitators, dropped specific regional markers and adopted a more general rural identity. For Jararaca and Ratinho, for example, this meant wearing felt instead of leather hats, and toning down the obviously northeastern parts of their repertoire. The duplas also grew increasingly bawdy, using the guise of the ignorant hick to tell jokes and act out situations that might not otherwise get past radio censors.[16]

The duplas remained popular but also incited a backlash among fans and radio critics. As one observer put it: "Catulo da Paixão Cearense is not folklore. The duplas caipiras are not folklore. It is necessary, above all, that radio stations organize authentic folklore programs, handing over the development of the programs to specialists." At the same time, other critics called not just for folklore but for a performance of that folklore that would be both professionally polished and popularly accessible. In 1941, *Diretrizes'* radio critic praised the initiative of popular vocalist Sílvio Caldas in bringing folk music back to Rio from his tour of the Northeast, and plugged his upcoming broadcast: "It will be a worthwhile program, for it will have the double advantage of the cultural side and the beauty of the interpretation, something that the scholars on radio often do not achieve."[17]

Folkloric initiatives from the government and independent scholars, high-cultural literary regionalism, grandiloquent pastorals, and hayseed ribaldry—all of these trends both demonstrated and stirred metropolitan interest in northeastern culture, but none of them included all the characteristics necessary to fuel a popular and commercial phenomenon of lasting influence. By the late 1930s, the stage was set for performers who could exploit the gap left by these trends, performers who possessed keen powers of folkloric observation and artistic savvy, and who could offer convincing, marketable performances of their own northeastern realness.

OUT OF BAHIA

Dorival Caymmi was born and raised in Salvador, passing his youth between the city and the outlying fishing village of Itapoan. He grew up in a middle-class family, exposed to both Brazilian and European literature and music, and was encouraged to study law and not to play the guitar (or at least not to be seen carrying one in the streets, for that was "a thing for hoodlums"). Nevertheless, as a teenager Caymmi tried to balance study and music. He quickly perceived that he would never stand out as a performer of the romantic songs popular in Salvador in the early 1930s, and he sought a different sound. He found it in the work chants of the fishermen of Itapoan and, in the mid-1930s, began writing songs that incorporated these chants, interspersing them with fragmentary descriptions of the fishermen's milieu.[18]

The subject matter was strikingly unusual—before Caymmi, not even fishermen had sung *about* fishermen, in the sense of describing everyday work—as was the technique. The combination of folkloric elements and illustrative detail gave the songs a resonance beyond reportage. The inclusion of Caymmi's own fatalistic observations about life in the fishing village ("It's sweet to die at sea . . ."), his rich vibrato tenor, and the minor and diminished chords he used in his guitar accompaniment suffused the songs with a sense of inescapable melancholy. The guitar parts were also innovative—Caymmi's unusual chord formations, on the edge of dissonance, in some ways presaged the *bossa nova* inventions that were still two decades away.

Even in unpolished form, these songs attracted the attention of local radio producers, and by 1937 Caymmi was performing fifteen minutes weekly on the city's leading station, Rádio Sociedade Bahia. The following year, he finished his preparatory studies and, after several brief and unsuccessful stints as a salesman, set out for Rio. His intent was to study law, to support himself through his skill as a trained draughtsman, and to make some effort to perform his music. Upon arriving in Rio at the age of 24, his career unfolded in a storybook manner. He suffered just enough hardship to provide some anecdotes of the hand-to-mouth camaraderie of the downtown pensions, and then became an overnight sensation. Within months of his arrival, Caymmi had, by exploiting a few well-placed contacts, impressed local radio producers with his *canções praieiras*, or beach songs. After a guest appearance at Rádio Nacional and a brief stint at Rádio Tupi, Caymmi signed a contract with Rádio Transmissora, one of the smaller Rio stations. The contract was not a lucrative one, but it enabled him to find an audience. He never went to law school.[19]

Once established in Rio, Caymmi began to compose, in addition to the moody canções praieiras, buoyant sambas describing life on the streets of Salvador. The samba was a *carioca* rhythm, native to Rio, but it had clear links to Bahia through the precedent of the Bahian batuque and the importance of the Baianas in nourishing the genre's growth. Caymmi strengthened these links by writing lyrics evoking the sensual charms of Salvador da Bahia. The first of this new genre, for example, "O que é que a baiana tem?" (What is it that the Bahian woman's got?), is basically an aural postcard of an exotic Bahian beauty.[20] The lyrics are rich in Bahian color, using local terms to describe the baiana's typical clothes and ornaments and praising her grace and beauty. At the same time, the musical structure blends influences of morro and cidade: Caymmi incorporated the carioca breque, or break, characeristic of the funky syncopation of informal samba within a sophisticated compositional structure of introduction, verse, chorus, and bridge. This combination placed "O que é que a baiana tem?" at the forefront of samba's musical evolution, making it perfect for the swinging orchestral treatment of the Estácio sound currently in vogue in Rio's studios.

Early in 1939 "O que é que a baiana tem?" came to the attention of the performer and producer Almirante, who was scheduled to appear in a film titled *Banana da terra* (Domestic banana). Although made in Rio's Sonofilm studio, the film was produced by Wallace Downey, and essentially followed the model of his Cinédia films—a paper-thin plot stringing together numbers by Rio's top musical performers. Carmen Miranda, the hottest vocal star in the country, was preparing for her solo segment, where she would appear in Baiana costume and perform Ari Barroso's "Na baixa do sapateiro," a samba about street life in Salvador. At the last minute, Barroso demanded more money. Downey and director João de Barro refused, and Barroso pulled out, leaving the movie with a Bahian street set and the appropriate costumes and no song. Almirante phoned Caymmi, Miranda sang "O que é que a baiana tem?" in the film, and Caymmi became the revelation of 1939.[21] His sudden stardom appeared to be just that serendipitous and frictionless. These qualities would become his trademark, contributing to his public image of sunny ease.

Aside from the tune's catchy melody, its evocative subject matter, and Miranda's charismatic performance, it had the ingredient that had previously been missing from commercial popular song—apparent folkloric authenticity. The lyrics include several local Bahian words, most notably *balangandãs*, a term that designated the charms that Bahian women attached to their bracelets, ornaments significant in the Afro-Bahian religion candomblé. The term was archaic even in Bahia, and in the rest of the country virtually unknown. Its sudden dissemination throughout Brazil in a popular film set off flurries of scholarly etymological inquiries into its origins and significance. It immediately entered into popular usage in the capital, quickly taking on the completely secular meaning of trinkets or baubles. Later in 1939, DIP intellectual Henrique Pongetti and popular composer Lamartine Babo cowrote a musical revue to benefit the charitable organizations of First Lady Darcy Vargas. The revue was virtually a command performance for the flower of Brazilian popular music, and the most prestigious event of the year. Picking up on the buzz created by "O que é que a baiana tem?," Babo wrote a composition titled "Joujoux e balangandãs," which also became the name of the show. The term's sudden cachet among the city's elite further secured Caymmi's growing stature, and implicitly linked that stature to his folkloric rediscoveries.[22]

Caymmi's star continued to rise. He and Miranda recorded a 78 of "O que é que a baiana tem?" together. He jumped from Rádio Transmissora, a struggling station, to Rádio Nacional, the pinnacle of Brazilian broadcasting. In 1941 he left Rádio Nacional for Rádio Tupi, a less prestigious station, but one that featured him in the prime slot of Friday nights at nine. Broadcasts and record sales quickly gave Caymmi national fame. When he traveled to São Paulo in 1943 to open that city's Rádio Tupi, fans broke down the studio wall attempting to gain entrance to the auditorium.[23]

CAYMMI'S METHOD AND ITS IMPLICATIONS

Sudden success did not alter Caymmi's approach. On his radio programs, he continued to perform alone, with minimal introduction of his selections. And in composition, he continued to write canções praieiras and sambas about Bahia. The method, too, remained the same—folkloric elements and exotic description packaged in a two-and-one-half minute marketable format. The 1942 samba "Vatapá," for example, ostensibly offers a recipe for the dish of the same name, an Afro-Bahian paste of cashews, dried shrimp, and fish fried in palm oil.[24] Before listing the ingredients, the lyrics advise the listener: "Procura uma nega baiana que saiba mexer" (find a black Bahian woman who knows how to stir). The refrain pleads suggestively for "um boca-dinho mais"—a mouthful more. Finally, the narrator confides, "Qualquer dez mil-reis e uma nega, faz um vatapá" (with any ten bucks and a black woman, you can make a *vatapá*). The lyrics make explicit some of the underlying principles informing Caymmi's work. Eventually, ingredients and procedure matter less than who is doing the stirring. Folklore, perhaps, can be learned, Caymmi's work suggests, but culture is inherited, and Bahian culture is carried principally by the Afro-Brazilian inhabitants of Salvador, in the noble work of men who fish and the erotic allure of women who dance and cook. Caymmi, the intermediary and mouthpiece, can explain that culture, but ultimately a metropolitan audience will have more success buying it than living it.

Caymmi emphasized both this distance between origin and audience and his own importance as bearer of folkloric authenticity in a 1943 interview: "From Itapoan, the fishing village of my homeland, I brought to the civilized world the legends of the men of the sea." Such assertions were only part of the way in which Caymmi affirmed his cultural legitimacy. He deliberately cultivated an image of indolence, frequently posing for press photographs lying in a hammock, idly strumming his guitar. Such images played into metropolitan stereotypes of the slow pace of Bahian life and its lazy inhabitants. Similarly, Caymmi frequently dressed in a stylized version of a fisherman's attire, with a tattered straw hat and canvas pants. And he began to bill his style of samba as *samba rebolado*, rolling samba, presumably describing a smooth, languorous Bahian sound in contrast to Carioca syncopation.

In reality, Caymmi played the standard Estácio rhythm on his guitar. He had a singular approach to melody, marked by a contrast between sprightly clusters of notes in the verse and soaring, romantic lines in the chorus, but his style was no more "rebolado" than that of any typical sambista.[25]

Caymmi's self-packaging was remarkably successful. In a 1950 feature on the composer, the *Revista do Rádio* praised his "typical and folkloric music," and asserted, "Caymmi's songs have a strange power that we can only attribute to the enchantment of the land of Our Lord of Bonfim" (the most famous church in Salvador, and one strongly associated with Afro-Bahian culture). This interpretation has proved persistent—a more recent scholar, for example, has highlighted "the Bahian indolence and leisure of Caymmi's music-making."[26]

Given the link drawn in Caymmi's lyrics between race and cultural inheritance—usually implicitly, but explicitly in works like "Vatapá"— it is not surprising that critics often invoke his own mixed background as evidence of his cultural authority. Caymmi's paternal grandfather, an Italian metalworker, emigrated to Bahia and married an Afro-Brazilian Baiana. This mixture of European and African was by no means unusual in middle-class Salvador, where few families could claim a pure European heritage, whatever their social pretensions. For Caymmi, this mixed heritage became a crucial element of his success. In an introduction written for a collection of Caymmi's music, for example, Jorge Amado stressed the "black blood and Italian blood he carries in his veins." Biographers Marília Barboza and Vera de Alencar take the observation and its implications back a generation: "His father was a handsome *mulato* named Durval. The European blood running in his arteries received affluents of African blood, and so he succumbed to the song of the Baianas." These authors by no means pulled their interpretations out of thin air: instead, they picked up on the Freyrean clues in Caymmi's music, his celebration of a sensual, erotic blend of African and European. He, after all, was a living example of the cultural recombination he celebrated—more so than Freyre or Amado—and this gave his project critical legitimacy. At the same time, Caymmi was light-skinned enough to enter into the cream of Brazilian society. He had no trouble breaking into the world of radio and film, when those careers were still closed to all but a few darker Afro-Brazilians.[27]

For the composer, constant reaffirmation of his Bahian roots proved fundamental to his success, but it had limiting and contradictory aspects as well. Caymmi has often seemed perplexed about the authorial ramifications of his method. Throughout his career, he has responded to questions about the sources of his songs with phrases like, "that was in the wind," and, "I heard it in the voice of the people." On some occasions he has suggested that his own aesthetic selection is the factor that gives his practice of mining Bahian folklore artistic legitimacy: "Every folkloric piece within my music is a poetic element that I appreciated."[28]

In other instances, he has seemed less certain. "A preta do acarajé" (The black acarajé vendor) is another Caymmi song describing the exotic charm of a Bahian woman selling Afro-Bahian delicacies—*acarajé* is a bean-paste patty, fried in palm-oil and stuffed with vatapá.[29] The song is built around the cries of a street vendor from the composer's Salvador neighborhood. His varying explanations of the song illustrate the imprecision of his enterprise. In a 1943 press interview, Caymmi stressed his own integrity as folklorist and composer: "I took the vendor's cry and the picturesque aspects of making the acarajé, put them together and made the song with the melody of the cry, without distorting it. I was honest and sincere." In a 1966 unpublished interview, he described the vendor's cry as "the voice of the people that pleased me." Two years later, in a book collecting his compositions, he tried to be more specific: "In truth, this song belongs more to that vendor . . . than it does to me."[30]

Caymmi's presumption to speak on behalf of an aggregate, essential, unchanging people of Bahia might appear less murky were it not accompanied by a tendency to smooth the rough edges of the material. His Bahia is utopian and carefree—history is merely a colorful backdrop. "Você já foi a Bahia?" (Have you been to Bahia?) fondly evokes "the memory of the maidens in the time of the emperor," untroubled that the emperor's time was also one of slavery.[31] Here, Caymmi parted ways with his friend Amado, a Communist Party member whose early novels portrayed bitter class conflict and exploitation of poor Afro-Brazilians in the Northeast. In this regard, Caymmi's work was more like Freyre's, depicting a closed, patriarchal world as a kind of destiny, where iconic figures like fishermen and Baianas play fixed and inviolable roles of cultural transmission. Modernization, because it threatened to disrupt that world, represented a danger. That danger, in turn, could only be overcome by drawing on the deep cultural reservoirs created and nourished within the confines of the archaic world. Cultural survival would then guarantee a uniquely Brazilian modernity. In this understanding, the time of the emperor was one to be remembered fondly as a period of cultural formation, not of brutal repression. Amado's later novels, less marked by the stamp of his early Marxist thought, moved closer to this emphasis on Afro-Brazilian cultural survival. In this respect, Caymmi influenced Amado at least as much as Amado had previously paved the way for Caymmi.

Despite the erotic tinge of his own depictions of Baianas, Caymmi was less willing than Freyre to acknowledge the earthy content of folkloric material. In 1955, he recorded a rendition of "Eu fiz uma viagem" (I made a journey), a Bahian folk song recounting a poor farmer's disastrous trip to market. The last line of the folk song puns on "The flour got moldy" and "I got screwed in the flour" (*mofo deu na farinha*). Caymmi's version transposed words to eliminate the second meaning (*deu mofo na farinha*).[32] This transposition was undoubtedly necessary to clear the song for airplay. But by eliminating the suggestion that the narrator has been cheated and restricting his misfortune to natural causes, it also rewrites folk material to conform to Caymmi's own vision of a harmonious Northeast.

OUT OF THE SERTÃO

Luiz Gonzaga grew up in a tiny provincial village on the outskirts of the small town of Exu, Pernambuco. The streams of the Araripe foothills kept Exu reasonably well irrigated in comparison with the drought-stricken surrounding area. As a result, unlike much of the poor population of the northeastern interior, the Gonzagas were not forced to migrate frequently in search of water and work. Relative comfort still amounted to scarcity, however, and the Gonzaga family of eleven did without plumbing, electricity, or access to formal education. Januário, Gonzaga's father, was regionally renowned for his skill on the *sanfona*, a homemade accordion with eight bass buttons. (Professional accordions generally have forty-one keys on the right side and as many as 120 bass buttons on the left side.) By age eight, Gonzaga had learned much of his father's repertoire, and within a few years they were playing together at country dances.

In 1930, at seventeen, Gonzaga left home for the city of Fortaleza and enlisted in the army. Following the so-called Revolution of 1930, which his regiment supported, like most of those in the Northeast, Gonzaga's battalion was sent back to the sertão as part of a mission to wipe out the *cangaceiros*. These bandits of the hinterlands roamed in packs, preying on ranchers and isolated villages, and occasionally working as guns for hire in local land disputes. Because they defied elite land-owners and redistributed some of their gains among the poor to maintain networks of protection and communication, they were occasionally celebrated as ambiguous folk heroes. The exploits of Lampião and Corisco, the most notorious of the cangaceiros, generated an extensive catalogue of tales of bloody gunfights, matched by its own iconography. The upturned leather hat with stars embroidered on the brim, the gun belts and rugged leather clothing, became symbols of outlaw glory. The cangaceiros thrived in the decentralized Old Republic, when the elites who controlled the northeastern states generally chose to appease rather than to confront them. The rise of strong centralization and a greater federal military presence in the interior under Vargas spelled their doom. In a turnabout typical of popular cultural packaging of outlaw style, Gonzaga would later dress like a cangaceiro onstage. The cangaceiro's image of rugged persistence became an integral part of his public persona.

In the army, Gonzaga honed his musical talent by playing cornet and guitar, learning from trained musicians familiar with both traditional military marches and the complex harmonies of choro. Only in 1936 did he again take up the accordion, this time a model much larger than the eight-bass sanfona he had played as a child. He used the extended range to incorporate the harmonic lessons he had learned on the guitar, and began playing the popular music he heard on the Rio radio stations—samba, choro, and Argentine tango. By 1939, he was also listening to Caymmi's programs and was struck by Caymmi's ability to translate northeastern flavor to a cosmopolitan audience. Nevertheless, it would be several years before Gonzaga discovered a parallel path.[33]

Gonzaga passed the 1930s stationed in various parts of the country, including the Northeast, Minas Gerais, and São Paulo. At the end of the decade, he was finally transferred to Rio. He immediately began to supplement his meager army salary by playing in bars in the Mangue, the red-light district adjacent to downtown Rio, and soon left the army altogether. In the Mangue he played, or attempted to play, whatever the patrons wanted, including the international hits requested by foreign sailors. He continued to listen to the local radio stations, and entered twice as a contestant on Ari Barroso's amateur show on Rádio Tupi. On both occasions, playing waltz and choro, he received low marks from the host.

Tales of sudden recovery of cultural identity are a genre unto themselves, and one rightfully viewed with skepticism. Gonzaga told his own with enough insistence and charisma that it has entered the lore of Brazilian popular music. A group of students from Ceará entered the Mangue bar where Gonzaga was playing, recognized his nordestino accent despite his attempts to mask it, and requested some northeastern folk tunes. Gonzaga had not played anything like that in nearly a decade and was unable to comply. He spent the next week relearning the songs he had played with his father, and when the students returned, he was able to grant their request with a show of nordestino accordion fireworks that stopped passersby in the street.[34]

Leaving the tale's cultural implications on hold for the moment, it is at least plausible in its details and certainly accurate in its broad trajectory. Gonzaga's subsequent return to Barroso's amateur show is well-documented: on a mid-1940 broadcast, he played a nordestino instrumental romp he called "Vira e mexe" (Turn and shake) and won the prize. His subsequent rise to national prominence, however, was not nearly as rapid as Caymmi's. His triumph on the amateur show gave him an entrance to radio, and over the next several years he played on a number of programas sertanejos and caipiras—the kinds of programs that invoked a general rural identity without local specificity and without apparent folkloric authenticity. He recorded "Vira e mexe" for RCA Victor in 1941, and over the next few years recorded dozens of mildly successful 78s, some of them nordestino music, most of them waltzes and choros. On both radio and in the recording studio, he remained only an instrumentalist—producers were not interested in the nordestino nasal twang of his singing voice.[35]

His reputation as an accomplished accordionist was growing, but his plans to build on the nordestino success of "Vira e mexe" were frustrated. He began searching for a partner who would help him translate the life of the nordestino people, as he described it, into song. In 1945, he met Humberto Teixeira, a lawyer from Ceará with similar ambitions. Teixeira became the lyricist Gonzaga required to create a more evocative portrayal of the sertão. In the next two years, the duo wrote "Asa branca" (White wing) and "Baião," songs that became the pillars of Gonzaga's enormous popular and critical success. The melody to the first was a haunting nordestino lay that he had played with his father as a child. Teixeira added new lyrics to the few fragments that Gonzaga remembered from his childhood, emerging with a hardbitten tale of drought and migration that might have served as the soundtrack for Vidas secas: "Por farta d'agua, perdi meu gado, morreu de sede meu alazão" (For lack of water I lost my cattle, my horse died of thirst).[36] By this time, Gonzaga was successful enough to impose his will to sing on the recording company. In his 1947 recording of "Asa branca," he exaggerated, rather than concealed, his nordestino accent, stressing regional pronunciation (the twangy *farta*, instead of the proper *falta*). He added rich harmonic shading on the accordion, moving skillfully between the keening whine of the sertão and full, triumphant major chords. The tune's drama of hardship and migration resonated with nordestino migrants, and the record sold tens of thousands of copies. It gradually became the unofficial hymn of the sertão and its displaced persons.

"Baião" experienced even greater short-term success, inspiring a dance craze that gripped Brazil through the early 1950s. As with "Asa branca," Gonzaga and Teixeira built the tune around a folkloric element—in this case, a simple, four-beat rhythm that nordestino guitarists used to introduce a ballad. Gonzaga transferred the rhythm to drum and accordion and repeated it throughout the song. Teixeira wrote lyrics that were at once manifesto and instruction manual: "Eu vou mostrar pra vocês, como se dança o baião, e quem quiser aprender é favor prestar atenção" (I'm going to show you how to dance the baião, and whoever wants to learn should pay attention). The 1946 recording by vocal group Quatro Ases e Um Coringa, with Gonzaga's accompaniment, became the biggest seller of the year. Gonzaga's own recording of the song three years later did almost as well.[37] More important, the baião became Gonzaga's staple rhythm: over the next decade he recorded dozens of top-selling records in the rhythm, becoming the most consistently popular recording artist in the country. In the words of Teixeira, "There was never such a perfect marriage. We ruled Brazil musically for five years."[38]

Over fifty years later, it is still easy to understand why these songs created such a stir. In addition to the nordestino realism of the lyrics and melodies, everything about Gonzaga as a performing and recording artist made him stand out from contemporary stars, who, for the most part, aspired to images of suave sophistication. His raw, unpolished voice often bent a half-note below the melodic line. His accordion work, similarly, was deliberately choppy and shaded with flat notes. And his shouts of exhortation exuded unrehearsed, backwoods charisma. The combination of these elements gave Gonzaga a homespun charm that metropolitan audiences found thoroughly winning. On Rádio Nacional, where he moved as soon as his career began to take off, he gained the tag-phrase "Luiz Gonzaga, sua sanfona e sua sim-patia" (his squeezebox and his congeniality, roughly).

BRINGING THE SERTÃO TO THE METROPOLIS

As in Caymmi's case, Gonzaga's success depended not only on his combination of folkloric elements with musical ability, but on success-ful marketing of his own cultural authenticity. To begin with, he and Teixeira emphasized the folkloric origin of the baião and minimized the adaptations they made in turning it into a dance rhythm for com-mercial popular music. As Teixeira described it in 1950, "The baião is as old as the sertão nordestino that gives it origin." At the same time, they underlined their own importance as intermediaries (a role which per-mitted, or even required, them to make minor alterations of folkloric essence in a process of civilization). Teixeira claimed in 1955, "The baião was a primitive rhythm . . . that we brought to the city in new clothes."[39]

Rádio Nacional stressed this folkloric mediation relentlessly in its advertisements for Gonzaga's show: "Luiz Gonzaga and Humberto Teixeira broke customs and taboos . . . to bring folkloric music to the big cities." "The baião was totally unknown in the capital. It came directly from the sertão to Rio, from whence it has spread throughout the nation." "The enthusiastic acceptance of this pair has brought as an agreeable consequence the implantation of northeastern folkloric mu-sic in the great urban centers." "A lawyer and an accordionist, the men who discovered the music that is sweeping the nation."[40]

And as in Caymmi's case, bringing this image to the public required careful self-packaging. Until the mid-1940s, Gonzaga had dressed in a tuxedo or linen suit for his performances, but his reinvention as the mouthpiece of the sertão necessarily involved a change in attire. At the same time, singer Pedro Raimundo was performing in the attire of the *gaúcho* cowboys of the southern plains, inspiring Gonzaga's transfor-mation. "The Carioca had his striped shirt, the Baiano had the straw hat, the southerner had those clothes that Pedro wore. But the nor-destino? I had the opportunity to invent his characteristics and the first thing that came to mind was Lampião." Gonzaga immediately im-ported a replica of the cangaceiro's enormous, decorated leather hat from the Northeast and brought it to Rádio Nacional. A costume evoking banditry as well as regional origin met with staunch opposi-tion at the station, and producers tried to prohibit Gonzaga from appearing in the auditorium dressed as a cangaceiro. His insistent cultivation of a public image in costume outside the studio, however, soon forced them to relent.[41]

In 1950 and 1951, Gonzaga and Teixeira collaborated with another nordestino, Zé Dantas, on a weekly Rádio Nacional program entitled *No mundo do Baião*—In the world of the baião. The program, which aired Tuesday nights at nine, was by far the most popular in its time slot and one of the most popular on the air. It featured musical selections from Gonzaga and guests, accompanied by a full orchestra, interspersed with folkloric investigations of life in the sertão. These took two forms—semischolarly, didactic explanations, and humorous or sentimental sketches. Teixeira played the role of the serious folklorist, and Dantas portrayed the nordestinos. To a degree, this reflected their personalities: Teixeira was a polished, cosmopolitan lawyer and, by this time, an elected congressman. Dantas was by no means a rube—his radio work only supplemented his career as an obstetrician—but he deplored city life and spent as much time in the sertão as possible. As Gonzaga described it, "Teixeira was more mixed up with the city, with the asphalt. And Zé Dantas came from the wild sertão. I used to say I could smell the stink of goat on his body." The exaggerated representation of these tendencies created the program's fundamental dynamic structure. Teixeira would offer a clinical explanation of a northeastern rhythm, or festival, or food. Dantas would follow with an imitation of two nordestinos discussing the drought, or a country dance. And then Gonzaga or one of the guests would perform.[42]

The pattern was a clever way to blend entertainment and instruction, and to vary emotional pitch, but it had larger implications. On the program, Teixeira, Dantas, and Gonzaga acted out the understanding of northeastern culture that underpinned Gonzaga's career. Teixeira's character could explain nordestino cultural expression, but his scholarly expertise distanced him from that culture. He was unable to participate and as a result occasionally became an absurd or pathetic figure. On a broadcast of late 1950, for example, he mocked his own pedantry by spinning pompous, evidently false definitions of folkloric phenomena—in the role of the professor, he was clearly missing the point, and concluded the segment by laughing at his own expense. The characters played by Zé Dantas had the opposite problem: their complete enclosure within the sertão precluded meaningful communication with the civilized world. They spoke in dialect so thick it was nearly unintelligible to metropolitan listeners, failed to understand the simple questions asked by the narrator, and often went on mumbling to themselves after the narrator had turned to other topics, seemingly unaware of the surrounding world. Only Gonzaga, the artist, could mediate between these extremes to transmit nordestino culture to a metropolitan audience. He pulled together folkloric understanding and cultural authenticity, delivering the essence of the sertão to the urban center in a comprehensible and compelling package.[43]

The cultural logic behind this format was so compelling that it seemed to rein in other impulses. In the first program of the series, from late 1950, Zé Dantas began to explain nordestino folklore in the same scholarly tones used by Teixeira. The narrator interrupted him and insisted, "None of that! You're talking like a professor—that doesn't work. I want you to tell the story like a *matuto*" (a rube). The show already had the professor and the artist—it needed the matuto to complete the circle.[44]

As in Caymmi's case, Gonzaga's self-packaging as "the authentic ambassador of sertanejo music" was so successful that it established parameters for critical reception of his music that persisted half a century later. When Gonzaga received the 1987 Shell Award for Lifetime Achievement, the most prestigious prize in Brazilian music, critic Nelson Xavier justified the award with reference not to Gonzaga's inventions but to his origins: "Luiz Gonzaga is telluric."[45]

Like Caymmi, Gonzaga was from a mixed racial background. But where Caymmi implicitly stressed the importance of his Afro-Brazilian roots, Gonzaga encouraged an understanding of *nordestino* as a race unto itself. As if to illustrate this notion, late in his career Gonzaga described the cultural transformation of his youth in terms of a racial transformation. Recounting his days as an entertainer in the Mangue, he identified himself as a "mulato gostoso"—a tasty, or hot, mulatto. This self-identification, however, was linked to cultural false-consciousness: "No one knew I was nordestino. . . . I threw in with the blacks, dressed like them, even sang samba . . . and tried to adopt the Carioca accent." In contrast, when recounting the days following his rediscovery of nordestino culture he described himself as "pure nordestino"—in other words, he had stopped identifying himself racially as a mulatto, and had stopped trying to pass for a Carioca, culturally. The implications of this new identification become apparent in the title of his 1974 album, *Sangue nordestino*—Northeastern blood.[46] The fiction of genetic racial heritage was combined with the fiction of regional cultural heritage, strengthening both.

For both Caymmi and Gonzaga, the fiction of a culture inherited in the blood was implicitly related to their folkloric borrowings and fundamental to their critical legitimacy—they are perceived as giving voice to a culture they cannot help but represent because it flows in their veins. For both artists, the ambiguity between folklore and authorship that surrounds their work is not incidental but fundamental, an inevitable consequence of their formal strategy in the construction of popular songs and their parallel understandings of cultural inheritance.

REGIONALISM AND COMMERCE

Emphasis on cultural authenticity often obscured the commercial aspect of the careers of Caymmi and Gonzaga. One prominent Brazilian critic has argued that Caymmi's songs "were made without the slightest commercial inclination, spurred by his born intuition, and not by anything he learned." The eager self-marketing of both performers plainly belies such statements. More interesting than the fact of their commercial enterprise, however, are its characteristics. Not surprisingly, both artists were extremely popular in the Northeast, and among fellow northeastern migrants to the major urban centers of the Southeast. Both cultivated that popularity through tours of the Northeast: they inaugurated many of the region's new radio stations and played on the others, and performed in theaters and in public plazas. Gonzaga continued this pattern for decades, spending much of his career on exhaustive tours of what he called "the half of Brazil stricken by drought." And certainly the influx of northeastern migrants into industrial jobs in Rio and São Paulo bolstered record sales for both artists.[47]

Their appeal was by no means limited to fellow northeasterners, however. In 1952, Caymmi was voted one of the most popular performers in the southern city of Porto Alegre, which at that time had received relatively few northeastern migrants. And Gonzaga was the most successful Brazilian recording artist for several years running in the early 1950s, eclipsing proven Carioca stars like Francisco Alves and Orlando Silva.[48] Clearly, their representations of the Northeast appealed not just to fellow northeasterners but to all Brazilians struggling to understand the nation's transition from archaic, rural, and enclosed to modern, industrial, and boundless.

For both artists, general appeal was partly built on sexual allure. Magazines like *Revista do Rádio* frequently ran photos of both performers in gallant and seductive poses, with captions calling attention to their physical charms. Radio advertisers were quick to exploit this attraction. *No mundo do baião*, for example, certainly aspired to broad appeal, but was commercially pitched to a middle-class, female audience. Its explicit targeting of a female audience was typical of daytime programs but less usual in the prime-time evening slot occupied by *No mundo do baião*. The show was sponsored by Fermentos Royal, a packaged-food company promoting its new line of dried mixes for cakes, gelatins, and puddings—"products that already form part of the good habits of the families of Brazil." Advertisements before, during, and after the program stressed the advantages of incorporating Royal products into a bourgeois domestic routine: "Make your cakes with Royal yeast—they will be fluffier and tastier. In my house it's already a tradition."[49] A program that dramatized the translation of rural tradition for a modern, urban audience featured advertisements that described modern, scientific commodities incorporated into domestic tradition. Both processes contained and assimilated the unfamiliar.

The Fermentos Royal advertisements imagined a woman's role dedicated to good, middle-class housekeeping, and to sensual allure: "What's the biggest worry of a good housewife? The flavor of her *quitutes*, of course!" Quitutes, a generic word for sweets, was also slang for a woman's sexual attributes. The advertisement's invitation of a double understanding showed a willingness to push bourgeois sensibilities where Caymmi's rendition of "Eu fiz uma viagem," for example, did not. But in this case, the sexual meaning merely reinforced the housewife's responsibility to satisfy in every regard. This duty was portrayed as being entirely compatible with the program's transmission of nordestino culture. The program's narrator, for example, encouraged listeners to send in folkloric questions and contributions about northeastern culture, promising in return a free pamphlet of Royal gelatin and pudding recipes. Trading folkloric knowledge for gelatin recipes was a way for listeners to possess both tradition and modernity at once.[50]

The harmonious coexistence of folklore and commerce was best exemplified in the good housewife's pastiche of "Baião" on a frequently aired Royal commercial: "Eu vou mostrar pra vocês, como se faz um pudim!" (I'm going to show you how to make pudding!) The rendition was painfully square: Gonzaga's accordion was replaced by a tame arrangement of piano and horns, and the actress playing the housewife sang in clear, round tones, right on key, lacking Gonzaga's slurred, soulful twang. But this did not obviate the advertisement's implications: the blend of "folkloric" popular music and commercial advertisement was as smooth as Royal pudding.[51]

REGIONALISM AND NATIONALISM

The northeastern projects of Caymmi and Gonzaga also accommodated the overarching nationalist concerns of the period. Despite the obvious exclusionary ramifications of their notions of a culture inherited only by some Brazilians, the regionalisms of Caymmi and Gonzaga were not separatist. They militated not for opposition to a larger Brazilian national character, but for a special place for the Baiano and the nordestino *within* that character. Their cultural projects only made sense in terms of the link they proposed to establish between region and nation: they rescued the vital folklore of the region for the edification of the metropolitan center and, by extension, of the nation. They communicated a part—a crucial part—to the whole. The implication was that only the chosen could live these cultures, but that all Brazilians could and inevitably did benefit from them, because they kept alive essential elements of the national soul.

Gonzaga, Teixeira, and Dantas expressed this idea through what they described as "the strong and moving theme of the nordestino cowboy." In an early broadcast of *No mundo do baião*, the narrator asks, "Can the man of the South form an accurate idea about the cowboy of the Northeast?" Much of the subsequent broadcasts was dedicated to insuring that listeners would be able to do precisely that, according to the prescriptions of the show's guiding trio. In songs, sketches, and descriptions, they constructed an image of the nordestino cowboy as noble, self-sacrificing, and stalwart: "Leather clothes, leather hat, this cowboy rides to the dense thicket of the scrub, ah, as dense as the thicket of his heart." Such elegies echoed the most famous line of Euclides da Cunha's *Os sertões:* "O sertanejo é, antes de tudo, um forte." The adjective *forte* here stands in for the adjective-noun combination strong man, and the line literally translates, "The sertanejo is, above all, a strong man." But *forte* can also mean fortress, and the line can be interpreted as implying that the sertanejo is a fortress, isolated and impervious. This implication was fundamental to the prevailing understanding of da Cunha's depiction of the sertanejo, echoed in *No mundo do baião*. And as in *Os sertões*, the nordestino cowboy of *No mundo do baião* represented the essential qualities of the region. In

Teixeira's description, "The nordestino cowboy grows giant in all the magnitude of his strength, and in these moments, he is the authentic and perfect symbol of the Northeast." The next, inevitable step was a claim for national relevance: "It is in these epics of hunger and drought... that the greatest Brazilian reveals himself in our cowboy."[52] Through his resilience in the face of hardship, the nordestino becomes the greatest Brazilian, imparting a lesson to the nation.

Once again, the popular press validated the efforts of the composers. A 1943 article in *Vamos Ler* (Let's read) provided the most eloquent testimony to the popularization of the concept of the Northeast as guardian of Brazil's folkloric past. It began by comparing Caymmi to Stephen Foster, the U.S. composer who had similarly popularized a folkloric, harmonious vision of an archaic order for a metropolitan audience. Waxing nostalgic, the article continued, "Bahia, repository of our folklore, reliquary of our imperishable traditions." A 1947 article praised Caymmi's "folkloric and typical interpretations, dedicated to the most Brazilian of popular themes." A critic of Gonzaga, similarly, commended him for "teaching the Brazilian the road to rediscovery of an entire northeastern culture."[53] Caymmi and Gonzaga saved the essence of the fading Northeast and brought it in a usable format to the modernizing Southeast, and then to all of Brazil.

As a result, far from creating tension with the Estado Novo's nationalist ambitions, for example, these regionalisms proved ideal fodder for nationalist propaganda. Nowhere is this more clear than in Caymmi's work for the Department of Press and Propaganda, or DIP. The DIP first used Caymmi's music in a short film from 1939 depicting the northeastern fishing industry. Like most DIP shorts, the film was competently produced but dry and created little in the way of popular reaction. Caymmi played a larger role in a later film, however, which became one of the DIP's most influential shorts.

Late in 1939, four fishermen piloted tiny *jangadas*, or rafts, from Ceará to Rio in a campaign to coax Vargas into creating a pension fund for fishermen. The unlikely voyage inspired significant press coverage, and by the time the fishermen arrived in Rio they were popular celebrities. The DIP attempted to minimize the potential negative fallout by incorporating the fishermen into Estado Novo propaganda. Vargas greeted the arriving *jangadeiros* on the steps of the presidential palace and offered grand promises to improve labor conditions in the fishing industry. Over the next two years, the DIP produced two related short films. The first, "Heroes of the Sea," included footage of the jangadeiros and Vargas, praising the former for their courage and the latter for his benevolence.[54]

The second film, *A jangada voltou só* (The raft came back empty), depended heavily on Caymmi's participation. It took its title from the Caymmi song of the same name, one mournfully narrating the death of two fishermen. Henrique Pongetti, the film's scriptwriter, based the film closely on the lyrics, merely adding a few narrative details. The talented cinematographer Ruy Santos shot the film in Ceará and took advantage of Caymmi's overlapping Northeast tour to cast him in the lead role.[55] Both film and song present a vision of the fishermen's life as elemental, tragic, and unchanging. The jangadeiros who sailed from Ceará to Rio campaigned for the modernization of labor relations, but the film's fishermen live in a circumscribed world where nature, rather than exploitative labor relations, presents the only threat. In the words of Caymmi's character in the second scene, "I have a jangada, a girl-friend, and my health. I'm happy."[56]

The film was one of the DIP's most ambitious, and quickly became its most popular. Caymmi's song and performance ratified the DIP's endeavor to present the fishermen of Ceará as local color, with a lesson to teach about resignation and noble suffering, rather than as labor activists. In *A jangada voltou só* they became another version of the nordestino cowboys of *No mundo do baião*: iconic figures whose destiny was to suffer, revealing and imparting a humble grandeur to the Brazilian people.

Rádio Nacional offered similar portrayals in its children's programming. In the early 1940s *Dicionário Toddy*, one of the stations most popular children's shows, ran a special on the jangadeiros, featuring Caymmi's compositions. Like the DIP film and Caymmi's songs, the show characterized the lives of the jangadeiros as picturesque and simple—they took to the sea each day not because they needed to feed their families but because they were "seduced by the green waves." Not surprisingly, the demands for labor reform presented by the four jangadeiros of Ceará were entirely absent from this story. Several years later, *Dicionário Toddy* ran a special on the Northeast, featuring music by Caymmi and Gonzaga. The show offered a similar portrait of a timeless land whose simple inhabitants spoke a nearly unrecognizable dialect and lived in blissful ignorance of the ways of the city. Such specials brought the most reductive lessons of *No mundo do baião* and *A jangada voltou só* to a younger generation.[57] Teixeira recognized this easy transition from picturesque regionalism to nationalism when he attempted to explain his success with Gonzaga: "The nationalist aspect, that our music was Brazilian, and pure . . . helped a great deal."[58]

This metropolitan portrait of a timeless, exotic Northeast corresponded fairly closely to an American vision of Latin America in general, one energetically endorsed by Good Neighbor Policy propaganda. It is no surprise, then, that when Orson Welles came to Rio in 1942 to film two segments of his never-completed Latin American opus, *It's All True*, he borrowed heavily from the DIP short *A jangada voltou só*. Welles planned a segment on the jangadeiros, recreating their journey to Rio, and hired Ruy Santos as an assistant. The reenactment ended tragically when Jacaré, leader of the jangadeiros, drowned in the waters off Rio. Welles pushed on with the filming, but most of the footage was subsequently lost. The surviving material suggests that Welles intended to follow the DIP script closely, with more ambitious photography and editing (indeed, the surviving footage is cinematically brilliant). Caymmi's character was played by another actor, but the storyline was the same. Welles reportedly intended to use Caymmi's music for the soundtrack, just as in the DIP film.[59]

Welles also planned a voiceover for the segment, providing Jacaré's chronicle of the fisherman's life. Undoubtedly, this would have breathed more realism into the segment, and perhaps salvaged the initial political intent of the four jangadeiros. It also bears noting that Welles's relationship with the DIP was contentious—the propaganda agency clearly feared coverage too sympathetic with the plight of the jangadeiros and other poor Brazilians.[60] Given this tension, Welles's adoption of the DIP script and Caymmi's romantic representation of the jangadeiros is even more striking. The regionalism of Caymmi and Gonzaga, promoting a vision of the Northeast as cultural museum and repository, proved amenable to both the developmentalist nationalism of the Estado Novo and the paternalist embrace of the Good Neighbor Policy.

Largely through their own talent and savvy, Caymmi and Gonzaga were able to position themselves at the nexus of three crucial trends— the great wave of northeastern migration to the Southeast, a growing interest in folklore in general and northeastern folklore in particular, and the rapid expansion of the radio and recording industries. That confluence made possible their commercial and critical success, and enabled them to exert enormous influence on popular conceptions of Baiano and nordestino identity. Their parallel projects of cultural construction brought them enormous critical success but also limited their careers. When Caymmi experimented with different styles in the early 1950s, he received negative reviews, universally suggesting he was better with regionalist material. As Gonzaga put it in a 1952 interview, "Dorival has gotten sucked in by the treacherous asphalt of Copacabana. He should stick with Bahian music." Caymmi dutifully returned to Bahian themes, although he has mined them with an infrequency that suggests he is wary of exhausting the lode: in sixty years of popular composition, he has written approximately one hundred songs. At least a dozen are generally acknowledged as classics of Brazilian popular music.[61]

Gonzaga followed an opposite path in terms of quantity—before his death in 1989, he wrote or cowrote over three hundred songs, and recorded many more. Stylistically, however, his repertoire was even more uniform than that of Caymmi. It has also had an even greater influence: the genre of Brazilian popular music today known as *forró*, a term describing music in various rhythms emphasizing the accordion and nordestino-tinged vocals, grows almost entirely out of the baião that Gonzaga developed in the 1940s and 1950s. It is not a stretch to say that without Gonzaga, forró could not exist. (The genre currently known as *música sertaneja*, it bears repeating, has very little to do with Gonzaga.)

While their music and their constructions of Baiano and nordestino identity did not change significantly over time, they were put to surprisingly different uses. Like the understanding of an idealized folkloric samba do morro as an essential national resource, the depiction of the Northeast as cultural repository has served, at different times, both to reinforce existing arrangements of economic inequality and to challenge them. The DIP, for example—the most fascistic wing of an authoritarian government—used Caymmi's music in short films that assimilated the jangadeiros into regime propaganda, masking its failure to address their material concerns. But as their parallel representations of the Northeast took root in Brazilian popular culture, Caymmi and Gonzaga—and other popular musicians following in their wake—acquired the authority to call attention to the region's material impoverishment, as well as to its cultural riches.

Beginning in the early 1960s, Gonzaga pushed the federal government for investment in irrigation projects in the sertão, revitalizing farms that had been lost to drought decades earlier. In 1970, he wrote the music for a *missa do vaqueiro*, a cowboy mass, celebrated by liberation theologist Catholic clergy outside the confines of the institutional

Catholic church. The missa do vaqueiro, celebrated annually throughout the 1970s, played a significant role in mobilizing impoverished nordestinos to participate in the drive for land reform spearheaded by the liberation theologists and allied agrarian organizers. João Câncio, the priest who organized the project, formed a successful alliance with Gonzaga, drawing a popular following and the attention of the national media. Beyond his own political participation, Gonzaga's music has served as the soundtrack and rallying cry for diverse movements for agrarian reform. "Asa branca," the story of a poor farmer forced off his land by drought, became the unofficial theme song for the land reform drives of the 1970s, sung at popular rallies throughout the Northeast. Over the past decade, it has been embraced again by the Movimento Sem Terra (MST, Landless Movement), an equally dynamic movement, and one national in scope. "Asa branca" is a standard at MST gatherings and teach-ins across the country.[62]

Just as Gonzaga began to push the military regime for more investment in the Northeast in the late 1960s, a younger generation of northeastern popular musicians began to celebrate him as the voice and conscience of the sertão. The rising star Gilberto Gil, who himself had migrated from Bahia to São Paulo, identified Gonzaga as "the first spokesperson for the marginalized culture of the Northeast."[63] At the moment, Gil and his fellow Bahian Caetano Veloso were leading a brash popular musical manifestation known as tropicalism, challenging both the repression of the military government and the narrow cultural assumptions of the Marxist political vanguard. Their embrace of Gonzaga was typical of their unorthodox stance. He was a radio star of a previous generation whose best years were behind him. His work for reform in the Northeast notwithstanding, he was scorned by the cosmopolitan left as a folksy relic; indeed, he was scorned in part because his engagement of the military dictatorship was reformist and not revolutionary. In hailing him as a pioneer, Gil and Veloso pushed for recognition of commercial popular culture as a form of politics.

As they recognized, the same impoverished nordestinos who cherished Gonzaga as a popular hero did not, for the most part, identify with the metropolitan radicals who claimed to speak in their name. For the tropicalists, hosting Gonzaga on their television program in 1968 was a way both to draw attention to his push for irrigation and to irk the orthodox left. After Veloso was exiled a year later, he recorded an emotional rendition of "Asa branca," giving another political overtone to the tune's tale of forced migration.[64]

Gonzaga's adopted son, known as Gonzaguinha, himself became a prominent rock musician in the 1970s, and was far more confrontational than his father with respect to the military regime. But Gonzaguinha was not one of the popular musicians to embrace his father's legacy. He was born and raised in Rio, eschewed northeastern music, and never cultivated a northeastern identity. Despite his name, he did not link his own career to his father's. His death in a car accident in 1991 foreclosed any opportunity of approximation to his father's legacy.

A host of younger nordestino performers, however, have followed the tropicalists in their reverence for Gonzaga. Every prominent forró artist, including Dominguinhos, Alceu Valença, Elba Ramalho, and Geraldo Azevedo has at some point paid tribute to the King of the Baião. Frequently these tributes take on political overtones. In 2000, for example, Zé Ramalho, a forró and rock performer from the northeastern state of Paraíba, released an album called *Nação nordestina*—Northeastern nation—a title that evokes Gonzaga's understanding of *nordestino* as a racial or ethnic category.[65] The album features several songs protesting the economic and political marginalization of the northeast, as well as a rendition of Gonzaga's "Pau de arara." In his construction of nordestino identity, Gonzaga and the critics who hailed him suggested that he was preserving something essential and bestowing it on the nation. Zé Ramalho's adaptation of Gonzaga demands in return that the nation incorporate nordestinos economically as well as culturally.

Caymmi's legacy has not acquired this political density. The northeastern migrants to the Southeast are primarily from the sertão, not from the coast. As a result, they perceive themselves, and are perceived by others, as nordestinos, and not Baianos, in the sense created and embodied by Caymmi. Because they continue to encounter discrimination and scorn as nordestinos, Gonzaga's formulation of nordestino identity still holds enormous power as a source of pride and self-definition. In contrast, Caymmi's construction of a coastal Baiano identity, while pervasive and influential, has not been taken up as a source of oppositional pride. Salvador da Bahia has nurtured a homegrown music of Afro-Brazilian protest over the past three decades, in the form of *bloco afro*, or Afro block, a style characterized by groups of dozens of percussionists playing variations of samba in unison. The style differs from the music of Rio's samba schools primarily in its rhythmic emphases, often incorporating the influence of reggae, and in its political stance, which frequently calls for Afro-Brazilian solidarity in opposition to the white elite. Perhaps because harmonious racial mixture is such a prominent theme in Caymmi's work, he has not been embraced by the *blocos afros* in their oppositional political manifestations.[66] He has, in contrast, been celebrated by those same blocos afros in more conciliatory moments. In February 2001, Salvador da Bahia's parade on the Sunday of Carnival—the highlight of that city's pre-Lenten festivities—featured an homage to Caymmi. A Bloco da Paz, or Peace block, concluded the now-traditional parade of blocos afros by performing his most famous compositions. Gil, Veloso, and their longtime collaborators Gal Costa and Maria Bethânia led the Bloco da Paz, joined by representatives from other blocos. Carrying white flags and singing Caymmi's *canções praieiras*, they exhorted revelers to enjoy a peaceful Carnival. The manifestation was an explicit reaction to violent episodes during the previous year's festivities. In contrast to recent uses of Gonzaga's music and image, Caymmi is pressed into service to conciliate and pacify.

On a critical level, as well, Caymmi's work has become a common ground of universal approbation. He is that rarest of creatures, the unanimously adored popular musician: beyond criticism of his early 1950s experiments, it is nearly impossible to find detractions of his work. Analysis of Gilberto Freyre's sins of commission and omission has been a scholarly industry for decades. But Caymmi, who did as much to popularize a Freyrean understanding of race in Brazil as anyone, remains sacrosanct. Jorge Amado, similarly, has been spurned by the Brazilian literati for his romantic depictions of Afro-Brazilian culture and his continual resort to a small universe of fixed, iconic characters. Caymmi's work shares these salient characteristics, but his reputation is unsullied, and indeed has never been higher. In 2001, Caymmi's granddaughter Stella Caymmi published a life of the composer that borders on hagiography.[67] The publication was universally greeted as an occasion for paying homage to the living legend. A glowing reviewer for a leading Rio daily, for example, rejoiced over "the adventures of this Baiano fascinated by the sea, by music, and by the people, who sailed through the radio age with his deeply rooted songs."[68] His critical immunity today springs from the same understanding that underpinned his glory sixty years ago: he is perceived at once as inventive composer and folkloric transmitter, and the music he passes on is to a certain extent beyond his own control. Although Gonzaga's music is currently put to different uses, his reputation still benefits from the same perception: as the original and authentic nordestino, he could not help but represent the concerns of all marginalized nordestinos. The critical constructions remain the same, even as the applications have diverged. Northeastern folklore continues to serve as fodder for Brazilian musicians. Gilberto Gil's 1997 album, *Quanta*, features a samba based on a Bahian folk rhyme, in a style remarkably similar to that of Caymmi. Gil's 2000 album, *Eu tu eles*, a companion to the soundtrack of the film of the same name, consists primarily of renditions of Gonzaga's classics. And within the last few years, a wave of northeastern bands and composers, including Chico Science e Nação Zumbi, Mestre Ambrósio, Lenine, Chico César, and Zeca Baleiro, has caught the attention of the national audience through the creation of strikingly innovative popular music blending folk elements with transnational influence. But these artists make no pretense to represent vast cultural identities, and no one describes them as télluric, or mistakes their commercial intent. In 1944, erudite composer Heitor Villa-Lobos enthusiastically told Caymmi, "Caymmi, you are creating Bahian folklore." It would be unimaginable for someone to say the same thing today. In 1944, it was not only imaginable, it was in a certain sense true.[69]

Getúlio Vargas and radio stars, 1939. Vargas is at center, in a white suit. Lamartine Babo looks over Vargas's shoulder. Almirante, in a gray suit, stands two to the left of Vargas, in the front row. Orlando Silva wears a white suit, on the far right of the front row. Dorival Caymmi, in a light gray suit, stands at far left. Vargas cultivated close ties with popular radio performers throughout his career. (Acervo MIS)

Adhemar Casé. Casé's variety show served as a laboratory for musical innovation throughout the 1930s. (Acervo MIS)

Radamés Gnattali at the piano, with a Rádio Nacional sax player. Gnattali changed the sound of samba by transferring rhythmic responsibilities to the horn section. (Acervo MIS)

Araci de Almeida in the 1930s. Araci was one of Noel Rosa's preferred interpreters in the 1930s, and played a key role in reviving his music in the 1950s. (Acervo MIS)

Ari Barroso. Barroso's "Aquarela do Brasil" initiated the wave of *samba-exaltação* in 1939. (Acervo MIS)

Dorival Caymmi performing on Rádio Nacional. Shortly afterward, Caymmi abandoned suit and tie and definitively adopted relaxed *Baiano* attire and attitude. (Acervo MIS)

Luiz Gonzaga as a *mulato gostoso*. Gonzaga in a white tuxedo, before reclaiming his nordestino roots. (Acervo MIS)

Luiz Gonzaga as nordestino. Gonzaga in the 1970s, wearing the exaggerated *cangaceiro* hat and leather gear that came to define his image. (Acervo MIS)

Pixinguinha and O Pessoal da Velha Guarda, 1950s. Straw boaters, bow ties, and white linen suits evoked the choro heyday of the 1920s. Like many choro ensembles, the Velha Guarda was highly racially integrated. (Acervo MIS)

Almirante and Pixinguinha at one of the São Paulo festivals, the height of the Velha Guarda experience. (Acervo MIS)

Amateur choro night, TV-Record, São Paulo, late 1950s. Seventy amateur musicians of every age and phenotype gather to perform Pixinguinha's "Carinhoso." Suits and ties indicate the serious nature of the enterprise. (Acervo MIS)

Marlene and rivals, *Programa César de Alencar*. César looks on as Marlene obscures Emilinha's face with the lyric sheet. Carmélia Alves, Linda Batista, and Heleninha Costa sing backup. (Acervo Rádio Nacional)

Ari Barroso's *Calouros* program, audience, late 1930s. Radio as respectable entertainment: live radio in the 1930s drew a predominantly white, middle-class crowd. Semiformal evening attire and polite applause, even at relatively boisterous amateur shows, were the order of the day. (Acervo MIS)

Programa César de Alencar, audience, 1950s. Radio as popular festivity: by the 1950s, the audience was younger, darker, less formal, and more exuberant. (Acervo Rádio Nacional)

Emilinha Borba and César de Alencar: Emilinha, festooned with streamers, seizes the microphone. (Acervo Rádio Nacional)

Getúlio Vargas broadcast, early 1950s. Vargas, on a flower-bedecked balcony, speaks to crowds gathering below and those listening at home. (Acervo MIS)

4 AMERICAN SEDUCTION

In mid-1931, Lamartine Babo composed and recorded a tune titled "Canção para inglês ver" (literally, Song for the English to see, and more figuratively and generally, A song just for show).[1] The lyrics are a thick bricolage of apparent nonsense in English, French, and Brazilian Portuguese: "I love you" rhymes with "whiskey off chuchu," which might be translated as chayote whiskey, and "Mon Paris je t'aime," in Brazilianized pronunciation, rhymes with "sorvete de creme," or vanilla ice cream. The foreign phrases seem to be pulled randomly from a stream of global pop culture where French films and American records intermingle and collide with the names of multinational enterprises like Standard Oil. They are presented without explanation or narrative, and are mixed and matched haphazardly with local elements of Brazilian culture, such as *abacaxí*, or pineapple, and the *bonde* Silva Manoel, a streetcar line in Rio de Janeiro. The melody is simple and direct, and the piano accompaniment on Babo's original recording is reminiscent of a Ziegfield Follies revue tune, emphasizing the downbeats of a mid-tempo 4/4 rhythm. In the Brazilian parlance of the period, it fell under the category of fox-trot, a generic term for American jazz and show tunes. The recording became an unlikely hit of the Brazilian winter season: thousands of 78 rpm recordings sold all over the country, and the tune inspired a successful live variety show, playing in a downtown theater, titled "Para inglês ver."

"Canção para inglês ver" was one of many popular Brazilian tunes of the early 1930s responding to increasing international cultural influence. The arrival of sound films from the United States and France, along with the growing availability of foreign popular music in recordings and on the radio, brought phrases like "good night" and "je t'aime" into usage in Brazil. Many Brazilians, including several influential composers, condemned this influence, perceiving it as a threat to Brazil's native culture. Others, like Babo, sought more complex relationships with the foreign, borrowing and reconfiguring international elements in creative and provocative ways. Even those who ostensibly condemned imitation of international pop often used nationalistic rhetoric as a cover for more subtle incorporations of foreign influence. In the process, they established patterns of response toward foreign— particularly U.S.—influence that would deeply influence both general perceptions of the cultural relationship between Brazil and the outside world and the development of Brazilian popular music over the next several decades.

Babo's curious fox-trot embodied this ambivalence toward foreign influence, and prefigured subsequent evolutions. To the degree that scholars have sought to explain the popularity of "Canção para inglês ver," they have considered it a fairly simple satire of those who sought to use foreign catchphrases, out of context, as currency in a new hip urban slang. All interpreters have seemed satisfied that Babo's tune is what it appears to be—clever fluff. Babo's biographer, Suetônio Soares Valença, describes "Canção para inglês ver" as a "masterpiece of non-sense."[2] Jairo Severiano and Zuza Homem de Mello, authors of a defi-nitive survey of the music of the period, also call attention to the tune's "nonsense" and its "absurd verses."[3] To a degree, these interpretations are incontrovertible: the lyrics are manifestly absurdist—which is not quite the same as absurd—defying immediate logical apprehension. And the tune's satire of shallow cosmopolitanism is also clear. But these easy interpretations miss deeper subtleties of "Canção para inglês ver" that mark it as an early high point in the development of a fertile tradition of Brazilian negotiation of foreign influence in the popular musical sphere.

On closer inspection, Babo's bricolage is not haphazard but follows a logic which contrasts the industrial commodities of the developed world with the raw materials and folklore of Brazil. On the interna-tional side, we find Studebaker, Underwood (referring to the type-writer manufacturer), Standard Oil, and Light and Power Ltd., the Canadian-financed company that controlled Rio's electric grid and its streetcar system. We also find the quotidian markers of a middle-class "American way of life"—sandwiches, boy scouts, and whiskey. On the Brazilian side, we find a zebu bull, *feijão tutu*—a thick black bean paste typical of the Brazilian interior—and *elixir de inhame*, or taro root elixir, a popular Brazilian physic reputed to cure syphilis. While bottled patent medicines evoke a growing international pharmaceutical indus-try which, in the early 1930s, was bringing products like Vicks Vapo-Rub to Brazil for the first time, elixir of taro root, considered sheer quackery by most educated Brazilians, seems primitive and antiscientific.[4] Similarly, the zebu bull and the bean paste bespeak a premodern agrarian culture. The word *tutu* derives from African sources, whereas *abacaxí* and *chuchu* derive from indigenous languages, as do Catumbi, Itaipiru, and Jaceguay, the Brazilian place-names listed in the lyrics. Babo contrasts a premodern Brazil, deeply influenced by indigenous and African roots and laughably incompetent in its attempts to create a modern medicine, with a slick, powerful, technologically sophisticated outside world. The lyrics further suggest that this contrast is, in some way, indicative of a larger truth of the modern Western civilization. The final verse tells us "Isto parece uma canção do Oeste" (this seems to be a song of the West).

Babo's rhetorical strategy in this regard is similar to those pursued earlier by the poet Oswald de Andrade in the 1920s, and later by the popular musicians of the Tropicalist wave of the late 1960s. In 1928, Andrade published the famous *Anthropophagist Manifesto*, declaring that in order to produce truly Brazilian art, local artists needed to cannibalize the foreign, thereby eliminating its threat while incorporating its power.[5] According to Andrade, this process of "deglutition" harkened back to the practices of Brazilian indigenous groups who symbolically stripped foreign invaders of their strength by capturing individual invaders and eating them. Is it an accident that "Canção para inglês ver" seems particularly preoccupied with eating, with its sandwiches, pineapples, bean paste, and other comestibles? Certainly Babo's lyrics seem perfectly anthropophagic, chewing up foreign phrases and spitting them out in strange combinations. It bears repeating, however, that the rhythm here is not samba but fox-trote: to audiences of the time, this certainly raised the question of whether Babo himself was not the one being digested. The dominant mood of the tune is one of amused ambivalence regarding foreign influence, seen as alluring, threatening, and inexplicably hilarious.

This ambivalence belies the title's assurance that this is a "song for the English to see." The popular phrase "para inglês ver" originated in the nineteenth century, and refers to facets of Brazilian life designed to look good in foreign eyes, but having no substance behind them. Brazil's 1831 law abolishing the slave trade, for example, was said to be a law "para inglês ver": it looked good on paper, but was completely unenforced. In contrast, "Canção para inglês ver" does not present a smooth surface of capability and modernity; rather, it invites us to observe a messy process of Oswaldian deglutition—one that would be impenetrable for the foreign observer.

The similarities of "Canção para inglês ver" and key compositions of the tropicalist movement of the late 1960s are even more apparent. Because of the international success of tropicalist music, these works are now far more familiar to a non-Brazilian audience than are Oswald de Andrade and Lamartine Babo. Caetano Veloso's works of the late 1960s, in particular, have been the subject of extensive international inquiry.[6] Their international relevance makes their similarity with Babo's composition worth exploring. As in Veloso's "Alegria, alegria" (1967) the narrator of "Canção para inglês ver" picks his way through a plethora of foreign and domestic signs, apparently in search of direction. As in Veloso's "Baby," (1969), he confronts the looming presence of hip slogans—on billboards in Babo's tune, and t-shirts in Veloso's. In both compositions, the advertised artifacts of an international consumer culture are depicted in an ambivalent manner. They are the markers of an alluring new lifestyle which comes complete with a specialized argot of foreign phrases, but which may well turn out to be entirely superficial. The same markers surface in both compositions: the speaker in "Baby" urges his interlocutor to eat ice cream and learn English, and concludes with the urgent insistence, "I love you," all elements in the bricolage of "Canção para inglês ver."

This is surely no accident: as Veloso himself has acknowledged, Babo deeply influenced his work. What previous scholars have underestimated, however, is the way "Canção para inglês ver" and other compositions of the 1930s and 1940s prefigure tropicalist negotiations of foreign influence. Tropicalism derived much of its critical energy from its renewal of the Brazilian Modernism of the 1920s, and in particular of Oswald de Andrade's anthropophagism. The tropicalists took Andrade's manifesto to heart and "cannibalized" American popular music, dismantling and incorporating the electric guitars, confrontational style, outlandish outfits, and politics of sexual liberation of late-1960s rock and roll into their own public personae. In doing so, they crafted densely provocative criticisms of a "Brazilian absurdity," in which archaic and modern elements confronted each other in a contradiction that informed every aspect of Brazilian life and which had no resolution. Several scholars have offered penetrating analyses of this tropicalist approach to the foreign. In contrast, the same strategies of cannibalistic incorporation and transformation have largely been overlooked in the popular music of the period between Andrade's *Anthropophagist Manifesto* and "Alegria, alegria."[7]

The Brazilian music of the 1930s through the mid-1950s—that is, all the music composed between the rise of radio as a popular medium and the emergence of bossa nova—has often been divided into two broad categories, one for traditional or nationalistic music rejecting foreign influence, and another for slavish imitations of American pop. Critics often disagree vehemently about which category a given recording or performer falls into: one listener's masterwork of national popular culture is another's sellout.[8] To a strong degree, this categorization follows almost inevitably from the rhetoric of the period itself, when critics and composers were quick to condemn work that appeared too Americanized. In doing so, they frequently invoked unwritten and supposedly understood standards of national musical expression, and characterized themselves as defenders of this tradition. Given the strength of this rhetoric, few composers and performers had the courage to admit freely to foreign influence and to accept the charges of selling out that would surely follow.

This is not to suggest that critical interpretations have not evolved: many of the performers widely denounced as sellouts in the 1940s are today considered in more nuanced terms, most famously in the case of Carmen Miranda. This Portuguese-born international superstar both fetishized and deeply distorted the markers of Brazilian popular cultural authenticity, using them as her passport to Hollywood success. Her willingness to cater to American tastes for the exotic outraged Brazil's musical nationalists, who rejected her as thoroughly Americanized, most notoriously in a 1940 episode analyzed below. The tropicalists of the late 1960s, engaged in their own confrontation with musical nationalists, perceived this very rejection as a badge of honor. At the same time that they celebrated Luiz Gonzaga as the voice of the marginalized sertão, they turned Miranda into a kind of patron saint of their movement, rejoicing in her reduction of nationalism to kitsch for a foreign audience. In doing so, however, they tended to emphasize the apparently unintentional nature of Miranda's transnational brilliance. In a well-known essay, for example, Caetano Veloso places great emphasis on a Hollywood photograph of the 1940s which revealed that the starlet wore no underpants beneath her short skirt. Veloso interprets the photo as emblematic of the shocking, unanticipated survival of the raw and essential in a glitzy and otherwise shallow setting.[9] By this influential interpretation, Miranda confounded the categories of national and international, but did so by accident.

But the composers and performers of the period, including Carmen Miranda, were more savvy in their appropriation of the foreign than this interpretation recognizes. Their subtle strategies, far from resulting in the dilution or destruction of local traditions, brought enormous vitality to Brazilian music, and served as a crucial counterweight to efforts at nationalist preservation. These strategies were deliberately transnational: they recognized the importance of national categories and their inescapability in the prevailing context, and sought not to obliterate them, but to traverse them in unexpected ways. Through most of this period, transnationalism required at least a superficial cloak of protectionism. For a brief period after the fall of the Estado Novo and the close of World War II, transnationalism could come out of the closet into the bright light of day. Only a few years later, in the early 1950s, it was forced to contend with a more xenophobic strain of cultural nationalism. By that time, the transnational strategies honed over the previous two decades had established durable patterns that would persist in the development of Brazilian popular culture.

LANGUAGE GAMES

Long before Carmen Miranda began wearing fruit headdresses and mixing rumba and samba for an American audience, she was a successful recording star in Brazil. In the early 1930s, her style was hip and urban. She was one of the few women to run with the samba crowd of downtown Rio, and the daringly flirtatious yet coy manner of her performances reflected this experience of a young woman among men. This was the tone she brought to "Goodbye," recorded late in 1932, one of her early hits. Composed by Assis Valente, "Goodbye" was one of the first Brazilian tunes to incorporate English phrases, although it did so ostensibly to ridicule them.[10] "Goodbye, boy," Miranda sings, "deixa a mania de inglês,"—forget this English-mania. "Fica tão feio para você moreno frajola, que nunca frequentou as aulas da escola" (It is so ugly for you, dapper brown one, who never attended school). The lyrics mock those Brazilians taken in by the fashion for English, particularly ambitious but undereducated young Afro-Brazilian men seeking to project an image of style and accomplishment.

The pejorative overtones of "boy" are not lost in the Brazilian usage—the English word was at the time becoming the preferred term for the errand runners of Rio's business community, most of them Afro-Brazilian. (Although by no means all—pasty Lamartine Babo had worked as a "boy" for Light and Power in the early 1920s.) As a homonym of *boi*, or bull, "boy" in Brazilian usage took on particular overtones of mental incapacity. As in the Jim Crow United States, "boy" in this sense could describe males of any age.[11] The apparent message of "Goodbye" then, could hardly be more conservative: back in your place, brown boy—English is not for you.

Yet Assis Valente, the composer, was himself just such a figure—a young Afro-Brazilian man of modest background seeking to rise in the world. He had come to Rio from Bahia, and by dint of talent and hard work was achieving considerable success in the nascent music industry. His dark skin made it unlikely that he would become a radio and recording star himself, but as a composer, he was fast becoming one of the professionals preferred by the singing stars of the day, including Carmen Miranda. Was Valente chiding young men from similar backgrounds who had sacrificed some kind of putative Afro-Brazilian authenticity in favor of a vain attempt at upward mobility in a white-dominated world? This seems unlikely. Valente was by no means a samba traditionalist, and he did not frequent the predominantly Afro-Brazilian samba circles of the *morros*, or favelas. He lived, worked, and circulated in the *cidade* below, where he was a key participant in a small circle of composers, performers, and producers of varying class and racial background who were rapidly changing the sound of samba, partly by adding sophisticated orchestral flourishes. He was an innovator, one of the first composers to write narrative sambas exploring complex characters.

Was Valente dramatically portraying the racist attitudes of Rio's elite, who mocked the pretensions of Afro-Brazilians like himself? This seems even less likely. The humor in "Goodbye" is infectious and good-natured, rather than caustic. Was he, then, mocking himself, or rather, intentionally putting words that mocked his own position in Carmen Miranda's mouth? This seems more convincing, although this self-mocking is also more complex than it initially appears. The lyrics to the second verse contend, "Já se desprezou o lampião do querosene, lá no morro só se usa luz da Light" (The old gas lamp is now disdained, up on the hill they only use the light from Light). In other words, even the residents of the hillside favelas have switched from gas lamps to electricity. Literally, this brings them into the web of the multinational corporation's power. Figuratively, it modernizes and therefore endangers the supposed redoubt of Afro-Brazilian cultural authenticity. Yet that danger may not be so pernicious after all: Valente knew that the popular audience for his composition would understand, and be delighted by, the bilingual closing pun—luz da Light. Similarly, while the samba ostensibly ridicules English foreign phrases, it uses them in the refrain of a catchy melody. Miranda's recording would only increase the popularity of these phrases. The deeper message of "Goodbye" is not one of xenophobia and defense of narrow tradition, nor of enforcement of Brazilian racial distinctions, but of bicultural mastery. Taken at face value, the lyrics are both nationalist and elitist. Considered in context, the recording celebrates transnational confidence at a popular level.

With "Goodbye," Assis Valente and Carmen Miranda had it both ways: they superficially embraced nationalist rhetoric while demonstrating cosmopolitan savvy that revealed such rhetoric to be something less than absolute. A variation on this dual approach would later become central to Carmen Miranda's international success, when she strategically played the part of the impulsive, hot-blooded Latina. More generally, it was a prototypical musical response to foreign influence, helping to establish a pattern for future responses.

Calculated self-ridicule of Brazilian underdevelopment, evident in "Canção para inglês ver" and implicit in "Goodbye," resurfaced in subsequent popular musical responses to foreign influence, most famously in the case of João de Barro's 1938 hit "Yes, nós temos bananas"(Yes, We Have Bananas).[12] Barro's *marcha*, or march, is a deliberate and crafty response to "Yes, We Have No Bananas," a U.S. success of the 1920s.[13] Although the lyrics to "Yes, We Have No Bananas" ridicule the malapropisms of a Greek-American grocer, the tropical commodity in the title and the mangled English of the chorus lent the tune to association with Latin America—it is a short step, after all, from "Yes, We Have No Bananas," to "banana republic." Barro's lyrics turn the joke on its head: the narrator of his marcha, implicitly representing Brazil, admits candidly that he comes from a banana republic, and wants nothing more. Coffee goes to France, he suggests, cotton goes to Japan, and if the crisis comes, no fear—we have enough bananas for everyone. Here, all the lyrics are in Portuguese except "yes," which rings throughout the tune like a gleeful, voluntary submission to underdevelopment. As in "Canção para inglês ver," the lyrics acknowledge Brazil's role as a supplier of raw materials and primary products for the developed world, and further suggest that this leaves the nation vulnerable to "crisis," a crash provoked by a sudden fall in commodity prices. This political reality is noted without being explicitly condemned. In contrast, it is celebrated to the point of obvious absurdity—an absurdity that calls the superficial meaning of the lyrics into question. A blithely offensive pop tune from the United States is chewed up, digested, and incorporated into a satirical comment on both Brazilian underdevelopment and American attitudes toward Latin America.

THE DOWNEY-EVANS CONUNDRUM

The Brazilian popular musicians and composers of the early 1930s and beyond believed themselves to be fighting off an invasion of foreign pop. They perceived, accurately, that U.S.-based marketers had targeted the Brazilian audience, and they trembled before the fearsome technological and administrative apparatus that enabled these marketers to place the polished products of an advanced popular cultural industry in the constant sight and earshot of the residents of Brazil's major cities. Nationalist rejection of these products was, on an economic level, a logical defense of their own market. At the same time, they were not immune to the charms of these products: the glamour of Hollywood productions and the sophisticated arrangements and crystalline sound of American popular recordings were self-evident. But professional, and more commonly semiprofessional, Brazilian musicians and composers could only take a guilty pleasure in such qualities. As a result, the 78 rpm records of American big bands that began to circulate on a small scale in Brazil in these years were seductive and repellent at the same time.

It bears noting, in this light, that Brazilian audiences of the early 1930s had relatively little exposure to hot jazz and swing. Instead, the American popular music that reached Brazil was mainstream and middlebrow, typified by the "sweet" bands of leaders like Kel Murray and Guy Lombardo, and the symphonic jazz-with-strings of Paul Whiteman. Even when swing became more popular in Brazil in the late 1930s, it did so primarily through the recordings of mainstream white bands like those of Tommy Dorsey and Glenn Miller.[14] All of these bands had in common an emphasis on complex arrangements and harmonic depth rather than on rhythmic swing or solo improvisations. As a result, Brazilian musicians came to perceive the muted, mellow brass of the Lombardo sound or the strings of the Whiteman band as evidence of a signature American predilection for lush arrangements. As suggested above, Brazilian musicians and audiences alike lumped all of this music under the heading of fox-trot, or merely *fox*, a generic, encompassing term which stood in direct contrast to their precise categorization of a number of discrete local rhythms.

This limited perception of the range of popular music from the United States derived primarily from the movies. Hollywood films were far and away the most important vehicles for popularizing American music in Brazil, and Hollywood favored Whiteman over Louis Armstrong as the *King of Jazz*—the title of a 1930 film starring Whiteman, a flop in the United States, but greeted in Brazil as the state of the art in musical cinema. Brazilian bandleaders and arrangers realized that they would need to approximate the polished sounds of Hollywood music soundtracks. If they wanted to supply the dance music for the ballrooms of Rio and the prime-time programs of its radio stations, they would need to offer audiences the same qualities of elegance, cultivation, and flawless execution offered by the popular orchestras of the United States.

Foreign producers helped persuade them that this was true. The recording industry in Brazil was not homegrown; instead, it was dominated from an early date by foreign corporations with local studios. These multinational corporations brought not only capital and technology but cultural influence. The Rio de Janeiro affiliate of the Odeon corporation, for example, was founded in 1913 by the Czech emigrant Friedrich (Frederico, in Brazil) Figner, who furnished his studios with the latest recording technology imported from Germany. Figner set early standards for recording clarity in the preelectric phase of the Brazilian recording industry. Eager to keep abreast of the latest popular musical styles, in 1926 Figner hired the conductor Simon Bountman, a Russian Jew who had come to Rio three years earlier as the bandleader for a Spanish *zarzuela* troupe, and who had stayed on conducting a popular orchestra at the luxurious Copacabana Palace Hotel. At Odeon, Bountman pioneered the incorporation of American jazz influences into recordings of Brazilian popular music, using lavish horn arrangements to back recordings by popular singers like Francisco Alves and Mário Reis. These orchestrations set a precedent for more extensive jazz borrowings in the subsequent decade.[15]

Odeon imported electromagnetic recording technology to Brazil in 1927, and Victor and Columbia soon followed suit. These three corporations would dominate Brazilian recording over the next decade.[16] The new technology vastly increased the possibilities of recorded music, allowing clear recordings of complex arrangements and vocal subtleties for the first time. In their quest to take advantage of these new opportunities, all three labels looked to the United States for models of popular musical orchestration in the recording studio. Partly as a result, they favored brass and strings over percussion. Recording sessions of the early 1930s, for example, rarely included the signature instruments of the Estácio sound, the cuíca, the surdo, and the tamborim. But this was not a conscious process of Americanization, and that was not the effect. Instead, each of the studios achieved innovative blends of cosmopolitan arrangements with local rhythms.

Two producers from the United States, Wallace Downey of Columbia and Leslie Evans of RCA Victor, played decisive roles in this process. Downey and Evans sought to foster both supply and demand in the Brazilian popular cultural market—each wanted to make stars of his label's vocalists, turning them into the universally recognizable and omnipresent icons of a domestic commercial popular culture. Toward that end, Downey hired Bountman as a conductor at Columbia, encouraging him to bring the hybrid arrangements he had pioneered at Odeon to the new recording process. The resulting records showed the influence of American sweet bands without losing the buoyancy of the Brazilian marcha. Downey apparently gave Bountman free rein in the studio and concentrated his own efforts on building the market. In order to promote his vision of a Brazilian Hollywood populated by the stars of the Columbia label, he branched out of the recording business into cinema. He produced his first cinematic musical revue, *Coisas nossas* (Our things) in 1932, through Columbia itself, along with its Brazilian partner Byington. (The film inspired the Noel Rosa samba "São coisas nossas," released shortly afterward.) For the next three, he joined forces with Adhemar Gonzaga's technically superior Cinédia studios. The resulting films, starring the top popular musical performers of the day, not only outgrossed imports from the United States, but spurred the growth of Brazilian entertainment at a pivotal moment.[17] They helped to create the film industry, promote the recording industry, and foster a vision of Brazilian popular music that was as glamorous and exciting as anything Hollywood had to offer. Instead of undermining Brazilian popular culture in favor of U.S. imports, Downey contributed decisively to the growth of a domestic popular music industry strong enough to withstand foreign imports.

Evans was even more influential than Downey in establishing the sound of Brazilian popular music in the 1930s. He has been richly lampooned in anecdotes suggesting he was deaf to samba, disdained percussion, looked down on popular musicians, and spoke Portuguese poorly. Composer Herivelton Martins, for example, suggests that Evans avoided shaking hands with musicians and spoke to them through a handkerchief in order to avoid contracting germs.[18] Fellow composer David Nasser alleges that Evans initially passed up the opportunity to record Ari Barroso's "Aquarela do Brasil" because he did not think humble samba deserved such grandiose treatment.[19] The recorded legacy of RCA Victor in the 1930s, however, does not support such anecdotes: under Evans's tenure, RCA Victor invested more heavily than any other Brazilian studio in samba and other Brazilian genres. The label recorded virtually every Brazilian performer of note in the period, and devoted little energy to importing fox-trote. Evans was gruff and supercilious. The performers he worked with knew him only as Mr. Evans—a forced formality decidedly out of step with the relaxed milieu of Rio's musical circles. But he was also a sharp judge of talent. Like Downey, he wanted to cultivate a Brazilian star system, and he did not wait for those stars to rise through other media. Instead, he maintained close contacts with a wide range of Brazilian musicians, from highly educated white composers like Barroso to working-class Afro-Brazilian musicians like Alcebíades Barcellos, relying on these interlocutors to connect him with emerging young talents. He produced some of the earliest Brazilian recordings to feature *samba de breque*, or samba with a break, emphasizing syncopation.[20]

Early in his tenure, Evans hired Pixinguinha as the studio's principal bandleader and arranger. Pixinguinha drew on his extensive experience with samba, choro, and the Brazilian march tradition to create a variety of orchestral styles for the studio. His use of large brass ensembles to support the label's most prominent vocalists helped to pioneer orchestral samba. His arrangements lacked some of the dynamics of the Bountman recordings of the same period, which were more successful at integrating a full range of instruments, but they were crucial in bringing a tradition of popular Brazilian counterpoint to the studio for the first time. In Pixinguinha's brass arrangements of the early 1930s, for example, the tuba plays simple contrapuntal runs, rather than just a repeating bass line. This approach, deeply rooted in the choro tradition, would later serve as a springboard for Pixinguinha's more adventurous contrapuntal improvisations in the 1940s.[21]

Later in the decade, Evans hired Radamés Gnattali, who largely took over Pixinguinha's responsibilities as the house arranger and bandleader. Gnattali was classically trained, and his own compositions sought to blend popular melodies and rhythms with an erudite approach to harmony. His experience as a radio bandleader for Rádio Nacional, however, required him to work with an extraordinary range of material, from samba to waltz. He brought this varied experience to bear on his work at Victor, writing intricate arrangements for large ensembles of brass, strings, and percussion. He was more deeply influenced than Pixinguinha by jazz, particularly the mellow swing of the Dorsey bands and, later, the subtle harmonies of Stan Kenton's big band. Gnattali seamlessly blended these influences with Brazilian rhythms, producing a swinging, orchestral samba that defined the sound of Brazilian popular music in the late 1930s and 1940s.[22]

In contrast to Downey, Evans maintained control over his recording sessions. He had the good judgment to hire Brazil's most talented musicians and composers but he did not allow them free rein—as the anecdotes about his dogmatic style demonstrate, he closely supervised Victor's recordings, passing final judgment on compositions, personnel, and arrangements. At the same time, he allowed both Pixinguinha and Gnattali to record their own instrumental work in various formats. Evans surely knew that these records would not be among Victor's top sellers, but he recognized that they might yield innovations for future arrangements.[23] This approach paid off most spectacularly in 1939, when Gnattali transferred a saxophone samba riff from one of his own instrumental compositions to the backing of Barroso's "Aquarela do Brasil."

Were Downey and Evans Americanizers? The answer to this crucial question must surely be no. Both wanted to make the Brazilian popular cultural market more like that of the United States. They sought to encourage the growth of a star system with qualities of glamour, sophistication, and up-to-the-minute hipness in order to fuel popular demand for their studio's products. And they brought some of the American markers of these qualities, like lush arrangements and high-gloss production numbers, to Brazilian recording and cinematic studios. But neither sought to promote the products of the popular cultural industry of the United States. And neither sought a simple substitution of those products with brazen Brazilian imitations. Instead, both sought to produce domestic products that would head off demand for the international by combining local elements with the gloss that typified foreign production. They were remarkably successful in this enterprise, making crucial contributions to the growth of a Brazilian music industry that turned singers like Carmen Miranda, Francisco Alves, and Silvio Caldas into stars, while the popular American singers of the early 1930s—figures like Rudy Vallee and Ruth Etting— had almost no repercussion in Brazil.

In the same period, Columbia, RCA Victor, and especially Odeon also released Brazilian covers of international pop tunes. These recordings, sung with lyrics translated into Portuguese, were known as *versões*, or versions. They were not exclusively versions of U.S. hits— Argentine tangos and Cuban and Mexican boleros, whose lyrics were easier to translate into Portuguese, often made the most successful versions—but most were tunes that the Brazilian audience encountered first through Hollywood movies. Most prominent lyricists of the period, including Lamartine Babo and João de Barro, wrote versions at some point in their careers. A few, such as Fred Jorge and Haroldo Barbosa, made it their specialty. Similarly, most bandleaders, including Gnattali, arranged versions, or included them in their repertoire, and many prominent singers recorded at least one or two versions. As such, versions could be a profitable sideline for musicians and composers who, in other respects, considered themselves to be defenders of Brazilian popular music. Strangely, only a few extremists perceived participation in the version trade as selling out. Purists were more energetic in their condemnation of Gnattali's blends of Brazilian rhythms and big band jazz arrangements than they were of versions, which rarely received any critical attention at all. In terms of critical attention, the Brazilian participants in the version trade seemed to disappear. Critics railed against a perceived growth in the popularity of foreign music in Brazil, but rarely noted that the best-selling foreign compositions in Brazil were recorded by Brazilian vocalists and musicians. The versions themselves were ephemeral, seeming to leave no lasting impression.

Downey and Evans, in contrast, were frequently perceived as foreign interlopers who might corrupt Brazilian music. Even the musicians who worked with them closely often shared this misperception, as the anecdotes concerning Evans suggest. Clearly, musicians were often uneasy with a gringo at the controls, and they tended to characterize the vitality of Brazilian music as a victory in spite of, rather than partially indebted to, the presence of producers from the United States. In recounting the early recordings of samba de breque, for example, Martins suggested that he needed to persuade a reluctant Evans to accept the new style.[24] Another revealing anecdote about Evans gives a clear indication of when and why musicians invoked the rhetoric of nationalist defense. In a 1974 interview, composer Hervê Cordovil recalled accompanying Carmen Miranda on piano in a recording session in 1934. Miranda was already a star, the best-selling female vocalist in the RCA Victor catalogue. Evans was producing the session and had been joined by the head of the label's South American operations, visiting from Argentina. Carlos Galhardo, an aspiring singer new to the Victor label, unintentionally interrupted the session, and the visiting producer sharply rebuked him. Miranda rushed to Galhardo's defense, declaring, "I won't sing anymore for that gringo. I won't sing for anyone who mistreats my countrymen. I am Brazilian. He [Galhardo] is Brazilian, and you have to respect us." Miranda stormed out of the studio. According to Cordovil, his admiration for her instantly grew immensely.[25]

It is possible that Cordovil exaggerated Miranda's reaction in order to give the anecdote more drama, but it seems plausible—Miranda was well known for her patriotic ardor. Whether accurate or no, the anecdote suggests the dynamics of what might be termed the staging of nationalism. Evans was ever an untrustworthy outsider, but at least he had established a working relationship with RCA Victor's performers. (Cordovil, in contrast to Martins and Nasser, suggests that Evans had even learned to play tambourine.) According to Cordovil's anecdote, however, the presence of another illustrious American in the studio tilted the balance, and Evans stood by while his countryman treated the performers in a disdainful, peremptory manner. This, in turn, prompted Miranda to act more stereotypically Brazilian—to come to the impassioned defense of a comrade, risking her career and economic security for the sake of national honor. As noted above, Miranda was born in Portugal. Galhardo, as it happens, was born in Argentina, the son of Italian immigrants. (He had Brazilianized his baptismal name, Catello Guagliardi, at the start of his career in order to mask his foreign origins).[26] When confronted with the stereotypical American capitalist seeking to trade in their talent, however, they instantly became ultra-Brazilian. Whether this was so in the moment or merely in the retelling, it indicates what Brazilian performers often felt was required in any interaction with the foreign—a vigorous if often superficial defense of national culture. The irony was that Miranda would later make a career out of playing the irrational, passionate Brazilian for a paying audience in the United States.

Reflexive nationalism, of course, was not limited to Brazilians, or to popular singers. What makes these episodes notable is the tension between nationalist rhetoric and transnational musical strategy, a tension that surfaces in different ways in compositions like "Canção para inglês ver" and "Yes, nós temos bananas." Versions and orchestral arrangements of samba were other manifestations of the same ambivalence—each was a way of incorporating and domesticating the foreign. The insipid nature of most versions shows that, Oswaldian theory notwithstanding, the act of incorporation itself was no guarantee of creative vitality. The versions were perhaps too faithfully translated for that—their meaning was not doubled but merely uncritically retransmitted. The creative reinterpretations of Gnattali's arrangements and the linguistic and political games of "Canção para inglês ver," "Goodbye," and "Yes, nós temos bananas," in contrast, thrust the multiple meanings of foreign influence before the listener, creating a densely layered blend of national and transnational expressions.

This approach was not limited to popular music. The Downey-Gonzaga cinematic musical revues of the Cinédia studio inaugurated a Brazilian tradition that quickly evolved into a signature approach to the filmed musical comedy. This tradition reached its apogee in the Atlântida studios in the 1940s. Like the Cinédia productions, the Atlântida films featured musical numbers stitched together by a loose comic plot. But the Atlântida plots were both more slapstick and more subtle— their low comic style often masked compelling, if ambiguous, criticisms of Hollywood's rise and influence. These films became known as *chanchadas*, a term suggesting vulgar, substanceless comedy. As João Luiz Vieira and Sérgio Augusto have shown, the chanchada directors often intentionally opted for apparently cheap cinematic effects in order to draw attention to the relative underdevelopment of Brazilian cinema in relation to Hollywood.[27] Deliberate parodies of Hollywood epics, moreover, suggested that what appeared to be classic and ennobling in the United States would inevitably be transformed into something chaotic and laughably ineffectual in the tropics. The chanchadas mocked Hollywood's self-importance and deliberately called attention to the insufficiencies of Brazil's own cinema at the same time. In doing so, they suggested that U.S. cultural influence was overbearing and potentially pernicious, but also seductive, and that the best way to mitigate its dominance was by turning it into comedy. Vieira has suggested that the impulse to self-parody was inevitable in cinema, where Brazilian studios could not hope to compete technically with Hollywood products. In popular music, in contrast, parody was only one option in an arsenal of responses to the foreign. A fuller appreciation of the range of these responses requires further analysis of the performer who built a career at the crossroads of Brazil and the United States, Carmen Miranda.

THE BOMBSHELL

Walking out of Evans's recording session did not, of course, end Miranda's career. She patched things up with her producer and continued to record for RCA Victor. She also sang regularly on Rádio Mayrink Veiga's programs throughout the 1930s and starred in Downey's films, giving her exposure in the three omnipresent new media of the day. She appeared in four Downey-produced films in all, the first three made in Adhemar Gonzaga's Cinédia studios, the last, in 1939, in Downey's new Sonofilmes studios. In contrast to later chanchadas, Downey's Carnival films—so-called because three of the four were brought out just before the pre-Lenten festivities—did not offer implicit criticisms of cultural and economic relationships between the first and third worlds. Like Hollywood screwball comedies of the 1930s, they offered good-natured reassurance that all foibles and pitfalls would eventually lead circuitously to the best possible resolution. Their production numbers were frequently glamorous, with grand sets, lavish costumes, and elegant choreography. The 1936 film *Alô, alô Carnaval* (Hello, hello Carnaval), features in its show-stopping number Carmen Miranda and her sister Aurora strutting grandly across a gleaming, tiered stage in silver, sequined tuxedos and top hats.[28] They sing "Cantoras do rádio" (Radio singers), a marcha by Babo, Barros, and Alberto Ribeiro whose lyrics describe the modern allure of radio and its ability to unite the nation: "We are the radio singers / our songs cross blue space / and unite in a big embrace / hearts from north to south." The Miranda sisters do not dance the marcha the way a Brazilian carnival dancer might, with syncopated elbow and hip movements, but instead high-step on the beat, in vaudevillian fashion. The overall effect is decidedly cosmopolitan, a page out of a contemporary Hollywood musical.

When Miranda eventually did appear in Hollywood she played a very different role—that of the comically exotic beauty ever awed by first-world ways. Honing that performance was a process greatly facilitated by the last film she did with Downey, *Banana da terra* (Domestic banana) of 1939.[29] The climactic scene here featured Miranda as a

Baiana, performing Dorival Caymmi's "O que é que a baiana tem?" Miranda did not wear blackface for the scene, as she had done in previous performances of sambas featuring an Afro-Brazilian character, but her costume was a greatly exaggerated version of typical Baiana attire. She wore a turban with a protuberant fabric bouquet, several kilograms of beads around her neck, and a two-pieced shiny dress that left her midriff bare. This, essentially, was the costume in which she would become internationally famous. The exotic tropical stereotype was already part of her repertoire before she left for the United States. Her stylized Baiana costume got progressively more extravagant in Hollywood, reaching intentionally absurd proportions in "The Lady in the Tutti Frutti Hat," from *The Gang's All Here*, of 1943, where Miranda appears to balance a gargantuan fountain of bananas on her head.[30] But this was merely an extrapolation from her role in the suggestively titled *Banana da terra*, not a different category. The rub was that her performance was so successful that Hollywood producers did not want her to play anything else.

Miranda left for the United States while *Banana da terra* was still filling theaters all over Brazil. By the end of 1939 she was reprising the scene on Broadway, to enormous success. The general trajectory of her career in the United States is well known—her speedy transition from Broadway to Hollywood in the early 1940s, her wildly popular but increasingly stereotyped roles over the next decade, her death from overdose and exhaustion in 1955.[31] A few key moments from that trajectory are enough to illuminate her strategies for negotiating international success while attempting to maintain the loyalty of her fans back home.

Within a few months of her arrival, Miranda was already having difficulties with her colleagues in Brazil. Downey, as a representative of the Associação Brasileira de Compositores e Autores (ABCA, Brazilian Association of Composers and Authors), a recently organized entity charged with collecting and distributing royalties to Brazilian composers, alerted Miranda that she would need to pay up for her successful performances of Brazilian tunes abroad. Downey demanded one hundred dollars a week. Broadway impresario Lee Shubert, Miranda's employer and sponsor in the United States, offered to pay fifty, and let Miranda know that she would need to make up any difference herself.[32]

Miranda wrote to her friends in Brazil urging them to restrain Downey. She argued that the composers would probably never see the royalties anyway, and complained that if Downey did not relent she would be forced to give up her Brazilian repertoire and sing in English or Spanish. Aloisio de Oliveira, Miranda's guitarist, also wrote to Brazil, reminding his musical colleagues that Miranda was dependent on Shubert, and counseling them to be patient, suggesting that Miranda's success would be good for all of Brazilian music. The obvious irony here is that the much-maligned American producer demanded that the self-professed Brazilian patriot pay her dues. Miranda, meanwhile, used *jeitinho*—a little crafty manipulation—to skirt a legal issue while maintaining a patriotic face. Her argument that there was no point in paying royalties because they would never reach the composers was a self-fulfilling prophecy. Miranda and her U.S. handlers continued to avoid remitting royalties whenever possible, setting a precedent for international attitudes toward Brazilian copyrights over the next several decades. Downey's work on behalf of the ABCA, meanwhile, shows that the economic and cultural ramifications of Brazilian-American engagement were neither simple nor predictable.

At the same time, Miranda's fear that economic circumstances might force her to drop her Brazilian repertoire was not idle: Shubert and her subsequent producers in the United States preferred her to sing in English, while relying on an exaggerated accent, costume, and choreography to give her performances Latin flair. While this could be accomplished with English translations of Brazilian compositions, faux-Latin romps by American composers and Cuban rumbas with translated lyrics served just as well, and were more accessible to audiences in the United States. Miranda faced a constant struggle in her attempts to keep Brazilian material in her repertoire and keep Brazilian musicians on the payroll. She was highly attuned to the charges from Brazil that she was not accurately representing Brazil's musical heritage. Such charges became more common once Miranda starting appearing in Hollywood films in the early 1940s. Brazilian audiences often found the stereotypes and inaccuracies of these films appalling, not least so in their confusion of rumba and samba.

Miranda sought to vindicate herself by systematically Brazilianizing her material. Even bland U.S. standards like "Chattanooga Choo Choo" took on samba's syncopated rhythmic dislocations and Brazilian Portuguese's sibilant texture in Miranda's renditions. It is tempting to see this consistent Brazilianization as a means of sending coded messages to a discerning Brazilian audience of Hollywood films—and this may at times have been the intent—but the clearest example comes from a film intended for viewing only by U.S. citizens. In 1942, Miranda sang the old sawhorse "K-K-K-Katy" in a short morale-booster intended for U.S. Marines. The tune is a bit of calculated small-town hokum, but Miranda's Brazilianized rendition included the lyrics "pegando a cuíca, eu sou brasileira, morena faceira, não posso negar" ("grabbing the cuíca"—a Brazilian percussion instrument used in samba—"I am Brazilian, a charming brown woman, I can't deny it").[33] In a context where almost no one would understand her, Miranda testified to her Brazilianness with references to her affinity for samba and an entirely fictive Afro-Brazilian ancestry. Apparently unscripted, or at least partially improvised, moments such as these are the most interesting in Miranda's films. They display her genuine talent for rhythmic phrasemaking and reveal the unresolved nature of her representational game. Which role was she playing—that of the defiant nationalist *sambista*, which she had learned back in Brazil, or that of the exotic and flighty Latin beauty, which she had perfected in Hollywood?

Coded messages or no, Brazilian fans were not always placated. Within months of learning of Miranda's success on Broadway and her initial foray into Hollywood, several Brazilian journalists began accusing her of selling out. Their columns, in turn, inspired readers to write, occasionally in defense of Miranda, but more frequently to accuse her of succumbing to Americanization.[34] This debate in the music columns of Brazil's newspapers continued for the remainder of her career—and long after. It rose and fell in intensity according to the movement of wider cultural currents regarding foreign influence in Brazil, but it reached its peak intensity quite early, in July 1940, during Miranda's first return visit to Brazil since her departure for Hollywood.

The initial return was triumphant: a horde of well-wishers awaited Miranda's ship, and then followed her convertible through the streets of downtown Rio. Only a week later, however, reactions turned sour. Miranda gave a concert at the posh Cassino da Urca to benefit the Casa des Meninas (House of Little Girls), a home for orphan girls and the pet charity of Darcy Vargas, wife of the ruling dictator. Miranda had performed at the Cassino many times before leaving for the United States—Shubert had first seen Miranda in a performance there. The well-heeled audience did not represent the popular core of Miranda's Brazilian fan base, but it was enthusiastically familiar with her pre-U.S. repertoire and her style. The presence in the audience of the first lady herself showed just how far samba had risen in the esteem of official Brazil. But the performance went horribly awry from the first moment. Miranda greeted the audience in English, provoking an icy response. She began the show with "South American Way," a Broadway rumba about the exotic charms of lazy, picturesque Latin America. The audience sat rigid and dismayed. Miranda proceeded to sing several more of her recent, foreign numbers before returning to her old Brazilian standbys. It was too late—the crowd's reaction remained hostile. Miranda retreated to her dressing room in tears, and canceled further appearances at the Cassino.[35]

Over the next several weeks, rumors of the disastrous performance and interpretations of the audience's reaction filtered through the city. Miranda herself blamed the failure on the audience's elitism, suggesting that the upper crust was enviously punishing her for her success abroad. At the same time, she admitted that a year in the United States had, indeed, Americanized her habits, and she needed time to readapt.[36] Other observers considered it the beginning of the end, judging that Miranda had clearly lost her rhythm and her appeal.

For two months, Miranda laid low, limiting herself to a few radio performances. In early September 1940, she returned to the Cassino da Urca. She was joined by Grande Otelo, Brazil's most famous Afro-Brazilian actor, a comic star of stage and chanchadas, in which the diminutive, bug-eyed Otelo always played the scheming but goodhearted man of the people. The pairing signaled a return to popular Brazilian entertainment, self-consciously celebrating Afro-Brazilian roots. Miranda unveiled a new repertoire, featuring several sambas with lyrics about leaving behind fame in foreign lands to return to "the cradle of samba." The best was "Disseram que voltei americanizada" (They said I came back Americanized), composed for her by Vicente Paiva and Luiz Peixoto.[37] The lyrics repeat the accusations that the singer has lost her swing and been corrupted by money, and then refute them with affirmations that her heart remains in the old-school samba circle, and that she could never betray her Brazilian ways. She closed the show with Dorival Caymmi's "Dengo que a nega tem," a samba featuring Miranda's favorite character, the Baiana, suggesting that the Baiana enchants because of her "dengo," a term of African derivation referring to a woman's ineffable sensuality. This time, the crowd went wild.[38]

The lesson is clear. Miranda won them over by distancing herself from her American success and reasserting her music's Afro-Brazilian roots. The audience demanded that she show them she would always love Brazil best. It was a lesson Miranda did not forget. Once back in Hollywood, she avoided return trips to Brazil, unwilling to subject herself to the constant test of nationalist commitment. But in her messages to Brazilian journalists and broadcasters, and in the coded, semi-improvisational moments in her films, she took pains to reassure her Brazilian fans that she had left her heart in Rio, but not her rhythm. Over the course of her career, Miranda successfully employed various strategies to make the cultural and geographic distance between Brazil and the United States work to her advantage. She could do a fine imitation of high-stepping first-world glamour, as in "Cantoras do rádio." She could pull strings backstage, as in her evasion of royalty payments. She could parody her own tropical outlandishness while winking at her Brazilian audience, as she did in her Hollywood films. And she could do indignant nationalism with the best of them. She was never able to reconcile these various strategies, however. And by the close of World War II, she had little hope of altering her wildly successful Hollywood persona. Nor was she ever able to allay the doubts of her Brazilian fans. Her death in 1955 provoked an outpouring of grief and lamentations from fans who suddenly felt that they had not loved her enough. But it did not erase a deep Brazilian ambivalence about her career.

PILGRIMS IN THE LAND OF PLENTY

In mid-1941, just as Miranda's Hollywood career was taking off, Heitor Villa-Lobos conducted a survey of prominent performers and composers of popular music, under the auspices of the intellectual magazine *Diretrizes* (Directives). The survey was designed to call attention to what Villa-Lobos believed to be the pernicious presence of foreign popular music in Brazil and to inspire a reaction against it. Villa-Lobos himself was conservatory trained and had built his career as a composer on the incorporation of Brazilian folkloric motives into Western classical structures. He was unwilling to tolerate similar transnationalism in the popular sphere, however, and insisted that Brazil's popular music remain resolutely and completely native and authentic. In particular, he resented the presence of foreigners like Downey and Evans, supposed agents of international corruption, and other foreigners who inexplicably appeared impervious to the charms of Brazilian music. The questions of his survey betray his anxieties: "Does Brazil, with all its original and excellent elements of popular manifestation, need the current influence of foreign popular music? Should foreigners who live in Brazil and reveal themselves to be indifferent to the items of this questionnaire be considered undesirable to our intellectual environment?"[39]

Most respondents took the bait, responding to the survey with the xenophobic indignation that its questions practically demanded. Ari Barroso, Brazil's most famous musical nationalist, was the only respondent to defend international musical influence. In a harshly worded rebuttal, Barroso mocked the survey and Villa-Lobos, and pointed out that international influence was inescapable. He responded with baffled derision to Villa-Lobos's implicit suggestion that foreigners who did not like samba should be exiled.[40] As the author of "Aquarela do Brasil," Barroso had the credentials to get away with such a response. The protectionist statements of his colleagues were far more typical. The editors of *Diretrizes* maintained a stance of supposed neutrality, but they gave ample space to Villa-Lobos and his xenophobic rant, implicitly supporting his position. Although the magazine's intellectual style was atypical of Brazilian journalism of the period, its attitude toward popular music was entirely standard. Journalists overwhelmingly praised apparently folkloric qualities, condemned international influence, and looked with disfavor on foreign professionals in the milieu—unless they concealed their foreign birth, like Miranda and Galhardo. Foreigners who professed their admiration for Brazilian popular music, and who expressed their appreciation of that music as folkloric and natural, in contrast, were celebrated as examples to be cherished.

At the time of Villa-Lobos's survey, musical tourists fitting this description were increasingly common. For economic and ideological reasons, these prominent visitors sought to ignore the commercial and professional aspects of Brazilian popular music, perceiving it instead as raw and authentic. Most of these travelers came under the auspices of the Good Neighbor Policy, Franklin Delano Roosevelt's strategy for hemispheric alliance, set in motion in the late 1930s in the face of oncoming war in Europe. Roosevelt named Nelson Rockefeller his Coordinator of Inter-American Affairs (CIAA), gave him an autonomous office within the State Department, and charged him with implementing the policy. Rockefeller viewed cultural exchange as critical and encouraged U.S. producers to create links to Latin America. Hollywood productions set in Latin America and featuring Carmen Miranda were one aspect of this policy. Brazilian junkets by American cultural power brokers were another.[41]

The first of these to visit Brazil was Leopold Stokowski, who was, in 1940, America's favorite celebrity conductor. As musical director of the innovative Philadelphia Orchestra, conductor of the score for Disney's recently released *Fantasia*, and a frequent radio presence, Stokowski was perhaps the best-known classical musical professional in the country. In the summer of that year, Stokowski took his All-American Youth Orchestra on a tour of South America, with their first stop in Rio de Janeiro. Stokowski used his contacts with Villa-Lobos to arrange an extraordinary recording session with local musicians. Although Columbia Records funded the session, it was not conducted in the label's downtown studios, where production was strictly oriented toward the Brazilian commercial market, but rather in the salon of the ocean liner *Uruguay*, docked in Rio's harbor. This was an unfortunate decision in terms of recording quality—the fidelity of the surviving recordings is far below the standards of Columbia's Brazilian releases—but Stokowski was interested in authenticity, not sonic fidelity. Toward that end, he instructed Villa-Lobos to bring him representatives of "the most legitimate Brazilian music." They opted primarily for semiprofessional sambistas—in particular, for the favela composers who commonly sold their best works to industry insiders—rather than the glamorous stars of Brazilian radio. The partial exceptions were artists like Jararaca and Ratinho, the Northeastern duo who emphasized their own rusticity, and the great Pixinguinha, who moved fluidly between professional radio orchestras and amateur choro circles.[42]

Brazilian journalists celebrated Stokowski's enthusiasm for local music as national vindication: the great maestro's high esteem for Brazilian rhythm demonstrated that national culture was naturally, inevitably bountiful. It did not require glossy production, which made it sound more like American music, to captivate receptive listeners. Columbia and Stokowski then turned around and marketed the recordings commercially in the United States, releasing them in a boxed set titled *Native Brazilian Music*, with Stokowski's name featured prominently on the cover. The liner notes characterized the recordings as folklore. For Columbia, this category made sense: it seemed to explain the poor recording quality, and appealed to an exotic interest on the part of Stokowski's customary audience. Potential buyers attracted by the imprimatur of Stokowski's name, after all, were likely to disdain commercial popular music. Folklore, on the other hand, was authentic, making it a useful marketing term. For the musicians, on the other hand, being

consigned to the category of folklore meant unpaid labor and anonymity. On the album cover and liner notes, almost all the composer
names and composition titles were botched, when not entirely omitted.
Few participants in the session received compensation, and none, apparently, received royalties.[43]

Walt Disney made similar use of Brazilian popular music, albeit
more successfully, and with greater acceptance of Brazilian professionalization. When Disney arrived in Rio in 1941, one of his first stops was
a visit to the favela of Mangueira, where he attended a samba performance of the Mangueira samba school. In his own productions,
Disney preferred orchestral gloss: he used Ari Barroso's "Aquarela do
Brasil" in the soundtrack to his 1942 film *Saludos, amigos*, and brought
Barroso himself to California to compose in the Disney stable. During Disney's visit, however, Brazilian journalists celebrated his visit
to Mangueira and its concomitant endorsement of samba do morro
above all other activities. His visit to the folkloric source justified a
commercial application.[44]

Orson Welles had more ambitious plans for Brazilian popular music
than either Stokowski or Disney. He also worked more closely with
Rockefeller and the CIAA, who had convinced RKO Pictures to sponsor
Welles's filming of a projected three-part Latin American epic, *It's All
True*. These relationships were far from harmonious—Welles squab-
bled continuously with both the CIAA and RKO, and the studio's lack of
confidence in his project ultimately prevented its completion. Soon
after Welles arrived, early in 1942, a trip to Mangueira—fast becoming
an obligatory stop for all enlightened tourists—convinced him that one
segment should portray the world of samba and carnival. He hired
Grande Otelo as a leading actor for the segment, enrolled a cast of
hundreds of extras for a carnival parade scene, and enlisted the aid of
some of Rio's best sambistas. Over several months of filming, Welles
became an assiduous fan of samba do morro, frequently spending days
filming and nights dancing in the favelas. This enthusiasm earned him
the adoration of most of the local press. He was one more illustrious
foreigner who got it, who recognized the raw vitality of samba in its
pure state. Even CIAA officials acknowledged that the Brazilian press
saw Welles as "the one visitor who most quickly understood Brazil, its
problems, and its people."[45]

No foreigner waxed more enthusiastic over the virtues of Brazilian
popular music than Waldo Frank, the left-leaning New York intellec-

tual. Frank's 1942 voyage to Brazil was subsidized by the State Department, but in contrast to Stokowski, Disney, and Welles, he had no immediate project linked to Rockefeller and the CIAA. He was a free agent, sent off with the guidance of the young poet Vinícius de Moraes, in search of the organic and spiritual heart of Brazil. Like most visitors, he was struck by Brazil's phenotypical mixtures, and he followed Gilberto Freyre in seeing this mixture as evidence of racial democracy and in suggesting that racial democracy was the secret of Brazil's cultural vitality. Almost inevitably, given this understanding, Frank perceived samba—which he knew from the by now obligatory observation of a Rio samba school—as a folkloric and essential expression of this racial democracy, and contrasted it with overly commercial American jazz. In Frank's understanding, jazz and swing embodied all the nervous tension, the forced hilarity, of a society intent on obscuring its class conflict with gaudy spectacle. Brazilian popular music, on the other hand, was "incredibly beautiful and profound . . . made of honey, soft petals and perfumed by flowers." Referring to the origins of this enchantment, Frank averred, "Brazilian music is not African or black. It is Brazilian. Its components—African, Portuguese and Indian—are organically united in a single body."[46]

Frank, in other words, was entirely taken in by the Freyrean surface of the spectacle of samba, perceiving it as racially democratic folklore, and failing to see the growth of an entertainment industry and the process of professionalization that produced that spectacle. (The participants in the samba schools for the most part were not paid, but by 1942 the schools themselves were a vital element in Rio's tourist industry, supported by the state and commercial sponsors.) The Brazilian press, meanwhile, portrayed Frank, Stokowski, Disney, and Welles as the foreigners who recognized the purity of the Brazilian soul in its musical form. These men had strikingly different projects and different understandings of Brazil. Welles, for example, was a serious student of samba, commissioning scholarly research into the origins of the genre. His unremitting enthusiasm for Afro-Brazilian cultural vitality proved one of the primary sources of friction in his relationship with RKO and the CIAA, preventing completion of his film.[47] Stokowski and Disney, in comparison, developed only a passing familiarity with Brazilian forms before moving on to more lucrative endeavors. But because all paid homage to samba do morro, all were celebrated in the same way by the Brazilian press. Evans and Downey, in contrast, were often portrayed as interlopers seeking to transform and profit from Brazil's musical soul. The irony of this contrasting reception was that it worked distinctly to the material advantage of Stokowski and Disney and against that of the popular musicians they employed.

A YOUNGER GENERATION

Miranda's Hollywood success and the stamp of approval from illustrious international arbiters made things easier on a younger generation of Brazilian performers. With the fall of the Estado Novo, knee-jerk nationalism temporarily came into disfavor. In the wake of a shared victory in World War II, moreover, many Brazilians felt a confidence regarding their role in the world order that they had not before. This was particularly true among members of the middle class who had opposed the Estado Novo and who now enjoyed new civil liberties and increased economic opportunities. Middle-class metropolitan youth were eager to sample the attractions of international popular culture, and impatient with nationalist scolds. This confidence would prove to be shortlived, but while it flourished, Brazilian performers were free to experiment openly with transnationalism with little fear of immediate condemnation. The musical protectionists did not entirely disappear from the scene, but their influence waned.

The beneficiaries of this new openness were artists like Augusto Duarte Ribeiro, a spirited young composer from the state of São Paulo who, like many ambitious young men looking to break into the recording industry, migrated to Rio de Janeiro in the early 1940s. Recognizing the changing attitudes toward foreign influence, Ribeiro adopted the Americanized pseudonym Denis Brean, and began writing hip, jaunty sambas celebrating a transnational youth culture. The most successful of these was "Boogie woogie na favela," a 1945 hit in the recording by vocalist Ciro Monteiro. The record begins with a swinging horn and piano riff, lifted straight from the music of boogie-woogie pioneers like Meade Lux Lewis (or, more likely, given the nature of international distribution, popularizers like the Andrews Sisters). It then settles into a fairly standard samba, with occasional flashes of barrelhouse piano. The lyrics describe samba returning from "the land of Uncle Sam" with a new swing, bringing "the new dance that's part of the Good Neighbor Policy." They go on to suggest that the craze is so infectious that in the favela, samba is now mixed with boogie-woogie.[48]

The record is a novelty. It inspired several imitations, including a few by Brean himself, but it did not start a movement for the blend of barrelhouse piano and samba. Beyond "Boogie woogie na favela," boogie-woogie itself had minimal repercussion in Brazil. But the novelty was not without ramifications. Residents of a new favela in the suburbs of Rio de Janeiro took to calling their impromptu development Favela Boogie Woogie. This unofficial designation was even accepted in court as neighborhood of residence for parties involved in a legal dispute.[49] Transnationalism, then, was not just for middle-class youth. Although this is an isolated instance, it does add complexity to the contemporaneous emergence of a new, critical samba written from the viewpoint of marginalized *favelados*. Geraldo Pereira used the notion of folkloric samba do morro to probe the contradictions in the rhetoric of racial democracy. The residents of Favela Boogie Woogie, in contrast, followed the white Paulistano Denis Brean in casting doubt on the assumption of the favela as natural home of samba.

Other performers took Americanization in a more romantic direction. Vocalist Farnésio Dutra was another young hopeful who changed his name to suit the new mood, in this case to Dick Farney. He adopted the crooning style of Bing Crosby and the stage persona of a world-weary high-society playboy. He had his biggest hit in 1946, recording João de Barro's "Copacabana," a mellow paean to the seaside neighborhood that was fast becoming the favorite playground of Rio's young elite. An enormous orchestra under the direction of Radamés Gnattali accompanied Farney on "Copacabana."[50] Gnattali, so pivotal in defining the orchestral samba in the late 1930s and early 1940s, was himself freed by the new openness to acknowledge greater influence by his American models. His arrangement for "Copacabana" was closely reminiscent of the Stan Kenton band's sophisticated harmonies and relaxed tempos. The recording became the soundtrack for a new postwar lifestyle—elegant and unabashedly cosmopolitan. Farney himself soon became the object of a fan club linking him to the swankiest star of the moment. The Farney-Sinatra Fan Club, founded not in Copacabana but in a basement in the middle-class suburb of Tijuca, was dedicated to the assiduous cultivation of transnational cool.[51]

Like Gnattali, the members of the vocal quartet Os Cariocas were deeply influenced by the Kenton band's harmonic explorations. In the late 1940s, they pioneered an urbane, vocal samba that set them apart from their contemporaries. Whereas vocalists like Ciro Monteiro emphasized rhythmic syncopation, Os Cariocas concentrated on subtle, modulating harmonies. In an irony savored by their fans, their biggest hit came with a 1948 recording of an ostensibly nationalist rejection of foreign influence. The narrator of Geraldo Jacques and Haroldo Barbosa's "Adeus, America" (Goodbye, America) insists that he is leaving America because he is tired of boogie-woogie, swing, fox-trote, and even "rocks"—probably the first Latin American reference to this nascent genre.[52] Drawn ineluctably by the call of samba, he must return to Brazil and play the cuíca. The lyrics recall the superficial protectionism of early 1930s sambas like "Goodbye," in which the composers protest foreign influence too much, thereby revealing their fascination with it. Here as well, the narrator is suspiciously up-to-date with U.S. popular culture for one supposedly fleeing from it. In contrast to the recordings of the early 1930s, however, in which that contrast remains muted, the Os Cariocas rendition of "Adeus, America" brings it to the fore. No one hearing the group's willfully cosmopolitan vocal harmonies could believe that Os Cariocas were running from jazz. Their hip urbanity reveals that the protectionism of the lyrics is just a convenient posture.[53]

The popular musicians of the 1930s sought to draw on the power of the foreign while at least pretending to protest against it. Ambivalence was a job requirement: expressing open enthusiasm for American music meant critical death, but ignoring American models meant falling behind their prospective popular audience. Composers like Assis Valente internalized that duality, making it a hidden but essential part of their creative work. Carmen Miranda externalized it, making it a crucial part of her performance. The stock character she played repeatedly in Hollywood films was one caught between the allure of American glamour and the deep pull of traditional Brazilian culture. But as her international fame grew in the early 1940s, her Brazilian fans demanded ever more vigorous declarations of fealty to the second half of that equation. Postwar artists, in contrast, could employ any of the transnational strategies used by Miranda, mixing and matching them with little fear of critical retribution. In 1945, Denis Brean wrote "Boogie woogie na favela," eagerly acclaiming American influence. Two years later, he wrote "Bahia com H," a samba more in the spirit of the 1930s, insisting on the protection of Brazilian tradition.[54] Both were hits, and no one called him on the contradiction.

Once established, these transnational strategies persisted, and resurfaced in later decades. The enthusiastic and open appropriation of cosmopolitan influence that marked the post–Estado Novo period returned in the late 1950s, during the presidency of Juscelino Kubitschek. As always, cosmopolitan influences were melded in striking hybrids to local forms: the construction of Brasília, for example, incorporated the latest innovations in international architectural design and urban planning into a self-consciously nationalist-developmentalist project to construct a new capital in the heart of the country. Simultaneously, a loose group of composers and performers in Rio combined the harmonic influence of the European avant-garde and the improvisational style of cool jazz with their own variation on samba. Their hybrid style was soon described as *bossa nova*, the new wave, and became Brazil's most famous contribution to international popular music. Tom Jobim, João Donato, and Johnny Alf, veterans of the Farney-Sinatra Fan Club, were pioneers of the new style, as were Os Cariocas.[55] Their eager approximation of foreign sounds in the late 1940s had paved the way for more adventurous explorations ten years later.

The ambivalence and language games that marked the 1930s and early 1940s resurfaced a decade after the emergence of bossa nova, when the tropicalists set out to reinvent Brazilian popular music in the late 1960s. In their celebration of Carmen Miranda, the tropicalists emphasized precisely the quality that had alarmed Brazilians back in her early Hollywood career—her over-the-top representation of infectious tropical sensuality. This representation, self-consciously extreme but still moved by an undeniable rhythmic flair, perfectly served the tropicalist project of interrogating notions of popular authenticity. Similarly, the tropicalists rerecorded the "nonsense" tunes of composers like Lamartine Babo and João de Barro. Caetano Veloso recorded a rendition of "Yes, nós temos bananas" in 1968.[56] In the same year, Os Mutantes, the experimental rock trio from São Paulo that had backed both Veloso and Gilberto Gil, recorded "Canção para inglês ver."[57] Both fit in perfectly with the tropicalist intent to expose a Brazilian absurdity, marked by the coexistence of the modern and the archaic, the cosmopolitan and the traditional, at the heart of national life. As Christopher Dunn has pointed out, Veloso in particular has frequently employed "palimpsest aesthetics," layering fragments of popular culture from earlier periods in the construction of his own work, creating a dense archaeology of popular song.[58] It is no surprise that he chose "Yes, nós temos bananas," and that his colleagues Os Mutantes chose "Canção para inglês ver." Both songs come from what is widely recognized as the golden age of popular music in Brazil, the period in the 1930s and 1940s when the national popular musical canon was established. And in their ambiguous language games, both cross willfully back and forth between the categories of national and international that appeared to other observers to be inviolable. Their transnational strategies, at once playful and subtly powerful, prefigured those of the tropicalists themselves.

But if transnationalism persisted, so did protectionism—these tendencies depended on one another. Defense of the national meant nothing without a perceived international threat, and transnational borrowing without some recourse to an apparently authentic local form was merely imitation. Even the robust hybrids of bossa nova and tropicalism required the prior existence of a strong strain of rhetorical insistence on the defense of an unchanging, essential national music. Before either manifestation emerged, in the early 1950s, that rhetoric reached its highest pitch. Cold War tensions and protectionist rhetoric in the political sphere added to a backlash against foreign influence in the popular cultural sphere. This backlash, however, did not result in a period of forced sterility on Brazilian popular music. Instead, as the next chapter explains, it inspired a choro revival that turned into one of the most stirring and vital musical phenomena of the 1950s.

5 INVENTING THE OLD GUARD

OF BRAZILIAN POPULAR MUSIC

In an April 1955 interview in the popular magazine *Radiolândia*, singer Araci de Almeida angrily proclaimed, "Certain sectors of the population, in particular those with greater acquisitive power, have distorted taste, and do not buy Brazilian music." She went on to attack those who played "Americanized" music, and lamented, "Brazilian popular music is decadent on radio and on records. It suffers from a pernicious foreign influence that did not affect us so much in the past."[1] That same week, in *Revista do Rádio* magazine, guitarist Antonio Rago made similar complaints about American influence, and insisted, "I am an enemy of any movement, even musical, that has as its objective the undermining of what is ours, of what is Joe Brazil, what is really, truly Brazilian."[2]

The declarations suggest that in the mid-1950s Brazilian popular music was endangered, that it was becoming more international and more homogenous, that neither performers nor fans were concerned with the preservation and cultivation of national traditions. In fact, nothing could have been further from the truth. 1955 was the high-water mark of a revivalist trend in Brazilian music. The defiant pronouncements by Almeida and Rago were manifestations of that trend, which drew much of its energy from rhetorical opposition to the supposedly relentless advance of Americanization. Almeida and Rago were part of a small but diverse cadre of musicians and producers who shaped that trend through performances, recordings, and broadcasts. Throughout Brazil, but particularly in São Paulo and Rio de Janeiro, audiences responded enthusiastically both to their extraordinary music and their protectionist sentiment.

Their movement—for, inchoate and polymorphous though it was, it was certainly a movement—began in the late 1940s, gathered momentum in the early 1950s, and peaked at mid-decade. It looked back to the music created in Rio de Janeiro between the late 1800s and the early

1920s and celebrated that music as the vital, authentic expression of Brazil's national soul. The revivalists, in other words, went back before the rise of samba in their historical search for a music unsullied by commercial transformations and modernization, for a music that would speak more clearly of a golden age past. As with any revivalist movement, their vision of the past was deeply influenced by contemporary fears and pressures, and in the process of ostensibly preserving old cultural expressions they developed new ones.

The revivalists were not entirely deluded about growing American influence. The interchange of the Good Neighbor Policy, and unusual postwar candor about the adoption of American influence had given American popular culture an explicit presence and an acceptability that it had not attained in earlier decades. The revivalists confronted this acceptance and, as the Araci de Almeida quotation suggests, did their best to beat it back. They were not terribly successful in this regard—adoption of American popular cultural models continued with no appreciable diminution. But in the process of their losing struggle, they created their own vital, creative musical trend, seizing the attention of an unexpectedly large audience. One of the curious aspects of the musical revivalism of the first half of the 1950s is this coexistence with eager cosmopolitanism. It also coexisted with Luis Gonzaga's rise to superstardom and the fad for the baião. The simultaneous flourishing of these diverse trends was an indication of the growth of the Brazilian broadcasting and recording industries. Far from losing out to American invaders, these industries became large enough and strong enough to support vigorous competing trends. Revivalism did not capture as large a share as some of its competitors in the market for popular entertainment, but it did find a healthy niche, and—precisely because of its nationalist rhetoric—commanded a disproportionate share of critical coverage.

Almirante (Henrique Foréis Domingues) was the pivotal individual in this revivalist movement. He had earned his nickname, Admiral, as a teenager in the Naval Reserves. Almirante emerged from the Bando de Tangarás of Vila Isabel to become the most influential radio producer and director of the late-1930s and 1940s. He had long demonstrated a keen interest in promoting Brazilian popular culture, creating programs on Brazilian folklore and the popular music of Rio de Janeiro. That interest reached its fullest expression in a program he created in the late 1940s titled *O Pessoal da Velha Guarda* (The personnel of the old guard, or, more colloquially, The gang of the old guard). As the name suggests, the program was designed to feature the old masters of Brazilian popular music, and to reaffirm their role as the true guardians of the nation's cultural soul.

Almirante's most important collaborator was Pixinguinha, the bandleader on *O Pessoal da Velha Guarda*. Pixinguinha (born Alfredo da Rocha Vianna) was one of the most influential musicians, composers, and arrangers of the 1910s through the early 1930s, but his star had faded since his days as the bandleader on the *Programa Casé*. His decline had coincided with waning interest in *choro*, or *chorinho*, his preferred genre. Defying that trend, Pixinguinha and Almirante made choro the featured rhythm of *O Pessoal da Velha Guarda*. Against all odds, the program became a tremendous success: it stayed on the air in weekly broadcasts for nearly seven years, surviving several changes in station and short hiatuses. Even afterward, it engendered music festivals, tours, television broadcasts, and records.

O Pessoal da Velha Guarda touched off the broader revivalist movement and remained at its heart. The program and the movement marked the birth of a new phase of choro, making the genre more popular nationally than it had ever been before, and expanding its musical possibilities. But these innovations were hidden by constant emphasis on tradition and the preservation of the nation's cultural riches. As a result, the movement also ultimately limited the genre. In imagining choro as an essential national form, it created an instant canon built around the compositions of Pixinguinha, encouraged the study and rehearsal of that canon, and discouraged further experimentation. In its emphasis on tradition and the protection of Brazilian culture, *O Pessoal da Velha Guarda* perfectly embodied an important transition in the evolution of Brazilian nationalism. The exalted patriotism of "Aquarela do Brasil" and the Estado Novo had lost its currency. *O Pessoal da Velha Guarda* expressed a new protectionism, defensive and resentful of foreign influence.

EARLY YEARS

As is the case with the names of most Brazilian musical genres, the term *choro* ostensibly denotes a rhythm, but in practice describes a combination of rhythm, instrumentation, and musical form. For choro, this combination began to coalesce in the last decades of the nineteenth century, when the term *choro* was first applied to small ensembles featuring strings and wind instruments of European origin and percussive instruments of African origin. There are several competing etymologies for the term. Most critics believe the term derives from the Portuguese verb *chorar*, to weep. A choro, by this etymology, would be a lament, in keeping with the generally plangent mood of the genre. Scholar Ary Vasconcellos, on the other hand, traces the term to the colonial Brazilian word *choromeleiro*, describing members of instrumental ensembles. *Choromeleiro*, in turn, derives from the Greek for "sweet music"—like *chorus*. Henrique Cazes casts doubt on this explanation and reasserts the importance of sentimental musical interpretation as a likely influence on the etymology. This disagreement over etymology begins to reveal the dynamics of the debate regarding choro: musicians, critics, and fans alike are deeply concerned with origins and establishing authenticity, and inclined to see the music as an intrinsically bittersweet evocation of a lost past. Regardless of its origins, the term gradually shifted from referring only to the ensembles to referring to the style of music they performed, in various rhythms.[3]

From its inception, choro lived on the borderline between erudite and popular music. Nineteenth-century composers like Ernesto Nazareth and Joaquim Antonio Callado combined the spontaneity of popular music, of both European and African origin, with the harmonic and melodic complexity of erudite chamber music, creating compositions that demanded technically skilled interpreters but were intended primarily for a popular audience. Not all of their music could be classified as choro, but much of it has become part of the standard repertoire of the genre. The blend of influences was subsequently codified by the City Fire Department Band in Rio in the 1890s, led by composer Anacleto de Medeiros. That band, distinguished by its professionalization and exacting rehearsals, was one of the first to give coherent and consistent expression to the growing body of work that later became known as choro, setting standards of instrumentation and execution.[4]

In addition to its mediation of erudite and popular influence, the Fire Department Band embodied two related truths of the emerging genre: its lower middle-class origins and its racial integration. Medeiros, like Callado before him, was of mixed-race background. His father was a medical doctor, his mother a freed slave.[5] Photographs of his band show that it included musicians of a broad range of phenotype. This integration was not unusual in the lower-middle- and working-class world of Rio de Janeiro, economic strata populated by low-ranking civil servants and clerks in merchant houses, and heavily concentrated in crowded downtown neighborhoods. These broadly integrated neighborhoods were clearly separate from the more precarious and less-urbanized housing of the overwhelmingly Afro-Brazilian poor and the leafy parks of the solidly white elite. The plazas of these lower middle-class neighborhoods became centers of a vigorous public life, and it was here that choro took root. Even in this context, however, choro was particularly integrated. The demands of the musical enterprise, perhaps, helped to create a zone less troubled by racism than was the encompassing society: anyone who had the chops was welcome to play along.

Not all choro groups were integrated. The same parties in the Praça Onze that gave birth to samba in the late 1910s also featured choro performances, and the musicians and the guests at these parties were overwhelmingly Afro-Brazilian.[6] Nor were choro and choro musicians unaffected by the racism of the broader society. Pixinguinha's influential choro group of the late 1910s was entirely Afro-Brazilian. When the group played at a posh downtown cinema in 1919, a number of elite white patrons were scandalized by both the nature of the music and the color of the musicians.[7] But the longstanding integration of choro ensembles meant that choro itself was not racially marked, as samba would later be. For Afro-Brazilian musicians, this lack of racial specificity may have held particular attractions: as Medeiros's success and influence suggest, choro was a realm where the child of a freed slave could rise to the pinnacle of an integrated musical hierarchy. This is not to say the process was open to all. In contrast to samba, whose basic percussive instruments could be made by hand from locally available materials, choro's leading instruments—woodwinds and strings—were relatively expensive. Becoming a choro soloist required an initial investment that limited the access of Rio's poorest residents. As a result, while those elite and middle-class Cariocas who aspired to a vision of pure Europeanness looked down on choro as rustic music, it was not, in general, perceived as either fundamentally African or intrinsically music of the poor. This protected it from the persecution and disparagement samba often experienced in the 1920s, but also precluded it from sharing in the initial elevation to national symbol that samba experienced in the 1930s.[8]

Pixinguinha, born in 1897, grew up in this relatively integrated world of choro musicians, or *chorões*. Like Medeiros, he was *mulato* by Brazilian standards and from a middle-class background—his father was a civil servant and amateur musician. By the early 1910s, Pixinguinha began to distinguish himself as a flautist, bringing a new sense of rhythm and a stronger attack to the choro flute. He was also one of the first choro musicians to improvise over more than a few bars, a practice which soon became characteristic of the genre, at roughly the same time that the same phenomenon was occurring in the evolution of jazz. He began to write music in the same years and soon showed even more promise in his composition than in his playing. By mid-decade, he was a prominent artist in the Carioca choro world, playing frequently in local bars and theaters.[9]

He was a regular in the Praça Onze, where he played frequently with the guitarist Donga and the percussionist João da Baiana, both of whom would continue to play with him over the next five decades. At the Praça Onze parties, all of these musicians moved easily from choro to samba: as Pixinguinha later recalled, "We played choro in the salon, and samba on the patio." The remark shows both the common ground of the genres and the class distinction beginning to emerge between them. That distinction was also one of style: from its inception samba lent itself both to dancing and singing. Choro, in contrast, remained more of a musician's genre—one demanding technical skill and giving great emphasis to instrumental improvisation, generally eschewing vocal accompaniment.[10]

The emergence of samba did not immediately threaten the popularity of choro. Pixinguinha's own career blossomed in the early 1920s. At the time, he led an influential band known as the Oito Batutas, or Eight batons (also punning on slang for "the eight clever ones"). The first incarnation of the Oito Batutas featured flute, three guitars, cavaquinho, mandolin, ganzá (rattle or shaker), and reco-reco (a hollow, grooved gourd rubbed with a stick, producing a sound similar to the washboard of Dixieland jazz). The line-up was occasionally varied to include clarinet, tambourine, and, less frequently, piano.[11] This instrumentation blended expensive and often imported melodic instruments with simple, often homemade percussive instruments. Within this blend, however, the melodic instruments—in this case, Pixinguinha on flute— definitely set the tone and commanded the audience's attention. The Batutas performed several times in São Paulo and toured Northeastern Brazil in 1922. Soon afterward, they played an extended engagement in a Paris nightclub, sharing the bill with American jazz bands. Their recordings and sheet music also began to circulate throughout Brazil.

Choro attained its first extensive national and international exposure through the music of Pixinguinha.[12]

In the late 1920s and throughout the 1930s, choro declined in popularity. The radio stations and recording companies of Rio heavily favored the Estácio sound, and as that style of samba flourished, choro languished. The decline by no means drove Pixinguinha out of the music industry: he worked as the bandleader on the Programa Casé and the head arranger at RCA Victor until the mid-1930s.[13] Nonetheless, he was clearly cognizant of the transition underway. In 1931, he led an ensemble at RCA Victor called the Grupo da Guarda Velha, or Group of the old guard. The group was essentially a new incarnation of the Batutas, performing the same style of choro. Its name shows that Pixinguinha was conscious of the fact that the music that had made him famous in the 1920s was now out of fashion, and that at the age of 34 he was considered outmoded. His colleagues Donga and João da Baiana were each about a decade older, giving them a slightly more logical claim to the name.[14]

Almirante and Pixinguinha first crossed paths during the same period, on the *Programa Casé*, where Almirante worked as the *contra-regra*, or assistant producer, contracting performers and stage-managing the show. There is no record of Almirante's reaction to the original Grupo da Guarda Velha, but he was undoubtedly familiar with its work. Fifteen years later, he would resuscitate the group's name, with a minor variation, making it the symbol of his revivalist drive.[15]

As choro dropped farther from public favor, Pixinguinha's own career declined. RCA Victor hired Radamés Gnattali as an arranger and bandleader, and Gnattali gradually took over most of Pixinguinha's duties at the label. By the late 1930s, he was no longer in great demand. In 1937, singer Orlando Silva recorded hit versions of two Pixinguinha compositions, "Carinhoso" and "Rosa," but these were choros Pixinguinha had written many years before.[16] The success of Silva's renditions was an anomaly in Pixinguinha's years of drought. Gnattali, in fact, had arranged the records, and was justifiably given much of the credit for their success. By the mid-1940s, Victor rarely called on Pixinguinha for arrangements, much less to make his own records. His radio exposure had dwindled to practically nil. He left a low-paying job at Rádio Mayrink Veiga, fell behind on his mortgage payments, and sank gradually into an alcoholic depression. In the words of a fellow musician, Canhoto, "Pixinguinha was forgotten. No one talked about him."[17]

Benedito Lacerda was widely known as the second-best flautist in Rio, a distinction that no doubt rankled him. He was several years younger than Pixinguinha, and, without overtly imitating him, had followed the older musician in nearly every step of his career. He distinguished himself early as a flautist and then became a renowned bandleader, forming the best *conjunto regional* on radio in the 1930s. *Conjunto regional* was the term used to describe radio back-up bands, most of them similar in formation to choro ensembles. And he was a skilled arranger, working frequently with the most popular sambistas of the era.[18]

Although Lacerda was not affected as deeply as was Pixinguinha by the decline of choro, by the mid-1940s he was struggling to keep his schedule full. According to a fellow musician, "Choro was stopped in 1946. Benedito Lacerda wasn't playing. Pixinguinha wasn't playing." Late in that same year, a record contract uniting the two great band-leaders for the first time initiated the revival. Lacerda brokered a deal with Pixinguinha and RCA Victor for a series of twenty-five 78 rpm records to be recorded over the next two years. In return for an advance on the contract, Pixinguinha agreed to two exacting conditions. First, Lacerda would be registered as a coauthor of all compositions the pair recorded, including those which Pixinguinha had originally composed decades earlier. Second, Lacerda would be the featured performer on flute, and Pixinguinha would play a supporting role on tenor saxophone.[19]

The first condition, which meant that Lacerda would get authorial royalties for compositions he had not written, was self-evidently exploitative but not unusual in an era when such rights were regularly transferred and violated more or less openly. The second condition was more alarming for Pixinguinha's admirers, but apparently did not trouble the composer himself. In his youth, he had been known for his strong "attack"—his ability to play complex runs with sustained strength and clarity—but he had lost confidence in his ability to pull off such feats. He had not recorded on the instrument since 1942, and may have looked on the contract with Lacerda as a relief, freeing him from the awkward spectacle of refusing requests to play flute.[20] Nonetheless, the switch did entail a musical sacrifice. Pixinguinha's skills as a saxophonist never equalled his talents on his first instrument: he brought the same melodic and harmonic genius to the sax, but his timbre was limited, bordering on monotonous.[21]

The Pixinguinha-Lacerda contract presented Almirante with a singular opportunity. Since leaving the *Programa Casé* in the late 1930s, Almirante had been creating radio programs that sought to present authentic Brazilian culture to a popular but discerning audience. His program *Curiosidades musicais* (Musical curiosities), begun in 1938, concentrated on facets of Brazilian popular and folkloric music. Early in 1939, for example, *Curiosidades musicais* commemorated the ten-year anniversary of the Mangueira samba school with a celebration featuring guest performances by school members.[22] His *Instantâneos sonoros do Brasil* (Sonic snapshots of Brasil) and *Aquarelas do Brasil* (Watercolors of Brasil), of the early to mid-1940s, were more explicitly about Brazilian folklore, including shows on fishermen's chants, capoeira, and the songs of the blind bards of the Northeast.

As the 1940s progressed, Almirante began to concentrate more heavily on urban music, both popular and erudite, and particularly on that which straddled those categories. His 1944 program *História das orquestras e músicos do Brasil* (The history of the orchestras and musicians of Brazil), presented short biographical sketches of nineteenth- and early-twentieth-century composers and musicians, and performances of their music. Inevitably, this brought Almirante to the roots of choro: one program, for example, featured Ernesto Nazareth, whose compositions prefigured choro; another was on Patápio Silva, widely reputed to be the greatest flautist before Pixinguinha. Unlike *Curiosidades musicais*, the musical biography program was not a popular success and did not last long. It did, however, receive critical acclaim, including a warm letter of praise from Luís da Câmara Cascudo, Brazil's most prominent folklorist.[23] For Almirante, there could be no higher compliment: Câmara Cascudo's enthusiasm undoubtedly strengthened his resolve to continue mining this lode.

The Pixinguinha-Lacerda contract, which brought the duo together with a small group of Rio's renowned chorões, gave Almirante the instant makings of a new program. Featuring Pixinguinha, Donga, and João da Baiana, moreover, would allow Almirante to improve on his most recent show. Rather than simply recreating the past through impressions, he would be rescuing it live, bringing the real characters of his investigations onstage. Despite the large cast necessary to produce the program—principally some twenty-five musicians—the preparations were fairly simple. Almirante had recently moved from Rádio

Nacional to Rádio Tupi, and quickly convinced his new station to hire Pixinguinha.[24] Lacerda was also already under temporary contract with Tupi, and the rest of the musicians followed eagerly—like Pixinguinha, if not more so, most had seen their fortunes decline in recent years, and were eager for the exposure.

CHORO AS NATIONAL TREASURE

O Pessoal da Velha Guarda debuted on 19 March 1947. Its format was simple and straightforward: Almirante introduced the orchestra and let it play, something it did marvellously well. On most selections, the entire band played collectively. On tunes arranged for smaller groups, Pixinguinha led an ensemble called Pixinguinha e a Turma dos Chorão (Pixinguinha and the Chorão Crew). In between the musical selections, he gave information about the composers and the rhythms, recounted anecdotes, and, as the program developed a regular audience, read from listeners' letters. From the beginning, he presented the program as a virtuous and patriotic exercise in the defense of national treasures. He introduced the program as "uma audição brasileiríssima," an extremely Brazilian broadcast, "perhaps the most Brazilian on radio," and praised "the noble work of this restoration of our authentic popular music." The logic behind such assertions was frankly circular: the program was authentic because it was Brazilian, and Brazilian because it was authentic, and noble because it was Brazilian and authentic.

The only way to give such logic any meaning was to stress the inviolability of traditional standards. Almirante complained of "those singers who dilute the melody of our songs," insisting that "the singer should not, for any reason, change the melody written by the composer." He affirmed that the Velha Guarda band would never do such a thing. On another evening, he declared, "Performers of popular music: the greatest benefit you can give to Brazilian popular music is to sing samba as samba, marcha as marcha. . . . none of this imitating the Bing Crosbys and Frank Sinatras. The effects they use for the fox-trot might be good for the fox-trot, *but not for our music*. On this point, The Personnel of the Old Guard plays our music with the greatest rigor."[25]

This defensive nationalism was not limited to music. Speaking of Vinhos Único, the vintner who sponsored the program for one stretch, Almirante proclaimed, "Brazilians now have confidence in the things that other Brazilians produce. They are confident that our industry has completely surpassed that of foreign industries."[26] Fortunately, the success of the program did not depend on the quality of Brazilian wine. In any case, Vinhos Único was soon replaced by another sponsor, a maker of a household analgesic. But if other things—wine, poetry, the plazas of downtown Rio—occasionally earned that adjective of highest praise, *brasileiríssimo*, popular music was, for Almirante, the truest expression of national character. And choro, in particular, communicated something essentially Brazilian. *O Pessoal da Velha Guarda* played various rhythms, including waltz, *lundu*, *xote*, and *maxixe*. Throughout the life of the program, however, its emphasis remained on choro, particularly on the style most closely associated with the chorões of the 1910s.

The program's emphasis on choro was not at all axiomatic: samba, after all, was a more popular genre, and one already deeply linked to nationalist sentiment. Choro, in contrast, remained primarily a local genre of Rio de Janeiro, despite the brief period of national prominence in the early 1920s and the continued existence of a small choro community in São Paulo. But in contrast to samba, which had progressed through several stages of evolution, choro had changed little in the previous thirty years. More important, it was noticeably in a state of decline, in danger of losing its elder practitioners and its remaining fans. These factors made it the perfect candidate for Almirante's curatorial attention. Each segment of the program, as a result, was billed not merely as a half-hour's worth of fine music, but as a journey into the past. As Almirante waxed romantically: "One more time, the melodies of the past return. . . . Join us on a voyage to the land of nostalgia."[27]

If the need for preservation provided the reason for the program's existence, it was the assertion of choro as an expression of a Brazilian essence that gave the project its importance. Again, this meant competing with samba on what had become its home turf, but Almirante did not flinch. He summed up his vision of choro as the carrier of national identity in a 1948 broadcast. Speaking with a passion that contrasted with his usual professorial tone, he confessed a belief in the power of popular music to pacify the world. "Therefore," he argued, "each of us should make sure that a good number of our songs crosses the world's borders, bringing to other peoples the certainty of our existence and a way to recognize our people." Samba had already traveled around the world, primarily via Carmen Miranda, but Almirante made no reference to Miranda's continuing success overseas (despite the fact that he was among her closest friends remaining in Brazil). Instead, he held Brazilians to an older standard, suggesting that when traveling abroad they identify themselves by whistling the most famous of all choros,

Pixinguinha's "Carinhoso."[28] Pixinguinha had written the melody in 1917, and first recorded it in 1927. By 1948, it already had the legitimacy conferred by the patina of age.

Almirante envisioned *O Pessoal da Velha Guarda* as the bulwark in a larger struggle for the survival of Brazilian music. For several weeks in 1948, he began the program with jubilant reports that the four most popular records on the Brazilian charts were all Brazilian compositions. Each week, he conveyed this news as if it were a surprise and a cause for celebration.[29] In fact, versions of foreign popular songs rarely broke the Top 10. *O Pessoal da Velha Guarda*, for its part, met the fox-trot head on and fared well. It generally aired at 9:30 p.m., moving from Wednesday to Friday and finally to Thursday nights—all prime slots, against popular competition. For most of its long run, the program averaged about an 8 percent audience share in Rio. This generally put it in second place, behind whichever program happened to be airing on Rádio Nacional at the moment—that station was so dominant that its leadership in prime-time was a foregone conclusion. The Rio broadcasts of *O Pessoal da Velha Guarda* also registered in audience polls in other cities, such as Salvador, rare for a Rio program not on Rádio Nacional. And occasional special broadcasts in São Paulo were even more popular, beating the competition in that city by a wide margin.[30]

BEYOND RIO

The popularity of the São Paulo broadcasts was not an aberration. In fact, the entire phenomenon of the Velha Guarda became even more popular there than in Rio, particularly through the Velha Guarda festivals of 1954 and 1955. The first, in April 1954, began with plans for a birthday tribute to Pixinguinha on Rádio Record of São Paulo. Paulo Machado de Carvalho, the owner of that station, arranged for two public concerts by the Velha Guarda, one in a local theater, the other in Ibirapuera Park, the city's principal space for outdoor, cross-class leisure, to be broadcast live on Rádio Record. The events, billed collectively as the Festival da Velha Guarda, were extraordinarily successful. Over ten thousand fans crowded into Ibirapuera for the free performance. The São Paulo papers gave prominent coverage to the event and to other performances by the Velha Guarda, including an unscheduled jam at a local bar that brought one reviewer to tears. Encouraged by this popular acclaim, the Velha Guarda organized another series of concerts back in Rio, playing an extended engagement at the exclusive Hotel Gloria. The Rio shows did well, but they did not provoke the same kind of clamor that had greeted the group in São Paulo. A similar reaction greeted the second Festival da Velha Guarda in São Paulo, in April 1955. Again, tens of thousands of fans turned out to hear the musicians at several public shows, and this time, local amateur musicians paid tribute to the Velha Guarda with performances of their own. Again, concerts in Rio after the second festival were only a moderate success. The Velha Guarda was embraced most passionately far from both the birthplace of the genre and the program that had set off the revival. A Rio critic noted the irony, writing: "This has created a paradox: these days whoever wants to hear Brazilian music in Brazil has to go to São Paulo."[31]

The critic's gripe reveals just how completely Rio had previously dominated the national music industry—he considered it shocking that the most exciting event in Brazilian music might take place somewhere else. São Paulo, in particular, seemed an unlikely site for the Velha Guarda's biggest events, given the strong emphasis on local color in its radio programming. The most curious facet of the success of Pixinguinha and cohort in São Paulo is that they were folded smoothly into an expression of Paulistano regional pride. In 1954, Machado de Carvalho incorporated the Festival da Velha Guarda into the city's quadricentennial celebration, officially commemorated on 25 January but celebrated throughout the year in a series of festivities. Pixinguinha and Benedito Lacerda shared the bill with schoolchildren's pageants of local history and politician's speeches honoring São Paulo's four hundred years of courage, independence, and industry.[32]

As Barbara Weinstein has shown, the quadricentennial festivities, as a general rule, obscured the role of Afro-Brazilians in São Paulo history and pushed them further to the margins of the city's industrial present. Those festivities also promoted an understanding of local exceptionalism, suggesting that São Paulo had always been more progressive and more industrious than the rest of Brazil, especially Rio de Janeiro.[33] But here were the Pessoal da Velha Guarda, led by the Afro-Brazilian Pixinguinha, performing Carioca music, embraced in the midst of this civic jubilee. On a general level, their success within the quadricentennial reminds us that popular culture is easily put to different uses by different audiences: the Paulistanos evidently borrowed what they needed from Almirante's rhetoric—the image of a living relic of an idealized past—and eschewed what they did not—the emphasis on

Carioca popular culture. Specifically, however, it is clear that choro was suitable where samba was not. Samba made its Afro-Brazilian roots explicit, and these were crucial to its appeal. Choro did not exactly obscure its Afro-Brazilian characteristics; it simply made no issue of them. Almirante, for example, never mentioned race in his discussion of nineteenth-century composers. The early integration of choro, one of its most distinctive characteristics, ironically permitted the question of race to disappear from critical accounts. Whereas samba was often perceived as a manifestation of racial democracy, choro—historically a more racially democratic genre—was perceived as racially blank. This, in turn, made it acceptable within the context of the São Paulo quadri-centennial.

DISGUISING INNOVATION

Onstage at the São Paulo festivals and the Rio concerts, the musicians dressed in a style evoking the 1920s, in white linen suits, straw boaters, and bow ties. The attire was presumably a visual reference to the choro heyday of the early 1920s, despite the fact that in 1922 the Oito Batutas had worn natty dark suits and dashing ties, striving for a sophisticated modern look.[34] The period costumes were only one of the ways in which the Velha Guarda sought to present everything they did as traditional. Inevitably, this emphasis on preservation hindered recognition of the group's innovations.

Greatest of these was the interplay of Lacerda's flute and Pixinguinha's sax. His limitations as a saxophonist not withstanding, Pixinguinha used his position as a supporting player to experiment more ambitiously with counterpoint. He had worked with parallel but distinct melodic phrases as early as 1919, and his Victor arrangements were rich in contrapuntal harmony. But the counterpoint he developed with Lacerda, in both written arrangements and improvisations, often created extended dual melodies played at the same time, intertwining like climbing vines. This contrapuntal invention became a hallmark of the genre. In the opinion of musicologist and composer Brasílio Itiberê, the counterpoint of Pixinguinha and Lacerda represented one of the most complex and important innovations in the history of Brazilian popular music.[35] On the program, however, the delicate, improvised conversation between the two instrumentalists, to the degree that it was recognized at all, was treated as a time-honored facet of the genre.

Similarly, the emerging talents of the younger or previously un-heralded musicians in the group, such as flautist Altamiro Carrilho and trombonist Raul de Barros, went largely unrecognized. Pixinguinha described them as "os novos da Velha Guarda,"—the young ones of the Old Guard—a phrase that, in its awkwardness, suggests the difficulty of acknowledging novelty within a performance designed to appear traditional. Mandolinist Jacob do Bandolim represented a special case in this regard. Although he had been a fixture on the amateur choro scene since the late 1930s, he had not had extensive broadcast exposure before *O Pessoal da Velha Guarda*. The program was an ideal showcase for the revelation of his talent, and he was often a featured instrumentalist. Almirante's rhetoric, however, fixed solely on tradition, was unable to accommodate the significance of this public revelation for the growth of the genre.

Despite constant evocation of an uncomplicated past, the Velha Guarda were entirely dependent on the modern media, and not only in terms of the radio broadcast itself. Members of the Velha Guarda re-corded over fifty 78 rpm records over the course of the program. As important, the Velha Guarda recorded three long-playing records for the Sinter label in 1955 and 1956, among the first LPs released in Brazil. Finally, the São Paulo festivals were broadcast to great fanfare on tele-vision, a medium in its infancy in Brazil, and in 1955 Pixinguinha and Lacerda were contracted to do an entire series on TV Record of São Paulo.[36]

THE WIDER REVIVAL

Even more surprising than the success of *O Pessoal da Velha Guarda* was the way it sparked a wider fad for the genre. As the program grew in popularity in the late 1940s, RCA Victor, Continental, and Odeon, the three major recording companies in Rio, began steadily increasing their choro releases. In 1949, Continental struck gold with Waldir Aze-vedo's "Brasileirinho," an infectious up-tempo choro featuring Aze-vedo's deft *cavaquinho*, or ukelele, picking. The record became the year's best-seller, a rare achievement for a composition with no vo-cals.[37] Interest in choro waxed further in the early 1950s: nearly every radio station in Rio broadcast at least one program entirely dedicated to choro, often featuring members of the Velha Guarda leading their own bands. Jacob do Bandolim, Antonio Rago, Altamiro Carrilho, and

Raul de Barros all had their own shows on different São Paulo and Rio stations.[38]

The most ambitious of the choro radio shows, beyond *O Pessoal da Velha Guarda* itself, was Rádio Nacional's *Instantâneos do Brasil*, or Snapshots of Brazil, broadcast in 1950 and 1951. Paulo Tapajós, a former assistant of Almirante's, produced the program in conjunction with writer Mário Faccini. Tapajós had recently inaugurated the Department of Brazilian Music at Rádio Nacional, a nucleus of producers, writers, and musicians organized with the expressed intention of defending the traditions of Brazilian music against a putative wave of Americanization. Like Almirante and the Velha Guarda, their approach concentrated on an ostensible rediscovery of the choro sounds of the past.

The format of *Instantâneos do Brasil* consisted of an imaginary voyage into a moment in Brazilian history. The time-traveling narrator, aided by his coachman and guide, described the sights and sounds of the past to the program's listeners. In a 1950 program, for example, the narrator lands in downtown Rio in 1901. Almost immediately, he hears the sound of an ensemble playing "Flor amoroso," a Joaquim Antonio Callado composition from the late nineteenth century. Chatting with a bystander, he praises the fine choro, puzzling his interlocutor. The narrator then realizes his mistake and explains to the audience that "choro" is not yet recognized as a genre, but that they can go hear some "chorões." The confusion is contrived—by 1901, any musically aware Carioca would have been familiar with the term *choro* and would not have been surprised to hear it applied to the music itself, rather than to the ensemble. But the plot device draws the listeners in, enabling them to witness the formation of the genre. The guide then leads the narrator across to a downtown plaza where they attend a rehearsal of Anacleto de Medeiros's City Fire Department Band—choro in its formative years is transmitted live to the radio audience of the 1950s. *Instantâneos do Brasil* was a smashing success, garnering a 20 percent audience share early in 1951.[39]

The radio critics and newspaper columnists of Rio and São Paulo gave prominent coverage to this spate of programs and records, playing a crucial role in fixing the lessons of revivalism. In 1954, Lúcio Rangel, the most sophisticated of these critics, founded the *Revista da Música Popular*, a critical review dedicated to analysis of recent and historical music. The first issue featured coverage of the Festival da

Velha Guarda. Rangel subsequently collected many of his own pieces in a 1961 volume titled *Sambistas e chorões*. The book's understanding of choro followed directly from Almirante's radio program, describing choro as a national treasure, unchanged over time and unsullied by commerce. It became a foundational work in the historiography of Brazilian popular music, influencing the interpretations of two generations of scholars.[40]

EFFECTS AND AFTERMATH

The choro revival saved Pixinguinha's career and consolidated his reputation. The publicity generated by *O Pessoal da Velha Guarda* also had immediate ramifications for Pixinguinha's more mundane source of income: in 1949, he was finally transferred from a long-held position as an inspector of public sanitation to the more appropriate post of administrative official in the city Department of Education, where he taught music and led the municipal band. The transfer was largely an issue of title and salary, as he had been directing the band for years and had never shown much concern for public sanitation. In 1952 the mayor of Rio promoted Pixinguinha to a more prestigious teaching and conducting position within the city's musical education program.[41] His employment in the civil service was not at all unusual. Many choro musicians held day jobs as civil servants, which guaranteed them a modest pension and health-care benefits. Even in the mid-1950s, at the height of the revival and its increased financial opportunities, most of the members of the Pessoal da Velha Guarda held on to their *ossos*—their bones, or day-jobs in the civil service. Jacob do Bandolim, for example, kept his job as a clerk in Rio's criminal court system until his death in 1969. Pixinguinha, the most famous chorão, finally retired from the civil service in 1966. He continued to play publicly until his death in 1973. By that time, his name had become incontrovertibly united with the genre of choro.

The other members of the Velha Guarda benefited as well. For musicians like Donga and João da Baiana, the revival was, in the words of scholar Sérgio Cabral, "a type of rebirth before the public." Once back in the spotlight, they carried on with the act that had brought them there, continuing to perform as the Velha Guarda until the ends of their careers in the mid-1960s. Benedito Lacerda, in contrast, always pursued other projects and never became completely identified with the Velha Guarda. The "young ones of the Old Guard" may have benefited the most. Jacob do Bandolim, Altamiro Carrilho, and Raul de Barros all went on to brilliant choro careers, defining the music for decades.

Perhaps because of the formative influence that *O Pessoal da Velha Guarda* had on their careers, the definitions they created were often quite restrictive. Jacob do Bandolim in particular was instrumental in establishing narrow parameters which continue to structure the way choro is played and appreciated.[42] In the late 1950s, when the revival faded, Jacob founded an ensemble known as Época de Ouro, or Golden Age. Like the Velha Guarda, Época de Ouro evoked a nebulous but glorious choro past in its name, and placed overwhelming emphasis on upholding tradition in its public performances. As the bandleader, Jacob required ceaseless rehearsal and insisted on playing a small repertoire with utter precision. Even more so than the Velha Guarda, the Época de Ouro concentrated on the compositions of Pixinguinha. In addition, it revived pieces by the ancestors of the genre, like Nazareth and Medeiros. The group continues to perform today, featuring some of its original personnel and largely the same repertoire.

In his radio broadcasts and in public pronouncements, Jacob regularly railed against any adulteration of the form. He attacked bossa nova, calling it a traitorous musical phenomenon, and arguing that its rhythm was inauthentic. He accused bossa nova guitarist Baden Powell—who had debuted as a teenager in the Festival da Velha Guarda—of corrupting choro: "Baden Powell brought inadmissible, jazzistic influence to choro. . . . In choro, there are no complications, no augmented ninths and I don't know what. They need to stop that, or it won't be pure choro." Like Almirante, Jacob advocated the protection of traditional choro at all costs: "If the so-called moderns try to adulterate choro, I, as composer and defender, will go to the public square to defend it. They are not going to do to choro what they did to samba. I will fight."[43] Jacob made explicit the contrast between a supposedly pure choro and a samba that had been changed too much to carry its former burden of national representation.

In the mid 1950s, Jacob organized amateur choro nights on Rádio Record and TV Record of São Paulo. He spent weeks preparing for the broadcasts, training his students in the rigors of his traditional interpretation. Then, in the climactic live broadcasts, he led his students in a harmonious rendition of choro standards. The 1956 show featured 133 amateur chorões playing "Carinhoso" in unison. Mass performance necessarily meant sacrificing the contrapuntal improvisation of the

Velha Guarda, but discipline, rather than innovation, was the point of the exercise.[44]

A handful of influential critics and scholars joined Jacob in burnishing the reputation of Pixinguinha and—almost as an inevitable corollary—condemning innovation in choro. Like Almirante, they saw Pixinguinha as "the most Brazilian of all Brazilian musicians," elevating him, in effect, to the category of national saint. In 1971 Hermínio Bello de Carvalho, a music journalist and a protégé of Jacob, produced an album titled *São Pixinguinha*—Saint Pixinguinha.[45] After Jacob died in 1969, he received similar critical treatment. His choro style was interpreted not only as being more authentic than that of pop chorões like Waldir Azevedo, but as being more Brazilian. In the words of fellow chorão Claudionor Cruz, "Jacob was one of our national perfections. His name is Jewish, but he was more Brazilian than any Brazilian. . . . He worked the national. That man never played a foreign note."[46]

This understanding of choro profoundly influenced the next flowering of the genre, in the mid-1970s, and as a result, that flowering was more limited in every way than the revivalism of the 1950s. The 1950s revival gave rise to a host of innovations, including the contrapuntal breakthroughs of Lacerda and Pixinguinha, the pop experimentation of Waldir Azevedo, and Antonio Rago's use of electric guitar. The choro of the 1970s, in contrast, revealed great instrumentalists but eschewed experimentation. More innovative chorões of the 1970s, such as Hermeto Paschoal and Paulo Moura, were pushed outside the genre and reclassified as Brazilian jazz musicians.

The *velhaguardismo* that emerged in the 1950s remains influential. Choro today is a genre made up predominantly of standards: most choro albums include several compositions by Pixinguinha, Nazareth, and Jacob, and rarely feature more than one or two new works. Recently, choro has once again begun to show signs of flexibility and openness to experimentation.[47] Still, the idea that choro communicates something essentially Brazilian and therefore must be protected without alteration continues to mark both the way choro is played and the way it is critically perceived. For example, a recent feature on the history of choro in a magazine dedicated to the genre bears the title, "The Musical Essence of the Brazilian Soul."[48]

O Pessoal da Velha Guarda was both the best thing and the worst thing to happen to choro. It was instrumental in reawakening the genre's popularity, saving it from years of decline and giving rise to some of its greatest innovations. But its protectionist rhetoric encouraged the adoption of narrow parameters of authenticity and acceptability, limiting the music for decades. *O Pessoal da Velha Guarda* had a greater influence on the subsequent development of Brazilian popular culture than other programs that were more commercially successful at the time. This was partly a result of its timing: *O Pessoal da Velha Guarda* achieved its greatest popular success in the early 1950s, when its rhetoric of the defense of Brazilian tradition found broader public resonance. The ardent protectionism of *O Pessoal da Velha Guarda* closely paralleled contemporary political rhetoric.

During his second presidency, begun in 1951, Getúlio Vargas and his supporters painted a stark contrast between his putative defense of national sovereignty and the *entreguismo*, or selling-out to foreign interests, of his political enemies. This rhetorical strategy reached fever pitch in the debate over the oil deposits of Brazil's Northeast. Vargas rallied support for his bid to establish a state oil company with the cry "o petróleo é nosso" (the oil is ours) and denounced the imperialist policies of companies like Standard Oil and Shell. Using language remarkably similar to Almirante on *O Pessoal da Velha Guarda*, Vargas urged Brazilians to defend their vital interests in Brazil's natural riches against the depredations of greedy imperialists. Behind the scenes, meanwhile, he worked to placate the multinationals and to maintain some foreign investment.[49]

Vargas by no means tailored his rhetoric to echo that of Almirante's successful program. Rather, both the program and the oil campaign responded to similar fears of internationalization, and inspired broad popular response with their call for the protection of endangered Brazilian resources. Both spoke to a larger anxiety about nationality, one fed by Brazil's ambiguous international position between Cold War superpowers. In contrast to the exalted patriotic fanfare of the Estado Novo, the nationalist rhetoric that both Vargas and Almirante emphasized in the early 1950s was thoroughly defensive and inward-looking, with more than a touch of xenophobia.

One notable irony of the rhetorical similarity between *O Pessoal da Velha Guarda* and "o petróleo é nosso" is that Almirante's show aired on Rádio Tupi, the flagship station of media magnate Assis Chateaubriand, a fervent supporter of multinational investors. The protectionists frequently derided Chateaubriand as the most vile *entreguista* in the country.[50] The relationship between cultural nationalism and international investment was not one of simple opposition. Standard Oil and Shell depended on Chateaubriand to defend their interests in Brazil, and supported him by advertising heavily in his newspapers. Chateaubriand depended on Almirante to produce popular programs, and Almirante and the Velha Guarda depended on Chateaubriand for exposure and employment.

These coincidences were evidence neither of hypocrisy on the part of Chateaubriand nor heroic resistance from within the *entreguista* fortress on the part of Almirante and the Velha Guarda. Instead, they demonstrate the expansion of Brazil's popular cultural arena. By the early 1950s, that arena was able to accommodate conflicting trends and diverse constituencies. Radio, in particular, had reached its peak of diversity and vitality. Rádio Tupi and RCA Victor could trade in both the cosmopolitan cachet of American pop and the nationalist pride of Brazilian tradition. These strategies were by no means mutually exclusive. As important, they did not necessarily appeal to exclusive subsets of the radio audience and record-buying public: Almirante's strict rhetoric notwithstanding, the same fans could and did listen to both American and Brazilian music. Within this diverse broadcasting field, however, the contemporary fears of international penetration made it almost inevitable that those broadcasters who embraced protectionist nationalist sentiment would achieve great critical resonance. Almirante's genius was to hook that rhetoric to a deceptively innovative musical phenomenon, revitalizing one of Brazil's richest musical genres.

6 FAN CLUBS AND AUDITORIUM PROGRAMS

We were fans, but it was not fanaticism. It was a conscious,
coherent choice, without fanaticism, without idolatry.
—Ciro Gaulo

If it is my destiny to be run over by an automobile, it would
not be so bad if it were at least Marlene's car.—Regina Silva

In a 1977 interview, radio producer Adhemar Casé mournfully pronounced, "The auditorium program killed Brazilian radio." Casé was
looking back at a long and brilliant career, one that had coincided with
the greatest days of Brazilian radio, trying to understand the medium's
decline. His *Programa Casé* had set the tone for popular broadcasting in
the 1930s. Designed to present popular music to its greatest advantage,
as an enterprise of artistry and sophistication, the program had remained on the air for decades, moving from station to station, and
inspired a host of imitations. But in the late 1940s, this type of programming appeared to lose its momentum; it no longer dominated nighttime ratings and lost its importance as a laboratory of popular culture.[1]

At the same time, the *programas de auditório,* or auditorium programs, were growing exponentially in popularity. These variety shows,
performed for a live studio audience, generally in the daytime, also
attracted considerable critical attention, albeit overwhelmingly negative. Criticism centered primarily on the noisy festivity of the auditorium, which often prevented listeners at home from hearing the
featured performers. One 1947 radio reviewer, writing in the name of
"good taste," lamented the "chaotic and ill-mannered nature of the
auditoriums." A few years later, another critic charged that "the auditorium program has ruined radio's ascendancy. . . . it is high time for
an auditorium that is less noisy, indeed, less ridiculous."[2]

Detractors blamed producers, sponsors, and, above all, the audience. As one observer put it, "the blame belongs entirely to those

listeners who take delight in degrading spectacles." While the home audience was charged with complicity, the studio audience bore the brunt of critical attacks. Pollsters described auditorium fans as members of a "professional audience" who had nothing better to do with their time, and whose rowdy manifestations of approval and disapproval could not be accepted as an indication of the reactions of a legitimate audience. One woman who frequented live radio programs in the early 1940s stopped attending later in the decade, explaining, "The audience changed. It was a different class of people. The auditorium lost its elegance."[3]

The new audience members were frequently members of fan clubs, societies for the adoration of the most popular singers. The fan clubs—passionate, demonstrative, and fervently loyal—fueled the rise of the auditorium programs, and occasionally turned them into chaotic battlegrounds between rival clubs. Their fans usually came from working-class or poor backgrounds, and were frequently women of color. They were not, generally, members of the industrial working class that had been incorporated into populist coalitions but members of a service working class—housemaids, in particular—that had largely been excluded from the political sphere. Many were from small towns in the interior or were recent migrants to Rio. Observers were frequently uncomfortable with their sudden emergence from the social margins into a public spotlight: one critic labeled them *macacas de auditório*—auditorium monkeys. The epithet stuck, marking both the fans and the programs for the next two decades. As one fan described it later, "the fan club had a negative image of fanaticism, of poor and unemployed people of low culture—a series of prejudicial stereotypes they created about us."[4]

The clubs were disparaged not only as lower-class but as socially deviant. Undoubtedly, these attacks responded in part to the prominent activity of gay men in the fan clubs. To the degree that this participation was recognized, however, it was apparently considered a subject unfit for public discussion. Critics frequently alleged that radio's social milieu was a hotbed of sexual transgression: in 1949, for example, a *Revista do Rádio* critic wrote a scathing diatribe against "the effeminates of radio," warning that some male radio stars "only have the characteristics of men but through their gestures and expressions imitate the other sex." But they did not wage specific campaigns against homosexual presence in the fan clubs: rather, outspoken criticism was limited to general condemnations of the clubs as socially pernicious. Partly as a result, the importance of the fan clubs as a semipublic social environment open to gay men has gone largely unrecognized, with the notable exception of James Green's excellent but brief introduction to the subject in *Beyond Carnival*.[5]

For the critics, the unsavory audience was an inevitable result of the crass nature of the programs themselves: they were perceived as a vulgar capitulation to the lowest common denominator rather than as authentically popular entertainment. In a 1955 interview, for example, producer Oswaldo Molles, who favored middlebrow literary adaptations in his own programs, assailed the pernicious influence of the auditorium program, and suggested that Brazilian radio needed to move on: "The shouting, the movement, the noise, the cheering sections, are already obsolete in radio." A picture accompanying the interview showed Molles with an Afro-Brazilian samba musician. In the photo, Molles holds a matchbox, often used as a percussive instrument in street samba, and appears ready to dance. The obvious implication was that he was defending Brazil's authentic popular culture against the base, superficial, commercial fad of the auditorium program. This critical position was typical: auditorium programs were assailed as a capitulation to internationalized mass culture and, hence, as a betrayal of Brazil's genuine popular traditions. Radio columnists also disparaged the auditorium programs for their failure to educate while entertaining—the mission of the medium, in their view. Railing against the programs, reviewers continually made comments like, "One must concede to popular taste—but not so much!" In short, the auditorium programs were widely described as mindless trash produced for an audience with "a mental age between ten and fourteen."[6]

The effects of this hostile critical reception were negligible. The auditorium programs climbed steadily in popularity throughout the first half of the 1950s, and remained the most prominent public face of radio throughout the decade. Nearly every Brazilian station of any size built its own auditorium and attempted to imitate the energy and enthusiasm of Rádio Nacional's auditorium programs. The fan clubs multiplied in number and in membership, and studio audiences grew ever rowdier. This popularity coincided with the height of radio's power: the medium brought in more money, reached more listeners, and exerted a larger cultural influence than it ever had before or ever would again, in relative terms. As a result, the auditorium programs left a lasting mark on Brazilian culture, establishing models of entertainment and sociability that resurfaced in the television era and continue to influence the Brazilian market for popular entertainment. Just as critics universally bemoaned the auditorium programs in their heyday, most have lamented their importance in shaping subsequent cultural expressions. One notable scholar, José Ramos Tinhorão, has rejected the overwhelming critical hostility toward the auditorium programs, adopting precisely the opposite interpretation. In a 1977 volume on the history of Brazilian popular music, Tinhorão described the programs and the fan clubs as a momentary triumph of the lower classes in Brazilian entertainment and argued that, lamentably, this triumph was quickly wiped out by a structural shift toward middle-class entertainment, both through the move to record-oriented, disc-jockey radio and the rise of television in the late 1950s and 1960s. This interpretation has the advantage of reversing elitist dismissal, but it seeks to impose a language of class struggle that seems ill-suited to the fun and games of the auditorium programs. Furthermore, despite his marked differences with Casé, Tinhorão agrees with his interpretation that the auditorium programs themselves provoked massive shifts in the structure of broadcasting, thereby underemphasizing factors such as the rise of niche marketing in radio programming and the growth of television.[7]

Other observers have paid closer attention to the programs and their stars, but none has investigated their relationship with the fan clubs in detail. Even among sympathetic interpreters, moreover, the members of these clubs are treated largely as exotic fauna. Scholars have explained the behavior of the fan clubs in terms of class conflict, in terms of false consciousness imposed by the industry, and—more persuasively—in terms of the creation of a ludic space for otherwise marginalized individuals. The fans themselves see their activity as the creation of a vibrant, enduring community.[8]

THE EMERGENCE OF A PROGRAMMING DIVIDE

In the mid-1940s, popular radio entertainment fell into two broad categories: ambitious, polished, semi-scholarly cultural programming like Almirante's shows, and melodramatic, unrepentantly commercial programming like soap operas. Almirante's didactic, self-consciously enriching entertainment set the tone for radio's most prominent shows, particularly on Rádio Nacional. Programs like Radamés Gnattali's *Um milhão de melodias* (A million melodies) and Almirante's *Aquarelas do Brasil* (Watercolors of Brazil) were designed to elevate Brazilian popular culture, presenting popular music in an atmosphere of sophistication and refinement. At the same time, Rádio Nacional also invested heavily in soap operas, children's adventure series, and women's beauty shows. These programs also had high production values, but, unlike Almirante's shows, they demonstrated negligible interest in Brazilian popular culture and were frequently copied unabashedly from Cuban and American models. Programs like *Um milhão de melodias* received favorable critical attention, occupied the prime-time slots, and were considered a fulfillment of radio's mission to educate and to spread authentic Brazilian culture while entertaining. The soap operas were characterized as women's programs and disparaged as subliterary, emotionally manipulative melodrama in the service of household cleansers and beauty creams. Their very commercial success was considered a sign of their lack of cultural integrity and a threat to quality programming. These programming categories were largely divided into night and day. Some soap operas, however, aired at night. By the early 1950s, prime-time soap operas were often the most popular shows on the air, establishing a well-known tradition that continues on Brazilian television.[9]

The gender labels applied to this programming division were misleading. Women did constitute a strong majority of daytime listeners, but they also constituted at least a bare majority of nighttime listeners. And some polls suggested that *Um milhão de melodias* and similar programs were more popular among women than they were among men. The characterization of soap operas as women's programming, then, was largely a way to dismiss them as unimportant, commercial vehicles filling up radio's wasted hours. The characterization of *Um milhão de melodias* as men's or family programming, conversely, was largely a way of conferring prestige and legitimating the genre as sophisticated, worthwhile, cultural radio. Needless to say, not every program fit neatly into one of these two categories. Sports broadcasts had none of the cultural trappings of the sophisticated prime-time shows, but were seen as healthy, masculine leisure programs, and were not denigrated like soap operas. Amateur talent contests, termed *calouro*, or rookie, shows, occupied a terrain somewhere between the crass and the cultural: some of the calouro shows consisted largely of mean-spirited joking at the expense of unpolished contestants, while others aspired to serve as a legitimate artistic proving ground for the finest local talent. Humor programs, likewise, ranged from coarse slapstick to theater of the absurd. While these programs did not fit neatly into either category of the programming divide, they did not upset its dynamics either. In general, the division between these categories defined the popular cultural arena in the 1940s.[10]

Critical reception did not reflect popular attitudes: indeed, the gap between critical disdain and popular acclaim was precisely what the critics lamented most fiercely. But as long as the soap operas and the culturally enriching musical programs occupied distinctly different terrain, the commercial success of the former did not endanger the prestige of the latter. An uneasy truce reigned in the broadcasting world.

A PROGRAMMING SHIFT

The booming popularity of the auditorium program late in the decade upset the dynamics of that truce. On the one hand, the auditorium programs were disparaged for the same reasons as the soap operas, albeit with even more intensity. But on the other hand, as they became the most popular musical programs on the air they encroached on the cultural ground of programs like *Um milhão de melodias*. Portions of the auditorium programs, after all, featuring glamorous singers performing the latest hits, were not unlike the overtly sophisticated programs. Formal similarities, however, only offset the drastic differences in tone between high-minded, if accessible, music appreciation and raucous festivity. In retrospect it is unsurprising that the deluxe musical showcases and the auditorium programs followed inversely proportionate trajectories. *Um milhão de melodias* declined in popularity and prestige just as the *Programa César de Alencar*, the most prominent auditorium program, ascended. One could chart these contrasting fortunes through advertising revenue, through audience polls, or through column inches in the radio press. But the larger transition is more difficult to pin down: the orchestral programs simply lost momentum, muscled into a smaller corner of the broadcasting stage by the newly powerful auditorium shows. The structure of radio entertainment shifted.

This shift responded to an expansion of the radio audience. The falling relative prices of radios in the postwar era, along with the expansion of the wage economy, vastly increased the size of the working class and poor radio audience, making it a target for the growing industries of mass-marketed household goods. Because of its expanded collective purchasing power, the working class became the target of mass-market radio advertising. At the same time, the falling price of radios dissolved the traditional middle-class family audience gathered in the living room that had been the target audience for *Um milhão de melodias*. Middle-class households became more likely to own two or more radios, allowing family members to choose separate entertainment. By the mid-1950s, moreover, middle-class families turned increasingly to television for nighttime leisure.

In the radio press, the expanding sector of the market was labeled the *suburbano* audience. The *subúrbios* of Rio always occupied a dramatically different social and economic space than the suburbs of American cities. In Rio in the 1940s and 1950s, the term applied to the outlying working-class and poor neighborhoods in the Zona Norte, or north zone, of the city. While they were not nearly as poor or lacking in amenities as the favelas, they were overcrowded and poorly served by public education. Even more important, they were relatively isolated from the cosmopolitan styles of the middle-class beach neighborhoods in the Zona Sul, or southern zone. Their inhabitants acquired a reputation as unpolished in their social behavior and unrestrained and unpredictable in their political and cultural choices, swayed by passion and crude emotional appeal rather than refined appreciation and rational affiliation. *Suburban* became a synonym for *lower-class* and *tacky*.

Not surprisingly, the suburbs had always been perceived as the ideal audience for unrefined, commercial radio. As early as 1941, playwright Nelson Rodrigues wrote an impassioned defense of everything that was garish and tasteless about radio titled, "Radio, the Poetry of the Suburbs." For Rodrigues, the suburban audience was entirely responsible for the rise of the bloody, melodramatic radio theater: "Don't say that the radio station corrupts the taste of the public. It is the public that corrupts the taste of the station. And the suburb is the fan. Our programs are suburban. Our broadcasting is suburban. Everything is suburban." For Rodrigues, the growth of "suburban" radio had enormous kitsch appeal: as he described it, "Radio is the world on top of a crochet mat." Other critics were not so generous: they described the suburban audience and its influence as radio's greatest nemesis.[11]

The auditorium programs were perceived as entirely suburban. Unlike soap opera authors, however, who frequently argued unsuccessfully for recognition of their creations as legitimate literature, the producers and stars of the auditorium programs reveled in their suburbanness. They made direct appeals to specific suburban neighborhoods, produced broadcasts live from suburbs around the city, and did everything possible to draw suburban fans to the auditoriums. Emilinha Borba, the most famous singer of the 1950s, built a career on her image of suburban simplicity. In the words of César de Alencar: "The public is the suburb, the neighborhood. Emilinha presented herself in those dresses that were really Madureira (a large Rio suburb), tacky, but the fact was that she identified with the public."[12]

The suburbs, and working class and poor listeners in general, responded. The auditorium programs became markedly more popular among these audiences than among the middle and upper classes. Audience polls, for example showed great numbers of listeners in Madureira turning on their radios, while listeners in Copacabana turned theirs off. With only rudimentary formal education and little interest in the cultural markers of middle-class sophistication, the majority of working-class and poor listeners found the revelry of the auditorium more entertaining than the cool didacticism of the musical showcases. As this audience grew, the radio industry shifted to meet its needs. Rádio Nacional led the way, and stations across Brazil followed suit. In 1951, Rádio Tamandaré opened in Recife under the slogan, "For the taste of the common man." A year later, Rádio Difusora of Porto Alegre announced that its new programming was "100 percent popular." The slogans themselves suggested that the days when everyone at least paid lip service to the ideal of educational broadcast entertainment had passed.[13]

THE NEW STYLE

The auditorium programs of the late 1940s attracted fans with an atmosphere of fun, games, and ecstatic celebration. Radio critics derided the programs as cheap and degrading, but fans responded to their celebratory mood and their encouragement of audience participation. As the *Revista do Rádio* described it, "Programs of this nature transmit happiness, infecting listeners and spectators, giving them prizes and messages of optimism."[14] Gláucia Garcia, a fan from the interior city of Birigui, São Paulo state, remembered, "I liked the auditorium programs more because they were more animated. When you had an audience there to make noise it was good." José Ramalho, another fan, used similar language: "The orchestra programs did not have the same energy. In the auditorium, we shouted, we sang along with the singer, the singer would stop and let the audience sing. It was happier. There was more interaction. We participated more."[15]

That participation quickly became a public ritual and, in its own way, an exercise in community-building. In the words of Ciro Gaulo, a longtime fan of the auditorium programs from the Rio suburb of Campo Grande, "The auditorium program was a festive atmosphere. It started at home with preparation, the mothers and daughters would prepare picnics, lunch baskets, all that preparation, for a party, a celebration, fraternization. People met each other there and became friends, and the fan clubs grew out of those contacts. It was in the auditorium that many people became friends."[16]

This atmosphere of festivity, occasionally edging into delirium, was precisely what distinguished the auditorium programs of the late 1940s and 1950s from their predecessors. Broadcasting before a live audience, after all, was not a novelty. Much of Brazilian radio, including *Um milhão de melodias*, had been performed before a live audience. But that audience had generally been encouraged to remain silent, or at most, to chuckle along with humor shows. Live radio in the early 1940s was not terribly different from a night at the theater. As one fan recalls, "We used to go to the auditorium in gowns and white gloves, the orchestra was all in tuxedos, and we listened attentively and at the end applauded politely." And although there were some shows which called for limited audience participation and involved the distribution of prizes, contact between performers and the audience was minimal, and audience noise rarely intruded on the broadcast. In some ways, the commotion of the auditorium program marked the release of a decade's pent-up energy.[17]

Admission policies changed along with the tone of the shows. In the early 1940s, admission was frequently limited to those with "invitations." These could be procured either from station employees or found as coupons in some of Rio's better magazines, effectively limiting audience membership to the middle class. With the rise of the auditorium programs, however, Rádio Nacional began handing out free tickets to all comers at the station. When the auditorium programs boomed, the station began charging a modest price for tickets. Prices increased throughout the 1950s. Still, demand remained so high that fans frequently camped out overnight to obtain tickets for the *Programa César de Alencar*.

The runaway success of this program defined the auditorium phenomenon and deserves further concentration. The host—the *animador*, or animator—César de Alencar, was born in the drought-stricken northeastern state of Ceará in 1917. His upper-middle-class, educated family moved to Rio when Alencar was still a teen, and he witnessed the growth of the broadcast industry in the capital first hand. By the early 1940s, Alencar was working regularly as a radio announcer and sportscaster. His break at Rádio Nacional came in 1945, when the station's directors offered him his own program on Saturday afternoons. It was one of the few time slots in the week in which Rádio Nacional did not dominate the competition, instead ranking second to Rádio Tamoio, a smaller station. Tamoio's Saturday afternoon schedule featured a low-budget auditorium program pitched at young listeners, a show that had proven an unexpected success. Rádio Nacional resolved to counter in kind, hiring Alencar to host an auditorium program from 3:00 to 5:00 p.m.[18]

The station was already familiar with the genre: radio actor Paulo Gracindo hosted a variety show on Wednesday afternoons. Gracindo, in fact, turned down the Saturday afternoon slot in order to leave his weekends free for traveling radio theater shows. Alencar, however, immediately brought a new energy to the format, demonstrating infectious good humor and a desperate desire to please the audience. He realized immediately that the key to success lay in emphasizing audience participation and appealing directly to a working-class and poor audience. On the air, he made frequent references to Rio suburbs, inviting listeners from those neighborhoods to attend the program.

Knowing that large sectors of Rio's working-class suburbs had immigrated from the Northeast, Alencar played up his own northeastern background and did special northeastern shows. These programs involved very little in the way of cultural references to the Northeast, depending principally on the presence of northeastern guests and occasional exclamations of regionalist pride. A show in honor of the impoverished state of Paraíba, for example, included a brief interview with a Paraíban politician, followed by Alencar extolling the civic virtues of that fine state, and repeating, "Paraibanos, this program is for you!" This attitude in itself stood in sharp contrast to increasing social bias against poor northeastern immigrants to Rio and São Paulo. Alencar sought to create a welcoming environment for those rejected by the polite classes because of their social and economic shortcomings. As he later claimed, "The truth was, I was in sync with the common people."[19]

Alencar played to the studio audience, letting listeners at home piece together what was happening in their imagination. He encouraged fans to be as noisy and demonstrative as possible, to join him in singing commercial jingles, to compete for prizes, and to scream their appreciation of favorite singers. Audience participation was the key, and the show's theme song hammered this point home: "Prepare your hands, and clap again, this program belongs to you!"[20]

The charismatic Alencar achieved tremendous success with this approach. Within a year, his program had overtaken Rádio Tamoio, and ratings continued to climb. By 1950, Rádio Nacional had expanded Alencar's slot until 7:00 p.m. In every fifteen-minute slot of his four-hour show he garnered at least a 20 percent audience share, beating the nearest competition by a wide margin. By 1953, the program had grown another hour, and ratings continued to climb, ranging between a 15 and 35 percent share. By 1955, the program was on for five and one-half hours, attracting more listeners and generating more advertising revenue than any other program on the air. Alencar's popularity, and the demand for his show in the interior, reached such heights that he often toured during the week, hosting shows around the country, returning to Rio only on Saturday. In 1951, he made weekly trips to his home state of Ceará to host an auditorium program in Fortaleza. These tours played an important role in bringing the latest metropolitan trends to the nation.[21]

This broadcasting juggernaut inspired a raft of imitations. In 1948, Rádio Nacional started another auditorium program, hosted by Manoel Barcellos, on Thursday mornings. Barcellos also achieved considerable success, dominating his time slot and boosting the careers of a cadre of young singers, but he never challenged Alencar's preeminence in the genre. Other stations also followed the model, often building auditoriums merely to initiate variety shows in the Alencar vein. By the early 1950s, the auditorium, and the auditorium program, became the mark of a station's status, and even small stations in interior towns built five-hundred-seat theaters, the same size as Rádio Nacional's. Rádio Tupi–São Paulo opened an auditorium with over a thousand seats.[22]

Stations also looked for ways to bring the excitement of the auditorium to the streets. In the late 1940s, Rádio Nacional began a program called *Ronda dos bairros*, or Neighborhood Patrol. The show was broadcast live each Sunday morning at 10:00 from a different neighborhood cinema in Rio. *Ronda dos bairros* was essentially a small-scale auditorium show, taken on the road. Almost invariably, the neighborhoods chosen were Zona Norte and suburban, such as Cascadura, Engenho de Dentro, and Grajaú. *A felicidade bate a sua porta* (Happiness knocks on your door), another program begun in the late 1940s, created a more spectacular meeting of auditorium and street. Every Sunday at 7:00 p.m., the host of the show announced the name of a street and a neighborhood. The cast of the show, featuring Emilinha Borba, then drove to a house on that street selected by lottery and knocked on the door. Residents who could produce the sponsor's products—household soaps, waxes, detergents, and cooking oils—won cash prizes. Neighbors also had a chance to win. Emilinha and company then closed the program with a performance live from in front of the chosen house. Like *Ronda dos bairros*, *A felicidade bate a sua porta* was pitched at a Zona Norte audience. Both programs show an evolution in the mainstream audience, away from the middle-class neighborhoods of the Zona Sul and toward the working-class neighborhoods of the Zona Norte.[23]

IN CÉSAR'S COURT

Imitations and variations of his program notwithstanding, Alencar remained the king of the genre. He owed much of his success to the talents of author and producer Fernando Lobo, another northeastern immigrant to Rio. Lobo had previously dedicated himself primarily to writing lyrics for popular music and writing and producing educational radio entertainment in the tradition of Almirante, occasionally with leftist political overtones. In the late 1940s, however, he sensed the change in the wind and signed up as Alencar's writer. Lobo created fifteen-minute segments involving games and contests to fill the first hours of Alencar's show. Lobo quickly demonstrated a keen sensibility for popular taste, and his segments provided Alencar with the perfect exercises in public participation to set up the climactic appearances of the featured singers later in the program.[24]

One Lobo segment, "A tendinha do Ali," or Ali's Tent, ostensibly evoked an Arab bazaar: Alencar donned a stylized turban and directed activity from beneath an open tent on stage. Beyond this vague nod to the exotic, there was nothing Middle Eastern about the segment. The Arabian theme was intended only to create an interesting visual spectacle and to suggest that anything could happen. The segment often featured letter-writing contests. One week, for example, Alencar asked three men in his studio audience to write a love letter to a woman named Odette. Later in the show, he invited a fan named Odette to read the letters aloud and to choose her favorite. If she could then pick the author of the letter from the group of three men, also on stage, the pair would be symbolically married on stage and win cash prizes. If she picked the wrong author, the wedding would be performed "vice versa": Odette would have to don a top hat, the man would put on a wig and bridal veil, and the couple would win a smaller prize. This ridicule of variation of gender roles presumably reinforced restrictive morality. Cross-dressing on stage, however, was precisely the sort of morally dubious tomfoolery to which conservative listeners objected so strongly. In an audience distinguished by at least a strong minority of gay men, moreover, laughter at the sight of a cross-dressing man did not necessarily carry the same sense of social stricture that it might have in another context.[25]

Alencar and Lobo improvised, incorporating regular audience members into the show. Upon discovering an amateur linguist in the audience, they dubbed him "Romário, the Dictionary Man," and, in subsequent shows, challenged other audience members to stump him with difficult words, competing, as always, for small cash prizes. Later, Alencar gave the nickname "Betty Grable" to a short, Afro-Brazilian, overweight woman who customarily sat in the second row. Whenever a heartthrob male singer—almost invariably young, white, and handsome—appeared on the show, Alencar invited Betty Grable to come onstage and dance with the guest. The spectacle was deliberately degrading: Alencar invited the rest of the audience to laugh at Betty Grable, implicitly appealing to racist attitudes that would construe any romantic pairing of a poor Afro-Brazilian woman with a famous white man as absurd. The carnivalesque atmosphere within the auditorium permitted both transgressions of social boundaries and unusually candid reinforcement of those boundaries through public ridicule. It also blurred the line between transgression and reinforcement, suggesting that all was in good fun, and nothing was to be taken seriously. Critics, at least, knew what to think, finding in such manifestations ample justification for attacking the program.[26]

Alencar did not give fans the opportunity to meditate on such interpretations—frenetic pace, or at least the illusion of frenetic pace, was one of the show's primary ingredients. The host spoke rapidly in breathless, excited tones, always urging contestants to respond more quickly. The band played musical numbers at least half again as fast as the orchestra on *Um milhão de melodias*. The host never paused to allow a moment of dead air, and the attractions continued for hours, passing at a dizzying clip. Rather than break for commercials, Alencar incorporated them into the fabric of the program, leading the audience, for example, in deafening chants of the martial jingle for the insecticide Detefon. Measuring time in a contest sponsored by Krush soft drink, he counted "one, two, three Krush, four, five, six Krush." Program and commercial became one, a single ceaseless parade.[27]

Alencar kept the chaotic nature of the program in check through his own perfectionism—he allowed the show to evolve in response to the demands of the audience, but carefully controlled its organizational aspects. He was particularly vigilant in regard to advertising, insisting on an unusual level of control over the contracting of sponsors for each of the show's segments. By 1950, he began to cut the length of segments in order to squeeze five-minute blocks between them. Much of the added advertising revenue from these shorter segments went into his own pocket. He also contracted the performers, usually for a pittance. Poorly paid radio gigs were nothing unusual—often singers worked for low salaries, making most of their money on tours of the interior and record sales. On Alencar's show, however, compensation was particularly disproportionate with the advertising revenue and the host's own salary. As a result, tension between performers and host often seethed beneath the show's celebratory facade. Emilinha Borba suffered particularly strained relations with Alencar, eventually joining a renegade tour company to escape his control, and extracting increased compensation through threatened walkouts. Emilinha had enough star power to win some of these battles. Most other singers felt lucky for the opportunity to appear on the program. Many performed for free for up to a year before Rádio Nacional and Alencar started paying them.[28]

In other ways, as well, the program offered less than ideal performing conditions. *Um milhão de melodias* demanded a well-rehearsed, polished performance from singers and in return offered the best in orchestral accompaniment and an atmosphere of complete respect and dedication to the music. On the *Programa César de Alencar*, in contrast, the band was small, unrehearsed, and barely audible over the crowd noise—even to the performers, who as a result often sang out of key. As Marlene, one of the biggest names of the era, described it, "Inside Rádio Nacional you had that shouting, those people, that auditorium. . . . I could not sing. As soon as I opened my mouth everyone shouted and applauded." When lesser stars took the microphone, Alencar remained onstage and continued to talk through the performances, singing along, exhorting both audience and performer, cutting off musical numbers after a couple of verses.[29]

As a result, performances were often sub-par. Many of the contests, moreover—such as musical chairs—were intelligible only to those in the auditorium. Critics charged that, in its focus on auditorium revelry, the program sacrificed regular listeners: "The auditorium program is produced for those two hundred people in the studio in detriment of the thousands listening at home." Again, fans disagreed completely. As José Ramalho recalled, "There in Recife, listening to the auditorium program, it was like we could see it, because when Marlene entered the auditorium there was such tremendous shouting that we knew the scene was fantastic, and we were envious. . . . we were on edge, we wanted to be there so much. It seemed like everyone was going crazy, and even without seeing it, I liked that."[30]

Ramalho was by no means atypical. No less an authority than Jairo Severiano, today one of the most eminent historians of Brazilian popular music, grew up an avid fan of the auditorium programs. When Severiano moved to Rio from the northeastern state of Ceará in 1950, he attended the César de Alencar show as soon as possible—he arrived in Rio on a Thursday, and was in the auditorium that Saturday. Years later, he remembered, "I was disappointed. It was more exciting listening at home in Ceará." The composer Caetano Veloso has described going through a similar process. He listened assiduously to the Rádio Nacional auditorium programs in the interior Bahian town of Santo Amaro da Purificação in the 1950s, and attended a live program as soon as he arrived in Rio. Unlike Severiano, he remained a fan.[31]

STAR QUALITY

The ecstatic reception of the featured singers described by Ramalho was the most visible manifestation of a new concept of stardom, one more dependent on personality, broadly defined, than on a narrow definition of artistic performance. Stars of the 1930s and early 1940s such as Orlando Silva and Carmen Miranda (before her relocation to the United States) depended on radio primarily to boost their record sales, to divulge their music. It is true that Silva was more than just a vocalist, becoming a sex symbol and a popular icon of his era. And Miranda was always recognized more for her great charisma than for her vocal talent. But to a large extent, their recordings were the measure of their careers. There was comparatively little public interest in their lives beyond music and no notion that the essence of their personality outweighed any questions of musical execution. In the 1930s, fans would not have applauded a performer singing out of key.

In the 1950s, in contrast, singers depended on radio to sell their personalities. Records were a secondary consideration, albeit still important. Emilinha and Marlene, at the height of their fame in the early 1950s, did not sell as many records as did Luiz Gonzaga during the same period. Instead, they made most of their money on tours, appearing on auditorium programs and giving concerts throughout Brazil. Fans no longer demonstrated their appreciation principally by purchasing records. Instead, they proved their loyalty by traveling great distances and suffering hardships in order to attend the auditorium programs and other live performances. They bestowed gifts, joined fan clubs, and in general made their favorite artists the objects of constant adoration. In return, they battled for symbolic pieces of their idol: performers were frequently in danger of having their garments torn off by crowds of admirers. Phrases in the radio press such as "The star's dress was nearly ripped to shreds" became a common shorthand description of enthusiastic reception. The singers became ersatz royalty, even semidivine creatures. As one fan recently described the young Marlene, eyes sparkling at the memory of packed auditoriums forty years ago, "it was like she was the queen of England."[32]

As focus shifted from music to personality, the artist's private life, or a well-crafted version of that life, became public, and that public persona itself became the artistic performance. Ari Barroso remarked sardonically on this transition on a 1953 radio show where he served as the guest host. When the famously exigent Barroso introduced Marlene to sing one of his compositions, the fans screamed and applauded feverishly, far more enthusiastically than they had for the composer himself. Shrugging at the crowd's frenzy before the singer had even appeared, let alone performed, he dryly observed, "you just have to say Marlene and they go wild, huh?"[33]

The *Revista do Rádio* was the principal engine and expression of this transformation. From its inception in 1948, the magazine praised and supported everything that the radio columnists of the major newspapers dismissed as crass, albeit not for its kitsch value, as Nelson Rodrigues had, but as glamorous entertainment. It gave extensive coverage to the auditorium programs and, above all, to their starring female singers. Everything about the magazine sought to propagate the idea that the world of radio in Rio de Janeiro was Brazil's Hollywood, inhabited by dazzling stars of the first magnitude.

Within a few years, the *Revista do Rádio* became Brazil's second-most popular magazine, and maintained that distinction until the late 1950s, when radio began to lose its hold on the popular imagination. During its decade of preeminence, the magazine was fundamental in establishing radio careers and tracking and creating trends. Alencar and Barcellos, for example, depended on the magazine to publicize their contests, to keep the names of their performers constantly before the public, and to put the journalistic stamp of apparently objective reporting on the star craze that made their programs a success. They could not have built and sustained their stunning levels of popularity without the constant publicity and support of the magazine.[34]

Much of the *Revista do Rádio* was dedicated to reporting on the quotidian lives of the stars. Every issue featured interviews with singers and musicians, asking them questions like, "What do you do to relax? Which is your favorite soccer team?" The social and moral opinions of the radio elite were also a constant topic: "Are you in favor of divorce? Should women smoke?" Articles such as "How the Stars Style Their Hair" were common. Close attention to radio programs themselves, on the other hand, was minimal. There were many articles describing new programs, but these were overwhelmingly promotional pieces rather than critical evaluations. The magazine did include acerbic record reviews and the occasional negative review of a radio program. Its emphasis, however, was on the endorsement of big-time radio programming, and on opening a window onto the lives of the stars.

Those lives were presented as fabulously exciting and luxurious on the one hand, and typical, even accessible, in their details, on the other. Articles about the grand estates of the stars were routine. Even more common, however, were portraits of the simplicity of the singer's life at home with her family, or accounts of the humble origins of the radio stars. Several performers wrote occasional columns chronicling their daily lives, covering both the elegance and exhilaration of the radio world and quotidian details such as walking the dog. Advertisements, meanwhile, emphasized the symbolic connection to stardom that purchase of the correct products offered. An ad for the bath soap Sabonete Big, for example, showed a drawing of an alluring blonde singer before a microphone, accompanied by the text "ELAS usam Big!" (They use Big). The magazine, above all else, sold a lifestyle, or the myth of a lifestyle.[35] The Revista do Rádio, perhaps even more than the auditorium programs themselves, contributed to the creation of a pantheon of pop divas, the idols of fan clubs across Brazil. The competition for preeminence within this pantheon became the primary concern of the magazine and the fan clubs.

THE PANTHEON

Emilinha Borba was the first star in the new mold, establishing fame by 1947. She grew up in a modest neighborhood of downtown Rio, and as a performer she cultivated the image of a common girl thrust into stardom unexpectedly, remaining close to her unpretentious roots. Marlene, Emilinha's greatest rival, emerged as a national star in 1949, adopting a contrasting style of elegance and daring. Emilinha cultivated her image of humility through her clothes, her mannerisms on stage, and her column in the Revista do Rádio, "The Life of Emilinha." The column combined memories of her youth with a diary of her current life as a star. Both aspects emphasized the universal and the unpretentious. Her childhood memories focused on the life of her working-class neighborhood and her relationship with her family. Her diary recounted the small pleasures of her life at home, the joys of watching her young son grow, and the comfort of her friendships with members of her fan club, presented as typical and uncomplicated by any inequality.[36]

At the same time, she sought to project a saintly quality that made her everyday humility exceptional. In one column, for example, she recounted the story of a small boy from the interior of Brazil who had pressed a medallion on her after a show. She asked for information on the boy's whereabouts so she could return the medallion. The story at once suggested her transcendent radiance (she was the object of unprompted gestures of fealty from innocent creatures) and her bound-less good-heartedness (she could not bear to see a child deprived of his prized medallion). Marlene later offered her own appraisal of this strategy: "Emilinha loved to play the saint. Every day fans would gather under her window, and she would bless them, sprinkling water on them, and they would say, thank you, my little saint."[37]

Marlene also came from a working-class background: she was the child of Italian immigrants to São Paulo, and her father was an iron-worker. Even as a schoolgirl, however, she sought a more glamorous image, abandoning her birth name, Vitória Bonaiuti, and taking the name Marlene for her appearances on local São Paulo talent shows. She hid her nascent musical career from her family and ran away to Rio as a teenager.[38] Once there, she landed a job singing at the nightclub of the Copacabana Palace, the city's fanciest hotel. At the Palace, Marlene honed her image of refinement and sophistication. Appearances in the nightclub brought her to the attention of Rádio Nacional's directors, and in 1948 they invited her to participate on the auditorium pro-grams. The invitation offered the opportunity of reaching a new au-dience, far larger and broader than that attending the Palace. As the singer described it, "I felt the need to sing for those people. I did not reject the elite guests at the Copacabana Palace, but in that moment of my career I judged that the common people at Rádio Nacional would be decisive. At the station I knew I would have intimate contact with the masses."[39]

Marlene's style proved successful in the auditorium. As one fan put it, "She was always the most elegant on the radio. She wore marvelous dresses, she never cursed, she was a person of class, of polish. That's what enchanted me." She adopted a bold, modern look, cutting her hair short and wearing long pants instead of a skirt, risking suspension from Rádio Nacional in the process. Later, she described her style as the foundation of a distinct relationship with the audience, although her vision for that relationship was hardly radical: "I was considered the liberated woman, more sophisticated, and Emilinha was the *sub-urbana*. . . . I think I inspired in the people a new sensation, that life was not only rice and beans . . . that there is something beyond that, perhaps a more sophisticated chicken that you can buy and that is not too expensive."[40]

Early in the 1950s, Angela Maria, another singer from Rio, reached similarly dizzying heights of fame. Still a teenager, she projected an air of innocence and enthusiasm. Dalva de Oliveira and Nora Ney occupied a slightly lower level in the radio pantheon. Dalva was as renowned for her marital turmoil as she was for her voice, and was seen as the mistreated but resilient woman of experience. Nora Ney was melodramatic and yet emotionally cool at the same time, and brought a worldly edge to her performance absent in the sunny optimism of Emilinha and Marlene.

A host of lesser divas filled out the rosters of the auditorium programs. Several of these, such as Hebe Camargo, Doris Monteiro, Ellen de Lima, and Heleninha Costa, achieved national fame and built long, successful careers, without ever provoking the frenzy of the top singers. Other contemporary female vocalists, such as Araci de Almeida, Carmen Costa, Linda and Dircinha Batista, and, of a somewhat younger generation, Elizeth Cardoso, left significant marks on the history of Brazilian popular music, but did not fall into the same category. They sang on the radio but were not *Cantoras do rádio* in the sense embodied by Emilinha and Marlene: they did not appear extensively on the auditorium programs, did not cultivate intimate ties to their fans in the same way as the pop divas, and, for the most part, stayed closer to the samba tradition established in the 1930s. (Linda Batista, to a certain extent, straddled both worlds.) Many other singers shot briefly across the firmament before returning to obscurity.

Male singers did not, in general, inspire the same kind of devotion. Francisco Alves was for many years Brazil's most popular male singer and sold more records than the female stars. His death in a car crash in 1953 provoked an outpouring of grief matched only by those for Getúlio Vargas and Carmen Miranda in the next two years. But he had no fan club, and his admirers did not snatch at his garments. Francisco Carlos and Cauby Peixoto attempted to mine the vein worked by Emilinha and Marlene, and experienced some success, but nowhere near the level of their female counterparts.[41]

The pop divas varied widely in talent and less so in style. Dalva de Oliveira and Angela Maria both had voices of extraordinary range and virtuosity. Dalva was famous for her vocal pyrotechnics and her command of tonal shadings. Angela Maria was less flamboyant but no less accomplished. Emilinha and Marlene, in contrast, depended primarily on charisma and energy, for neither had a spectacular voice. Nora Ney had a voice of limited range but compelling timbre, and a unique delivery.[42] Stylistically, all of the radio singers worked in a number of rhythms and formats, including baião, samba, and Brazilian versions of American popular songs. Above all else, however, they sang *samba-*

canção and bolero. The samba-canção is a slow samba, usually with a melody of greater length and range than a Carnival samba, and almost inevitably featuring melodramatic lyrics. Although the genre first became popular in the 1930s, the spare arrangements common in that decade bore little relation to the orchestral flourishes of the 1950s. The singers of the 1950s pushed the rhythm's capacity for emotional drama to the limit, resulting in a style music historian Sérgio Cabral has termed *samba pastoso*, or gummy samba. The bolero, Cuban in origin but prominent in Brazil mostly in the more histrionic Mexican variety, was equally melodramatic. In the repertoire of the pop divas, the two rhythms became almost interchangeable. Orchestras on one program played Dalva's "Tudo acabado," for example, as a samba-canção, and on another as a bolero. In some cases, they melded the rhythms into a *sambolero*.

The lyrics to these songs invariably concerned traumàtic love. Frequently, they were conservatively moralist, condemning infidelity, particularly on the part of women, and upholding the sanctity of marriage. Lyrics to the material in other rhythms, like samba and baião, were, in contrast, largely optimistic and celebratory. The overwhelming majority of the material, both lyrically and musically, conformed to well-established models—the music of the pop divas offered few surprises. But its merits as music were almost beside the point. Serious fans moved quickly beyond consideration of musical expression to adulation of the star and everything associated with her. A Marlene fan could recognize no shortcomings in Marlene, and no virtues in Emilinha—grudging respect for other singers was sometimes conceded, although usually in a backhanded manner.

THE FAN CLUBS AND THEIR RIVALRY

The fan clubs were the incubators for this new concept of stardom. Their concurrent emergence with the auditorium programs and the *Revista do Rádio* was not a matter of chance, for the three institutions were interdependent from the start. The fan clubs seized on both the festive mood of the auditoriums and the magazine's vision of a brilliant world of radio stars. In turn, they exercised a significant influence on the programs and the careers of their idols. The Emilinha Borba Fan Club of Rio de Janeiro was founded in November 1948 "with the single goal of seeing, hearing, applauding, and promoting our singer." The club charged a moderate, but by no means insignificant, entrance fee and low monthly dues. In return, members received an occasional newsletter, published entirely by fan members. The newsletter was a simple mimeographed affair of a few pages, featuring accounts of club activities and notices of upcoming dates such as public performances and club member birthdays. Members also gained access to the modest club headquarters in downtown Rio and came one step closer to their idol. This step was not illusory: from the beginning, the fan club established close ties with the singer, gaining the privilege of greeting her personally after the programs and, eventually, visiting her at home. Members of the club became official *Emilinistas*. Aided by acknowledgement on the *Programa César de Alencar* and publicity in the *Revista do Rádio*, the organization spread quickly throughout Brazil. Individual clubs adopted their own names, such as Emilinista League, Emilinista Party, Emilinha Borba Football Club, and their own rules and internal hierarchy, and turned a portion of their dues over to the main club in Rio.[43]

Marlene fans began collaborating to support their idol in 1949 but did not formally establish a club until 1951. Like its Emilinista counterpart, the organization had its headquarters in Rio, published a newsletter, required dues, distributed membership cards, and organized gatherings at which the fans could meet the star. And like the Emilinha club, it quickly spread throughout the country. By 1955, at least a dozen other singers had fan clubs, but the Emilinha and Marlene clubs remained the most prominent, locked in bitter rivalry. Early on, that rivalry was fueled by a publicity gimmick propagated by Rádio Nacional, the *Revista do Rádio*, and the singers themselves. It had its origins in a 1949 contest for the Rainha do Rádio, or Queen of the Radio, sponsored by the Brazilian Radio Workers Association. Voters purchased ballots for one cruzeiro, approximately fifty cents, with proceeds donated to the construction of a hospital for radio workers. Emilinha was the overwhelming favorite, and undoubtedly would have won a fair contest, but Marlene struck a deal with Antárctica, the powerful Brazilian soft drink and beer corporation, that predetermined the outcome. She attracted the attention of an Antárctica executive one night at the Copacabana Palace and asked him to buy a vote in support of her candidacy for Rainha do Radio. Instead, he bought her the whole contest. Antárctica worked out a promotional scheme with Rádio Nacional—the radio station promoted the contest extensively, and Antárctica wrote a blank check to cover as many votes as Marlene would need to win.[44]

At the same time, Antárctica made Marlene the poster girl in its advertising campaign for Guaraná Caçula, the popular Brazilian soft drink, marketed for the first time in small bottles to encourage individual consumption. The strategy was part of Antárctica's response to Coca-Cola's rapid takeover of a large share of the Brazilian soft-drink market. Print advertisements featured a drawing of Marlene's head emerging from a foaming bottle of Guaraná, accompanied by the legend, "The Queen of Radio and the King of Soft Drinks."[45] Backed by Antárctica, Marlene won handily. Emilinha's fans cried foul, to no avail, while Marlene's followers celebrated and denied any tampering. Recognizing the passions stirred by the rivalry, the singers used it to their own advantage, alternately pretending to squabble and to reconcile, always keeping the press and fans guessing as to their real relationship. At the same time, they were not above using the emotions surrounding the rivalry to make each other look bad. Marlene claims, "I suffered terribly with Emilinha. When we were in the auditorium, she had ploys to signal her fans to boo me. Codes that she had worked out beforehand, like gathering her skirt in her left hand."[46]

More so than the singers, the fans took the rivalry to heart. Not infrequently, fights between Marlenistas and Emilinistas broke out in the hallways of Rádio Nacional after auditorium programs. Occasionally, the programs themselves erupted into brawls. And, without fail, Marlene's fans booed Emilinha thunderously when she took the stage, and vice versa. When the singers engaged in a display of reconciliation, the fans protested, pulling them away from each other, into opposing camps. The fans made it clear that they wanted to remain vigorously partisan, and that they wanted their partisanship to be both visible and decisive, influencing both the programs and appearances outside the studios. Impassioned public rivalry offered a way to make their presence felt.[47]

Many other contests followed the 1949 Queen of the Radio election (Queen of the Singers, Best of Radio, Favorite of Radio, Most Elegant of Radio). Most were sponsored by large corporations and heavily publicized by the *Revista do Rádio*. Ciro Gaulo, the Marlene fan from Campo Grande, remembers collecting hundreds of sugar sacks from a local café to stockpile voting coupons in a contest sponsored by a sugar company. Emilinha, however, had the backing of a local supermarket chain and won that round. Gaulo, today a high school sociology teacher, recognizes that his avid participation in the contest, in effect, provided unpaid labor and free advertising for the sugar company. But for him, the social role of the clubs outweighs any taint associated with the commercial nature of the contests. He insists, "The contests were valuable. They made us work hard, they united us."[48]

Today, a few Marlene fans are objective enough to admit that the 1949 election was a sham. Most prefer not to speak of that aspect. Even now, many avoid mentioning Emilinha by name, calling her only *a outra*—the other woman—the echo of the language of infidelity is not entirely coincidental. As one Marlene fan recalled, "The rivalry with *a outra* was serious, a bitter feud." The implication was that one chose a favorite for life and that vacillation was treason. Club members expected favorites to develop a special bond with them that would not be easily extended to more casual fans. When I informed one Marlenista of my aspiration to interview both Marlene and Emilinha during the course of my research, he remarked, "A outra é tão vulgar que você a consegue em qualquer esquina" (The other one is so vulgar you can get her on any street corner).[49]

JOINING THE CLUBS

For many fans, the first trip to the auditorium was a form of initiation, not only into the world of radio, but into metropolitan public life. Glaúcia Garcia, for example, grew up in the small agricultural center of Birigui, in the northwestern reaches of São Paulo state. She first came to Rio at age fourteen to see Marlene on the Manoel Barcellos show, and recalls, "You cannot imagine what it was like growing up in the interior and then coming to Rio, to be confronted with the world of radio in the era of glory. It was extraordinary." Following that first trip, Garcia returned every year for Marlene's birthday program. Even for local fans, the programs created an opportunity to experience a different side of the city. As Lúcia Soares, an Emilinha fan from the Rio suburb of Cascadura, recalls, "The first time I went to the city by myself was to see the *Programa César de Alencar*. I had only been to the center two or three times before. I was just a poor girl from the suburbs. That first time, I got lost coming home and had to take a taxi back to the railroad station. But after that, I went nearly every weekend."[50]

Many fans signed up for membership in the clubs on their first trip to the auditorium, paying their initiation fee and the first of their monthly dues. In the early 1950s, these ranged from approximately fifty cents to three dollars a month. For a struggling young woman of the suburbs, contributing up to three dollars a month meant doing without other luxuries like Carnival costumes or records, or even necessities. Economic sacrifice, however, was seen not as an unfortunate burden but as one of the defining aspects of true fandom: homage to the star became meaningful partly through tribute, work, and a certain amount of renunciation.[51] The clubs carried this idea to lavish extremes in the gifts they bestowed on their favorites. After every program, club leaders presented the singers with sashes, usually bearing legends such as "Queen of the Radio" or "Favorite of Rio." Special occasions required special sashes, sewn with gold filigree or adorned with jewels. As the 1950s went on, gifts became more elaborate—Emilinha, for example, received a platinum brooch, a silver tea set, a washing machine, a refrigerator, and a silver bedstead from her fans. The fans, in the vast majority, could not have acquired such presents for themselves. They belonged either to a fantasy of royal luxury, like precious jewelry, or a vision of upper-middle-class domesticity, like household appliances. These were both worlds that most of the fans could approach only through their attachment to the star: "Giving things to Marlene that we, as individuals, could not afford was a way to express our collective force and our collective appreciation. The luster we gave to her shined back on us."[52]

Not all the singers were comfortable with these practices. Nora Ney, for example, instructed her fan club not to give her presents and to dedicate its energies instead to literacy drives and occupational instruction. Faced with what it considered a lukewarm reception from the singer, the club soon disbanded.[53]

Charitable activities were the flip side of tribute. Throughout Brazil fan clubs donated clothes, school supplies, and food to the poor. Their focus was on providing clothing and food for infants in need, usually at Christmas. In some cases, fans met at club headquarters to sew the clothes themselves. In others, they reserved part of their dues to donate to charity. These endeavors were consciously intended to balance and to justify the celebratory activities of the clubs. According to the Emilinha Borba Fan Club handbook: "Organizing parties and contests are not our only activities. We systematically promote our philanthropic and social efforts." At the same time, they also allowed fans to participate in an activity generally reserved for wealthier classes. As Soares put it, "As someone from a working family, it made me feel better to be able to do something for people poorer than I was. It showed that not just rich people could do charity."[54]

Hierarchical organization was another fundamental principal for the fan clubs. Presidents, vice presidents, and financial officers were chosen in yearly elections, open only to dues-paying members. The frequency of elections insured a rapid turnover, permitting new members to rise to positions of authority quickly. The clubs permitted a type of social advancement largely blocked to their members in other areas. It would be hard to name another organization in 1950s Brazil in which a poor girl from the suburbs, or any woman of color, could rise to an elected post within two years of activity. The rules and by-laws of elections, membership, and procedure, moreover, gave the clubs a formal structure, reaffirming their importance for the members. As Gaulo describes it, "The fan club was a family, a social group, an institution, bound by rules and affection."[55]

Club solidarity was closely tied to the collective emotional release inspired by the favorite's performance. In the words of José Ramalho, "When it was time for Marlene to perform, we were transformed. We entered into a state of ecstasy." At the same time, fans expected these emotions to be at least partially reciprocal and were disappointed if the singers did not burst into tears of appreciation for their gestures of devotion. Recognizing the importance of such emotional displays, the *Revista do Rádio* gave them prominent coverage. In one example, the magazine gave the title "Marlene Really Cried" to an article describing an airport fan-club reception for the singer.[56]

The most immediate benefit of joining the clubs was the contact they afforded with the star. When Marlene performed in Birigui, for example, she stayed in Garcia's home, as a gesture of appreciation for Garcia's activity in the fan club. Garcia recalls: "My mother received her with all the honors. That boosted my own fame in Birigui, of course, and even in the surrounding towns." Even today, fans proudly point to the intimacy with their idols that they achieved through years of activity in the fan clubs: "I came to Rio, joined the fan club, and became Marlene's friend. Now, almost every New Year's Eve, I go to a party at her house, for the most intimate fans, those who grew closest to her." As another fan describes it, "I gradually became her friend. Today it is more of a friendship, a fan that became a friend." As these quotations suggest, fans expected stars not only to acknowledge them but, eventually, to welcome them into their lives. The singers were called on to attend the birthday celebrations of club leaders and to visit ailing members at home. These mutual gestures among fans and between fans and stars knit the clubs together. As Ramalho put it, "It's a family. We call it a family."[57]

Critics dismissed such contacts as scripted and insincere, and lamented the fan clubs as a monumental waste of energy that might be better spent elsewhere. Several fans, however, reaped immediate professional benefits from participation in the clubs. Regina Silva, for example, was an early leader of Marlene's fan club—she was the fan, quoted in the epigraph, who suggested that getting hit by Marlene's car would not be such a bad thing. At the time, Silva was an Afro-Brazilian teenager of working-class background. Within a few years, she turned her exposure to show business through the club into her own performing career, bypassing the usual round of amateur talent shows. While Silva's proclamation of loyalty was intentionally extreme, in effect she used the social network of the fan club effectively as a means of upward mobility. More recently, Ciro Gaulo wrote and directed a revue about the golden years of radio. The play ran for four years in his own suburb of Campo Grande—significantly removed from the sophisticated downtown theaters of Rio de Janeiro, but precisely in the suburban Zona Norte region where Marlene's fans are still thickest on the ground. Other fans became business managers and promoters for their favorites. And Soares credits her experience teaching basic literacy to fellow Emilinistas in a course organized by the club with inspiring her to return to school herself, where she earned a teaching certificate. But the fans regard these concerns as tangential to the real nature of the clubs. For them, the greatest long-term benefit of participation in the clubs was the creation of an extended social network, largely unaffected by external class and social divisions.

DECLINE

The auditorium programs reached a peak of popularity in the early to mid-1950s, and then began to decline rapidly. They faced competition from new television variety shows, which demanded a far more orderly audience and did not welcome the radio fans. Radio stations, for their part, grew unwilling and unable to invest in the rotating cast of stars the programs demanded. Radio station personnel also grew uncomfortable with the noisy manifestations of popular leisure in the auditoriums. The programs had encouraged working-class women to leave their homes and join in raucous festivity not only in a public space but, given national broadcast prominence, in a practice that made many observers uneasy. In 1958, composer Miguel Gustavo wrote a hit marcha titled "Fanzoca de rádio," or Big Radio Fan. The lyrics mock the title character for attending the auditorium programs and chastise her for abandoning her duties as housemaid: "She's an Emilinha fan, she never leaves César de Alencar. . . . It's a sash over here, a sash over there, and meanwhile in my house, no one can find the maid."[58] The marcha is typical of a growing hostility toward the social disruptions fostered by the programs.

The fans, for their part, were quick to react when Rádio Nacional treated them as second-class citizens. A 1952 letter to the *Revista do Rádio* complained that fans were asked to ride in the freight elevator, rather than the social elevator, when attending the programs at Rádio Nacional. Elevators have traditionally been an easy vehicle for social exclusion by class and race in Brazil. Shunting unwanted visitors to the freight elevator is a well-worn tactic for suggesting they are beneath polite society. Rádio Nacional justified the move on the basis of extraordinary traffic, created by the fans themselves. But the author of the letter was not assuaged, particularly in light of rising ticket prices. She warned that eventually the hosts of the programs would suffer the consequences of alienating their audience.[59]

Conflict between hosts and audience was not unusual, and it increased in the latter half of the 1950s. Often, as César de Alencar attempted to conduct a contest onstage, the fan clubs would break out into a rousing samba, overpowering the host. On several occasions, Alencar stopped the program when fights broke out between Marlenistas and Emilinistas, or when he simply lost control of the proceedings. In response, Alencar and Rádio Nacional administrators attempted to enlist the support of the singers in reining in the audience. In 1958, Emilinha published an "Appeal to the Fans" in the *Revista do Rádio*: "Your enthusiasm disturbs the programs a bit, you know? . . . The station would like you to continue applauding with the same enthusiasm as always, but conserving a bit of silence during the performance. Can I count on you one more time?"[60] Later that year, Emilinha joined Marlene, a handful of other popular singers, and the hosts of the programs in issuing "The Ten Commandments for the Fans." The document, published in the *Revista do Rádio* and circulated in the studios, again encouraged fans to restrain themselves in the auditorium.

These appeals had no effect: the programs had encouraged a rowdy festivity that was not easily checked. By the end of the decade, Rádio Nacional, under a new administration, raised ticket prices beyond the means of most working-class fans. Even more dramatically, the station installed a retractable glass partition separating audience and performers. The live audience had become more of a hindrance than a benefit. Rádio Nacional clung to live programming longer than most stations, and César de Alencar's show remained one of the most popular on the air. But after the 1964 military coup, the new regime radically scaled back Rádio Nacional's budget and fired much of the remaining cast. Alencar, moreover, alienated many of his colleagues with his outspoken support of the coup. Live radio, moribund for several years, was all but terminated.[61]

EFFECTS

The most immediate effect of the growth of the fan clubs in the early 1950s was the boost they gave to the careers of the singers. The clubs served not only to organize and encourage fans but also to publicize and guide the star's activities. As Marlene put it, "They were our local entrepreneurs. We got invitations [from fan clubs] from every place imaginable." Fan clubs in the interior rented cinemas, convinced local radio stations to support their efforts, and largely took over the production of shows and appearances by their favorites. Often, these arrangements required the club to guarantee certain attendance figures beforehand. The clubs created such an effective system of communication, however, that they could always rely on bringing in fans from vast surrounding regions for local shows. As José Ramalho put it, "We went from Recife to Paraíba, and through all the towns in the interior, following Marlene."[62]

The larger ramifications of the fan clubs and auditorium programs are more difficult to measure. To begin with, these phenomena created a forum for public opinion in which the desires and inclinations of members of otherwise marginalized sectors were fundamental. This in itself was significant: the fan clubs welcomed women from a service working class, poor women, and gay men at a time when most other ostensibly public fora were, in effect, closed to individuals from those social sectors. This reduced range of opportunities begins to explain why fans invested in the auditorium programs and the clubs with such fervor. In Soares's words, "It was like they were our country club, our jockey club."[63]

The presence of poor and working-class women was both immediately apparent and much discussed, but the presence of gay men was not. The fans, on the other hand, describe that participation as vital and stress the importance of the clubs as one of the few social spaces in

1950s Brazil that welcomed gay men. Paulo Azevedo, a Marlene fan from suburban Rio, describes his own entrance into the clubs: "In the 1950s I was a gay teenager in a society that only let gay people come out at Carnival. The fan club was like a new world for me, one where I could meet people like me, where I could be open without any fear."[64] The nature of the available evidence does not permit a reliable estimate of the extent of gay participation, but several of the fans suggested gay men made up as much as 25 percent of the club membership. Most agreed that, while the network of gay sociability within the fan clubs had been firmly established by the mid-1950s, their importance in that regard became even more pronounced in the 1960s and more recently. None hesitated to discuss the subject, and all defended the clubs as free of prejudice, a place where gay and straight could meet and interact openly without restraint. According to Garcia, "Yes, of course, there are many gay men in the club. But there is no prejudice, and I think that is very lovely, and very important. Knowing that we are all fans of Marlene, we can establish intimate friendships. It is a way for everyone to get to know each other. It is almost as if, within the fan club, there is a kind of protection."[65]

The stars themselves welcomed gay presence in the clubs. In the late 1950s, Emilinha confronted gay-bashing ruffians who had assaulted her fans outside the studios of TV Tupi. Emilinha was also known to give her old gowns to gay fans for their Carnival costumes. And in a 1973 interview, Marlene attested to the presence of gay men in the auditorium as evidence that the epithet *macacas de auditório* was inaccurate as well as hostile: "We didn't just have little housemaids. We had high-school students, college students, queers, we had everything."[66] For the star, gay presence was precisely a way of defending fans in general from racist prejudice. This made the fan clubs highly unusual within the context of 1950s Brazil. As James Green has shown in *Beyond Carnival*, gay men were forced to navigate between zones of apparent tolerance and harsh repression. Carnival, with its celebration of excess and liberation, permitted relatively free transgression of social strictures. When Carnival ended, however, zones of tolerance were narrowed, and gay men enjoyed few spaces of public leisure, and none of public achievement and power. The fan clubs offered at least a semipublic arena of gay sociability and achievement where homosexuality could be expressed openly, among insiders. The fan clubs, then, fulfilled a similar function for gay men and for working-class and poor women, creating an arena marked by solidarity and achievement for otherwise marginalized Brazilians. Their role as social network was even more important to gay men, who had few other opportunities for establishing connections with new peers.

As contemporary observers noted, the clubs shared structural and stylistic similarities with populist political organizations: like the populist parties, they were hierarchical, zealous, characterized by a sense of mission, and given to noisy public display. A 1953 *Revista do Rádio* article on the clubs, for example, described a public commotion "that looked like a march of striking workers, carrying great banners bearing provocative slogans. . . . But it was not a strike, or a political party waiting for its leader. It was just a fan club, preparing a demonstration for its adored artist." On a superficial level, there was little distinction between celebratory affiliation with a politician and with a singer, or a soccer team, for that matter. One fan suggested as much in a 1954 letter to the *Revista do Rádio:* "In our house, there are three things we cannot do without—Dalva, Getúlio, and Flamengo." Like populist parties, moreover, the fan clubs were simultaneously accessible and exclusive: the strength of their common bond depended on the fervor of their opposition to all dissenters.[67]

The names of fan club chapters, such as Emilinista Party and Emilinha Borba Football Club, make this similarity even more explicit. Populist parties, fan clubs, and football clubs with open membership— a phenomenon that emerged contemporarily with the fan clubs—all offered at least a sensation of popular ownership of a larger phenomenon. Like voters who supported populist parties, fans that paid dues to the Emilinha club or the Vasco da Gama football club invested in these institutions, and publicly claimed a stake in their direction. The fan clubs, more so than the populist parties or the football clubs, responded to these demands. They had no upper tiers of educated bureaucrats or wealthy executives—their administrative ranks were truly a hierarchy of peers.

Scholars have interpreted the similarities between the clubs and populist parties as evidence that the fan clubs were parapolitical phenomena, a substitute for political expression for groups shut out of the formal political sphere.[68] There is undoubtedly some truth to this: fans clearly seized the opportunity to rise through the hierarchy of the fan clubs, an experience of power foreclosed in other arenas. But the fan clubs did not simply imitate populist parties in structure and style. Rather, both, along with the growing football clubs, grew out of deeper tendencies of popular organization in this period, influencing both politics and pop culture. Industrialization and urbanization made the working class, for the first time, a consistently powerful force within the political arena, rather than an intermittently powerful force exercising influence largely through the disruption of formal politics. These same phenomena gave the working class a growing share in an expanding market for cultural goods. The makers of household cleaners, beauty products, and nonprescription remedies who sponsored the bulk of radio programming from the mid-1940s through the mid-1950s, for example, sought to reach an audience that gradually moved from predominantly middle-class to predominantly working-class. The emergence of working-class citizens as cultural consumers and producers, rather than only producers, lagged somewhat behind their political emergence, for it required more than voting power and demographic growth. Also necessary was economic growth, facilitating the increased availability and relatively lower prices of nondurable commercial goods and, likewise, the increased availability and relatively lower prices of cultural goods such as magazines, records, and radios. These trends, clearly related, were established by 1950. The incorporation of the working class into the political and cultural dialogue of the nation first focused on the industrial working class, encompassing the service sector somewhat later.

At the same time, the rapid growth of the radio industry enabled the immediate transmission of cultural and political messages to enormous audiences. In realms of both culture and politics, individuals with an understanding of the advantages of the medium and the changing nature of the audience succeeded in crafting charismatic appeals of enormous resonance. In both realms, these appeals inspired massive public manifestations of adhesion, the rapid growth of supporting organizations characterized by hierarchy and division into local cells, and, above all, fierce exclusivity among followers and hostility toward real and imagined enemies. The growth of these political and cultural movements had contradictory implications, expanding the opportunities for popular participation in the public sphere, while placing fairly narrow limitations on the nature of that participation. Again, in both realms, these phenomena provoked criticism from observers who condemned participants for their lack of sophistication and their emotional, irrational behavior. The structure of populist movements and the fan clubs were similar. Their meanings, however, were not. The fans, to begin with, had no illusion that the clubs were a substitute for formal political participation. In the words of Ciro Gaulo, "I was, and am, a staunch Marlene fan. But outside the auditorium, I made other political choices."[69] Instead, the fan clubs fulfilled a different social role. One clue to that difference is their contrasting fate: no populist party survived the 1964 coup. The fan clubs, however, are still going strong decades after the auditorium programs closed their doors.

In a 1981 study of the *cantoras do rádio*, scholar Miriam Goldfeder interprets the fan clubs as "mystifying," and as "demobilizing mobilization." Goldfeder suggests that members deluded themselves, "seeing themselves, in an illusion, as participants in a universe that, at the level of reality, was definitely closed to them."[70] Again, there is some substance behind this interpretation. Rituals of tribute and charity served to connect fans to economic strata from which they were largely excluded. But as conversations with the fans themselves reveal, these rituals were not evidence of false consciousness; they were self-consciously symbolic acts, serving primarily to unite the fan clubs. Fans had no illusion that they were becoming wealthy by bestowing jewels on their favorite, or that they were becoming middle-class by working for charitable causes. Rather, they experienced such rituals as moments of transcendence of existing economic position achieved through group solidarity, and as strengthening that solidarity in turn.

The bond of the fan clubs had its costs. Advertisers, producers, and stars extracted considerable wealth from the auditorium programs and their related phenomena, while the fans made heavy financial sacrifices. Beyond the financial commitments of dues, contests, and gifts to the star, the clubs demanded the sacrifice of certain opportunities. They became tight-knit, impassioned communities for their members, but only at the expense of dividing those members from other fans, who were similar in every respect but their chosen favorite. The rituals of audience participation in the auditorium programs, similarly, promoted a sense of community partly by separating a few fans and exposing them to degrading ridicule. Community existed only in tension with exclusivity.

As Goldfeder notes, moreover, the auditorium programs placed great emphasis on the appearance of popular representation without conceding much in the way of real control or influence to the popular participants—another similarity with populist political organizations. The fan clubs, in contrast, were and are controlled solely by the fans themselves. And they have long outlived any connection to those programs, or to Queen of the Radio contests promoted by advertisers. Their survival depends on the emotional, affective bonds forged forty years ago, and these bonds have proven the salient and defining feature of the larger phenomenon.

When asked to explain their participation, fans who had joined the clubs in the 1950s overwhelmingly referred to the festivity of the auditorium and the warmth of the club's social network. The importance of these characteristics to individuals otherwise consigned to the margins of Brazilian public life cannot be underappreciated, and it explains the persistence of the fan clubs. With the support of the clubs, the singers have been able to continue their careers long past their prime, without any extensive promotional campaigns. The relationship between fans and star became a self-perpetuating phenomenon. Marlene, Emilinha, and Angela Maria virtually disappeared from the mainstream media long ago, but they are still in great demand for shows throughout Brazil. These appearances are organized and publicized entirely by the fan clubs. The clubs are smaller than they were in their prime, but they still meet regularly, pay dues, and defend the reputation of their favorites, and they are still bound by rules and affection.

7 ADVERTISING AND AUDIENCE

FRAGMENTATION

In September 1948, Auricélio Penteado, director of the Brazilian polling organization IBOPE, wrote an article in praise of Coca-Cola, describing the beverage as "the symbol of a new economic, political, and social order." Penteado contrasted Coca-Cola and its associations with "light, health, strength, and faith in a better future for Brazil" to *cangaço*, or backwoods banditry, the symbol of an archaic and corrupt old regime. "Coca-Cola," he asserted, "is a democratizing element par excellence . . . exalting the man in shirtsleeves. . . . It is progress. . . . It is against the bare foot, against yellow fever, against *cachaça* (cane liquor) . . . against bad roads, against *cangaço*." He concluded: "Wherever Coca-Cola penetrates there is an air of renovation, of progress, of youth, of cleanliness, and of efficiency."[1]

Penteado published his effusion in the advertising trade journal *Publicidade*. IBOPE and *Publicidade* were both founded in the early 1940s, a period of intense growth and rapid evolution in the Brazilian advertising industry. Both organizations subscribed to the same fervent belief in advertising and market research as the supreme forces of democracy and modernity. As Penteado's attitude toward Coca-Cola suggests, theirs was a religion of progress through Americanization, which they understood to mean the spread of democracy through the cultivation of individual ambition and consumption of the mass-marketed goods of modern industry. They shared this creed with a host of American advertising professionals who came to Brazil during the war to work in the local offices of American advertising agencies. These agencies and their Brazilian imitators redefined Brazilian advertising in the 1940s and early 1950s. Along the way, they drastically changed the way popular music was packaged and sold.

In the late 1930s, advertising agencies had little control over what happened inside the radio studios. Most had little interest, concentrating their resources on the print media. By the early 1950s, every major agency had its own radio department. Several had their own studios as well and produced prerecorded programs, which they sent to the stations ready for broadcast. Some stations virtually ceded programming control to the agencies. Others maintained their own extensive casts and production facilities, but all became increasingly beholden to the sponsors and the advertising agencies. The agencies, meanwhile, relied ever more on the polls to tell them what to do. The advertising professionals considered the rigorous collection and analysis of this poll data the key to their scientific understanding of popular culture and the audience's desires. Consequently, they looked with some disdain on the apparently impressionistic methods of radio programmers and performers. Through their role as the middlemen between the sponsors and the stations they exercised increasing influence over broadcasting content.

Based on what the polls were telling them, the advertising agencies pushed stations to devote more airtime to soap operas and auditorium programs. Although critics complained, this counsel did not threaten the vitality of Brazilian radio programming. The auditorium programs, in particular, fueled previously unforeseen audience engagement with broadcasting, spurring the growth of the fan clubs. And advertising agencies continued to support the prime-time musical programs that played such a crucial role in consolidating trends in popular music. Radio programming was never more diverse and vital than in the early 1950s, when advertising agency involvement was at its peak.

Shortly thereafter, however, the agencies began to invest heavily in niche marketing, concentrating on inexpensive programs pitched at narrow sectors of the audience. Stations were forced to cut their expenses, firing musicians and producers in favor of recorded music or prepackaged agency shows. The rapid growth of television made this trend irreversible. Agencies drained their funds from radio and poured them into the new medium, and radio stations could not recover. Television, the fragmentation of the radio audience, and the demise of live musical programming brought to an end the enormously fertile period of broadcast musical experimentation that had begun in the early 1930s.

THE GROWTH OF AN INDUSTRY

In the early 1930s, just as broadcasting emerged as a medium for popular entertainment and the record industry honed its ability to reproduce and deliver the sounds of popular music, advertising in

Brazil began a rapid transformation of its own, marked by the rise of powerful agencies. The concept of the advertising agency was not itself new to Brazil. Ecléctica, the first Brazilian advertising agency, was founded in 1914.[2] But before the 1930s, the few existent agencies were essentially clearinghouses for transactions between commercial firms and newspapers. They did little in the way of production and did not conduct any market studies. The 1929 arrival in São Paulo of the American agency J. Walter Thompson (JWT) began to change advertising practice. JWT expanded to Brazil largely at the behest of General Motors, which had opened an assembly plant in São Paulo in 1925 and had been producing its own ads. GM pledged its account to JWT, giving the agency the anchor client it needed to expand to Brazil. JWT arrived with the intent of selling American products and, more generally, an "American way of life," defined by middle-class consumption, that had become the principal theme of the advertising industry in the United States.[3] But the Brazilian market was more limited in every way, with fewer potential consumers, confined to a smaller geographic ambit and comprising a smaller percentage of the nation's economically advantaged. As a result, in its early years in Brazil, JWT was largely limited to advertising GM's cars and related products, such as Goodrich tires and Atlantic Motor Oil, to São Paulo's upper class. It ran the vast majority of its ads in the *Estado de São Paulo* and a few other publications with well-heeled readerships.[4]

Even these limited efforts had immediate effects. JWT's striking graphic spreads and its inventive campaigns set new advertising standards, and Brazilian firms and other new American arrivals soon imitated its methods. The advertising agencies began to claim an ever larger share of print advertising and expanded their operations. JWT opened a Rio office in 1931. McCann-Erickson and N. W. Ayer, two other prominent American advertising agencies, also expanded to Brazil, opening Rio and São Paulo offices in the 1930s. And Brazilian agencies such as Inter-Americana changed their approaches in order to compete with the Americans.

For several years after the 1932 legalization of commercial broadcasting, radio advertising remained predominantly local: independent bakeries, clothiers, and furniture stores sponsored programs and rarely contracted advertising agencies to serve as their middlemen. This changed rapidly in the late 1930s: as national and international firms began to turn to radio advertising, they relied on the same agencies that handled their print exposure. Several agencies established radio departments to meet their needs. Standard Propaganda even built its own radio studio in 1937, broadcasting a few programs directly, through hookups with local stations.[5] U.S. advertising agencies brought American radio specialists to Brazil to train a cadre of local disciples in the latest advertising methods. The most influential of the new arrivals was Richard Penn, who came to Brazil to direct Colgate-Palmolive's local marketing in 1940. Penn had already worked extensively in U.S. radio, and he immediately began to play a far greater role in radio production than any advertising professional in Brazil had played previously. In addition to producing ads, he designed the programs that would serve as their vehicles. Penn also took responsibility for the creation of jingles away from the radio stations, hiring his own employees expressly for that purpose.[6]

His most significant initiative was bringing the soap opera, or *novela*, as it soon came to be known, to Brazil. In June 1941, working with Standard Propaganda, Penn contracted with Rádio Nacional to sponsor *Em busca da felicidade* (In search of happiness). The program was a direct translation of a successful Cuban soap opera, with minor adjustments to names and locations to give it local verism. It soon turned into a runaway success, dominating its late-morning time slot.[7] *Em busca da felicidade* established a precedent. Soap operas derived directly and unashamedly from international models and entailed extensive agency involvement. Musical programming, in contrast, often invoked nationalist rhetoric, concealed transnational influence, and remained relatively independent of direct agency involvement.

EVALUATING THE MARKET

Throughout the 1930s, advertising professionals lamented the absence of any reliable gauge of the audience. Polling and market analysis had already become a sophisticated and indispensable auxiliary branch of the advertising industry in the United States. In Brazil, in contrast, market analysis barely existed. JWT had undertaken a few studies, but the agency only had thirty-five employees in Brazil in 1933, leaving it desperately shorthanded in any effort to track audience response. In 1939, J. Winsor Ives, cultural attaché of the U.S. embassy, called specifically on Brazilian entrepreneurs to fill the need for a polling organization to measure radio audiences.

In 1942, Auricélio Penteado finally responded to the call, founding

IBOPE (Instituto Brasileiro de Opinião Pública e Estatística, or Brazilian Institute of Public Opinion and Statistics).[8] Penteado had previously tried his hand at the production side of radio, investing in Rádio Kosmos, a São Paulo station that billed itself as "the broadcaster to the elite." The station failed miserably and was unable to compete with popularly oriented stations for advertising funds. Unable to rise above the vicissitudes of popular taste, Penteado resolved to track them. He sold shares in IBOPE to a host of those with the greatest interest in the project—directors of advertising agencies and major commercial firms—hired a staff of presentable and articulate young men, and sent them into the streets of São Paulo to ask questions. The following year, Penteado opened a Rio office, which soon became the headquarters of his growing operations.[9]

IBOPE divided the population into three classes: Class A was "well-off," class B "middle," and class C "poor." Class determination was based entirely on residential location. IBOPE mapped Rio and São Paulo by neighborhood, ranking each neighborhood by class. Within each neighborhood, pollsters visited only those streets considered "typical," a system given to imprecision.[10] In fact, IBOPE's neighborhood denominations were dubious: the Rio neighborhoods that IBOPE identified as poor, such as Méier, Andaraí, and Engenho de Dentro, were primarily working-class suburbs. The organization did not poll at all in Rio's growing favelas. Just as those favelas were acquiring an enormous importance in defining the nation's popular music, they were being left out of market calculations entirely, a practice that reflected and magnified their economic marginalization. It was not until the 1960s that pollsters began identifying a class D encompassing this population.[11]

During the first few years of IBOPE's existence, the polls determining total audience share gave equal proportional representation to each class, counting A, B, and C each as one-third of the total population. Naturally, the results were skewed, giving the data from the wealthy neighborhoods a weight far beyond their true proportion in Brazilian society.[12] The organization began to adjust for this disproportion in 1947, establishing a 1:3:2 class ratio for most of its polls. While the new ratio was still skewed in terms of real economic makeup of Rio and São Paulo, it was now skewed decidedly in favor of the middle class. This focus reflected the philosophy of both IBOPE and the advertising agencies, who conceived of the middle class as the key sector in their vision of progress through consumption. It was to play a prominent role in the subsequent abandonment of live radio by advertisers in the mid-1950s.

In the first years, the polls were elementary, offering only total audience figures for each station, without differentiation by day and hour. But by late 1944, IBOPE provided daily and hourly audience breakdowns for prime-time slots. IBOPE polls quickly became a necessary resource for both advertisers and broadcasters. From the organization's inception, all the major advertising agencies subscribed to its monthly reports, and within a few years most radio stations subscribed as well. Before long, popular stations began using IBOPE results in their bid for advertisers. In ensuing decades, IBOPE became so deeply identified with audience measurement that *ibope* became common slang for star quality, and promoters still speak of bringing celebrities to an event in order to "give it more ibope."[13]

The organization's growth was largely limited to Rio and São Paulo. Penteado conducted sporadic consumer surveys in a few other major cities and made vague pronouncements about expanding his radio polling operations but was unwilling to take on the initial costs of such a venture. The advertising agencies, meanwhile, seemed content with coverage of the two largest markets. IBOPE did not conduct its first radio poll in Recife, the country's third-largest city, until 1948. Rio, in particular, became the constant focus of IBOPE's analysis. As Penteado wrote in his introduction to a 1950 survey, "For the sake of this study, we understand Rio de Janeiro to be a synthesis of Brazil, because populations from all the states are represented here."[14] IBOPE's practices intensified Rio's dominance of the nation's cultural market. If a trend did not surface in Rio, it simply had no ibope.

THE PRIESTHOOD

For many aspiring, qualified young men—and the profession was overwhelmingly male in this period—fresh from Rio and São Paulo's expanding institutions of higher education, advertising offered the perfect blend of the social status of the white-collar world and the limitless possibilities of expanding industry. The advertising industry grew tremendously through the mid-1950s, attracting a diverse array of former journalists, would-be artists, and underemployed intellectuals. Some of the most ambitious minds of a rising generation turned to careers in advertising.[15] Because the rapid advancement that characterized the profession seemed to rest on general growth more than on competition within the field, advertising was marked by a greater sense of collegiality than rivalry across agencies. The ad men considered themselves brothers in a common struggle.[16]

For these young professionals, progress, advertising, market research, and democracy were inseparable. As the title of a June 1944 *Publicidade* article put it, "Advertising is the fulcrum of civilization."[17] They refrained from expressing these beliefs too vigorously under the Estado Novo, but once the regime fell avowals of advertising's democratizing effects became a leitmotif of the industry. In a rambling 1949 speech before the Brazilian Advertising Association, Penteado gave this belief its most candid expression, describing market research and advertising as the keys to the development of radio as a force for teaching Brazilian's democratic habits: "Commercial advertisement itself already educates, when it teaches the new habits of hygiene, of nutrition, of apparel, when it awakens in the public a little ambition, arising from the desire to acquire new commodities and utilities."[18] In bringing the message of progress and modernity into the Brazilian home, advertising fostered individual acquisitive ambition, the key to democracy.

This process, however, depended on the constant attentions of the enlightened stewards of public opinion.[19] As a result, while the new professionals viewed advertising as a democratic force, they considered the guidance of that force the exclusive responsibility of a technically skilled elite, or even an indoctrinated priesthood. Again, Penteado expressed this sentiment most clearly. In an editorial published with the September 1944 IBOPE radio polls he wrote, "We prefer to present our data in more or less hermetic character, inaccessible to laymen, comprehensible only to those who are accustomed to handling it. The principal reason for this is that the data constitutes a precious fund for those who understand it, but in inexperienced hands it could become dangerous."[20] The danger inherent in this rich fund of information lay in the key it offered to the public mind. Only industry insiders, imbued with a common spirit and endowed with common skills, could be trusted to use it wisely. To that end, in 1950, IBOPE started publishing a weekly collection of political and commercial surveys designed for advertising professionals and the nation's political elite. The title of the journal revealed its foundational tenets of exclusivity and solemn responsibility—*Boletim das Classes Dirigentes* (Bulletin of the guiding classes).

The yearly conferences of the Brazilian Advertising Association, founded in 1937, served to instill this doctrine of exclusivity and purpose. The 1951 establishment of the postbaccalaureate School of Advertising in São Paulo attached to it an advanced degree and a codified set of skills. At the same time, in making professionalization concrete, the foundation of the school signaled an end to the days when self-taught moonlighters could cultivate several specialties and rise rapidly through the ranks.

SELLING MODERNITY

As several scholars have observed, the late 1920s and the 1930s witnessed the rise in the United States of a style of advertising designed to provoke the insecurities of potential consumers and to suggest to them that the solutions to these insecurities lay in the purchase of the right products.[21] While this suggestion might take any of several forms, all of these implicitly sought to teach several basic lessons to consumers: that despite current difficulties and inequalities, a brilliant, democratic future lay just around the corner; that the only way to ensure success in that future was to create the right impression, one based on the careful public projection of a winning personality; and that children were particularly vulnerable in the ceaseless competition of the modern world, giving parents everything to gain for their offspring from welcoming the proper corporations into their lives and everything to lose if they did not. The historian Roland Marchand describes these lessons as "the parables of advertising," and argues that these parables "invited readers to a new 'logic of living' in which the older values of self-discipline, character-building, self-restraint, and production-oriented achievement were subordinated to the newer values of pleasure, external appearance, and achievement through consumption."[22]

By the mid-1940s, these parables were as firmly entrenched in Brazilian advertising as they were in the United States, with only minor variations. Despite the considerable differences between the American and Brazilian markets, the American advertising professionals and their Brazilian trainees largely imported U.S. methods to Brazil wholesale. The campaigns of the 1940s and 1950s emphasized vibrant images of modernity, holding out to the Brazilian public the promise of a radiant and plentiful future. Ads urged consumers to jettison the past in favor of the future and suggested that those commodities most closely linked to images of modernity—cars, radios, appliances—were precisely the ones that needed to be updated as frequently as possible.

As a 1951 advertisement for Assunção Radios put it, "Don't fix your old radio! Trade it in for a new one!"[23] Why cling to the past when the future offered an ever expanding cornucopia of goods?

The advertising professional's foremost strategy was to suggest that the proper purchases could place the consumer on the crest of the peaking wave of modernity, and to that end advertisers ever stressed the new, the modern, the latest, the future. A 1949 ad for Phillips toothpaste, for example, described the product as "The Ultramodern Toothpaste" and urged consumers to "Move to the front. Move to Phillips."[24] Pond's Vanishing Cream, a major JWT account, was sold as the beauty cream of "the modern woman."[25]

At the same time, advertisements also acknowledged that modernity could have ominous implications, threatening to swallow up individuals in an ever widening circle of faceless anonymity, impersonal relationships, and uncertainty. Hence, the ads suggested, in a well-known paradox, that the commodities of the mass market were the remedy for the ills of modernity. The correct choice of products enabled consumers to express individual taste and refinement, or enhance personality. A 1948 Mirta perfume spot, for example, promised "a perfume that accentuates your personality even more."[26]

Advertisements emphasizing individual ambitions and a future of rapid transformation played an important role in the emerging popular music. Many of the signature musical programs on Brazilian radio were, in effect, backward-looking, and evoked a communal spirit. *O Pessoal da Velha Guarda*, for example, looked to a past golden age of amateur popular musicians. *No mundo do baião* looked to the rural roots of nordestinos. The predominant message of advertising presented a clear contrast to such programs, matching competitive but auspicious modernity to soothing, nourishing tradition. Both messages became defining themes in the new popular music. The advertisements were not merely vehicles that used popular music to sell toothpaste: they were also *part* of popular culture. As such, they lacked the best qualities of the popular music itself—its grace and subtlety, its deep roots, its democratic creation. But their message of modernity provided a crucial counterweight to the pull of nostalgia. The tension between these themes gave the new popular culture its depth and relevance to Brazilians living through a period of rapid urbanization and industrialization. The counterpoint between advertisements pushing consumers into modernity and nostalgic programs pulling them into the past was merely another expression of the counterpoint that existed within much of the music itself, for example in a samba like "Aquarela do Brasil," whose lyrics evoking a golden past are accompanied by up-to-the-minute orchestration. In both cases, the contrast suggested that Brazilians not only could have both tradition and modernity, but that they needed both in order to be fully Brazilian and fully modern.

Advertisements overwhelmingly depicted a middle-class public. Often, they promised a product of elite quality, but always with the caveat—either expressed or implied—that for the first time such luxury was available to all. One 1930s advertisement, for example, described an aristocrat chauffeured around the city in a Rolls-Royce. The aristocrat suddenly abandons his hobby of hunting for antiques when he sees the "modern objects" offered by Casas Pekin, a store selling moderately priced home furnishings.[27] This advertisement, like many others, implied that the modern world would make luxury affordable and thereby blur the distinctions between elite and middle class. The poor, on the other hand, simply did not appear in advertisements, and the working class did so only rarely.

This made sense, as the advertisers of mass-market commodities were primarily attempting to reach the growing middle class. As Brian Owensby has shown, members of that class spent a far greater percentage of their income on the commodities of the expanding mass market than did the poor and the wealthy. They were willing to go into debt to do so, partly in order to bolster their social status through conspicuous consumption.[28] More interesting is the way the class distortion in advertisements mirrored the population's self-representation. A *Boletim das Classes Dirigentes* survey of 1952 found that in wealthy, middle-class, and poor neighborhoods alike, residents overwhelmingly identified themselves as middle class.[29] In São Paulo, residents of "A" neighborhoods were more likely to identify themselves as middle class than were their "class B" counterparts. Advertising's focus on the middle class not only reflected the economic standing of the target audience, but responded to broader tendencies of self-perception, or at least self-representation, across classes. Linking depictions of middle-class consumption to an idea of democratic modernity was an effective way to sell to the working class and the elite, as well as to the middle class.

Advertisements were even more overwhelmingly white than they were middle class. Print ads of the era rarely showed a black face, and when they did, it was almost invariably in order to depict a housemaid. This absence apparently resulted from a twofold racism. To begin with, advertising agencies avoided employing people of color. A 1967 study found that fewer than 1 percent of the employees of Brazilian advertising agencies were Afro-Brazilian.[30] On a more subtle level, moreover, the advertisements implicitly, and at times explicitly, sold whiteness. Because of the nonvisual nature of the medium, this strategy can be difficult to identify on radio, but there are some striking examples: the Pond's Cream radio campaign for "the modern woman," for example, promised that the cream would make one's skin lighter (*mais alva*).[31]

Undoubtedly, this approach spoke to the insecurities and prejudices of the audience: because wealth in Brazil overwhelmingly corresponded to whiteness, emphasizing whiteness was yet another way for advertisers to "awaken ambitions" for prosperity. In this aspect as well, then, advertisements played in counterpoint to the emphasis on Afro-Brazilian popular culture within prime-time musical programs. In this case, however, advertising practice also reflected the failure of the American advertising professionals and their Brazilian trainees to grapple with the reality of the Brazilian audience. In the 1940s, Afro-Brazilians constituted a large and growing percentage of the radio audience, and these listeners purchased the products advertised on the air, notwithstanding their concentration in the working and poor classes. The failure to craft a message that would speak to their experiences—beyond suggesting that one could look whiter if one purchased the proper products—suggests that the agencies suffered from significant blind spots in evaluating their market.

At the same time, the advertisements demonstrated some awareness that the Brazilian middle-class nuclear family did not function entirely like its American counterpart. The Brazilian radio advertisements of the 1950s often recognized the domestic politics between housewife and maid, implicitly charging middle-class female listeners with the duty of both disciplining and appeasing household servants. In a famous campaign of the early 1950s, for example, Josefina the maid bubbles over with glee about the Bombril steel wool pads purchased by her *patroa* (female employer).[32] Proper consumption ensures the harmony of domestic labor relations. Radio left one to assume that the housewife was white and the maid Afro-Brazilian, by far the most common arrangement. (Josefina was played by a white actress, but this was also true of most Afro-Brazilian soap opera roles.) The Bombril campaign ran on the prime-time musical programs that celebrated Afro-Brazilian popular music as the cultural essence of the nation. The programs suggested that popular culture was a democratic realm, while

the advertisements reminded listeners of the need for discipline, hierarchy, and patronage in the home and workplace.[33]

SELLING AMERICA, PROGRAMMING BRAZIL

The relationship between program and advertisements was by no
means always a clear contrast between tradition and modernity. The
auditorium programs, for example, offered fans the opportunity to
create community as they entered modernity. Perhaps for this reason,
the line between advertisement and program on these shows often
blurred, with audiences singing along to studio jingles, occasionally
changing their words in the process. *Um milhão de melodias* (A million
melodies), Rádio Nacional's flagship musical program through most of
the 1940s, also offered a subtle variation on the counterpoint of tradition and modernity, Brazilian and international. In 1942, a McCann-
Erickson's executive visited Radamés Gnattali, the orchestral director
of Rádio Nacional, and proposed that the station produce a hit parade
sponsored by Coca-Cola, which was just entering the Brazilian market.
Coca-Cola was already internationally recognized as one of the foremost symbols of the American way of life. McCann-Erickson's campaign called for linking that lifestyle's images of democratic consumer
plenty to a sophisticated, polished orchestral program. Gnattali accepted the offer on the condition that Brazilian music be the centerpiece of the show. He had built his reputation on presenting polished,
sophisticated orchestrations of samba and considered it his mission to
bring Brazilian popular music, in its most elevated form, to a large
radio audience—seeing no contradiction between that mission and his
incorporation of American jazz influences. For Gnattali, Coca-Cola's
sponsorship was merely a means to a higher end.[34]

Um milhão de melodias first aired in January 1943, Wednesday nights
at 9:30.[35] Immediately, the program revealed a dual nature—the advertisements offered a distinctly Americanized vision of domestic
abundance, and the program's announcer praised the superiority of
Brazilian popular music—and the featured music was always Afro-
Brazilian. The ads sold Coca-Cola as the hallmark of a gracious, but not
necessarily luxurious, home: "My lady, if you don't have Coca-Cola at
home, go get some emergency bottles, for only 1.50 cruzeiros." "Coca-
Cola is the drink of family and cordiality, and it costs only 1.50."[36]
This picture of middle-class attainment, along with the hint of competition—clearly anyone who did *not* have emergency bottles of Coca-

Cola on hand had failed to become successfully modern—perfectly distilled the advertising industry's doctrine of progress through Americanization. Coca-Cola was the spearhead of that advance. As Penteado put it in his 1948 essay on Coca-Cola versus cangaço, "Coca-Cola is the symbol of new commercial methods, of a new American civilization, of a new order of ideas."[37]

At the same time, the program became a showcase for Brazil's top composers and performers, and a forum for musical nationalism. This was not the defensive nationalism, bordering on xenophobia, that characterized *O Pessoal da Velha Guarda*. Instead, the rhetoric and programming strategy of *Um milhão de melodias* suggested that Brazilian music did not need to be defended, for its superiority would inevitably shine through in any fair presentation. Gnattali's orchestra played American music, often devoting segments of the show to recent American hits. But pride of place was always given to Brazilian selections, and most frequently to samba-exaltação. The orchestra itself became more Brazilian: Gnattali added *cuíca*, *tamborim*, and *cavaquinho*, giving Brazilian accents to the European symphonic tonal palette. The relationship between the depiction of a recognizably American way of life in the advertisements and the program's celebration of Brazilian cultural grandeur was portrayed as entirely harmonious. On the fifth anniversary special, for example, the announcer stressed that only on the program of Coca-Cola could the listener hear majestic arrangements of Brazilian folk tunes.[38] Americanization represented no danger, because as the American way of life was imported it became Brazilianized. The middle-class Brazilian family—the program's target audience—could enjoy the advantages of both democratic consumer plenty and deep Afro-Brazilian folk roots. Coca-Cola, rather than a symbol of a blandly nefarious American imperialism that would undermine Brazilian culture, became an ingredient of modernity that could be safely balanced by the proud cultivation of Brazilianness.

This formula proved spectacularly successful. *Um milhão de melodias* achieved a cultural influence far beyond its short-term commercial success, shaping the way Brazilian popular music was performed, broadcast, and recorded. Gnattali's incorporation of Brazilian percussion into the orchestra set the tone for the sound of Brazilian popular music, particularly in studio recordings, over the next two decades. His orchestra's professionalism and inventive arrangements became hallmarks of Rádio Nacional's supremacy. The program's special segments highlighting the music of specific Brazilian composers—including Ari

Barroso and Dorival Caymmi—helped construct the canon of Brazilian popular music. The program's orchestral requirements and numerous guests made it one of the most expensive to produce on Brazilian radio. Despite these high costs, McCann-Erickson and Coca-Cola remained enthusiastic. After the program's one-hundredth show, the president of McCann-Erickson in Brazil wrote to Rádio Nacional to thank Gnattali and his team, describing *Um milhão de melodias* as, "incontestably, the best musical program on Brazilian radio."[39] *Um milhão de melodias* represented the high point of the relationship between sponsor, agency, and station. McCann-Erickson presented its goals to Gnattali and then gave him complete control. He used the opportunity to craft a powerful popular cultural expression with enduring significance. Coca-Cola drew economic benefits from this creation, but in the process Coca-Cola itself was domesticated, incorporated into the process of Brazilian popular cultural invention.

SHAPING BROADCASTING CONTENT

By the mid-1940s, it became a commonplace in the advertising industry that advertising professionals were far better judges of the popular audience than were radio station personnel. As Penteado put it, "The agencies have human elements of greater vision than those of the radio stations."[40] Radio stations, for their part, became increasingly dependent on the money channeled through the agencies. The combined result of these factors was that agencies gradually assumed greater control over programming.

In particular, agencies pushed auditorium programs and soap operas, or novelas. The former were relatively impervious to agency control, since they depended on live performance and responded to audience participation. The latter, in contrast, presented agencies with the perfect opportunity to take over programming responsibilities. By the mid-1940s, radio stations often found it difficult to keep up with the demand for new novelas. Agencies soon realized that they could organize production more efficiently by hiring their own writers and sending completed novela scripts, including advertisements, to the stations. They found it easy to lure writers away from radio stations, which generally did not pay as well.[41] And as recording equipment became more sophisticated and less expensive, agencies took the logical step of hiring actors and recording their own novelas, sending them to stations ready for broadcast.[42] The consequences of this trend were obvious: agencies grew, as radio stations shrank. While provincial stations and second-rank stations in the major cities were the first to cut personnel, the top stations were not far behind.

Rádio Nacional was an exception in this regard, at least temporarily. As the nation's most popular station, Rádio Nacional was powerful enough to insist on producing its own novelas while it weighed competing bids for sponsorship. Victor Costa, director of radio theater in the 1940s and then executive director in the early 1950s, maintained a large, high-profile cast of actors and a productive stable of writers.[43] But if Rádio Nacional's authority guaranteed it a certain amount of independence in times of prosperity, it did not make its programming fundamentally different from that of other stations. Rádio Nacional invested heavily in novelas in the 1940s, just like its competitors—in fact, the other stations largely imitated Rádio Nacional in this respect, as in most others. And the station's maintenance of a large cast partially masked a growing dependence on agency sponsorship that became all the more devastating when those agencies deserted radio in the mid-1950s.

These trends greatly accelerated in the late 1940s and early 1950s. According to *Publicidade* studies, advertisers spent five times as much on radio sponsorship in 1953 as they had in 1947.[44] The agencies, which controlled this flow, gained increasing leverage over programming decisions. A 1951 article in *Boletim das Classes Dirigentes* noted that radio stations increasingly accepted the dictates of the agencies "even when it hurts the homogeneity of the station."[45] That same year, *Publicidade* estimated that the radio departments at JWT and McCann-Erickson produced about 60 percent of the shows their clients sponsored, either by themselves or in close conjunction with the station.[46] By the early 1950s, many stations became entirely dependent on the advertising funds controlled by a handful of major agencies. Even Rádio Nacional, which had greater flexibility in its choice of sponsors than any other station, failed to guard against this tendency. By some estimates, 70 percent of Rádio Nacional's advertising receipts in 1954 came through just three agencies, JWT, McCann-Erickson, and Sidney Ross.[47] Any change in advertising strategy at these organizations placed the majority of the station's budget at risk. Other stations, lacking Rádio Nacional's capital and its significant tax and rent indulgences, were in more vulnerable positions. To make matters worse, the clubbish nature of the ad game practically foreordained large-scale migratory trends in the industry, rather than varying responses to new market conditions. The advertising professionals tended to follow leaders like Penteado or Penn in pursuit of the latest trend. In the mid-1950s, that habit of mass pursuit would lead them quickly away from radio.

FRAGMENTATION AND TV

In 1951, Rádio Relógio Federal (Federal clock radio) was founded in Rio de Janeiro. The station's programming was breathtakingly simple: once a minute it broadcast the correct time. Interspersed with these announcements were brief advertisements and curious factoids (such as, "the hummingbird beats its wings fifty times a second"). The implications of this innovation were not immediately obvious. Advertisers did not flock to Rádio Relógio. IBOPE admitted that it did not know how to reckon with the new station, and completely left it out of radio poll results until 1954.[48] The notion of a station that sought to attract listeners for a minute at a time seemed foreign to the rest of the broadcasting world, where the half-hour block was still the standard programming unit. But Rádio Relógio's advertising space was inexpensive—a tiny fraction of Rádio Nacional's—and advertisers began to realize they had nothing to lose by purchasing time on the new station.[49]

At the same time, IBOPE realized that its general audience polls were not necessarily the most efficient tools for advertisers. In the 1950s, in addition to regular audience polls, the organization began to conduct its own narrowly focused surveys. Typically, these concentrated on a single aspect of broadcasting, such as radio journalism or erudite music, and gave detailed results, breaking the audience down by sex and class. The intent of such surveys was to give agencies more precise knowledge of audience habits, enabling them to craft their programming "for greater penetration in this or that sector of the audience."[50] The concept of individual programs pitched at a specific sector of the audience was not new, and for many years sponsors had chosen specific programs, and shaped them, in order to reach target audiences. But the Rádio Nacional model, pursued by all the major stations, called for all kinds of programs at one station. The evolution that IBOPE sought to keep up with in 1952 was the growth of stations entirely devoted to a single niche.

The first niche stations sought to attract the economic elite and the upper middle class. In the early 1950s, Rádio Globo, an affiliate of the Rio daily newspaper *O Globo*, began to invest heavily in a new form of radio journalism pitched at middle-class opponents of the Vargas government. The station slashed its musical and radio theater budgets, moved almost entirely to recorded music and news, and began to climb steadily in the polls.[51] In the same years, Rádio Jornal do Brasil—also affiliated with a newspaper oriented toward the middle class—began to concentrate exclusively on recorded classical music. It did not reach as large an audience as Rádio Globo, but it promised advertisers that it reached the right audience: "Rádio Jornal do Brasil profits with class programming. Our programs are created for a determined public—that which can buy the best products."[52] In 1956, the station commissioned a special survey from IBOPE, with instructions to poll only in upscale neighborhoods.[53] The majority of the potential audience became irrelevant to its strategy.

Soon, key stations in both Rio and São Paulo did the same with sports programming, putting most of their budgets into sports coverage and slashing all other departments. Like Rádio Globo, these stations filled in the gaps with recorded music. They began to challenge Rádio Nacional for its popular audience in certain time slots. Once included in IBOPE's polls, even Rádio Relógio began to show a slow growth in its percentage of the total radio audience, although remaining in the single digits. These trends presented advertising agencies and potential sponsors with three options: they could pay a pittance to Rádio Relógio to reach a small audience that constantly renewed itself; they could pay somewhat more to Rádio Jornal do Brasil to reach a small but well-defined audience; or they could pay hefty sums to Rádio Nacional to reach a large and diverse—but shrinking—audience.

The rise of television further complicated matters for large radio stations. Talent fled to the new medium, and the quality of radio programming began to suffer. More important, despite the small size of the nascent television audience, advertising agencies were even more eager about TV than they were about niche marketing on radio. Paulo Tapajós, one of the architects of Rádio Nacional's influential live musical programming, summed up this process in a 1982 interview: "When television came, there was a commercial exodus. Sidney Ross had almost all its budget invested in Rádio Nacional, and it began to pull it out and put it in television. Budgets were cut and profits disappeared."[54] Rádio Nacional was still powerful enough to maintain some semblance of its former glory. It cut many of its employees but retained a diminished orchestra. It could no longer demand exclusive contracts from its stars—they insisted on working on television as well—but it continued to air a wide variety of live music, featuring some of the country's most famous performers. Most other stations gave in to the changing tenor of the times. In a 1953 interview, José Scatena accurately assessed the transformation in its early stages: "In any economic crisis . . . advertising money is the first to retreat. Having in advertising its principal source of funds, a radio station is generally unstable." As Scatena noted, stations began solving their problems with drastic cuts in personnel and a switch to inexpensive recorded programming.[55]

Within a few years, television consisted primarily of the same types of programs that the agencies had favored on radio—auditorium programs and novelas. But the auditorium programs were far more contained in their new incarnation, their noisy exuberance reduced to telegenic, scripted displays. Novelas made the transition with remarkably little alteration and soon moved into prime time, where they have remained for the last five decades. In contrast to radio, television did not become a fertile laboratory for popular musical experimentation and innovation. Its high production costs dictated emphasis on established stars performing preapproved numbers. *Jovem guarda* (Young guard), for example, a program of the early 1960s, introduced rock and roll to many Brazilians. By the time it took the air in 1965, however, Roberto and Erasmo Carlos, its stars, were already proven market quantities. In retrospect, the program's explicit self-definition, in contrast to *O Pessoal da Velha Guarda*, appears ironic—under cover of tradition, Almirante's program was at least as musically innovative. But *Jovem guarda* was remarkably successful at reaching a well-defined audience of middle-class youth, and advertisers supported it strongly. Other televised musical programs adhered to these general rules.[56]

As they fired their musicians, meanwhile, radio stations began to promote a new kind of performer, the disc jockey. Programs of recorded music introduced by announcers had existed since the birth of Brazilian radio, but the new shows offered something different—a personality, filling breaks with friendly patter, responding to the requests of individual listeners and addressing those listeners as old friends. "Request programs," as they were called, became some of the most popular on the air. Rádio Tamoio of Rio de Janeiro, a station that had never managed to rise above mid-level in the city's ratings despite experimentation with numerous formats, switched to disc-jockey programming in the mid-1950s and suddenly shot up in the radio polls. For the few stations that maintained orchestras and large casts of performers, this was a maddening and ominous development. Rádio Tupi of Rio de Janeiro succumbed in 1955, firing its orchestra and moving almost entirely to recorded music. Rádio Nacional witnessed its ratings slide despite its continued investment in live radio. Even it began to fill late-night hours with recorded music.[57]

These trends were buttressed by another momentous radio development, the appearance of the transistor in 1956. Radio suddenly became portable, casual, and peripheral, where it had once been stable, formal, and essential. The cathedral radio that had served as a centerpiece of family life in the 1930s and early 1940s was consigned definitively to nostalgia; new radio designs emphasized portability and sleek, modern lines. Radio in the 1930s and 1940s had promised to take listeners anywhere on an imaginary voyage; in the mid-1950s the new promise was that listeners could take their radios anywhere. The transistor fostered unscheduled, temporary listening. In response, most stations concluded that the traditional half-hour feature program no longer made sense. Instead, they turned to format radio, maintaining a similar sound, directed at a target audience, throughout the day. This transition reversed the relationship between radio stations and recording companies. For over twenty years, the radio stations had been the dominant partner in their mutual expansion. With the rise of disc-jockey radio, recording companies exercised new leverage. *Jabuculê*, or payola, the practice of paying disc jockeys to promote certain songs, became a chronic feature of the music market. Many radio stations became heavily dependent on these regular subsidies.

Advertising professionals did not create these trends. Television, the transistor, and the disc jockey were inevitable. The flight of the advertising agencies away from live radio in the mid-1950s merely speeded the transition from one model to another. The new model by no means put an end to innovation in the popular musical arena. Bossa nova, the most significant Brazilian musical expression of the second half of the century, emerged just as live radio died and television took its place. But this transition clearly brought to an end a period of ferment and consolidation. The rise of bossa nova, a genre which derived from classic samba and arose in reaction to the melodramatic samba-canção of the mid-1950s, itself demonstrates the passage from a foundational period to one of experimentation based on existing forms, within previously established patterns.

Advertising agencies experienced a boom in the mid-1950s, precisely as live radio declined.[58] After the initial rush to television in the mid-1950s, advertising money continued to drain slowly out of radio over the next twenty years. An independent study of the late 1970s estimated that by 1975, 54 percent of the advertising money in Brazil went into television, compared with 9 percent for radio.[59] Advertising remains one of the most vital industries in Brazil. The top Brazilian agencies and the Brazilian branches of multinational agencies are among the most sophisticated and competitive in the world, and they regularly win international industry awards. They have shown themselves to be remarkably hardy and flexible. They succeeded in adapting to the growth of a single dominant television network, to the relative lack of a vigorous print culture, and to a radio industry gutted partly by their own desertion of the medium in the mid- to late 1950s. They also adapted to, and flourished under, the long reign of a brutal military regime. They failed to demonstrate that advertising is the fulcrum of civilization. They did succeed in making Brazil somewhat more like the United States, in the sense that they nurtured the growth of transplanted consumer habits and the language used to describe those habits. This transplant, however, was always subject to Brazilianization, the adaptation of a loose gospel of the American way of life to local demands and conditions. More important, they helped to build the national audience in the 1930s and 1940s, and then to break it into fragments in the 1950s. By that point their messages of middle-class modernity and individual ambition were as deeply embedded in Brazilian popular culture as the invocations of Afro-Brazilian communal roots to which they ran in counterpoint.

CONCLUSION

It is 13 July 1950, and nearly two hundred thousand Brazilians, along with a handful of foreigners, have crowded into the brand-new Mário Filho Stadium, in the downtown Rio neighborhood of Maracanã, to see a World Cup match between Brazil and Spain. The Brazilians are coming off a 7–1 trouncing of Sweden and know that a victory against Spain will put them one game away from the coveted Cup. They rise to the occasion, playing their signature game of balletic grace and breathtaking improvisation. The Spaniards are stopped in their tracks, humiliated. Early in the second half, the score is already 4–0, the Brazilians are playing keep-away, and the fans are shouting "Olé!" every time a Spaniard lunges ineffectually for the ball. And then the fans start singing—first a few, then a section, then, improbably, the entire stadium, belting out a string of percussive nonsense symbols from an old carnival hit. "Boom parará chim poom boom, Boom parará chim poom boom / Eu fui as touradas em Madri / Parará chim poom, boom boom parará chim poom boom / E quase não volto mais aqui / Para ver Peri beijar Ceci." (I went to the bullfights in Madrid / and I almost didn't come back here / to see Peri kiss Ceci.) The gentlemen pull out their handkerchiefs and wave, as if inciting a bull to charge. The fans sing chorus after chorus, untiring, as the score runs up to 6–1. Millions more listening at home on the radio feel the pull of Maracanã and emerge into the streets to celebrate and sing along. No one knows it, but this is the high point of national popular communion. As the fans file out of the stadium, they breathlessly anticipate a final game against Uruguay three days later. Surely, that will be the apotheosis—Brazil will take the Cup for the first time and savor victory for four years.[1]

Instead, fortune turned the other way. Uruguay won, 2–1, breaking millions of hearts. Brazil had to wait eight more years for its Cup, finally winning in Sweden, far from Maracanã and its cauldron of popular energy. By 1958, the popular audience had splintered. Brazil would be incapable of celebrating as it had celebrated after defeating

Spain, or suffering as it had suffered after losing to Uruguay. The loss has been the subject of endless hand-wringing, fictional and documentary accounts, and more than one tearful memoir.[2] The victory that came before it is almost as resonant in the popular memory but has received less attention. Its combination of soccer, popular music, and nationalist effusion would seem contrived if it had not actually occurred. How was it that two hundred thousand fans with no rehearsal and no conductor came to sing in unison, impassioned and—if reports are to be believed—on key? And why did they sing what they did?

"Touradas em Madri" (Bullfights in Madrid) was not a chart-topper of the moment. It was twelve years old, written by João de Barro and his collaborator Alberto Ribeiro for the Carnival of 1938.[3] The original recording by Almirante—his last hit record as a vocalist—was released in January of that year. It was a marcha, a genre as prominent as its close relative, samba, in the Carnival hit parade. But its onomatopoetic refrain, sung by a chorus and echoed by the woodwinds and percussion section, evoked the castanets and stamping feet of a Spanish *paso doble:* boom parará chim poom boom. The Simon Bountman arrangement, typical of his work, blends Brazilian rhythm with cosmopolitan flourish. The lyrics recount the narrator's comically heroic struggle to remain loyal to Brazilian culture. He goes to Spain to see the bullfights and meets a Catalonian woman who tries to convince him to play the castanets and grab a bull with his fingernails. Aghast, he insists to her that he is faithful to samba and intends to run directly back to Brazil. He concludes by invoking a Brazilian folksaying, "Isso é conversa mole para boi dormir," literally, "that is soft conversation to put the bull to sleep." Figuratively, the phrase refers to any smooth tale concocted to achieve ulterior motives. The implication is that he, the good Brazilian, will not be seduced by any Spanish ruse. If there is *conversa mole* to be deployed, he will be the one doing the talking.

The fans in Maracanã, then, sang "Touradas em Madri" because it was uniquely suitable for the purpose of gloating over the hapless Spaniards. The Brazilians on the field were manipulating their opponents with deadly grace, like a toreador before the kill. But the unpredictability of this occasion reveals a great deal about the workings of Brazilian popular culture. The fans did not choose to sing "Aquarela do Brasil," much less the official national anthem. Instead, by means of impromptu common consent, they chose a tune at once more appropriate to the situation on the field and more lighthearted in its patriotism, befitting a mood of festivity rather than exaltation.

The unscripted performance in Maracanã recalled earlier, less voluntary choral spectacles. Under the Estado Novo, the erudite composer Heitor Villa-Lobos had directed an ambitious state project to instruct Brazilian schoolchildren in *Canto orfeónico*, or orpheonic song—the lifting of thousands of voices in unison to the greater glory of the nation. On a superficial level, exhibitions of canto orfeónico looked a great deal like the scene in Maracanã—thousands of Brazilians filling the bleachers of a soccer stadium, their voices raised in patriotic song. But these occasions were orchestrated, with participation commanded by the authorities and Villa-Lobos himself out front waving a baton. In the wake of the Estado Novo, they tended to be remembered with embarrassment, if not outright resentment. Villa-Lobos's orpheonic arrangements of Brazilian folk songs failed to take root in the popular tradition.

Many of the fans in Maracanã were undoubtedly veterans of these orpheonic performances. But the song they chose in 1950 was one that would have given Villa-Lobos fits. Its refrain betrayed a clear Spanish influence, and it had been written expressly for the Carnival market. It bore the double taint of the foreign and the commercial, the two characteristics Villa-Lobos abhorred in popular music. Indeed, in 1938, "Touradas em Madri" was disqualified from a government-sponsored Carnival competition on the grounds of insufficient Brazilianness.[4] Nonetheless, "Touradas em Madri" had settled into the popular imagination in a way that orpheonic song clearly had not.

The mass performance of "Touradas em Madri" could not have been predicted, but it did conform to fundamental rules of the popular music that emerged in the Vargas period. The tune itself, in both lyrics and music, embodied the productive tension between the national and the transnational. Its persistence in the popular memory demonstrates the fertility of the commercial musical market during its period of initial expansion, and it shows the importance of popular choice, as opposed to state imposition, in the construction of a popular musical canon. Its consecration in Maracanã is perhaps the best example of the voluntary, uncontrolled nature of popular participation in the creation of the new popular music.

The loss to Uruguay three days later, shattering though it may have seemed, was not enough to bring the period of popular cultural formation to a close. Instead, the next several years witnessed the consolidation of the popular cultural themes and patterns established over the previous two decades. By the mid-1950s, samba was recognized as both celebration of the nation and inquiry into its failures. The parallel constructions of Baiano and nordestino identity undertaken by Dorival Caymmi and Luiz Gonzaga had taken deep root, inspiring successors and imitators. Transnational strategies like those pioneered by Lamartine Babo and Denis Brean were an inextricable part of popular musical construction and appreciation. The choro revival and its protectionist rhetoric were in full swing, as were the auditorium programs and the fan clubs they nurtured, and they had inspired a level of popular mobilization that would guarantee their survival.

In the mid-1950s, a combination of transformations brought this period to a close. Politically, the populist coalition that had returned Getúlio Vargas to power in 1950 fell apart, initiating a decade of internecine struggle that would be repressed, but not resolved, by the inauguration of military dictatorship in 1964. Economically, debt and inflation disrupted the period of rapid industrialist development that had played such a crucial role in creating both an audience and the cultural industries to serve it. The rise of television and niche marketing signaled the demise of live radio, for years the most fertile laboratory for popular musical formation.

Two crises symbolized these deeper transformations. On the morning of 24 August 1954, Getúlio Vargas, enmeshed in a political scandal on the verge of forcing him from office, shot himself in the heart. He left behind a stirring *carta testamento*, or testament letter, reminding the humble citizens of Brazil that he had struggled on their behalf, and urging them to resist the forces of international rapacity and their domestic agents. As Rádio Nacional broadcast repeated readings of the letter over the next day, tens of thousands of mourners crowded outside the presidential palace and waited to file past the glass-lidded coffin of the former dictator. The crowds then followed the cortege that carried Vargas's body up Flamengo Beach to the Santos Dumont airport, where it was loaded into a waiting airplane and flown to his ranch in Rio Grande do Sul.[5]

A little less than a year later, crowds of similar size gathered to file past the coffin of another fallen icon. Following her death in Hollywood, Carmen Miranda's body was flown back to Rio and mourned in a public wake in a downtown federal building. This time, the crowds followed the opposite trajectory, following Miranda's cortege down Flamengo Beach toward the São João Batista cemetery.[6] Photographs of the two occasions, showing streams of distraught mourners clogging the road along the rocky waterfront, are hauntingly similar. In both cases, the collective outpouring of grief pushed more ambivalent observers to the margins, allowing the illusion of universally shared remorse for the passing of a hero insufficiently adored in life. These spectacles of mourning for the two most recognizable and polarizing personalities of the period served as grimly fitting symbols of its conclusion.

The themes and patterns consolidated over the previous years did not die with Vargas and Miranda but endured to structure subsequent popular cultural growth. Their continuity at times creates an illusion of sameness, but their meanings continue to evolve. It is impossible to dip into Brazilian popular music, however lightly, for example, without encountering some affirmation of samba's importance as the expression of national identity. Because these affirmations are so plentiful, it is easy to perceive them as an unchanging blur, but each responds to specific circumstances, and often carries a specific critical charge.

To choose but one notable example, "Querelas do Brasil" (Complaints about Brazil, or Indictments of Brazil), a 1978 samba by Maurício Tapajós and Aldir Blanc, puns on the title of Barroso's "Aquarela do Brasil." The arrangement of the original 1978 recording by vocalist Elis Regina intentionally evokes Gnattali's lush, rhythmic horn ensembles from "Aquarela."[7] Gnattali himself, at the end of his long career, arranged the horns on a subsequent recording of the samba, using the same methods he had used in 1939. But here the lyrics tell a different story, or rather they avoid telling a story at all. They begin with, "O Brazil não conhece o Brasil / o Brasil nunca foi ao Brazil." ("Brazil does not know *Brasil* / *Brasil* has never been to Brazil." The difference in pronunciation between the Portuguese and English pronunciations of Brazil is subtle, but clear.) Immediately, the samba calls attention to a gap between the real nation—*Brasil*—and the image it produces for export—Brazil.

This gap had existed even under the Estado Novo, as reactions toward Carmen Miranda's exotic representations attest, but it was particularly notable in the late 1970s. The military dictatorship had borrowed massive sums to fuel the so-called Brazilian economic miracle earlier in the decade, and Brazil continued to project an image of tropical exuberance for tourists, similar to the one honed by Miranda, only showing more flesh. Meanwhile, those living behind the projection witnessed firsthand the failure of the economic miracle, in addition to a thoroughgoing campaign of repression, torture, and censorship. The gap between *Brasil* and Brazil had never been more politically charged, but censorship precluded open discussion of its existence. As a result, the subsequent verses of "Querelas do Brasil" avoid declaration of any kind and are limited primarily to a string of indigenous words, including names of tropical plants and animals. These indications of native bounty again recall samba-exaltação, but the tone is deadpan and absurdist rather than exalted. Sprinkled in this list are names of popular composers, authors, working-class Rio suburbs, and a few remnants of international pop culture—the flotsam and jetsam of a ruined nation. The list degenerates into rote recitation of meaningless filler—"blah blah blah, ba fa fa."—before the samba concludes with a more dire message: "Do Brasil, S.O.S. ao Brazil" (From Brasil, S.O.S. to Brazil). The real nation, silenced and suffering, sends out a cry for help to its more successful image. Again, samba-exaltação turns into caustic political criticism, conveyed by means of a superficially good-natured and eminently hummable popular song.

The other patterns established in the Vargas period have generated similarly self-conscious, tongue-in-cheek reiterations. They are so entrenched in the popular culture that they can be invoked with a gesture and can accommodate parodic renderings that nevertheless perpetuate their basic form. The 2000 Zé Ramalho album *Nação nordestina* (Northeastern nation), for example, relies heavily on Luiz Gonzaga's construction of nordestino identity to fashion a criticism of inequality and discrimination in Brazil. As noted in chapter 4, Ramalho includes a rendition of a Gonzaga standard chronicling migration under duress, along with his own compositions calling attention to continued marginalization of the Northeast. The album's cover art is a parody of the Beatles' famous *Sgt. Pepper's* album, showing several generations of nordestino musicians and popular icons cut-and-pasted into a triumphal assemblage. At the center is Gonzaga, in cangaceiro hat, wielding his *sanfona*. To his left is Zé Ramalho himself. And hovering behind Ramalho's shoulder is the bandit Lampião. The parody of the Beatles is clearly a joke, but the message of nordestino solidarity and persistence through several generations is entirely serious.[8]

The persistence of these patterns at times creates a striking circularity. In 1997, Virgínia Rodrigues, an Afro-Brazilian vocalist from one of Salvador da Bahia's poor neighborhoods, recorded her first album. In an almost obligatory homage to the founding father of Bahian popular music, she included a rendition of one of Dorival Caymmi's standards, "Noite de temporal" (Night of the tempest).[9] The *canção praieira* describes the demanding labor and peril faced by fishermen heading out to sea on a stormy night. Like many Caymmi compositions, it is based on the work chants of the fishermen of Itapoã and includes local Afro-Brazilian vocabulary. Caymmi's original guitar accompaniment intentionally evoked the sound of the *berimbau*, a single-stringed bow that produces a twangy, hollow reverberation, and an instrument strongly associated with capoeira, the Afro-Brazilian martial art played in the streets and on the beaches of Salvador. Caymmi's 1940 recording of "Noite de temporal" was one of the first attempts to evoke the sound of this rustic instrument in a recording studio. Rodrigues's rendition goes back to the source of that sound, prominently featuring a berimbau playing one of the rhythms of capoeira.

The song was the first single from what soon turned into a best-selling album. For the video, Rodrigues used footage from the fishing village segment of Orson Welles's *It's All True*. The song and the video, in turn, have played a crucial role in structuring Rodrigues's image, one that has been marketed more successfully abroad than it has in Brazil. This international success can be attributed in part to an ambitious promotional campaign backed by powerful patrons with international critical influence, like Caetano Veloso. But it also rests on Rodrigues's apparent authenticity, her Baiana realness. Joe Boyd of Hannibal/Rykodisc, Rodrigues's American record label, has suggested that the international audience now cares more than the Brazilian audience about authenticity: "The public in Brazil . . . seems to want a slick, modern sounding samba. But the World Music audience wants classic Brazilian music. And so there is a disconnection between what Brazil is producing and what the outside world wants. Virgínia is fascinating because she is almost like post-modern samba, like a return to the roots."[10] In fact, Rodrigues rarely sings samba, and her recordings rely on the same kinds of studio manipulation as those of other popular singers. If her performance appears more rooted, it is because she draws on the same folkloric elements used by Caymmi, and also by Welles. In other words, Rodrigues's performance *is* deeply rooted, but not in a vague, timeless tradition. Instead, like *Nação nordestina* and "Querelas do Brasil," her work has its roots in the popular music of the 1930s and 1940s.

Caymmi borrowed the work songs of the fishermen and the Baianas, and reconfigured them within his own framework, constructing a Baiano identity that could be marketed to the nation. The DIP used Caymmi's music to add folk substance to its incorporation of jangadeiro labor activists into Estado Novo propaganda. Orson Welles appropriated the plot of the DIP's short film in his frustrated plan to depict a ruggedly noble Brazil to an American audience. And now Rodrigues has borrowed from Welles and reinterpreted Caymmi in packaging her own version of Baiana authenticity. The circle is now complete, having moved from Baiana to composer to bureaucrat to filmmaker and back to Baiana. But it will continue to roll along, taking on new inflections as it goes.

Apparent folk authenticity remains a valuable asset and continues to exist in productive tension with transnational strategies. After the tropicalists forced fans and critics to grapple with their brash combinations of the Brazilian and the foreign in the late 1960s, these strategies lost much of their power to shock. Traditionalists among musicians, critics, and fans can always be relied on to bemoan the corruption of authentic national forms, but such lamentations have not prevented cross-pollination. Transnational experimentation, however, is not unmoored from tradition, but instead has come to follow recognizable rules stemming from the tropicalist experience, itself founded on the models of the 1930s and 1940s. In "Canção para inglês ver," for example, Lamartine Babo brought to popular music the modernist literary technique of juxtaposing archaic Brazilian elements with highly modern international ones in an absurdist collage. The tropicalists revived this approach in the late 1960s, using it to disrupt a real political stasis imposed by the military dictatorship and an illusory cultural stasis imposed by the orthodox left. Over the last decade, neotropicalists like Chico Science, Lenine, and Zeca Baleiro have turned the same approach into a set of codified practices. Their innovation within these parameters and their use of absurdist juxtaposition to call attention to new manifestations of unequal development in Brazil prevents these practices from becoming entirely formulaic. *Brazilian Popular Music and Globalization*, a collection edited by Christopher Dunn and Charles Perrone and published in 2001, provides ample evidence of the fruits of transnational experimentation over the last twenty years.[11] Analyzing manifestations as diverse as samba-reggae, Brazilian rap and funk, and neotropicalism, the authors demonstrate that transnationalism remains among the most fertile themes of Brazilian popular culture.

Choro continues to be regarded as the most traditional of Brazilian musical genres. As a result of its small share of the overall musical market, it continues to accommodate relatively fluid crossover and collaboration of amateur and professional. In massive contrast to samba, for example, the amateur *chorão* is just a jam session away from sitting in with the genre's top performers. At the same time, choro has become more academic, particularly since the second revival of the 1970s. This trend of formal training and performance in controlled settings has reinforced the tendency toward inflexibility established in the 1950s. Until recently, choro seemed to be devolving into a closed repertoire for formalist interpretation, rather than a genre in a constant process of evolution. The foundation of the Acari label in Rio de Janeiro in 1999, however, has signaled a new stage of growth. Acari has released a small collection of excellent choro discs ranging from solidly traditional performances to openly experimental pieces, pushing the genre's boundaries of instrumentation, form, and improvisatory style. Since the 1970s, musicians following this course have usually been forced outside the category of choro and classified as experimental or as Brazilian jazz. By blending their innovation seamlessly with obvious gestures toward tradition, and by marketing their own works explicitly as choro, the Acari musicians have been able to stay within the genre, which bodes well for its expansion and renewal.[12]

Over fifty years after their foundation, the Marlene and Emilinha fan clubs still bring together members from all over the country for annual celebrations. Local chapters continue to devote their energies to manifestations of partisanship and works of charity. If the fans are no longer quite as passionate as they were in the 1950s, the importance of the clubs as networks of solidarity and mutual assistance is more apparent than ever.

These cultural themes and patterns remain powerful partly because of the context of their creation: they emerged in the midst of a rapid burst of industrialization, urbanization, and bureaucratic centralization, interrelated phenomena that favored the equally rapid growth and definition of domestic culture industries and their audiences. But they also remain powerful because, taken collectively, they are coherent, interdependent, and not easily disaggregated. They offer counterbalanced messages of cultural citizenship: they celebrate inclusive racial democracy and lament its absence. They invoke burnished tradition and praise glittering modernity. They affirm the value of group identity and summon the awakening of individual desire. They look back lovingly on the rural hinterland as they speed toward the bustling metropolis. These messages pull against one another in productive tension. They have accepted invigorating adaptation but have proven deeply resistant to fading away.

This book takes its title from *Alô, alô Brasil*, the Wallace Downey-produced Cinédia film of 1935, set in the enchanted world of radio stars. But it also calls to mind the 1979 Carlos Diegues film *Bye-Bye Brasil*, and the song of the same title from its soundtrack, composed by Roberto Menescal and Chico Buarque.[13] Diegues intentionally reversed the title of Downey's film, and also its message. *Alô, alô Brasil* depicted the creation of a glamorous, modern Brazilian popular culture bringing together radio singers and their adoring fans, and Diegues's film seemed to say goodbye to all that. In *Bye-Bye Brasil*, a troupe of itinerant popular entertainers wanders the sertão and the Amazon in search of an audience innocent enough to be impressed by their shopworn act. But everywhere they encounter the dreaded fish skeletons—television antennae—and their message of cheap, cosmopolitan pop culture. Specifically, they find themselves competing with a televised soap opera set in a flashy discotheque. Similarly, the narrator of the Menescal-Buarque composition is a trucker who roams the Brazilian heartland and encounters a Brazil undergoing rapid transformation, where the Bee Gees, pinball, and Lee Jeans are the common marks of reference. "Aquela aquarela mudou"—that watercolor has changed—the narrator remarks, in yet another reference to "Aquarela do Brasil."

"Bye-Bye Brasil," then, says goodbye to a homegrown, authentic popular culture, lost in a flood of cheap imports. But in both film and song, the farewell is premature. The film's *sanfoneiro* becomes a successful *forró* performer in Brasília, wearing the obligatory *cangaceiro* hat. The rest of the troupe gets a new truck with flashing colored lights and dancing girls and takes to the road with an updated version of its old show. And in the song, as in so many transnational Brazilian compositions, the music transforms the meaning of the lyrics. The arrangement played over the film's closing credits incorporates the electronic drum machines and synthesizers of disco but mutes them and folds them into a harmonic bed of subtle shifts and complex intervals.[14] Menescal's ingenious approach to harmony is firmly rooted in the best Brazilian tradition, recalling Tom Jobim, Pixinguinha, or even Villa-Lobos—though surely the old maestro would disavow anything remotely connected to disco. In both film and song, Brazilian popular culture demonstrates its capacity to incorporate and reconfigure the foreign, thereby guaranteeing its own survival.

A quarter century later, the song remains the same. Brazilian popular culture is by no means static—it shows a tremendous capacity to regenerate and transform itself. But overwhelmingly, innovation occurs within the patterns established between the late 1920s and the mid-1950s. After fifty years of reiteration and revision, these patterns have acquired a range of meanings and the density of tradition. They are rooted deeply enough to accommodate varying and even contradictory interpretations. They are now inescapable and instantly recognizable features of Brazilian life, a network of roads leading back to the heart of Brazil.

NOTES

INTRODUCTION

1   Lamartine Babo, "História do Brasil," RCA Victor, 1933.

2   Alencar, *O guarani*.

3   Carlos Gomes, *O guarani*, libretto by Antonio Scalvini, Milan: G. Ricordi, 1870–79? Gomes's *O guarani* premiered at the Scala in Milan in 1870.

4   For analysis of this process at the level of high culture, see Borges, "The Recognition of Afro-Brazilian Symbols and Ideas, 1890–1949."

5   For an overview of pre–twentieth-century Brazilian popular music, see Tinhorão, *História social da música popular brasileira*; and Fryer, *Rhythms of Resistance*.

6   Vianna, *The Mystery of Samba*, 8.

7   Decreto número 5,492, 16 July 1928, *Anuário das leis da República dos Estados Unidos do Brasil*, Rio de Janeiro: Imprensa Nacional, 1928.

8 Cabral, *A MPB na era do rádio*, 32.

9 For an overview of Vargas's fractious second regime, see D'Araujo, *O segundo governo Vargas, 1951–1954*.

10 See, for example, Cabral, *No tempo de Ari Barroso*, 217, 301.

11 The key analytical political history is Skidmore, *Politics in Brazil, 1930–1964*. Also helpful for understanding the political and economic foundations of the modern nation are Levine, *The Vargas Regime, 1934–1938*; and Wirth, *The Politics of Brazilian Development*. For analysis of high cultural and political nationalist formulations, see Burns, *Nationalism in Brazil*; Lauerhauss, *Getúlio Vargas and the Triumph of Brazilian Nationalism*; Oliveira, *Elite intelectual e debate político nos anos 30*; Oliveira, Velloso, and Gomes, *Estado Novo*; and Martins, *The Modernist Idea*.

12 On the rise of *trabalhismo*, the formation of an industrial working class, and its place in the Vargas regime's projects, see Gomes, *A invenção do trabalhismo*; French, *The Brazilian Worker's ABC*; and Wolfe, *Working Women, Working Men*. On the relationship between shifting honor codes and nation building, see Caulfield, *In Defense of Honor*. On the rearticulation of patriarchal structures, see Besse, *Restructuring Patriarchy*. On legal structures of exclusion written into the new nation, see Fischer, "The Poverty of Law." On the role of nationalist projects in primary education, see Dávila, "Perfecting the Brazilian Race." On the foundation of a tradition of agrarian protest, see Welch, *The Seed Was Planted*. On the emergence of an urban middle class and its ambivalent position, see Owensby, *Intimate Ironies*. On conflict between indigenous Brazilians and the state, see Garfield, *Indigenous Struggle at the Heart of Brazil*. On patterns of immigration, assimilation, and ethnic construction, see Lesser, "Immigration and Shifting Concepts of National Identity during the Vargas Era"; and idem, *Negotiating National Identity*. On gay men and their negotiation of a place within Brazilian identity, see Green, *Beyond Carnival*.

13 See in particular Williams, *Culture Wars in Brazil*; Miceli, *Intelectuais e classe dirigente no Brasil, 1920–1945*; and Schwartzman, Bomeny, and Costa, *Tempos de Capanema*.

14 There is a rich historiography on Brazilian popular music from 1920 through the 1950s, and that body of work has established a crucial foundation for this book. That work has tended to concentrate almost entirely on individual artists, however, rather than on broader context and meaning. For fundamental contributions, see Tinhorão, *Música popular*, and other works by the same author; Cabral, *No tempo de Almirante*, and other works by the same author; Severiano, *Yes, nós temos Braguinha*, and other works by the same author; and Máximo and Didier, *Noel Rosa*.

15 See, for example, Vianna, *The Mystery of Samba*; Shaw, *The Social History of the Brazilian Samba*; Seigel, "The Point of Comparison"; Sandroni, *Feitiço decente*; Frota, *Auxílio luxuoso*; and Davis, *Avoiding the Dark*.

16 For categorical statement of the co-optation thesis, see Raphael, "Samba and Social Control"; Goldfeder, *Por trás das ondas da Rádio Nacional*; and Oliveira, "Quando canta o Brasil." For nuanced analysis that still reaches a conclusion of successful state direction of popular culture, see Shaw, *The Social History of the Brazilian Samba*; Melo Souza, "Ação e imaginário de uma ditadura"; and Davis, *Avoiding the Dark*.

17 Williams, *Culture Wars in Brazil*, 24–25.

18 Augusto, *Este mundo é um pandeiro*, 91–93.

19 There are no extant complete copies of *Alô, alô Brasil* and *Estudantes*. I have gleaned these plot summaries from film histories. See, for example, Augusto, *Este mundo é um pandeiro*, 85–102.

20 Rebelo, *A estrela sobe*.

21 Ibid.

22 Hobsbawm, *The Jazz Scene*, 137. It was perhaps the scandalous nature of such assertions that initially led Hobsbawm, in the 1950s, to publish his jazz writings under the name Francis Newton.

23 Andrade, *Música, doce música*, 281–82. I am grateful to José Roberto Zan for leading me to this passage.

I RADIO AND ESTADO NOVO

1 Lourival Fontes, 1936 interview in *A Voz do Rádio*, as cited in Saroldi and Moreira, *Rádio Nacional*, 13.

2 CPDOC, GC, 34.09.22-A, Genolino Amado to Getúlio Vargas, 2 Sept. 1942.

3 Gurgueira, "Integração nacional pelas ondas."

4 For analysis of competition within the regime, see Oliveira, Velloso, and Gomes, *Estado Novo*, 31. On the ideology and architecture of the Estado Novo, see Lauerhauss, *Getúlio Vargas and the Triumph of Brazilian Nationalism*; Lenharo, *A sacralização da política*; and Schwartzman, Bomeny, and Costa, *Tempos de Capanema*.

5 My assessment of the failure of direct government broadcasting stands in stark contrast to many assertions of a putative state dominance of broadcasting under the Estado Novo. For extreme statements of this position, see Lilian Perosa, "A hora do clique," 47; Carmona and Leite, "Rádio, povo e poder"; and Fernandes, "65 anos de radiodifusão no Brasil." For a more nuanced analysis that still ascribes enormous influence to direct regime broadcasting, see Gurgueira, "Integração nacional pelas ondas."

6 Williams, *Culture Wars in Brazil*, 26, 60–79.

7 For accounts of Brazil's first broadcast, see Calabre de Azevedo, "Na sintonia do tempo," 42–44; and Moreira, *O rádio no Brasil*, 15.

8 On Roquette-Pinto and early educational goals on radio, see Moreira, *O rádio no Brasil*, 16–22; see Owensby, *Intimate Ironies*, 47, for discussion of a representative 1928 radio speech.

9 For analysis of Roquette-Pinto's racial thought, see Skidmore, *Black into White*, 185–90.

10 IBOPE, *Pesquisas Especiais*, vol. 2 (1945); vol. 7 (1948), 368; *Boletim das Classes Dirigentes* 1.2 (1950): 1, 7; IBOPE, *Registros de Audiência de Rádio*, Rio de Janeiro, Jan. 1947. See Owensby, *Intimate Ironies*, 112–15, for insightful analysis of radio's symbolic importance in a process of rapid commodification. For worker acquisition of radios, see Velloso, *Mário Lago*, 140.

11 AERJ, DGIE, Geral 11, Pasta 1, Departamento de Correios e Telégrafos, data on radio transmitters in Brazil, 10 Sept. 1942; Ortiz, *A moderna tradição brasileira*, 40.

12 Arquivo Multi-Meios, Centro Cultural de São Paulo, Arnaldo Câmara Leitão, depoimento, 1984.

13 Câmara Leitão, depoimento; Museu da Imagem e do Som–São Paulo, *Nossa cidade*, see undated cassette of program, late 1940s, cassette 31.6. For further information on regionalist broadcasting in São Paulo, see Krausche, *Adoniran Barbosa*. For a fascinating study of the growth of São Paulo's popular music scene, see Vinci de Moraes, *Metópole em sinfonia*.

14 For an overview of IBOPE's history, see Gontijo, *A voz do povo*.

15 RCA acquired the Victor label and its multinational enterprises shortly after Victor expanded to Brazil; Tinhorão, *Música popular*. José Roberto Zan is currently revising his thesis in the history department at Universidade Estadual de Campinas, in São Paulo state, that will add greater detail to our understanding of the early growth of the recording industry in Brazil; Zan, "Do fundo de quintal á vanguarda," 1997.

16 AN, MJNI, 1933–39, Cx. 287, anonymous letter of 30 Oct. 1934; Gurgueira, "Integração nacional pelas ondas," 27, 137.

17 Tota, *A locomotiva no ar*, 129–31.

18 CPDOC, GC, rolo 45 (0248), anonymous letter to Gustavo Capanema, July 1934.

19 AN, Agência Nacional, Lata 185, Lourival Fontes to Getúlio Vargas, 16 Dec. 1940; AERJ, DGIE, Setor Administração, Pasta 13, Assunto DIP, Relação dos funcionários do DIP, 1940.

20 AN, Arquivo Sonoro, cassettes 597, FC 67; 598, FC 71; and 602, FC 67, Vargas speeches from *Hora do Brasil*.

21 Melo Souza, "Ação e imaginário de uma ditadura," 197; Goulart, *Sob a verdade oficial*, 68.

22 AN, Arquivo Sonoro 386, FC 21; Melo Souza, "Ação e imaginário de uma ditadura," 201; *Hora do Brasil*, 10 Nov. 1943; AN, Agência Nacional, Cx. 189, Lourival Fontes to Amilcar Dutra de Menezes, 21 June 1945.

23 Cabral, *As escolas de samba de Rio de Janeiro*, 127.

24 Several scholars have called attention to this episode. Hermano Vianna has adduced it as evidence of the growing acceptance of samba as a symbol of national identity. This is certainly true, although as chapter 2 will demonstrate, the regime did not so much direct popular understandings in this regard as follow them. Raphael interprets the incident as evidence of the state's successful co-optation of a popular genre. This is more dubious: a single broadcast, differing dramatically from the regular programming on the *Hora do Brasil*, does not constitute a successful policy of government appropriation of popular culture, much less a transformation of that culture's meaning. Vianna, *The Mystery of Samba*, 91; Raphael, "Samba and Social Control," 105.

25 IBOPE, *Relatório dos registros de Audiência de rádio do Rio de Janeiro*, April 1950; *Publicidade*, Oct. 1944; CPDOC, José de Segadas Viana, interview.

26 Actor and author Mário Lago, for example, recalls close supervision of his radio theater scripts by the censors. Significantly, the incident Lago recalls most clearly occurred under the Dutra government, not the Estado Novo (and thus after the DIP had ceased to exist) and did not result in any redaction of his scripts; MIS-Arquivo, Mário Lago, depoimento.

27 Occasionally, these papeletas concerned prohibitions of large scope and long duration. In September 1942, for example, the DIP prohibited broadcasts of any material in German or Italian, a decree that wreaked havoc on the opera programming at Rádio MES, the broadcast platform of the Ministério da Educação e Saúde (Ministry of Education and Health). The great majority of the surviving papeletas, however, prescribed temporary prohibitions, and concern relatively minor and arcane matters. A papeleta on 4 Nov. 1942 recommended, "Comments on rabies should be laconic"; AERJ, DGIE, Setor Administração, Pasta 13, Assunto DIP, Papeletas of 1942.

28 Claudia Matos provides an excellent analysis of the effects of this campaign on samba composers who chronicled life on the urban margins; Matos, *Acertei no milhar*, 107–28. For an interpretation that ascribes greater influence to DIP censors, see Davis, *Avoiding the Dark*, 133, 139.

29 *Diretrizes*, 22 May 1941, 22.

30 AERJ, DGIE, Setor Administração, Pasta 13, Assunto DIP, confidential

memorandum of 23 Nov. 1940, Polícia Civil; Relação dos funcionários do DIP, 28 Aug. 1941, Polícia Civil; and memorandum of 11 Oct. 1941, Polícia Civil.

31 AERJ, DGIE, Setor Administração, Pasta 13, Assunto DIP, Relação dos funcionários do DIP, 28 Aug. 1941, Polícia Civil; and confidential memorandum of Polícia Civil do Distrito Federal, 23 Nov. 1940.

32 AN, Agência Nacional, Cx. 191, memorandum from Júlio Barata to Agamemnon Magalhães, 20 June 1945.

33 For analysis of Capanema's ideals and methods, see Williams, *Culture Wars in Brazil*, 61–82; Gurgueira, "Integração nacional pelas ondas," 94; CPDOC, GC, 4.8.30, Carlos Drummond to Gustavo Capanema, 4 Aug. 1930.

34 Gurgueira, "Integração nacional pelas ondas," 111; CPDOC, GC, 36.12.00 (0020/2; 0033/2), Gustavo Capanema to Getúlio Vargas, 21 Dec. 1937 and 24 Feb. 1938.

35 Arquivo Rádio MEC, Rádio MEC: história, unindexed file.

36 CPDOC, GC, rolo 45 (001), Capanema, speech accepting donation of Rádio Sociedade, 8 Sept. 1936.

37 CPDOC, GC, rolo 45 (0014), Ruth de Assis to Getúlio Vargas, undated; CPDOC, GC, rolo 45 (0185), Fernando Tude de Souza, *Relatório do funcionamento da Rádio MES* do ano 1945 (submitted in March 1946); CPDOC, GC, rolo 45 (0146), Tude de Souza to Vargas, 29 Sept. 1944.

38 In a February 1938 letter, Capanema wrote to Vargas, "The possibility of transferring this station to the Ministry of Justice does not appear advisable. . . . That ministry does not need it . . . it needs, instead, all the stations . . . in the country, during the day and the night." Capanema recommended that the DPDC be granted a certain number of obligatory broadcast minutes, and that it prepare brief segments to be aired on every station throughout the day. If Justice were to take over Rádio MES, in contrast, "the station will have no audience, because everyone, even the friends of the government, will tune in to other stations"; CPDOC, GC, rolo 45 (0033/2), Capanema to Vargas, 24 Feb. 1938.

39 Arquivo Rádio MEC, Alvaro Salgado to Rádio MES, 28 Sept. 1937; and Alvaro Salgado petition for leave of absence, 20 May 1941. The station known as "Rádio MES" in the Vargas period became known as "Rádio MEC" later, when its supervising ministry dropped "Saúde" and added "Cultura."

40 Arquivo Rádio MEC, scripts of *Como falar e escrever certo*, esp. scripts for programs 13, 43, 44, and 51.

41 Arquivo Rádio MEC, unsigned letter to Rádio MES, 22 March 1938; Arquivo Rádio MEC, Sylvio Moreaux to Rádio MES, 1938; CPDOC, GC, rolo 45 (0088), Tude de Souza to Capanema, 13 Aug. 1943.

42 CPDOC, GC, rolo 45 (0162; 0185–0200), Tude de Souza, *Relatório do funcionamento da Rádio* MES do ano 1945.

43 Melo Souza, "Ação e imaginário de uma ditadura," 205.

44 Saroldi and Moreira, *Rádio Nacional*. On the foundation of Rádio Nacional and early personnel, see 16–22.

45 For an example of a scholarly perception of Rádio Nacional as state radio, see Haussen, "Rádio e política."

46 Saroldi and Moreira, *Rádio Nacional*, 26–27.

47 On Vargas's early contemplation of incorporation of the Estrada de Ferro São Paulo–Rio Grande, see Calabre de Azevedo, "Na sintonia do tempo," 37. Ortriwano, *A informação no rádio.*

48 The incorporated enterprises were not entirely free from requests for political patronage. At Rádio Nacional, singers who were imposed on the station through political channels were shunted to a half-hour program at 4:00 p.m. called *Programa Alfa.* The program was broadcast only via medium wave (not via short wave), limiting its exposure. It was one of the station's few unsuccessful shows and was essentially maintained as a political sacrifice; MIS-Arquivo, Paulo Tapajós, depoimento, 1982; MIS-Arquivo, St. Clair Lopes, depoimento, 1978.

49 Profits went from 190,000 cruzeiros to 15 million cruzeiros, in a period of relatively low inflation. Rádio Nacional, *20 anos de liderança a serviço do Brasil*, 22.

50 MIS-Arquivo, St. Clair Lopes, depoimento; "A semana em revista," Rádio Nacional weekly program guides, Jan.–Dec. 1944.

51 "O Rádio no Brasil," *Boletim das Classes Dirigentes*, 11–17 May 1952; IBOPE, *Pesquisas Especiais* 17.81 (1954).

52 For Câmara Cascudo's letters to Almirante in 1944–46, see Cabral, *No tempo de Almirante*, 224, 229, 232.

53 IBOPE, *Registros de Audiência de Rádio*, Rio de Janeiro, March 1947; "Rádio Nacional," *Revista do Rádio*, 26 Feb. 1955, 50.

54 Paulo Tapajós interview with Luiz Carlos Saroldi, 1977, MIS-Arquivo.

55 Gilberto Andrade, "A semana em revista," Rádio Nacional weekly program guide, 17 July 1943.

56 In understanding Gilberto de Andrade's approach to directing Rádio Nacional, it bears noting that after leaving the station in 1946 he became the executive director of Rádio Tupi, giving further evidence that he was more interested in the possibilities of commercial radio than in state propaganda or policy.

57 Saroldi and Moreira, *Rádio Nacional*, 48.

58 MIS-Arquivo, Lourival Marques, depoimento, 1985.

59 Genival Rabelo, interview with Victor Costa, *Publicidade*, 20 May 1954, 6–7.

1   In 1974, Sérgio Cabral published a history of the samba schools of Rio de Janeiro, concentrating on the musical evolution of carnival samba, drawing scholarly attention for the first time to samba's progression. Six years later, American anthropologist Alison Raphael wrote a dissertation arguing that the federal government had co-opted samba, robbing it of its authenticity and using it to mask social control. José Ramos Tinhorão, another Brazilian historian of music, published several volumes in the 1970s and 1980s, all of them attentive to the economic processes that transformed preindustrial folk musics into the products of a modern music industry. Cabral, *As escolas do samba de Rio de Janeiro*; Raphael, "Samba and Social Control"; Tinhorão, *Música popular*.

2   Vianna, *The Mystery of Samba*; Shaw, *The Social History of the Brazilian Samba*; Shaw, "São Coisas Nossas: Samba and Identity in the Vargas Era, 1930–1945." John Chasteen's work on carnival dancing should also be mentioned in this regard, for its contribution to understandings of the context in which samba emerged; Chasteen, "The Prehistory of Samba." Frota's *Auxílio luxuoso* contributes sophisticated analysis of samba's place within a growing entertainment industry. Davis's *Avoiding the Dark* explores connections between high cultural modernism, government propaganda, and the rising symbolic importance of Afro-Brazilian contributions to soccer and popular music.

3   Sandroni, *Feitiço decente*.

4   For early scholarly rebuttal of "the myth," see Fernandes, *The Negro in Brazilian Society*. For analysis of Fernandes's importance in stimulating further rebuttals, see Hanchard, *Orpheus and Power*.

5   See, in particular, Sheriff, *Dreaming Equality*, 218–24. For analysis of this recent trend in the scholarship on race in Brazil, see French, "The Missteps of Anti-Imperialist Reason."

6   The best sources for the early emergence of samba and its relationship to maxixe are Fryer, *Rhythms of Resistance*, 154–58; and Sandroni, *Feitiço decente*, 62–130.

7   Both sources are cited in Sandroni, *Feitiço decente*, 66.

8   Sandroni, *Feitiço decente*, 97.

9   MIS-Arquivo, Radamés Gnattali, depoimento, 1975.

10 Sandroni, *Feitiço decente*, 218–19.

11 This schematic explanation, of course, leaves out many complexities. For further details on the origins of samba, see Roberto Moura, *Tia Ciata e a Pequena África no Rio de Janeiro*, and Tinhorão, *História social da música popular brasileira*.

12 Foreis Domingues, *No tempo de Noel Rosa*, 61–66. Although the bass thump in "Na Pavuna" worked well within the Estácio sound, it was not itself an example of percussive syncopation, since its accents fell on the strong beats.

13 Cabral, *No tempo de Almirante*; Severiano, *Yes, nós temos Braguinha*; Máximo and Didier, *Noel Rosa*.

14 Casé, *Programa Casé*, 44–46.

15 Ibid., 45, 56–60.

16 Cabral, *Pixinguinha*, 127.

17 MIS-Arquivo, Marília Batista, interview with Luis Carlos Saroldi, 1977.

18 Casé, *Programa Casé*, 58–59.

19 Moreira da Silva, interview with Rafael Casé cited in Casé, *Programa Casé*, 53.

20 On samba de breque, see Tinhorão, *Pequena história da música popular*, 161–68; and Matos, *Acertei no milhar*, 199–200.

21 Casé, *Programa Casé*, 51–52, 58–59. The samba, titled "De babado," incorporated references to the textile retailer O Dragão (The dragon). The following Rosa quatrain, for example, fills in the verse with a plug for the store: "Quando andei pela Bahia / pesquei muito tubarão / Mas pesquei um bicho um dia / Que comeu a embarcação / (Não era peixe, era Dragão)." (When I went to Bahia / I caught many sharks / But I caught a beast one day / that ate the whole boat—It wasn't a fish, it was a Dragon).

22 Batista, depoimento; Máximo and Didier, *Noel Rosa*, 105.

23 Marília Batista, "Me larga," RCA Victor, 1932.

24 MIS-Arquivo, Batista, depoimento.

25 Noel Rosa, "Coisas nossas," Columbia, 1932.

26 For extended analysis of the progression of Rosa's nationalism, see McCann, "Noel Rosa's Nationalist Logic." For complete lyrics to Rosa's compositions, see Máximo and Didier, *Noel Rosa*; for further interpretation, see Shaw, *The Social History of Brazilian Samba*, 90–143.

27 Rosa, "Não tem tradução," original recording by Francisco Alves, Odeon, 1933.

28 Máximo and Didier, *Noel Rosa*, 209–15.

29 Batista, "Lenço no pescoço," original recording by Silvio Caldas, RCA Victor, 1933.

30 Rosa, "Rapaz folgado," 1933, original recording by Araci de Almeida, RCA Victor, 1938.

31 Batista, "Mocinho da Vila," 1934. For recorded versions of "Mocinho da Vila" and subsequent contributions to the polemic, see Cristina Buarque and Henrique Cazes, *Sem Tostáo* vol. 2, Kuarup.

32 Rosa and Vadico, "Feitiço da Vila," original recording by João Petra de Barros, Odeon, 1934.

33 Rosa, interview in *Diário Carioca*, Rio de Janeiro, 1 Jan. 1936, as cited in Máximo and Didier, *Noel Rosa*, 357.

34 Rosa, "Palpite infeliz," original recording by Araci de Almeida, RCA Victor, 1936.

35 "Palpite infeliz" underpinned Rosa's emphasis on the importance of both morro and cidade. Of the neighborhoods mentioned, Vila Isabel and Osvaldo Cruz were cidade; Salgueiro, Mangueira, and Matriz were favelas, and Estácio contained both morro and cidade.

36 Luís da Câmara Cascudo, *Som*, July, 1937, as cited in Cabral, *No tempo de Almirante*, 133.

37 Cabral, *As escolas de samba de Rio de Janeiro*.

38 For analysis of transactions between favela composers and recording stars, see Sandroni, *Feitiço decente*, 147–51.

39 Cabral, *As escolas de samba de Rio de Janeiro*, 28, 37–40.

40 On the evolution of the surdo and the cuíca, see Cabral, *As escolas de samba de Rio de Janeiro*, 41–42.

41 Sandroni, *Feitiço decente*, 174

42 Raphael, "Samba and Social Control," 98–101; Vianna, *The Mystery of Samba*, 124; Cabral, *A MPB na era do rádio*, 53; on Paulo da Portela's importance, see Cabral, *As escolas de samba de Rio de Janeiro*, 100–112; 127.

43 The best introduction to the historical growth of the samba schools remains Cabral's *As escolas de samba de Rio de Janeiro*.

44 Vianna dedicates his book to investigation of the transformation of intellectual opinion regarding samba, concentrating primarily on Freyre. See, in particular, Vianna, *The Mystery of Samba*, 19–36, 75–94. In his sharply critical review of Vianna, Jeffrey Needell adds significant complexity to the portrait of Freyre's intellectual evolution; Needell, review of *The Mystery of Samba*. This criticism notwithstanding, Vianna's depiction of a general intellectual shift in the first half of the 1930s toward a new appreciation of Afro-Brazilian cultural influence remains accurate. For literary background on pre-Freyrean precedents for that shift, see Borges, "The Recognition of Afro-Brazilian Symbols and Ideas, 1890–1940."

45 Carlos Lacerda, *Diário Carioca*, Feb. 1936, cited in Cabral, *As escolas de samba de Rio de Janeiro*, 109.

46 "Café Nice," *Diretrizes*, 28 May 1942, 24.

47 Rosa was by no means completely forgotten. As Darien Davis has shown, in 1940 Júlio Barata, director of the DIP's radio division, attempted to incorporate Rosa into the regime's commemoration of the founding of Rio de Janeiro. Barata implausibly suggested that Rosa did not celebrate the urban margins. This unconvincing attempt, however,

was decidedly out of step with Estado Novo propaganda. See Davis, *Avoiding the Dark*, 139.

48 The debate, originally published in the pages of *A Noite* and *O Jornal* in June and July 1939, is reproduced in Cabral, *A MPB na era do rádio*, 70–72.

49 Mário de Andrade, as cited in Cabral, *A MPB na era do rádio*, 72.

50 Matos, *Acertei no milhar*, 42–44, 67–87.

51 For analysis of the effects of this campaign on the most prominent malandro sambistas, see ibid., 107–28.

52 For details on the number of compositions censored, see ibid., 90.

53 Composers may also have felt some loyalty to Vargas for defending their interest in legislation requiring radio stations to pay royalties for the music they broadcast; Velloso, *Mário Lago*, 115–17.

54 Castelo, "Rádio," 292; Matos, *Acertei no milhar*, 91.

55 Severiano and Homem de Mello, *A canção no tempo*, 196.

56 Vianna, *The Mystery of Samba*, 124; Raphael, "Samba and Social Control," 111.

57 For biographical detail, see Cabral, *No tempo de Ari Barroso*.

58 Ibid., esp. 153–74.

59 Ibid., 161, 94.

60 Sandroni, *Feitiço decente*, 98–99.

61 Murce, *Bastidores do rádio*, 42–44; Cabral, *No tempo de Ari Barroso*, 153; MIS-XV, Arquivo Ari Barroso, obituary for Barroso.

62 Ari Barroso, "Aquarela do Brasil," original recording by Francisco Alves, RCA Victor, 1939.

63 Ari Barroso, interview with Marisa Lira in *Diário de Notícias*, 1958, as cited in Severiano and Homem de Mello, *A canção no tempo*, 177–78, and Cabral, *No tempo de Ari Barroso*, 179.

64 For the lyrics to "Aquarela," see Chediak, *Songbook Ari Barroso*.

65 Cabral, *No tempo de Ari Barroso*, 180, 186.

66 Ibid., 182–83. "Aquarela do Brasil" had been performed in public once before its official debut in *Joujoux e Balangandãs*. Shortly before that spectacle, "Aquarela do Brasil" was included in a failed musical revue in a downtown theater, but that performance passed without significant notice.

67 Didier, *Radamés Gnattali*, 18. For critical analysis of Gnattali's incorporation of American swing, see Tinhorão, "Cinquenta anos a serviço de jazz."

68 Cabral, *No tempo de Ari Barroso*, 185–86.

69 Heitor Villa-Lobos, in a feature on the composer in *Diretrizes*, 27 Mar. 1941, 12–13.

70 Documents relating to accusations of plagiarism against Villa-Lobos

brought by the executors of the estate of poet and composer Catullo de Paixão Cearense, CPDOC, GC, rolo 89 (0862, 0873). For more on Villa-Lobos's association with popular music, see Garcia, "The Choro, the Guitar, and Villa-Lobos."

71 Moraes, *Recordações de Ari Barroso*, 58.

72 MIS-XV, Arquivo Ari Barroso, David Nasser, "Cabelos brancos," 1950s magazine interview with Ari Barroso, source unnamed.

73 Gnattali might well be added to this list. See Didier, *Radamés Gnattali*, esp. 90.

74 Máximo and Didier, *Noel Rosa*, 467.

75 MIS-Arquivo, Tapajós, depoimento.

76 *Cruzeiro*, "Um dia com Ari Barroso," 6 Jan. 1940; on Alves's appearances on the *Hora do Brasil*, see Cabral, *As escolas de samba de Rio de Janeiro*, 127.

77 Moraes, *Recordações de Ari Barroso*, 69–70.

78 Marques Rebelo, "Discoteca crítica," *Diretrizes*, 17 July 1941, 23; Castelo, "Rádio," 292; Severiano and Homem de Mello, *A canção no tempo*, 197.

79 MIS-Arquivo, *Quando canta o Brasil*, esp. cassette 119.

80 Assis Valente, "Brasil pandeiro," original recording by Anjos do Inferno, Colombia, 1941; Severiano and Homem de Mello, *A canção no tempo*, 197.

81 Ari Barroso and Luis Peixoto, "Brasil moreno," original recording by Cândido Botelho, Odeon, 1941; Chediak, *Songbook Ari Barroso*.

82 Barroso, speech before the Câmara dos Deputados, Jan. 1948, as cited in Cabral, *No tempo de Ari Barroso*, 247.

83 MIS-Arquivo, feature on Ari Barroso, *Um milhão de melodias*, 1 Sept. 1948.

84 MIS-Arquivo, *Gente que brilha*, 1950, cassette 218.

85 MIS-Arquivo, "O morro de Mangueira," *Dicionário Toddy*, cassette 269.

86 Cabral, *No tempo de Ari Barroso*, 207–40.

87 Part of a 1942 RKO broadcast is reproduced at the close of *It's All True*, the 1993 film documenting Welles's unfinished epic of the same name. The recording is also available at the archive of the Museum of Television and Radio in New York City.

88 For a foundational analysis of the concept of racial democracy, see Skidmore, *Black into White*, 216–17.

89 MIS-Arquivo, Sérgio Cabral, "Samba pos-40," lecture in course "História da música popular brasileira," 1973, reel 2.

90 Noel Rosa and Hervê Cordovil, "Triste cuíca," original recording by Araci de Almeida, RCA Victor, 1935.

91 Herivelton Martins, "Laurindo," original recording by Trio de Ouro, Odeon, 1943.

92 Martins himself had grown up in the favela of São Carlos in the Estácio neighborhood, and he later claimed to have a particular musician from that community in mind.

93 Campos et al., *Um certo Geraldo Pereira*, 185–89.

94 Batista had collaborators in each case, composing "Lá vem Mangueira" with Haroldo Lobo and Jorge de Castro, original recording by Deo, Continental, 1943; "Cabo Laurindo" with Haroldo Lobo, originally recorded by Jorge Veiga, Continental, 1945; and "Comício em Mangueira" with Germano Augusto, original recording by Carlos Galhardo, RCA Victor, 1945.

95 Wilson Batista and Geraldo Pereira, "Acertei no milhar," original recording by Moreira da Silva, Odeon, 1940.

96 Geraldo Pereira, "Falsa baiana," original recording by Ciro Monteiro, RCA Victor, 1944.

97 Geraldo Pereira, Cristóvão de Alencar, David Nasser, "Golpe errado," original recording by Ciro Monteiro, RCA Victor, 1946.

98 Campos et al., *Um certo Geraldo Pereira*, 119.

99 Geraldo Pereira and Arnaldo Passos, "Ministério da Economia," original recording by Pereira, Sinter, 1951.

100 Geraldo Pereira and Arnaldo Passos, "Escurinha," original recording by Pereira, Sinter, 1952.

101 Geraldo Pereira and W. Vanderley, "Cabritada malsucedida," original recording by Pereira, RCA Victor, 1953.

102 Luiz da França, as quoted in Campos et al., *Um certo Geraldo Pereira*, 103.

103 For a pathbreaking revelation of racial discrimination in radio in São Paulo in the 1960s, see Pereira, *Cor, profissão e mobilidade*.

104 A case might be made for a small number of other singers. Luiz Gonzaga was perceived not as Afro-Brazilian but as nordestino, a phenomenon analyzed extensively in chapter 3. Jackson do Pandeiro was also perceived primarily as nordestino and had not yet attained the fame he would acquire a few years later. Jamelão, the definitive carnival singer of the period, had little broadcast and recording exposure before the late 1950s. (Like Blecaute, Jamelão bore a nickname that called attention to his color: the jamelão is a dark purple fruit of northern Brazil.) Among female vocalists, several, such as Angela Maria, were clearly Afro-Brazilian, but none had dark skin. Carmen Costa and Ellen (or Helen) de Lima, the first dark-skinned female singers to attain the vocal pantheon, were still several years away from the height of their fame.

105 For excellent analysis of Alves and his career, see Shaw, *The Social History of the Brazilian Samba*.

106 Geraldo Pereira and Arnaldo Passos, "Que samba bom," original recording by Blecaute, Continental, 1949.
107 *Revista do Rádio*, 5 Feb. 1955, 3.
108 Wilson Batista, "Chico Brito," original recording by Dircinha Batista, Odeon, 1950.
109 Geraldo Pereira, "Escurinho," original recording by Ciro Monteiro, Todamérica, 1955.
110 Nelson Pereira dos Santos, *Rio, 40 graus*, 1955.
111 For an excellent account of the importance of Pereira dos Santos's early films in the cinematic portrayal of race in Brazil, see Stam, *Tropical Multiculturalism*, 160–66.
112 Zé Keti, "A voz do morro," original recording by Jorge Goulart, Continental, 1955.
113 Nelson Pereira dos Santos, *Rio, Zona Norte*, 1957.
114 For the best presentation of the former strain of analysis, see Shaw, *The Social History of the Brazilian Samba*. For a pathbreaking presentation of the latter, see Vianna, *The Mystery of Samba*.

3 RISE OF NORTHEASTERN REGIONALISM

1 For the epigraph, see Dorival Caymmi, interview, *Jornal do Brasil*, 7 April 1984, caderno B; MIS-XV, Arquivo Luiz Gonzaga, Luiz Gonzaga, interview with Capinan, undated. Caymmi recorded "Peguei um Ita no Norte" for Odeon in 1945.
2 Luiz Gonzaga and Guio de Morais, "Pau de arara," original recording by Luiz Gonzaga, RCA Victor, 1952.
3 Ramos, *Vidas secas*.
4 MIS-Arquivo, *Um milhão de melodias*, Rádio Nacional, January 1949.
5 MIS-XV, Arquivo Dorival Caymmi, doc. 13A, Jorge Amado, undated interview; Tárik de Souza, *Jornal do Brasil*, 20 April 1981, caderno B, 10.
6 For estimations of the importance of Caymmi and Gonzaga, see Sidney Miller, *Jornal do Brasil*, 26 June 1971, caderno B, 4. Miller argues that Caymmi and Gonzaga, as founders of two rich, coherent genres, are among the four most influential Brazilian popular composers.
7 AN, Arquivo Sonoro, 624 FC8, Getúlio Vargas, speech, 11 Nov. 1937; AN, Arquivo Sonoro, 624 FC8, Vargas, speech 11 Sept. 1940. For analysis of the flag burning, see Williams, *Culture Wars in Brazil*, 9–10, 177, 196.
8 AN, MJNI, correspondência, 1940, Lourival Fontes letter to Câmara Cascudo.
9 CPDOC, Arquivo Agamemnon Magalhães, microfilm 2 (0982), Agamemnon Magalhães letter to Vargas, 1938.
10 For analysis of Andrade's initial project and its eventual results, see Williams, *Culture Wars in Brazil*, 98–134.

11 Andrade, *Cartas de Mário de Andrade a Luís da Câmara Cascudo*, 149.
12 Da Cunha, *Os sertões*.
13 Freyre, *Casa grande e senzala*.
14 Lins do Rego, *Pedra Bonita*; Queiroz, *O quinze*; América de Almeida, *O Boqueirão*; Amado, *Jubiabá* and *Mar Morto*; for the first chapters of the collective novel, see *Diretrizes*, March 1941.
15 Murce, *Bastidores do rádio*, 89–90.
16 Braucks, *Jararaca e Ratinho*; *Publicidade*, "Coluna de rádio," 1 July 1950.
17 Manoel Diegues Jr., "Folclore e Rádio," *Publicidade, Anuário do Rádio*, 1953, 86; *Diretrizes*, "Rádio," 26 June 1941, 22.
18 Barbosa and Alencar, *Caymmi*; MIS-Arquivo, Dorival Caymmi, depoimento, 1966.
19 Barbosa and Alencar, *Caymmi*, 23; Cabral, *A música popular brasileira na era do rádio*, 67.
20 Dorival Caymmi, "O que é que a baiana tem?," original recording by Carmen Miranda and Dorival Caymmi, Odeon, 1939.
21 MIS-Arquivo, Caymmi, depoimento; Cabral, *A MPB na era do rádio*, 68–69.
22 MIS-Arquivo, Caymmi, depoimento; Caymmi, *Cancioneiro da Bahia*, 86.
23 MIS-Arquivo, Caymmi, depoimento; Barbosa and Alencar, *Caymmi*, 69.
24 Dorival Caymmi, "Vatapá," original recording by Anjos do Inferno, Columbia, 1942.
25 *Vamos Ler*, 30 Dec. 1943.
26 *Revista do Rádio*, 2 May 1950, 40; MIS-XV, Arquivo Dorival Caymmi, Ricardo Cravo Albim, transcript of radio special on Caymmi, undated (but apparently from the early 1970s).
27 Amado, introduction to Caymmi, *Cancioneiro da Bahia*, 4; Barbosa, *Caymmi*, 28.
28 MIS-Arquivo, Caymmi, depoimento.
29 Dorival Caymmi, "A preta do acarajé," original recording by Carmen Miranda and Dorival Caymmi, Odeon, 1939.
30 *Vamos Ler*, 30 Dec. 1943; MIS-Arquivo, Caymmi, depoimento; Caymmi, *Cancioneiro da Bahia*, 158.
31 Dorival Caymmi, "Você já foi a Bahia?," original recording by Anjos do Inferno, Columbia, 1941.
32 Caymmi, *Cancioneiro da Bahia*, 164.
33 Dreyfus, *Vida do viajante*; MIS-Arquivo, Gonzaga, depoimento, 1978.
34 For slightly varying versions of the tale, see Dreyfus, *Vida do viajante*, 80–85; and Gonzaga, depoimento.
35 Gonzaga registered the 1941 recording of "Vira e mexe" as a "xamego," a nordestino exclamation of enthusiasm. Despite the nordestino style of

the accordion solo, however, the tune is, rhythmically, a choro. In addition to Gonzaga's own fiery solo, furthermore, it features a buoyant ukelele solo, distinctly within the choro tradition, by guitarist Garoto. For a complete list of Gonzaga's recordings, see Dreyfus, *Vida do viajante*, 317–49.

36 Luiz Gonzaga and Humberto Teixeira, "Asa branca," original recording by Luiz Gonzaga, RCA Victor, 1947; Gonzaga, depoimento; Dreyfus, *Vida do viajante*, 105.

37 Luiz Gonzaga and Humberto Teixeira, "Baião," original recording by Quatro Ases e um Coringa, Odeon, 1946; recording by Luiz Gonzaga, RCA Victor, 1949.

38 MIS-Arquivo, Teixeira, participating in Luiz Gonzaga, depoimento, 1978.

39 MIS-Arquivo, NMdB, Rádio Nacional, 17 Oct. 1950; *Radiolândia*, interview with Humberto Teixeira, 30 April 1955.

40 MIS-Arquivo, NMdB, 31 Oct. 1950; NMdB, 7 Nov. 1950; NMdB, 9 Jan. 1951; *Revista Rádio Nacional* 1.6, 1951.

41 Saroldi and Moreira, *Rádio Nacional*, 39; Dreyfus, *Vida do viajante*, 134; MIS-Arquivo, Gonzaga, depoimento.

42 Saroldi and Moreira, *Rádio Nacional*, 41.

43 MIS-Arquivo, NMdB, in particular 14 Nov. 1950 and 28 Dec. 1950.

44 MIS-Arquivo, NMdB, 17 Nov. 1950.

45 MIS-Arquivo, NMdB, 31 Oct. 1950; MIS-XV, Arquivo Luiz Gonzaga, Nelson Xavier, untitled interview.

46 MIS-Arquivo, Gonzaga, depoimento; Dreyfus, *Vida do viajante*, 81; Gonzaga, *Sangue nordestino*, Odeon, 1974.

47 MIS-XV, Arquivo Dorival Caymmi; Zuza Homem de Mello, "Dorival Caymmi, sesenta anos," *Estado de São Paulo*, 29 April 1984; MIS-Arquivo, Gonzaga, depoimento.

48 *Publicidade, Anuário do Rádio*, 1951–53; *Publicidade*, 1 April 1951, 29.

49 *Revista do Rádio*, 5 Feb. 1955, 26–27; *Revista do Rádio*, 30 Oct. 1951, 48–49; *Cine Rádio Jornal*, "A jangada voltou só," 4:176, 19 Nov. 1941, 6; MIS-Arquivo, NMdB, 2 Jan. 1951.

50 MIS-Arquivo, NMdB, 16 Jan. 1951.

51 Ibid.

52 MIS-Arquivo, NMdB, 31 Nov. 1950, 2 Jan. 1951, 16 Jan. 1951.

53 *Vamos Ler*, 30 Dec. 1943; Sebastião Braga, *Rádio visão*, 15 Aug. 1947, 45; João Máximo, booklet enclosed in *50 anos de chão*, 1996 RCA collection of Gonzaga's music.

54 Melo Souza, "Ação e imaginário de uma ditadura," 389–90.

55 Ibid., 390–94; *Cine Rádio Jornal*, "A jangada voltou só," 6.

56 *Cine Rádio Jornal*, "A jangada voltou só," 4:176, 19 Nov. 1941, 6.

57 MIS-Arquivo, *Dicionário Toddy*, Rádio Nacional, cassettes 4, 18, 21.

58 MIS-Arquivo, Gonzaga, depoimento.

59 MIS-Arquivo, Ruy Santos, depoimento. The segment based on *A jangada* forms the bulk of a 1993 documentary on Welles's unfinished film, released with his original title. The original dialogue and soundtrack were lost, and the 1993 soundtrack has no Caymmi music. But Caymmi was in close contact with Welles during the filming, and has subsequently reported that the director intended to use his music in the soundtrack; Stella Caymmi, *Dorival Caymmi*, 207.

60 On the planned voiceover, see Stam, *Tropical Multiculturalism*, 130. On Welles's difficulties with the DIP, see ibid., 127–28.

61 MIS-XV, Arquivo Caymmi, doc. 27; MIS-XV, Arquivo Gonzaga, *Publicidade*, "O padre Cícero do baião," 1 Jan. 1952.

62 Dreyfus, *Vida do viajante*, 147–52; Thais Agular, "Aula de revolução," 31 July 2001, available online at www.no.com.br/revista/noticiavinculada paraimpressao/1591/998507141000.

63 Dunn, *Brutality Garden*, 56.

64 Luiz Gonzaga and Humberto Teixeira, "Asa branca" (1947), recording by Caetano Veloso, Philips, 1969.

65 Zé Ramalho, *Nação nordestina*, BMG Brasil, 2000.

66 For an excellent introduction to *bloco afro*, see Perrone and Dunn, *Brazilian Popular Music and Globalization*.

67 Stella Caymmi, *Dorival Caymmi*.

68 Sílvio Essinger, "Caymmi sem mitos," *Jornal do Brasil*, 7 Dec. 2001, caderno B, 2.

69 Gilberto Gil, "Vendedor de caranguejo," *Quanta*, Atlantic, 1997. This samba by the composer Gordurinho is strikingly similar to Caymmi's work in both its formal construction and its depiction of local color. For representative work of the latest treatment of northeastern folk influence, see Chico Science e Nação Zumbi, *Da lama ao caos*, Chaos, 1995, and *AfroCiberdelia*, Chaos, 1996; Mestre Ambrôsio, *Terceiro samba*, Sony, 2001; Lenine, *Na pressão*, RCA International, 2000; Zeca Baleiro, *Vô Imbolá*, MZA Records, 2000; MIS-XV, Arquivo Caymmi, doc.13A.

4 AMERICAN SEDUCTION

1 Lamartine Babo, "Canção para inglês ver," Odeon, 1931.

2 Soares Valença, *Tra la lá*, 66.

3 Severiano and Homem de Mello, *A canção no tempo*, 105.

4 Brazilian poet Carlos Drummond de Andrade also invokes elixir de inhame in his 1940 poem "Brinde no Juízo Final" (A toast at the Final Judgment). The poem celebrates, and also gently mocks, the popular poets of Brazil, the poets of the street, of the streetcar and the radio, the poets of taro root elixir. Like Babo, Drummond seems to play a double

game: his invocations of the streetcar and elixir de inhame, as well as Light, the power company, in a poem praising the poets of the radio suggest a clear reference to Babo and "Canção para inglês ver." Implicitly, then, the poem celebrates the cohort of inventive popular musical lyricists of the 1930s, whose sophistication belied their popular status. But Drummond also uses "elixir de inhame" in the same way Babo does—to invoke a less sophisticated popular sector likely to accept the claims made for quack medicines at face value; Drummond de Andrade, *Sentimento do mundo* (1940).

5 Oswald de Andrade, *Manifesto antropófago*, in Mendonça Teles, *Vanguarda européia e modernismo brasileiro*, 353–60.

6 Caetano Veloso, "Alegria, alegria," Philips, 1967, and "Baby," Philips, 1969. For critical evaluation of Veloso's career, see Dunn, *Brutality Garden*. For specific analysis of "Alegria, alegria" and "Baby," see 65–66, 109, 204–6.

7 Dunn's introduction is an exception in this regard, offering brief but illuminating analysis of the tension between foreign and domestic in Carmen Miranda's career and in bossa nova, demonstrating the way these manifestations prefigured tropicalist concerns; Dunn, *Brutality Garden*, 27–35. Micol Seigel has developed a superb analysis of transnationalism in the 1910s and early 1920s, tracking the intertwining fates of early jazz and samba; Seigel, "The Point of Comparison."

8 Among the extremists who have characterized most commercial popular music as unacceptably tainted by the foreign are José Ramos Tinhorão and Vagalume. See, in particular, Tinhorão, *Do gramofone ao rádio*; and Guimarães (Vagalume), *Na roda de samba*. For more moderate appraisals that uphold the supposed sanctity of the national, see Cabral, *A MPB na era do rádio*, as well as Severiano and Homem de Mello, *A canção no tempo*.

9 Veloso, "Carmen Mirandadada." On the tropicalist use of Miranda's image, see Dunn, *Brutality Garden*, 35–36, 90–92.

10 Assis Valente, "Goodbye," original recording by Carmen Miranda, RCA Victor, 1932.

11 This usage of the English word *boy* to describe errand runners of any age remains common in Brazil. Its pejorative associations, if anything, have deepened over time.

12 João de Barro and Alberto Ribeiro, "Yes, nós temos bananas," originally recorded by Almirante, Odeon, 1938.

13 Frank Silver and Irving Cohn, "Yes, We Have No Bananas," recorded by Bailey's Lucky Seven with Irving Kaufman, Gennet, 1923.

14 For an indication of popular music from the United States that reached Brazil, see Severiano and Homem de Mello, *A canção no tempo*, 109, 117, 125, 133, 141.

15 Ulhôa, "Música Brasileira Popular."

16 Parlophon and Brunswick also opened branches in Rio in these years, but Parlophon merged with Odeon, and Brunswick produced far less than the other companies, leaving Odeon, Columbia, and Victor to control the market until the foundation of Continental in the early 1940s; Severiano, *Yes, nós temos Braguinha*, 24–25.

17 Augusto, *Este mundo é um pandeiro*, 91–93.

18 MIS-Arquivo, Herivelton Martins, depoimento.

19 Cabral, *No tempo de Ari Barroso*, 180–81.

20 For a representative recording, see Raul Marques and Moacir Bernardino, "Risoleta," original recording by Luiz Barbosa, 1937. For details on Evans's early interest in samba de breque, see MIS-Arquivo, Herivelton Martins, depoimento. Even Martins's deprecatory account shows Evans's appreciation of Brazilian syncopation.

21 See, for example, Pixinguinha, "A vida é um buraco," RCA Victor, 1930.

22 Didier, *Radamés Gnattali*, 18.

23 See, for example, Radamés Gnattali, "Recordando," originally recorded by the Trio Carioca, RCA Victor, 1937.

24 MIS-Arquivo, Martins, depoimento.

25 Recording of a 1974 interview on TV Cultura, São Paulo, released on compact disc as Cordovil, *A música brasileira deste século por seus autores e intérpretes*.

26 Severiano and Homem de Mello, *A canção no tempo*, 44. Evans had given Galhardo his first recording contract in 1933, and Galhardo's rise to fame in the world of Brazilian popular music depended heavily on Evans's support.

27 The term *chanchada* has etymological roots in the Italian *ciancata*, for vulgar comedy. For analysis of the formal rules of chanchada, see Vieira, "From *High Noon* to *Jaws*," 256–68; Augusto, *Este mundo é um pandeiro*.

28 Adhemar Gonzaga, Wallace Downey, *Alô, alô Carnaval*, Cinédia, 1936.

29 Wallace Downey, *Banana da terra*, Sonofilmes, 1939.

30 Busby Berkeley, *The Gang's All Here*, Twentieth Century Fox, 1943.

31 For further detail on Miranda's success in the United States, see Gil-Montero, *Brazilian Bombshell*; and Mendonça, *Carmen Miranda foi a Washington*. For musicological analysis of Miranda's Hollywood appearances, see Clark, "Doing the Samba on Sunset Boulevard."

32 Mendonça, *Carmen Miranda foi a Washington*, 78–80.

33 Ibid., 101. This footage is included in Helena Solberg's documentary, *Bananas Is My Business*, International Cinema Productions, 1994.

34 See, for example, *Correio da Manhã*, Rio de Janeiro, 1 Oct. 1940, 11.

35 For versions of this notorious episode, see Solberg, *Bananas Is My Business*; Mendonça, *Carmen Miranda foi a Washington*, 122–25; and

Cabral, *No tempo de Almirante*. Solberg's documentary includes an interview with producer Caribé da Rocha suggesting that the Cassino da Urca crowd disliked Miranda because they were elite snobs who had never appreciated samba. Mendonça quotes her own interview with Rocha to the same effect. But this analysis is incorrect: the crowd consisted of the same elite clientele that commonly attended shows at the Cassino da Urca. Miranda had performed at the venue many times before her departure for the United States, always to great success. The crowd was deeply familiar with samba and accustomed to seeing and applauding the top samba performers of the day. Before Miranda took the stage that night, the same crowd applauded the back-up band for an opening performance of samba. Clearly, the crowd objected to Miranda's performance, and not to samba itself.

36 Mendonça, *Carmen Miranda foi a Washington*, 125.

37 Vicente Paiva and Luiz Peixoto, "Disseram que voltei americanizada," original recording by Carmen Miranda, Odeon, 1940.

38 Mendonça, *Carmen Miranda foi a Washington*, 126–29.

39 Villa-Lobos survey, *Diretrizes*, 15 May 1941, 12–13.

40 Ari Barroso, *Diretrizes*, 12 June 1941, 9.

41 For a thorough account of the Good Neighbor Policy's Brazilian manifestations, see Tota, *O imperialismo sedutor*, 28–39, 41–90.

42 By far the most thorough treatment of the Stokowski episode is Daniella Thompson's illuminating account, posted on her excellent Web site on Brazilian music, *Daniella Thompson on Brazil*, daniv.blogspot.com; see Thompson, "Stalking Stokowski," originally published in *Brazzil* online magazine, February 2000, www.brazzil.com. See also the report on Stokowski's visit in *O Globo*, Rio de Janeiro, 8 Aug. 1940, 1; and Cabral, *Pixinguinha*.

43 Thompson, "Stalking Stokowski."

44 For accounts of Disney's Brazilian visit, see Cabral, *No tempo de Ari Barroso*, 192; and Tota, *O imperialismo sedutor*, 68–70, 135–39.

45 Brazilian Division, CIAA, 27 May 1942, as cited in Stam, *Tropical Multiculturalism*, 112. For an account of Welles's experience in Rio, see Stam, *Tropical Multiculturalism*, 107–32.

46 Frank, *South American Journey*, 43. For further analysis of Frank's Brazilian voyage, see Tota, *O imperialismo sedutor*, 157–68.

47 Stam, *Tropical Multiculturalism*, 124–27.

48 Denis Brean, "Boogie woogie na favela," original recording by Ciro Monteiro, RCA Victor, 1945.

49 Fischer, "The Poverty of Law," 407–8.

50 João de Barro and Alberto Ribeiro, "Copacabana," original recording by Dick Farney, Continental, 1946.

51 Castro, *Chega de saudade*, 31–46.

52 Haroldo Barbosa and Geraldo Jacques, "Adeus América," original recording by Os Cariocas, Continental, 1948.

53 On these pre–bossa nova experiments, see Castro, *Chega de saudade*, 60, 96.

54 Denis Brean, "Bahia com H," original recording by Francisco Alves, Odeon, 1947.

55 For a detailed history of the emergence of bossa nova, see Castro, *Chega de saudade*.

56 João de Barro and Alberto Ribeiro, "Yes, nós temos bananas," recorded by Caetano Veloso, Philips, 1968.

57 Lamartine Babo, "Canção para inglês ver," recorded by Os Mutantes, Philips, 1969.

58 Dunn, *Brutality Garden*, 167–68.

5 INVENTING THE OLD GUARD

Portions of this chapter were previously published in "The Invention of Tradition on Brazilian Radio" in *The Brazil Reader*, edited by Robert M. Levine and John J. Crocitti (Durham: Duke University Press, 1999) and are used here by permission.

1 Araci de Almeida, *Radiolândia*, 23 April 1955, 4–6.

2 Antonio Rago, interview, "Rago e seu regional," *Revista do Rádio*, 16 April 1955, 16–17.

3 Cazes, *Choro*, 19.

4 The best basic treatment of the history of the genre is Vasconcellos, *Carinhoso*. For analysis of specific figures, see Rangel, *Sambistas e chorões*. For an analysis of Heitor Villa-Lobos's choro foundation that also includes discussion of formation and basic characteristics of the genre, see Garcia, "The Choro, the Guitar, and Villa-Lobos."

5 *Enciclopédia da música brasileira: Samba e choro* (São Paulo: Art Editora, 2000), 145; Cazes, *Choro*, 29.

6 For detailed discussion of the Praça Onze scene in the 1910s, see Moura, *Tia Ciata e a Pequena África do Rio de Janeiro*.

7 Cabral, *Pixinguinha*, 45.

8 Cazes, *Choro*, 23–34; Barreto, *O triste fim de Policárpio Quaresma*; Chasteen, "The Prehistory of Samba."

9 Cabral, *Pixinguinha*, 13–49; Sérgio Cabral and Henrique Cazes, lecture on Pixinguinha in series *Desde que o choro é choro*, Casa Rui Barbosa, Rio de Janeiro, July 1997.

10 For Pixinguinha's participation in the Praça Onze house parties, see Cabral, *Pixinguinha*, 40; Cazes, lecture on Pixinguinha in series *Desde que o choro é choro*, Casa Rui Barbosa, Rio de Janeiro, July 1997.

11 Cabral, *Pixinguinha*, 45.

12 Choro was certainly known in São Paulo before the Batutas played there, primarily through the music of flautist Patápio Silva. But the genre remained predominantly Carioca.

13 Cabral, *Pixinguinha*, 127.

14 Ibid., 131–33.

15 Casé, *Programa Casé*, 67–70.

16 Pixinguinha composed both "Carinhoso" and "Rosa" in 1917. João de Barro wrote lyrics for "Carinhoso" in 1937, and the choro was recorded by Orlando Silva for RCA Victor later that year. Otávio de Souza wrote the lyrics for "Rosa" before 1920, but they were not recorded until Orlando Silva's 1937 recording, also for RCA Victor.

17 On Pixinguinha in the late 1930s and early 1940s, see Cabral, *Pixinguinha*, 161; Pixinguinha (Alfredo da Rocha Vianna) record of employment, AN, Mayrink Veiga archive, Arquivo Particular 24, cx. 25; Cazes, lecture on Pixinguinha in series *Desde que o choro é choro*, Casa Rui Barbosa, Rio de Janeiro, July 1997; author interview with Jairo Severiano, Ipanema, June 1997; MIS-Arquivo, Jacob do Bandolim, depoimento, 1967.

18 Máximo and Didier, *Noel Rosa*, 290.

19 MIS-Arquivo, Jacob do Bandolim, depoimento, 1967; by the terms of the contract, for example, beginning in 1946, Lacerda appeared as co-author of "Um a zero," a Pixinguinha choro of 1919 and earned royalties for all subsequent recordings of the work; Cabral, *Pixinguinha*, 160–61; MIS-Arquivo, Alcebíades Barcellos, depoimento.

20 Cabral, *Pixinguinha*, 160.

21 This is the one aspect in which the Pixinguinha-Lacerda recordings of 1946–47 sound less sophisticated than American music of the same era. In comparison with Ben Webster or Lester Young, Pixinguinha's tone on tenor sax was predictable and unimaginative. This was doubtless a consequence of the absence of a vibrant saxophone tradition in choro or in Brazilian popular music in general. Pixinguinha played the sax much the same way it had been played in American jazz in the mid-1920s—largely as a bass instrument designed to offset the featured soloist. The reverse was true of flute: Lacerda, and Pixinguinha before him, played that instrument with a range and imagination unequalled in American popular music of the same era. Clarinetist and soprano saxophonist Luis Americano Rego was, to my knowledge, the only Brazilian of the period to experiment with a broader range of timbre on the saxophone.

22 Almirante inaugurated *Curiosidades musicais* as a segment of the *Programa Casé* in 1935, but did not produce it as an independent program until 1938. Cabral, *No tempo de Almirante*, 361. For details on the Mangueira episode, see Cabral, *As escolas de samba de Rio de Janeiro*, 123.

23 MIS-Arquivo, *Curiosidades musicais, instantâneos sonoros do Brasil* and *Aquarelas do Brasil* cassettes 195, 197, 214. See also Cabral, *No tempo de Almirante,* 227–29.

24 Cabral, *No tempo de Almirante,* 241.

25 MIS-Arquivo, PDVG. The dates listed on the *fichas técnicas* of the PDVG cassettes are unreliable, and only in a few cases have I been able to determine the precise date from contextual information. Cited above, in order, are audiotapes PDVG 3:A; 8:B; 4:B; 4:A; 1:A; and 1:B. Tapes 4:A and B are from 26 Nov. 1947 and 21 Jan. 1948, respectively.

26 MIS-Arquivo, PDVG, 4:A, 26 Nov. 1948.

27 MIS-Arquivo, PDVG, 4:B, 21 Jan. 1948.

28 MIS-Arquivo, PDVG, 5:B, 1948.

29 MIS-Arquivo, PDVG, 1:B; 4:B, 21 Jan. 1948.

30 IBOPE, *Registros de Audiência de Rádio,* Rio de Janeiro. See, for example, Oct. 1947; May 1948; Jan. 1951; Jan. 1952. For São Paulo, see *Registros de Audiência de Rádio,* São Paulo, April–June 1954. Questions of audience share are complicated by the fact that the program often aired on Rádios Tupi and Tamoio at the same time. In order to arrive at a true indication of the program's success, one must add those audience shares. In May 1949, for example, the program averaged a 4 percent share on Tupi, and a 3 percent on Tamoio. (Both stations were owned by Assis Chateaubriand and in general had separate programming schedules.) In 1952, Almirante moved to Rádio Clube. Shortly thereafter, Pixinguinha followed, and they began a new phase of the program, which fared similarly well. The São Paulo broadcasts were on Rádio Record, São Paulo.

31 Mário Cabral, *Tribuna da Imprensa,* April 1955, as cited in Cabral, *No tempo de Almirante,* 293.

32 Cabral, *Pixinguinha,* 174; Porto, "Festival da Velha Guarda."

33 Weinstein, "Celebrating Modernity."

34 For a comparison of photos of the different groups, see Barbosa Silva, *Filho de Ogum Bexinguento,* illustrations; and Vianna, *O mistério do samba,* cover.

35 Itiberé, *Mangueira, Montmartre e outras favelas;* for an example of the Pixinguinha-Lacerda recordings, see "Um a zero," RCA Victor, 1946.

36 Ary Vasconcellos, *O cruzeiro,* 1955, as cited in Cabral, *Pixinguinha,* 177; *Radiolândia,* 9 April 1955.

37 Severiano and Homem de Mello, *A canção no tempo,* 267.

38 Altamiro Carrilho had his own program on Rádio Mauá in 1950. At the same time, Jacob do Bandolim hosted a program on Rádio Guanabara. Raul de Barros had a show on Rádio Nacional in 1954, and in São Paulo Antonio Rago worked first on Rádio Nacional São Paulo, then on Rádio and TV Record. For all program schedules and audience shares, see IBOPE, *Registros de Audiência,* Rio de Janeiro and São Paulo, 1950–55.

39 MIS-Arquivo, *Instantâneos do Brasil*, 1950, 1:A; IBOPE, *Registros de Audiência*, Rio de Janeiro, Feb. 1951. See also, MIS-Arquivo, Rádio Nacional, twentieth anniversary broadcast, 1956.

40 *Revista da Música Popular* 1.1; Rangel, *Sambistas e chorões*. Rangel's work established the foundation and the model for the music historians of the next generation, including Sérgio Cabral and Jairo Severiano.

41 Cabral, *Pixinguinha*, 162, 167.

42 Paz, *Jacob do Bandolim*; and Cazes, *Choro*, 129–34; 159–66. For his own polemical opinions on the state of choro in 1967, see MIS-Arquivo, Jacob do Bandolim, depoimento.

43 MIS-Arquivo, Jacob do Bandolim, depoimento.

44 Paz, *Jacob do Bandolim*, 106; MIS-Arquivo, Jacob do Bandolim, depoimento.

45 *São Pixinguinha*, originally released as *Som Pixinguinha*, Odeon, 1971.

46 Claudionor Cruz, as quoted in Paz, *Jacob do Bandolim*, 40. Jacob's given name was Jacob Pick Bittencourt. His mother was a Polish Jew who emigrated to Brazil early in the twentieth century. Cruz thus suggested that Jacob's musicianship enabled him to overcome parentage that ordinarily would have marked him as an outsider and to become fully Brazilian.

47 There are a host of musicians experimenting with the genre, including Paulo Moura, Paulo Sérgio Santos, Maurício Carrilho, Zé Nogueira, Cristóvão Bastos, and Pedro Amorim. Henrique Cazes (his fine work in recreating the arrangements of Pixinguinha notwithstanding) has argued for greater experimentation within choro and has recorded works by innovators like Hermeto Paschoal.

48 Aratanha, "A essência musical da alma brasileira."

49 D'Araujo, *O segundo governo Vargas, 1951–1954*, 92–102.

50 Chateaubriand was himself a figure of enormous complexity, not least in his attitudes toward Brazilian cultural heritage. For a richly detailed biography, see Morais, *Chatô*.

6 FAN CLUBS AND AUDITORIUM PROGRAMS

1 MIS-Arquivo, Adhemar Casé, depoimento, 1977. For epigraphs, Ciro Gaulo, interview with the author, Rio de Janeiro, tape recording, 11 June 1997; Silva, "Galeria das fanáticas," *Revista do Rádio*, 1 Jan. 1954, 15. See also Avancini, "Nas tramas da fama," 96–97.

2 Tinhorão, *Música popular*, 83; Osvaldo Molles, *Revista do Rádio*, 26 Feb. 1955, 40–41.

3 "Notícias de Rádio," *Publicidade*, Sept. 1948, 24; IBOPE, *Registros de Audiência de Rádio*, Rio de Janeiro, May 1949; D. Norma Tapajós, interview with the author, Rio de Janeiro, tape recording, Nov. 1996.

4   Bonaiuti, *A vida de Marlene*, 95; Ciro Gaulo, interview with the author, Rio de Janeiro, tape recording, 11 June 1997.

5   Green, *Beyond Carnival*, 162–64.

6   Osvaldo Molles, *Revista do Rádio*, 26 Feb. 1955, 40–41; Floriano Faissal, interview with Luís Carlos Saroldi, 1979, MIS-Arquivo; Arnaldo Câmara Leitão, depoimento, Arquivo Multi-Meios, Centro Cultural de São Paulo. The Juvenile Court of Rio attempted on several occasions to impose a ban on the attendance of minors at the programs. Each time, the measure failed. Many parents, however, took matters into their own hands, forbidding their children to attend; "Carta do editor," *Revista do Rádio*, 3 April 1951, 3; Bonaiuti, *A vida de Marlene*, 95.

7   MIS-Arquivo, Linda Batista, depoimento; Tinhorão, *Música popular*, 69.

8   Miriam Goldfeder, Alcir Lenharo, and Marta Avancini have all taken up the subject of the auditorium programs and their related fan clubs. In *Por trás das ondas da Rádio Nacional*, Goldfeder argues that the audience was manipulated by media magnates, and only occasionally established breaches allowing for limited democratic interpretation and participation. Lenharo, in *Cantores do radio*, presents a detailed and sensitive biography of two radio singers and analyzes their milieu and the context of their success. He emphasizes the celebratory nature of the auditorium programs but does not analyze them in detail. Avancini's analysis in "Nas tramas da fama" is largely consonant with Lenharo's, understanding the auditorium as a ludic space for the underprivileged.

9   "A voz de beleza," *O Malho*, 11 July 1935. See also "Notícias de rádio," *Publicidade*, June 1943, 15, for a contrast between *Um milhão de melodias* and comedy programs.

10 For insightful analysis of a programming divide in the United States, see Hilmes, *Radio Voices*, particularly chaps. 6, 7, and 8.

11 Nelson Rodrigues, "Rádio: Poesia dos subúrbios," *Diretrizes*, 11 Dec. 1941, 18–19.

12 Vieira, *César de Alencar*, 46.

13 IBOPE, *Boletim das Classes Dirigentes* 1.24 (1951): section 2, 1–3; IBOPE, *Pesquisas Especiais* 21.13, 1956; *Publicidade*, 1 Jan. 1951, 30.

14 *Revista do Rádio*, 23 Oct. 1951; also cited in Avancini, "Nas tramas da fama," 61.

15 Gláucia Garcia, interview with the author, São Paulo, tape recording, July 1997; José Ramalho, interview with the author, Rio de Janeiro, tape recording, June 1997.

16 Ciro Gaulo, interview with the author, Rio de Janeiro, tape recording, 11 June 1997.

17 The live audience became a part of Brazilian radio by the early 1930s. In the earliest days of the medium, programs were produced in precarious,

tiny studios. Soon large stations expanded their facilities and installed "fish bowls": studios behind glass partitions. Often the rooms on the other side of the glass were large enough to accommodate small audiences, admitted free of charge. (The *Programa Casé*, for example, was performed in a fish-bowl studio throughout the 1930s.) As radio became a bigger business and as technological improvements enabled better broadcasts from open theaters, the largest stations built auditoriums. As early as 1934, Rádio São Paulo opened an eighty-seat auditorium. By the end of the decade, several stations had theaters that seated over a hundred people. Radio dramas and orchestral programs were increasingly performed before live audiences. In the late 1930s, many of these programs cultivated the trappings of high culture, even when their material consisted overwhelmingly of popular music. Radio Kosmos in São Paulo, for example, billed itself as "the station of the elite" and encouraged formal wear for members of the audience at the most prominent shows.

18 MIS-Arquivo, César de Alencar, depoimento, 1985. Alencar's move to the Saturday afternoon variety show also marked a radical shift in his own broadcast personality, from "sober and elegant" to noisy and rigorously unpretentious; *A Manhã*, 13 July 1945.

19 MIS-Arquivo, *Programa César de Alencar*, 1949, cassette 1; Vieira, *César de Alencar*, 159.

20 MIS-Arquivo, *Programa César de Alencar*, 1949, cassette 1.

21 MIS-Arquivo, Alencar, depoimento.

22 IBOPE, *Registros de Audiência*, December 1953.

23 Tinhorão, *Música popular*, 80; Ciro Gaulo, interview with the author, Rio de Janeiro, tape recording, 11 June 1997; IBOPE, *Registros de Audiência*, Jan. 1951; MIS-Arquivo, *A felicidade bate a sua porta*; *Revista do Rádio* 1.1; Avancini, "Nas tramas da fama," 74.

24 MIS-Arquivo, Fernando Lobo, depoimento, 1994.

25 MIS-Arquivo, *Programa César de Alencar*, 1948, cassette 3; Ramalho, interview.

26 MIS-Arquivo, *Programa César de Alencar*, cassette 3.

27 MIS-Arquivo, "De tudo um pouco," *Programa César de Alencar*, cassette 3 and 4.

28 MIS-Arquivo, Alencar, depoimento.

29 MIS-Arquivo, *Programa César de Alencar*, cassette 3; MIS-Arquivo, Marlene, depoimento.

30 Tinhorão, *Música popular*, 85; Câmara Leitão, depoimento; José Ramalho, interview with the author, Rio de Janeiro, tape recording, June 1997.

31 Jairo Severiano, interview with the author, Rio de Janeiro, July 1997; Veloso, *Verdade tropical*, 502–3.

32 MIS-Arquivo, Marlene, depoimento. *Revista do Rádio*, 8 Jan. 1955, 3–5; José Ramalho, interview with the author, Rio de Janeiro, tape recording, June 1997. For analysis of the new concept of stardom, see Avancini, "Nas tramas da fama," 79.

33 Barroso's distaste for the trend of smooth, melodramatic samba (of which Marlene was one of the foremost proponents) was well-known. The acerbic composer once remarked, "Samba para mim tem que ter teleco-teco" (samba, for me, has to have teleco-teco, or syncopation); MIS-Arquivo, *Aqui está o Ary*, 1953.

34 *Cruzeiro*, a general affairs magazine modeled on *Life*, was the nation's most popular magazine in this period.

35 Like the *Programa César de Alencar*, the *Revista do Rádio* inspired imitations. *Radiolândia*, a similar magazine with higher graphic production values, began publishing in the early 1950s and achieved moderate success. Other radio fanzines had shorter runs, overshadowed by the *Revista do Rádio*'s dominance; *Publicidade*, 1 Aug. 1951, 26–27; *Revista do Rádio*, 5 Feb. 1955, 7.

36 "A vida de Emilinha," *Revista do Rádio*, 8 Jan. 1955, 11.

37 "A vida de Emilinha," *Revista do Rádio*, 5 Feb. 1955, 11; Bonaiuti, *Vida de Marlene*, 73; Goldfeder, *Por trás das ondas da Rádio Nacional*, 63.

38 Marlene also took a stage name to avoid tainting her family with any connection to the dubious world of musical entertainment. As she described it later, "Today, I would use my baptismal name as an artistic name. But in the era when I started I could not, because I did not want to involve my family in all that . . . my concern was to leave the family's name out, not to involve it in the image of a radio singer"; Bonaiuti, *Vida de Marlene*, 54.

39 Bonaiuti, *Vida de Marlene*, 57, 63.

40 MIS-Arquivo, Marlene, depoimento; José Ramalho, interview with the author, Rio de Janeiro, tape recording, June 1997; Bonaiuti, *Vida de Marlene*, 77.

41 In 1951, Francisco Carlos and Cauby Peixoto, instructed by their press agents, attempted to cultivate a marketable rivalry. They taunted each other in the press and staged a fight outside a prominent nightclub ("snapshots" of the fight were featured the following week in the *Revista do Rádio*). According to some reports, Peixoto and his manager went the extra step of commissioning poorly sewn clothes that would fall to shreds as soon as admirers clutched at him.

42 Marlene frankly admits that her voice was never brilliant, and that her success depended on charisma and personality; Bonaiuti, *Vida de Marlene*, 121, 124. See Lenharo, *Cantores do rádio*, for an excellent study of Ney.

43 Fan Club Emilinha Borba, folheto.

44 MIS-Arquivo, Marlene, depoimento. At Rádio Nacional, Manoel Barcellos supported Marlene's candidacy on his program while Alencar supported that of Emilinha.

45 Even without calculating the money spent on buying the contest for Marlene, Antárctica's publicity campaign for Guaraná Caçula was the most expensive Brazilian advertising campaign of 1949; *Publicidade*, 15 July 1950, 22–23, 28.

46 For satire of the rigged contest, see MIS-Arquivo, *PRK-30*, cassette 3; MIS-Arquivo, Marlene, depoimento; Bonaiuti, *Vida de Marlene*, 75.

47 For a related discussion of the rivalry, see Avancini, "Nas tramas da fama," 82–83.

48 Bonaiuti, *Vida de Marlene*, 77; Ciro Gaulo, interview with the author, Rio de Janeiro, tape recording, 11 June 1997; Goldfeder describes the contests as "an openly mystifying vertex of radio and a propagator of false expectations"; Goldfeder, *Por trás das ondas da Rádio Nacional*, 159.

49 José Ramalho, interview with the author, Rio de Janeiro, tape recording, June 1997; João Batista, interview with the author, Rio de Janeiro, tape recording, June 1997.

50 Gláucia Garcia, interview with the author, Rio de Janeiro, tape recording, July 1997; Lúcia Soares, interview with the author, Rio de Janeiro, tape recording, May 1997.

51 Gláucia Garcia, interview with the author, Rio de Janeiro, tape recording, July 1997.

52 Goldfeder, *Por trás das ondas da Rádio Nacional*, 59; Avancini, "Nas tramas da fama," 90; Ciro Gaulo, interview with the author, Rio de Janeiro, tape recording, 11 June 1997.

53 MIS-Arquivo, Nora Ney, depoimento, 1994.

54 Fan Club Emilinha Borba, folheto; Lúcia Soares, interview with the author, Rio de Janeiro, tape recording, May 1997.

55 Ciro Gaulo, interview with the author, Rio de Janeiro, tape recording, 11 June 1997.

56 José Ramalho, interview with the author, Rio de Janeiro, tape recording, June 1997. The emotional tie with the singer was considered ennobling in its purity. One Emilinha fan from the southern state of Paraná won a *Revista do Rádio* contest with this description of the effects of Emilinha's singing: "Emilinha's voice is like the revivifying sun that causes the blessed flower of hope to blossom in my heart"; *Revista do Rádio*, 26 Feb.1955. "Marlene chorou de verdade," *Revista do Rádio*, 26 Feb. 1955, 8–9; Avancini, "Nas tramas da fama," 87.

57 Gláucia Garcia, interview with the author, Rio de Janeiro, tape recording, July 1997; José Ramalho, interview with the author, Rio de Janeiro, tape recording, June 1997; Antonieta de Carvalho, interview with the

author, Rio de Janeiro, tape recording, June 1997; Ciro Gaulo, interview with the author, Rio de Janeiro, tape recording, 11 June 1997.

58 "Opinião dos fãs," *Revista do Rádio*, 18 Dec. 1951, 22; *Revista do Rádio*, 20 Nov. 1951, 20. Velloso, *Mário Lago*, 139. "Fanzoca de rádio" became a hit in its interpretation by Carequinha and the Altamiro Carrilho band, Copacabana, 1958.

59 Goldfeder, *Por trás das ondas da Rádio Nacional*, 157.

60 *Programa César de Alencar*, cassette 4, 1952, MIS-Arquivo; Goldfeder, *Por trás das ondas da Rádio Nacional*, 174; "A vida de Emilinha," *Revista do Rádio*, 5 Feb. 1955, 11.

61 Goldfeder, *Por trás das ondas da Rádio Nacional*, 177–78. Alencar has been widely accused of joining in the military regime's witchhunt immediately after the coup, informing on Communists and leftists working at Rádio Nacional; MIS-Arquivo, Mário Lago, depoimento, 1992; MIS-Arquivo, Brasini, depoimento. Alencar denied the accusations, but documents uncovered by his biographer show that they had at least some foundation; Vieira, *César de Alencar*. It seems likely that the regime had already identified its targets within the cast of Rádio Nacional, and that Alencar's indication merely provided the military with justification to act against those individuals it perceived as subversive. Alencar's reputation in the artistic community suffered gravely and never recovered.

62 Bonaiuti, *Vida de Marlene*, 83; José Ramalho, interview with the author, Rio de Janeiro, tape recording, June 1997; Gláucia Garcia, interview with the author, Rio de Janeiro, tape recording, July 1997. Fans expected their idols to visit and socialize with local fan clubs, and failure to meet these expectations met with energetic disapproval. In 1950, for example, fans in Vitória, Espírito Santo, wrote to the *Revista do Rádio* to chastise Emilinha for failing to live up to her commitment to the fan club to participate in a local soccer match. Through the organization of such activities and the insistence on their fulfillment, fans, to a significant degree, produced the spectacle in which they participated; "A carta da semana," *Revista do Rádio*, 9 May 1950, 40; Avancini, "Nas tramas da fama," 85.

63 Lúcia Soares, interview with the author, Rio de Janeiro, tape recording, May 1997.

64 Paulo Azevedo, interview with the author, Rio de Janeiro, tape recording, June 1997. (I have used a pseudonym at the interviewee's request.)

65 Goldfeder, Avancini, and Lenharo largely ignore male members of the fan clubs. Goldfeder writes, "While the suburban man excluded himself from these manifestations . . . the woman occupied this space entirely." Avancini mentions "a minority of boys" but goes on to identify fans almost exclusively in the feminine; Goldfeder, *Por trás das ondas da*

Rádio Nacional, 169; Avancini, "Nas tramas da fama," 80. Gláucia Garcia, interview with the author, Rio de Janeiro, tape recording, July 1997; José Ramalho, interview with the author, Rio de Janeiro, tape recording, July 1997. My own conclusions regarding percentages are based primarily on a series of interviews with current and former members of the fan clubs.

66 Marlene in *Pasquim*, 20 Aug. 1973, 14–20. Marlene used the term *boneca*, or doll, a common euphemism for gay, often carrying derogatory implication.

67 Avancini, "Nas tramas da fama," 83; Goldfeder, *Por trás das ondas da Rádio Nacional*, 157. The fan alluded to Dalva de Oliveira, President Getúlio Vargas, and Flamengo, the popular Rio soccer team.

68 See, in particular, Goldfeder, *Por trás das ondas da Rádio Nacional*, 140–60.

69 Ciro Gaulo, interview with the author, Rio de Janeiro, tape recording, 11 June 1997.

70 Goldfeder, *Por trás das ondas da Rádio Nacional*, 144.

7 ADVERTISING AND AUDIENCE FRAGMENTATION

1 Auricélio Penteado, "Coca Cola e cangaço," *Publicidade*, Sept. 1948, 20.

2 Reis, "São Paulo e Rio," 302–3.

3 Woodard, "Marketing Modernity." See also JWTA.

4 Woodard, "Marketing Modernity"; JWTA, J. Walter Thompson Company do Brasil, "Investigation for Lehn and Fink," May 1931, microfilm 223.

5 On the general growth of radio advertising, see Leite, "Rádio, 'uma voz que vai de um fim a outro fim do mundo.'"

6 Richard Penn, letter to the editor, *Publicidade*, June 1949, 6–8.

7 Ibid.; MIS-Arquivo, Floriano Faissal, interview with Luiz Carlos Saroldi, 1975; Saroldi and Moreira, *Rádio Nacional*; Calabre de Azevedo, "Na sintonia do tempo."

8 Before IBOPE, the trade journal *Publicidade*, founded in 1940, had conducted some scientific market research, but its studies were minimal in comparison with similar enterprises in the United States or with those carried out by IBOPE beginning in 1943.

9 For a general overview of IBOPE's growth, see Gontijo, *A voz do povo*, 207–57.

10 *Publicidade, Anuário do Rádio*, 1956; IBOPE, *Registros de Audiência do Rádio*, Rio de Janeiro, April 1945. See Owensby, *Intimate Ironies*, 102, for discussion of Penteado's original intent to poll based on income and educational level.

11 IBOPE, *Registros de Audiência do Rádio*, Rio de Janeiro, June 1942; IBOPE, *Registros de Audiência do Rádio*, Rio de Janeiro, April 1947, May 1949.

12 IBOPE, *Registros de Audiência do Rádio*, Rio de Janeiro, April 1945.

13 IBOPE, *Registros de Audiência do Rádio*, Rio de Janeiro, Aug.–Dec. 1944; *EMASS: Boletim das Emissoras Associadas* 1.1 (1953), 3.

14 IBOPE, *Pesquisas Especiais* 7.1 (1948); *Boletim das Classes Dirigentes* 1.19 (1950) and 1.1 (1951).

15 Prominent would-be literati who turned to advertising included Ricardo Ramos, son of the novelist Graciliano Ramos and a writer with literary aspirations of his own, who became a JWT executive. Foreign intellectuals who had immigrated to Brazil were also attracted to the profession: the German expressionist painter Hans August Rey, after fleeing the rising Nazi menace in the 1930s, worked as an ad man in Brazil. Rey subsequently moved to New York, where he used his Brazilian experience as fodder for a children's book about a curious monkey.

16 Ramos, *Do reclame a comunicação*, 42. For the trajectory of one advertising professional, and for a discussion of the sense of mission shared among advertising professionals, see Owensby, *Intimate Ironies*, 79, 94, 111.

17 "Propaganda, a pedra angular da civilização," *Publicidade*, June 1944, 22–24.

18 Penteado, address to Associação Brasileira de Propaganda, May 1949, reproduced in IBOPE, *Registros de Audiência do Rádio*, Rio de Janeiro, May 1949.

19 Ibid.

20 Penteado, editorial, in IBOPE, *Registros de Audiência do Rádio*, Rio de Janeiro, September 1944.

21 As late as 1929, top JWT executives objected to "psychology in advertising," favoring what they considered a no-nonsense, practical approach of offering the right information about the product to the right audience. The success in the 1930s of what JWT personnel termed "the psychological approach," however, quickly convinced any remaining doubters that advertising was an art of persuasion, not merely an effective means of conveying information; JWTA, J. Walter Thompson Company, minutes of staff meeting, 10 April 1929, Box 1, Folder 7.

22 Marchand, *Advertising the American Dream*, esp. 231, xv–xxii; Lears, *Fables of Abundance*.

23 Rádios Assunção advertisement, *Publicidade*, 15 March 1951, 27, 32.

24 Pasta Dental Philips advertisement, *Noite de estrelas*, cassette 149, MIS-Arquivo.

25 MIS-Arquivo, *Rádio melodia Pond's*, cassette 1.

26 MIS-Arquivo, Perfumaria Mirta Sociedade advertisement, *Balança mas não cai*, cassette 1.

27 Casé, *Programa Casé*, 47–48.

28 Owensby, *Intimate Ironies*, 109–10, 128.

29 The survey found that in Rio 66 percent of the residents of A neighborhoods considered themselves middle class; 80 percent of the residents of B neighborhoods considered themselves middle class; and 56 percent of the residents of C neighborhoods considered themselves middle class. In São Paulo, 92 percent of the A residents, 84 percent of the B, and 60 percent of the C identified themselves as middle class; *Boletim das Classes Dirigentes*, 24–30 Aug. 1952, section 2, 7–10.

30 The Afro-Brazilian actor Grande Otelo complained vociferously about the absence of blacks in advertisements in a 1951 interview with *Publicidade*, arguing that the advertising industry harbored an ugly racial prejudice. Surprisingly, the editors of *Publicidade* were sympathetic enough to his complaint to give it ample space, but the diatribe changed nothing: advertisements remained almost completely white for decades; Grande Otelo, *Publicidade*, 15 Feb. 1951, 15. For a groundbreaking study of race in radio and advertising, see Pereira, *Cor, profissão e mobilidade*, 105.

31 MIS-Arquivo, *Rádio melodia Pond's*, cassette 1.

32 MIS-Arquivo, Bombril advertisement, *Gente que brilha*, cassette 216.

33 Print advertisements made the racial underpinnings of the typical middle-class housewife's supervision of the maid far more explicit. As Owensby has shown, a print campaign of the same period showed a white housewife literally jackhammering consumer sensibility into the head of her Afro-Brazilian maid; Owensby, *Intimate Ironies*, 125. For more extensive discussion of the responsibilities thrust on middle-class housewives by advertisements, see ibid., 119–29.

34 MIS-Arquivo, Radamés Gnattali, depoimento, 1977.

35 IBOPE, *Registros de Audiência de Rádio*, Rio de Janeiro, Oct. 1943.

36 MIS-Arquivo, advertisements for Coca-Cola, *Um milhão de melodias*, cassettes 3–7.

37 Auricélio Penteado, "Coca Cola e cangaço," *Publicidade*, Sept. 1948, 20.

38 MIS-Arquivo, *Um milhão de melodias*, 5 Jan. 1949, cassette 2.

39 Letter from McCann-Erickson to Gilberto de Andrade, reproduced in *Rádio Nacional* program guide, "A semana em revista," 9 Dec. 1944; "Notícias de Rádio," *Publicidade*, June 1943, 15.

40 Auricélio Penteado, "Influências nas audiências de rádio," IBOPE, *Registros de Audiência do Rádio*, Rio de Janeiro, Nov. 1951.

41 Pereira, *Cor, profissão e mobilidade*, 85–86.

42 Arquivo Rádio Nacional, *As mães não tem destino*, program scripts.

43 MIS-Arquivo, Edmo de Valle, depoimento, 1977; MIS-Arquivo, Fer-

nando Lobo, depoimento, 1994; interview with Victor Costa, *Publicidade*, 15 April 1951, 31.

44 In 1947 advertising agencies and corporations invested 750 million cruzeiros (approximately 37 million dollars) in advertising in Brazil. By 1953, that figure reached 3.5 billion cruzeiros, growth of nearly 500 percent; Lima, "O negócio de publicidade no Brasil," *Observador Econômico*, July 1954, 53–63. The largest agencies, meanwhile, directed approximately 40 percent of their clients' funds to radio throughout this period; "Como as agências de publicidade resolvem seus problemas de rádio," *Publicidade, Anuário do Rádio*, 1951; *Anuário de Publicidade*, Dec. 1951, 120–26.

45 Penteado, editorial, *Boletim das Classes Dirigentes* 2.56 (1951).

46 "Como as agências de publicidade resolvem seus problemas de rádio," *Publicidade, Anuário do Rádio*, 1951; "A indústria que deixou de ser rendosa," *Anuário do Rádio*, 1954, 52.

47 MIS-Arquivo, Paulo Tapajós, depoimento, 1982.

48 IBOPE, *Registros de Audiência do Rádio*, Rio de Janeiro, July 1951.

49 Interview with Victor Costa, *Publicidade*, 15 April 1951, 31.

50 Paulo Montenegro, editorial, *Boletim das Classes Dirigentes*, 23–29 March 1952.

51 For detail on Rádio Globo's strategy, see McCann, "Thin Air and the Solid State," 96–108.

52 Rádio Jornal do Brasil feature, *Publicidade*, 20 April 1955, 39.

53 IBOPE, *Pesquisas Especiais*, 21 Jan. 1956. Survey on musical preference commissioned by Rádio Jornal do Brasil.

54 MIS-Arquivo, Paulo Tapajós, depoimento.

55 Interview with José Scatena, *Publicidade, Anuário do Rádio*, 1953.

56 *O fino da bossa*, for example, also inaugurated in 1965, presented a slick style of bossa nova, eschewing innovation. The tropicalist program *Divino maravilhoso* was the exception that proved the rule. It was so innovative and experimental that it was pushed off the air after a handful of episodes in 1968. For analysis, see Dunn, *Brutality Garden*, 144–46.

57 For the general surge in the popularity of recorded music programs, see IBOPE, *Registros de Audiência do Rádio*, Rio de Janeiro, 1953–1956. Particularly interesting in these radio polls is the sudden rise in popularity in the mid-1950s of request programs on Rádios Mauá, Continental, and Tamoio, stations that in previous years had generally trailed in audience polls. Also notable is the appearance in late 1953 of a Rádio Nacional program on Saturday nights at 10:00 p.m. titled *Audição longplay*—an indication of the decline of live programming.

58 Ramos, *Do reclame a comunicação*, 69–71.

59 Leite, "Rádio, 'uma voz que vai de um fim a outro fim do mundo,'" 231.

1 For accounts of the spectacle in Maracanã, see Severiano, *Yes, nós temos Braguinha*, 84–85; and Severiano and Homem de Mello, *A canção no tempo*, 169–70.

2 For an excellent summary of the place of the 1950 defeat in the Brazilian psyche, see Bellos, *Futebol*, 43–76.

3 João de Barro and Alberto Ribeiro, "Touradas em Madri," original recording by Almirante, Odeon, 1938.

4 Severiano, *Yés, nós temos Braguinha*, 50–51.

5 For a range of perspectives on the suicide and its consequences, including analysis of journalistic coverage, see Gomes, *Vargas e a crise dos anos 50*.

6 Mendonça, *Carmen Miranda foi a Washington*, 162–64. For images of Miranda's cortege, see Helena Solberg's documentary film, *Bananas Is My Business*, 1994.

7 Maurício Tapajós and Aldir Blanc, "Querelas do Brasil," original recording by Elis Regina, Philips, 1978, recording by Tapajós and Blanc, SACI, 1984.

8 Zé Ramalho, *Nação nordestina*, BMG Brasil, 2000.

9 Dorival Caymmi, "Noite de temporal," original recording by Dorival Caymmi, Odeon 1940; recording by Virgínia Rodrigues, Natasha, 1997.

10 Bruce Gilman, "From Sacred to Samba," *Brazzil*, Sept. 1998, *www.brazzil.com*.

11 Perrone and Dunn, *Brazilian Popular Music and Globalization*.

12 See, in particular, Maurício Carrilho, *Maurício Carrilho*, Acari, 2000; and Pedro Amorim, *Violão tenor*, Acari, 2001.

13 Carlos Diegues, *Bye-bye, Brasil*, Carnaval Unifilm/Gaumont/Aries Cinematográfica Argentina/Embrafilme, 1979; Roberto Menescal and Chico Buarque, "Bye-bye, Brasil," original recording by Chico Buarque, Polygram, 1979.

14 Severiano and Homem de Mello, *A canção no tempo*, 254–55.

BIBLIOGRAPHY

ARCHIVES CONSULTED

Arquivo Edgar Leuenroth, Universidade Estadual de Campinas, São Paulo
Arquivo Estadual do Rio de Janeiro
Arquivo Multimeios do Centro Cultural de São Paulo
Arquivo do Museu da Imagem e do Som, Rio de Janeiro
Arquivo Nacional, Rio de Janeiro
Arquivo da Rádio MEC, Rio de Janeiro
Arquivo da Rádio Nacional, Rio de Janeiro
Biblioteca de Música, Biblioteca Nacional, Rio de Janeiro
Biblioteca Nacional, Rio de Janeiro
Centro de Pesquisa e Documentação (CPDOC), Fundação Getúlio Vargas,
    Rio de Janeiro
J. Walter Thompson Archives, John W. Hartman Center for Sales, Advertis-
    ing, and Marketing History, Duke University, Durham, North Carolina
Museu da Imagem e do Som, Rio de Janeiro
Museu da Imagem e do Som, São Paulo

PRINCIPAL SERIALS CONSULTED

Aspectos
Boletim das Classes Dirigentes
Cine Rádio Jornal
Correio da Manhã
Cultura Política
Diário Carioca
Diário de Notícias
Diretrizes
EMASS: *Boletim das Emissoras Associadas*
Estado de São Paulo
O Globo
IBOPE, *Pesquisas Especiais*
IBOPE, *Registros de Audiência de Rio de Janeiro e São Paulo*
O Jornal

Jornal do Brasil
O Malho
A Noite
Pasquim
Publicidade
Rádiolândia
Revista do Rádio
Tribuna da Imprensa
Vamos Ler

BOOKS AND ARTICLES

Alencar, José de. *O guarani*. 1857. Reprint, São Paulo: Cultrix, 1968.

Amado, Jorge. *Jubiabá*. Rio de Janeiro: Olympio, 1935.

———. *Mar morto*. São Paulo: Livraria Martins, 1936.

Amaral, Aracy A. *As artes plásticas na semana de 22: Subsídios para uma história da renovação das artes no Brasil.* 5th ed. São Paulo: Editora 34, 1998.

América de Almeida, José. *O Boqueirão*. São Paulo: José Olympio, 1935.

Andrade, Mário de. "A linguagem radiofônica." In *O empalhador de passarinhos*. São Paulo: Livraria Martins, 1972.

———. *Música, doce música*. São Paulo: Livraria Martins, 1976.

———. *Cartas de Mário de Andrade a Luis da Câmara Cascudo*. Belo Horizonte: Villa Rica, 1991.

Aratanha, Mário. "A essência musical da alma brasileira." *Roda de choro* 1.2 (March 1996): 12–15.

Augusto, Sérgio. *Este mundo é um pandeiro*. São Paulo: Companhia das Letras, 1989.

Avancini, Marta Maria Picarelli. "Nas tramas da fama: As estrelas do rádio em sua época áurea, Brasil, anos 40 e 50." M.A. thesis, Universidade Estadual de Campinas, 1996.

Barbosa, Marília T., and Vera de Alencar. *Caymmi: Som, imagem, magia.* Salvador: Fundação Odebrecht, 1995.

Barbosa Silva, Marília Trindade. *Filho de Ogum Bexinguento*. Rio de Janeiro: Funarte, 1979.

Barreto, Lima. *O triste fim de Policárpio Quaresma*. São Paulo: Scipione, 1994.

Bellos, Alex. *Futebol: Soccer, the Brazilian Way*. New York: Bloomsbury, 2002.

Besse, Susan K. *Restructuring Patriarchy: The Modernization of Gender Inequality in Brazil, 1914–1945.* Chapel Hill: University of North Carolina Press, 1996.

Bonaiuti, Vitória (Marlene). *A vida de Marlene: Depoimento.* Rio de Janeiro: Rio Cultura.

Borges, Dain. "The Recognition of Afro-Brazilian Symbols and Ideas, 1890–1940." *Luso-Brazilian Review* 32.2 (1995): 59–78.

Braucks, Sônia Maria. *Jararaca e Ratinho*. Rio de Janeiro: Funarte, 1989.

Buarque de Holanda, Sérgio. *Raizes do Brasil*. 1936. Rio de Janeiro: José Olympio, 1989.

Burns, E. Bradford. *Nationalism in Brazil: A Historical Survey*. New York: Praeger, 1968.

Cabral, Sérgio. *No tempo de Almirante: Uma história do rádio e da* MPB. Rio de Janeiro: Livraria Francisco Alves, 1990.

———. *No tempo de Ari Barroso*. Rio de Janeiro: Lumiar, 1993.

———. *As escolas de samba de Rio de Janeiro*. 2d ed. Rio de Janeiro: Lumiar, 1996.

———. *A* MPB *na era do rádio*. Rio de Janeiro: Moderna, 1996.

———. *Pixinguinha: Vida e obra*. 2d ed. Rio de Janeiro: Lumiar, 1997.

Calabre de Azevedo, Lia. "Na sintonia do tempo: Uma leitura do cotidiano através da produção ficcional radiofônica, 1940–1946." M.A. thesis, Universidade Federal Fluminense, 1996.

Campos, Alice Duarte Silva de, Dulcinéia Nunes Gomes, Francisco Duarte Silva, and Nelson Matos (Nelson Sargento). *Um certo Geraldo Pereira*. Rio de Janeiro: FUNARTE, 1983.

Carmona, Elisabeth, and Geraldo Leite. "Rádio, povo e poder: Subservência e paternalismo." In *Populismo e comunicação*, edited by José Marques de Melo. São Paulo: Cortez/Intercom, 1981.

Casé, Rafael. *Programa Casé: O rádio começou aqui*. Rio de Janeiro: Mauad, 1995.

Castelo, Martins. "Rádio." *Cultura Política* 1.13 (1942): 292–93.

Castro, Ruy. *Chega de saudade: A história e as histórias da bossa nova*. São Paulo: Companhia das Letras, 1990.

Caulfield, Sueanne. *In Defense of Honor: Sexual Morality, Modernity, and Nation in Early-Twentieth-Century Brazil*. Durham, N.C.: Duke University Press, 2000.

Caymmi, Dorival. *Cancioneiro da Bahia*. São Paulo: Círculo do Livro, 1984.

Caymmi, Stella. *Dorival Caymmi: O mar e o tempo*. São Paulo: Editora 34, 2001.

Cazes, Henrique. *Choro: Do quintal ao municipal*. São Paulo: Editora 34, 1999.

Chasteen, John. "The Prehistory of Samba: Carnival Dancing in Rio, 1840–1917." *Journal of Latin American Studies* 28.1 (1996): 19–47.

Chediak, Almir, ed. *Songbook Ari Barroso*. Vol. 2. Rio de Janeiro: Lumiar, 1994.

Clark, Walter Aaron. "Doing the Samba on Sunset Boulevard: Carmen Miranda and the Hollywoodization of Latin American Music." In *From*

Tejano to Tango: Latin American Popular Music, edited by Walter Aaron Clark. New York: Routledge, 2002.

Cordovil, Hervê. *A música brasileira deste século por seus autores e intérpretes*, Vol. 13.13. Sound recording. São Paulo: SESC, 2001.

Da Cunha, Euclides. *Os sertões*. Rio de Janeiro: Laemmert, 1902.

D'Araujo, Maria Celina Soares. *O segundo governo Vargas, 1951–1954: Democracia, partidos e crise política*. Rio de Janeiro: Zahar, 1982.

Dávila, Jerry. "Perfecting the Brazilian Race." Ph.D. diss., Brown University, 1999.

Davis, Darien J. *Avoiding the Dark: Race and the Forging of National Culture in Modern Brazil*. Aldershot, England: Ashgate, 1999.

Didier, Aluísio. *Radamés Gnattali*. Rio de Janeiro: Brasiliana, 1996.

Dreyfus, Dominique. *Vida do viajante: A saga de Luiz Gonzaga*. São Paulo: Editora 34, 1996.

Drummond de Andrade, Carlos. *Sentimento do mundo*. 1940. Reprint, São Paulo: Record, 2002.

Dunn, Christopher. *Brutality Garden: Tropicália and the Emergence of a Brazilian Counterculture*. Chapel Hill: University of North Carolina Press, 2001.

Fernandes, F. Assis. "65 anos de radiodifusão no Brasil." *Revista Brasileira de Comunicação* 10.56 (June 1977).

Fernandes, Florestan. *The Negro in Brazilian Society*. New York: Columbia University Press, 1969.

Fischer, Brodwyn. "The Poverty of Law: Rio de Janeiro, 1930–1964." Ph.D. diss., Harvard University, 1999.

Foreis Domingues, Henrique de (Almirante). *No tempo de Noel Rosa*. Rio de Janeiro: Livraria Francisco Alves, 1963.

Frank, Waldo. *South American Journey*. New York: Durrell, Sloan, and Pearce, 1943.

French, John D. *The Brazilian Workers' ABC: Class Conflicts and Alliances in Modern São Paulo*. Chapel Hill: University of North Carolina Press, 1992.

———. "The Missteps of Anti-Imperialist Reason: Pierre Bourdieu, Loïc Wacquant, and Michael Hanchard's *Orpheus and Power*." Working paper, Duke/University of North Carolina Latin American Studies Colloquium, 1999.

Freyre, Gilberto. *Casa grande e senzala*. Rio de Janeiro, 1933.

Frota, Wander Nunes. *Auxilio luxuoso: Samba símbolo natcional, geração Noel Rosa e indústria cultural*. São Paulo: Annablume, 2003.

Fryer, Peter. *Rhythms of Resistance: African Musical Heritage in Brazil*. Hanover, N.H.: Wesleyan University/University Press of New England, 2000.

Garcia, Thomas. "The Choro, the Guitar, and Villa-Lobos." *Luso-Brazilian Review* 34.1 (1997): 57–66.

Garfield, Seth. *Indigenous Struggle at the Heart of Brazil: State Policy, Frontier Expansion, and the Xavante Indians, 1937–1988.* Durham, N.C.: Duke University Press, 2001.

Gil-Montero, Martha. *Brazilian Bombshell: The Biography of Carmen Miranda.* New York: Donald I. Fine, 1989.

Goldfeder, Miriam. *Por trás das ondas da Rádio Nacional.* Rio de Janeiro: Paz e Terra, 1981.

Gomes, Angela de Castro. *A invenção do trabalhismo.* São Paulo: Vértice/Editora Revista dos Tribunais, 1988.

——, ed. *Vargas e a crise dos anos 50.* Rio de Janeiro: Relume Dumará, 1994.

Gontijo, Silvana. *A voz do povo: O IBOPE do Brasil.* Rio de Janeiro: Objetiva, 1996.

Goulart, Silvana. *Sob a verdade oficial: Ideologia, propaganda e censura no Estado Novo.* São Paulo: Marco Zero, 1990.

Green, James N. *Beyond Carnival: Male Homosexuality in Twentieth-Century Brazil.* Chicago: University of Chicago Press, 1999.

Guimarães, Francisco (Vagalume). *Na roda de samba.* 2d ed. Rio de Janeiro: FUNARTE, 1978.

Gurgueira, Fernando Limongeli. "Integração nacional pelas ondas: O rádio no Estado Novo." M.A. thesis, FFLCH–Universidade de São Paulo, 1995.

Hanchard, Michael. *Orpheus and Power: The Movimento Negro of Rio de Janeiro and São Paulo, 1945–1988.* Princeton, N.J.: Princeton University Press, 1994.

Haussen, Doris Fagundes. "Rádio e política: Tempos de Vargas e Perón." Ph.D. diss., Escola de Comunicações e Artes, Universidade de São Paulo, 1992.

Hilmes, Michele. *Radio Voices: American Broadcasting, 1922–1952.* Minneapolis: University of Minnesota Press, 1997.

Hobsbawm, Eric. *The Jazz Scene.* 3d ed. New York: Pantheon, 1993.

Hobsbawm, Eric, and Terence Ranger. *The Invention of Tradition.* Cambridge: Cambridge University Press, 1983.

Itiberé, Brasílio. *Mangueira, Montmartre e outras favelas.* Rio de Janeiro: Livraria São José, 1961.

Johnson, Randal. "The Dynamics of the Brazilian Literary Field, 1930–1945." *Luso-Brazilian Review* 31.2 (1994): 5–22.

Johnson, Randal, and Robert Stam, eds. *Brazilian Cinema.* 2d ed. New York: Columbia University Press, 1995.

Joseph, Gilbert, and Daniel Nugent, eds. *Everyday Forms of State Formation: Revolution and the Negotiation of Rule in Modern Mexico.* Durham, N.C.: Duke University Press, 1994.

Krausche, Valter. *Adoniran Barbosa.* São Paulo: Brasiliense, 1985.

Ladeira, Cesar. *Acabaram de ouvir: Reportagem numa estação de rádio.* São Paulo: Companhia Editora Nacional, 1933.

Lauerhauss, Ludwig, Jr. *Getúlio Vargas and the Triumph of Brazilian Nationalism*. Los Angeles: UCLA Press, 1972.

Lears, T. J. Jackson. *Fables of Abundance: A Cultural History of Advertising in America*. New York: Basic Books, 1994.

Leite, Manuel L. "Rádio, 'uma voz que vai de um fim a outro fim do mundo.'" In *História da propaganda*, edited by Renato Castelo Branco, Rodolfo Lima Martenson, and Fernando Reis. São Paulo: T. A. Queiroz, 1990.

Lenharo, Alcir. *A sacralização da política*. Campinas: Papirus, 1986.

———.*Cantores do rádio: A trajetória de Nora Ney e Jorge Goulart e o meio artístico de seu tempo*. Campinas: Editora da Universidade Estadual de Campinas, 1995.

Lesser, Jeff. "Immigration and Shifting Concepts of National Identity in Brazil during the Vargas Era." *Luso-Brazilian Review* 31.2 (1994): 27–48.

———. *Negotiating National Identity: Immigrants, Minorities, and the Struggle for Ethnicity in Brazil*. Durham, N.C.: Duke University Press, 1999.

Levine, Robert. *The Vargas Regime: The Critical Years, 1934–1938*. New York: Columbia University Press, 1970.

Lima, Melo. "O negócio de publicidade no Brasil," *Observador Econômico*, July 1954, 53–63.

Lins do Rego, José. *Pedra bonita*. Rio de Janeiro: José Olympio, 1938.

Marchand, Roland. *Advertising the American Dream: Making Way for Modernity, 1920–1940*. Berkeley: University of California Press, 1985.

Martins, Wilson. *The Modernist Idea: A Critical Survey of Brazilian Writing in the Twentieth Century*. New York: New York University Press, 1971.

Matos, Claudia. *Acertei no milhar: Samba e malandragem no tempo de Getúlio*. Rio de Janeiro: Paz e Terra, 1982.

Máximo, João, and Carlos Didier. *Noel Rosa: Uma biografia*. Brasília: Editora Universidade de Brasília/Linha Gráfica, 1990.

McCann, Bryan. "The Invention of Tradition on Brazilian Radio." In *The Brazil Reader*, edited by Robert Levine and John Crocitti. Durham, N.C.: Duke University Press, 1999, 474–82.

———. "Thin Air and the Solid State: Radio, Culture, and Politics in Brazil's Vargas Era." Ph.D. diss., Yale University, 1999.

———. "Noel Rosa's Nationalist Logic." *Luso-Brazilian Review* 31.1 (2001): 1–16.

McCann, Sean. *Gumshoe America: Hardboiled Crime Fiction and the Rise and Fall of New Deal Liberalism*. Durham, N.C.: Duke University Press, 2000.

Melo Souza, José Inácio de. "Ação e imaginário de uma ditadura: Controle, coerção e propaganda nos meios de comunicação durante o Estado Novo." M.A. thesis, ECA–Universidade de São Paulo, 1990.

Mendonça, Ana Rita. *Carmen Miranda foi a Washington*. Rio de Janeiro: Record, 1999.

Mendonça Teles, Gilberto. *Vanguarda européia e modernismo brasileiro*. Petrópolis: Vozes, 1982.

Miceli, Sérgio. *Intelectuais e classe dirigente no Brasil, 1920–1945*. São Paulo: Difel, 1979.

Moraes, Mário de. *Recordações de Ari Barroso*. Rio de Janeiro: Funarte, 1979.

Morais, Fernando. *Chatô: O rei do Brasil*. São Paulo: Companhia das Letras, 1994.

Moreira, Sonia Virgínia. *O rádio no Brasil*. Rio de Janeiro: Rio Fundo, 1991.

Moura, Roberto. *Tia Ciata e a Pequena África no Rio de Janeiro*. Rio de Janeiro: FUNARTE, 1983.

Murce, Renato. *Bastidores do rádio: Fragmentos do rádio de ontem e de hoje*. Rio de Janeiro: Imago, 1976.

Needell, Jeffrey. Review of *The Mystery of Samba*, by Hermano Vianna. *Journal of Latin American Studies* 32.2 (1999): 561–62.

Oliveira, Claudia Maria Silva de. "Quando canta o Brasil: A Rádio Nacional e a construção de uma identidade nacional popular, 1936–1945." M.A. thesis, Pontífica Universidade Católica do Rio de Janeiro, 1996.

Oliveira, Lúcia Lippi, ed. *Elite intelectual e debate político nos anos 30*. Rio de Janeiro: Editora da Fundação Getúlio Vargas, 1980.

Oliveira, Lúcia Lippi, Mônica Pimenta Velloso, and Angela Castro Gomes. *Estado Novo: Ideologia e poder*. Rio de Janeiro: Zahar, 1982.

Ortiz, Renato. *A moderna tradição brasileira: Cultura brasileira e indústria cultural*. São Paulo: Brasiliense, 1991.

Ortriwano, Gisela Svetlana. *A informação no rádio: Os grupos de poder e a determinação dos conteúdos*. São Paulo: Sumus, 1983.

Owensby, Brian. *Intimate Ironies: Modernity and the Making of Middle-Class Lives in Brazil*. Stanford, Calif.: Stanford University Press, 1999.

Paz, Ermelinda. *Jacob do Bandolim*. Rio de Janeiro: FUNARTE, 1997.

Pereira, João Batista Borges. *Cor, profissão e mobilidade: O negro e Rádio de São Paulo*. São Paulo: Pioneira/Editora da Universidade de São Paulo, 1967.

Perosa, Lilian. "A hora do clique: Uma análise sobre o programa oficial de rádio *Voz do Brasil* na Velha e na Nova República." M.A. thesis, ECA–Universidade de São Paulo, 1991.

Perrone, Charles, and Christopher Dunn, eds. *Brazilian Popular Music and Globalization*. Gainesville: University of Florida Press, 2001.

Porto, Sérgio. "Festival da Velha Guarda," *Revista da Música Popular* 1.1 (1954): 5–7.

Queiroz, Rachel de. *O quinze*. Author edition. Fortaleza: Estabelecimento Graphico Urania, 1930.

Rádio Nacional. *20 anos de liderança a serviço do Brasil*. Rio de Janeiro: Rádio Nacional, 1956.

Ramos, Graciliano. *Vidas secas*. Rio de Janeiro: José Olympio, 1938.

———. *Memórias do cárcere*. São Paulo: Livraria Martins, 1969.

Ramos, Ricardo. *Do reclame a comunicação: Pequena história da propaganda no Brasil*. São Paulo: Atual, 1985.

Rangel, Lúcio. *Sambistas e chorões*. Rio de Janeiro: Francisco Alves, 1961.

Raphael, Allison. "Samba and Social Control: Popular Culture and Racial Democracy in Rio de Janeiro." Ph.D. diss., Columbia University, 1980.

Rebelo, Marques (Eddy Dias da Cruz). *A estrela sobe*. São Paulo: Livraria Martins, 1939.

Reis, Fernando. "São Paulo e Rio: A longa caminhada." In *História da Propaganda no Brasil*, edited by Renato Castello Branco, Rodolfo Lima Martensen, and Fernando Reis. São Paulo: T.A. Queiroz, 1990.

Sandroni, Carlos. *Feitiço decente: Transformações do samba no Rio de Janeiro (1917–1933)*. Rio de Janeiro: Jorge Zahar, 2001.

Saroldi, Luiz Carlos, and Sonia Virgínia Moreira. *Rádio Nacional: O Brasil em sintonia*. Rio de Janeiro: Martins Fontes/FUNARTE, 1984.

Schwartzman, Simon, Helena M. Bousquet Bomeny, and Vanda M. Ribeiro Costa. *Tempos de Capanema*. Rio de Janeiro: Paz e Terra/Editora da Universidade de São Paulo, 1984.

Seigel, Micol. "The Point of Comparison: Transnational Racial Construction, Brazil and the United States, 1918–1933." Ph.D. diss., New York University, 2001.

Severiano, Jairo. *Yes, nós temos Braguinha*. Rio de Janeiro: Martins Fontes/FUNARTE, 1987.

Severiano, Jairo, and Zuza Homem de Mello. *A canção no tempo: 85 anos de músicas brasileiras*. Vol. 1, 1901–1957. São Paulo: Jardim Europa, 1997.

Shaw, Lisa. "*São Coisas Nossas*: Samba and Identity in the Vargas Era, 1930–1945." *Portuguese Studies* 14 (1998): 152–69.

———. *The Social History of the Brazilian Samba*. Aldershot, U.K.: Ashgate, 1999.

Sheriff, Robin. *Dreaming Equality: Color, Race, and Racism in Urban Brazil*. New Brunswick, N.J.: Rutgers University Press, 2001.

Skidmore, Thomas E. *Politics in Brazil, 1930–1964: An Experiment in Democracy*. New York: Oxford University Press, 1967.

———. *Black into White: Race and Nationality in Brazilian Thought*. New York: Oxford University Press, 1974.

Soares Valença, Suetônio. *Tra la lá*. Rio de Janeiro: Funarte, 1981.

Stam, Robert. *Tropical Multiculturalism: A Comparative History of Race in Brazilian Cinema and Culture*. Durham, N.C.: Duke University Press, 1997.

Thompson, Daniella. *Daniella Thompson on Brazil*. Accessed online at http://daniv.blogspot.com, 24 June 2003.

——. "Stalking Stokowski." *Brazzil* (www.brazzil.com), Feb. 2000. Accessed online at www.brazzil.com/musfeb00.htm, 24 June 2003.

Tinhorão, José Ramos. *Pequena história da música popular: Da modinha a canção do protesto*. Petrópolis: Vozes, 1974.

——. "Cinquenta anos a serviço de jazz." *Jornal do Brasil*, 14 Nov. 1975.

——. *Música popular: Do gramofone ao rádio e TV*. São Paulo: Ática, 1981.

——. *História social da música popular brasileira*. Lisbon: Caminho, 1990.

Tota, Antonio Pedro. *A locomotiva no ar: Rádio e modernidade em São Paulo, 1924–1934*. São Paulo: P. W. Gráficos/Secretaria da Cultura do Estado de São Paulo, 1990.

——. *O imperialismo sedutor: A americanização do Brasil na época da Segunda Guerra*. São Paulo: Companhia das Letras, 2001.

Ulhôa, Martha Tupinambá de. "Música brasileira popular: Uma reflexão sobre o brasileiro e o popular." Working paper, Universidade de Rio de Janeiro Colloquium on Popular Music, 1999.

Vasconcellos, Ary. *Carinhoso*. Rio de Janeiro: Gráfica, 1984.

Velloso, Monica Pimenta. *Mário Lago: Boemia e política*. Rio de Janeiro: Fundação Getúlio Vargas, 1997.

Veloso, Caetano. *Verdade tropical*. São Paulo: Companhia das Letras, 1997.

——. "Carmen Mirandadada." In *Brazilian Popular Music and Globalization*, edited by Charles Perrone and Christopher Dunn. Gainesville: University of Florida Press, 2001.

Vianna, Hermano. *O mistério do samba*. Rio de Janeiro: Jorge Zahar/Editora Universidade Federal do Rio de Janeiro, 1995.

——. *The Mystery of Samba*. Chapel Hill: University of North Carolina Press, 1999.

Vieira, João Luiz. "From High Noon to Jaws: Carnival and Parody in Brazilian Culture." In *Brazilian Cinema*, edited by Randal Johnson and Robert Stam. 2d ed. New York: Columbia University Press, 1995.

Vieira, Jonas. *César de Alencar: A voz que abalou o mundo*. Rio de Janeiro: Valda, 1993.

Vinci de Moraes, José Geraldo. *Metrópole em sinfonia: História, cultura e música popular na São Paulo dos anos 30*. São Paulo: Estação Liberdade, 2000.

Wade, Peter. *Music, Race, and Nation. Música Tropical in Colombia*. Chicago: University of Chicago Press, 2000.

Weinstein, Barbara. "Celebrating Modernity: São Paulo's Quadricentennial and the Historical Construction of Regional Identity." Unpublished manuscript, David Rockefeller Center for Latin American Studies Colloquium, Harvard University, 2002.

Welch, Clifford. *The Seed Was Planted: The São Paulo Roots of Brazil's Rural Labor Movement, 1924–1964*. State College: Pennsylvania State University Press, 1999.

Williams, Daryle. *Culture Wars in Brazil: The First Vargas Regime, 1930–1945*. Durham, N.C.: Duke University Press, 2001.

Wirth, John D. *The Politics of Brazilian Development*. Stanford, Calif.: Stanford University Press, 1970.

Wolfe, Joel William. *Working Women, Working Men: São Paulo and the Rise of Brazil's Industrial Working Class, 1900–1955*. Durham, N.C.: Duke University Press, 1993.

Woodard, James. "Marketing Modernity: The J. Walter Thompson Company and North American Advertising in Brazil, 1929–1939." *Hispanic American Historical Review* 82.2 (May 2002): 257–90.

Zan, José Roberto. "Do fundo de quintal á vanguarda: contribuição para uma História Social da Música Popular Brasileira." Ph.D. diss., Campinas, SP, IFLCH/UNICAMP, 1997.

Zolov, Eric. *Refried Elvis: The Rise of the Mexican Counterculture*. Berkeley: University of California Press, 1999.

INDEX

Bryan McCann is an Assistant Professor in the Department
of History at Georgetown University.

Further information
on the music analyzed in *Hello, Hello Brazil* may be accessed at
http://www.georgetown.edu./departments/history/faculty/mccann.html.